USE THE POWER OF
"finger-tip control"
TO MAKE YOUR GARDENING
PLANS *flower into reality*

Here is the book that busy homeowners the country over have long waited for. Now at last, whatever your project or problem, you can quickly flip the pages to find the specific information you need without laborious hunting.

Giving full consideration to differing soil and climate conditions of various parts of the continental United States, this book fully justifies the words of the Louisville *Courier-Journal*:

"In spite of the fact that I always approach warily any book that contends it is 'complete' or 'encyclopedic,' I'll have to admit that F. F. Rockwell and his wife have come up with one that comes as near living up to the claim as any recent one ... They write with the air of authority possible only with those who can draw on their own experiences, their broad knowledge and their basic common sense."

ABOUT THE ROCKWELLS: F. F. Rockwell and Esther C. Grayson (Mrs. Rockwell) are among America's most famous garden authorities. Mr. Rockwell has won distinction as garden editor of such publications as *The New York Sunday Times, Farm Journal* and *Flower Grower*. Esther Grayson has been a celebrated lecturer, writer and flower-show judge for many years. Each has won the Citation for Horticultural Achievement of the American Horticultural Society in recognition of the notable books on which they have colaborated. The Rockwells currently live and garden in Orleans on Cape Cod.

Other Signet Books of Related Interest

☐ **THE HANDY BOOK OF GARDENING** by Albert E. Wilkinson and Victor A. Tiedjens. A complete, fully-illustrated handbook on growing flowers, vegetables, fruits and house plants; using insecticides; caring for lawns; and landscaping.
(#T3422—75¢)

☐ **HOW TO KNOW THE BIRDS** by Roger Tory Peterson. In this compact handbook, a noted ornithologist and artist describes over 200 species of birds, including flying style, body outline, field markings, habits, peculiarities and legends. 72 color illustrations and over 400 black-and-white drawings. (#P2784—60¢)

☐ **HOW TO KNOW THE MINERALS AND ROCKS** by Richard M. Pearl. An authoritative guide to important gems, ores, and metals of the mineral kingdom. Many full-color and black-and-white illustrations. (#Q3456—95¢)

☐ **HOW TO KNOW THE AMERICAN MARINE SHELLS** by R. Tucker Abbott. A quick guide to the most abundant and colorful shells of America's Atlantic and Pacific coasts, which includes a digest of shell-fishery laws, a list of shells by locale, and full-color photos. (#KT375—75¢)

☐ **OVER 2000 FREE PUBLICATIONS: YOURS FOR THE ASKING** edited by Frederic J. O'Hara. A comprehensive listing of free or inexpensive government publications available to any interested citizen on a wide variety of subjects from baby care to workmen's compensation.
(#Q3691—95¢)

THE NEW AMERICAN LIBRARY, INC., P.O. Box 2310, Grand Central Station, New York, New York 10017

Please send me the SIGNET BOOKS I have checked above. I am enclosing $_____(check or money order—no currency or C.O.D.'s). Please include the list price plus 10¢ a copy to cover mailing costs. (New York City residents add 5% Sales Tax. Other New York State residents add 2% plus any local sales or use taxes).

Name_____

Address_____

City_____State_____Zip Code_____

Allow at least 3 weeks for delivery

The Rockwells'
COMPLETE GUIDE TO SUCCESSFUL GARDENING

The homeowners' step-by-step counselor in planning, laying out, planting, and caring for his place; and monthly reminders of what to do in his particular region, including direct page references on how to do it; lists of plant material for specific purposes and regions.

With photographs by the authors (except as otherwise noted); and more than a hundred line drawings by Virginie Howie, to supplement the text.

FREDERICK F. ROCKWELL
AND ESTHER C. GRAYSON

A SIGNET BOOK
PUBLISHED BY THE NEW AMERICAN LIBRARY

Copyright © 1965 by Frederick F. Rockwell and Esther C. Grayson

All Rights Reserved. For information address Doubleday and Company, Inc., 277 Park Avenue, New York, New York 10017.

Library of Congress Catalog Card Number: 64-13854

This is an authorized reprint of a hardcover edition published by Doubleday and Company, Inc.

ACKNOWLEDGMENTS

Grateful acknowledgment is made to the following for the use of copyright material:

JONATHAN CAPE LIMITED
"The Villain" from *The Complete Poems of W. H. Davies*. Reprinted by permission.

NORMA MILLAY ELLIS
"Northern April" and "The Hardy Garden" from *Collected Poems*, Harper & Row, Publishers. Copyright 1928, 1955 by Edna St. Vincent Millay and Norma Millay Ellis. Reprinted by permission.

ESTHER GRAYSON
"October Ale." Reprinted by permission.

THE MACMILLAN COMPANY
"The Buds," "The Petal of a Rose," "In Green Ways," "The Wind." Copyright 1915 by The Macmillan Company, renewed 1943 by James Stephens. "Spring 1916," copyright 1916 by The Macmillan Company, renewed 1944 by James Stephens. All from *Collected Poems* by James Stephens. Reprinted by permission of The Macmillan Company, Macmillan & Co. Ltd., The Macmillan Company of Canada Limited, Mrs. James Stephens and St. Martin's Press, Inc.

THE NEW YORK TIMES
"Across the Plains of April" by F. F. Rockwell. Reprinted by permission.

CARL ROSE
"It's Broccoli, dear." "I say it's Spinach, 'and I say the Hell with it'"! Copyright © 1928, 1956 by *The New Yorker Magazine, Inc.* Reprinted by permission.

CHARLES SCRIBNER'S SONS
"The Heavenly Hills of Holland" from *The Poems of Henry Van Dyke* by Henry Van Dyke. Copyright 1911 by Charles Scribner's Sons; renewal copyright 1939 by Tertius Van Dyke. Reprinted by permission.

SIGNET TRADEMARK REG. U.S. PAT. OFF. AND FOREIGN COUNTRIES
REGISTERED TRADEMARK—MARCA REGISTRADA
HECHO EN CHICAGO, U.S.A.

SIGNET BOOKS are published by
The New American Library, Inc.,
1301 Avenue of the Americas, New York, New York 10019

First Printing, March, 1969

PRINTED IN THE UNITED STATES OF AMERICA

DEDICATION

To our good friend Arno Nehrling, who, as long-time executive secretary of the Massachusetts Horticultural Society, director of its publication *Horticulture,* and manager of the Annual New England Spring Flower Show, has contributed so much to the advancement of distinguished gardening in America.

CONTENTS

Foreword   xv

PART I. YOUR HOME GROUNDS: HOW TO PLAN, PLANT, AND MAINTAIN THEM

1. Planning the New Place   19

The importance of having a long-range plan. How to set about making a plan. The preliminary work: existing features, divisions, elevations. The important areas: utility, play and rest. Screening and protection: hedges, fences, walls, shrubbery. Special gardens: flower beds, borders, rock and wall gardens, vegetables and fruits.

2. The Soil and How to Manage It   29

Over-all importance. Possibility of altering. Types of soil and their origins: clay, sand, loam, humus. Subsoil and its importance. Drainage. Special area soil types: peat, gumbo, muck, adobe. Remaking and maintaining soils.

3. The Plant and How It Grows   52

Plant anatomy: roots, stems, leaves. Reproduction: how plants grow: air, water, food, light, temperature. Deterrents to growth: light, air, cold, heat, drought, pests, old age.

4. New Plants from Old: Methods of Propagation   65

Growing from seed: timing, control of conditions, the mechanics of sowing, equipment for seed sowing, sterilizers, watering, temperature, transplanting, repotting. Asexual propagation: layering, divisions, cuttings, grafting, budding.

5. Keeping Plants Vigorous and Healthy   85

The gardener's job: temperature, micro-climates, light, moisture, mulches, watering, watering equipment, wind barriers. Feeding plants: fertilizers, manures, green manures. Soil preparation: organic gardening, fertilizers and fertilizer formulas. Plant pests, diseases. Weeds and their controls.

6. Pruning and Training Plants   102

Definitions. Pruning objectives: renewing old plants, increasing yields of flowers, fruits, repairing injured or diseased plants. Training objectives: controlling size, habit of growth, shape. Pruning equipment, pruning techniques.

CONTENTS

7. Coldframes and Hotbeds — 112

Definitions: types of frames, types of sash; location, drainage, building the frame, soil for frames. Frame management, temperature control, planting, watering, ventilation, feeding, shading. The hotbed: construction, methods of heating, management.

8. Tools and Equipment — 122

Tools for many purposes: the question of quality. Hand tools for many tasks. Power tools. Tools for transplanting, cultivating, pruning. Equipment for training and supporting plants: fences, trellises, arbors; for dusting, spraying, lawn care.

PART II. SPECIAL GARDENS, AREAS, AND PLANT MATERIALS

9. Trees, Shrubs, and Vines — 137

Dominent and permanent features of the landscape plan: advantages of establishing them early, possibilities of a home nursery and its advantages, problems of selection. Suggestions for deciduous, evergreen, and ornamental subjects. Shrubs for various purposes. Vines and other climbers. Supports.

10. Lawns and Turf Areas — 152

The lawn, an important feature: what type of lawn to use. Preliminary preparations: grading, drainage, preparation of seedbed, sowing. After care, sodding, stripping, plugging, sprigging, and other methods of lawn making. Lawn renovation. Lawn maintenance: mowing, feeding, rolling, pests, diseases, weed control. Lawns and grasses for hot climates, for cool climates, for dry lawn areas. Ground-cover substitutes for grasses.

11. Flower Beds and Borders — 172

Placement. Backgrounds. A definite plan. Annuals from seed: setting out plants, culture, support for, fall clean-up. Biennials. Perennials. Planning the border. Buying plants. Dividing and replanting. Bulbs: selecting, planting, storing.

12. Rock, Bank, and Wall Gardens — 192

Specialized gardens have many advantages. Rock garden location, preliminary work, background trees and shrubbery, a definite plan, construction, rock plants, culture. The bank garden. The wall garden.

13. Pools, Streams, and Water Gardens — 204

The fascination of water. Importance of good design, location, construction, water supply, water control, winter care. The question of fish.

CONTENTS ix

14. The Patio Garden, Mobile Gardening, Window Boxes 210

Definitions. Location. Suitable plants. Added protection. Plants for walls. Lilies and other bulbs for succession of bloom in pots. Patio pools. Modern mobile gardening. Window boxes.

15. Roses and Rose Gardens 218

The Queen still reigns! The all-purpose flower. Various types of roses. Their selection for different purposes. Preparation of soil. Supports. Fall *vs.* spring planting. Planting techniques. Culture: feeding, pruning, pruning climbers. Spring care. Pest control. Winter protection.

16. Vegetables for Better Eating 232

Why "grow your own"? Location. Size. What to grow. A definite plan. Soil preparation. Planting. Cultivation. Thinning. Fertilizing. Mulching. Harvesting. Winter storage. Detailed culture for popular vegetables.

17. Tree Fruits, Small Fruits, and Berries 253

Definitions; and again, why "grow your own"? Locations. Planting. Pruning. Spraying. Harvesting. Storing. Tree fruits: apples, pears, plums, peaches, figs, grapes. Bush and cane fruits: blueberries, raspberries, strawberries.

18. The Home Greenhouse 271

Year-round gardening. Uses and types of construction: even span or lean-to. Work space. Heating. Ventilation. Shading. Watering. Greenhouse operations: timing, sowing dates, soil mixes, seed sowing, transplanting, watering. Pots, potting, and repotting. Pest control. Propagation.

PART III. SELECTIVE, COUNTRY-WIDE MONTHLY CALENDAR

How to Use the Calendar 287
Alphabetical List of States Showing Areas 290
The Calendar 295
Notes on Country-wide Gardening Problems: 378
    West Coast, Southwest, Mountain, Intermountain, Great Northern Plains, Central Plains and Heartland, North Central, Northeast, East Central, Mid-Atlantic, South Central, Upper South, Lower South and Gulf Coast, Seashore.

PART IV. APPENDIX

Hardy trees and shrubs 399
Trees, shrubs, and other plants for very cold climates 411
Trees, shrubs, and other plants for the South and
    for reclaimed desert lands 420
Trees, shrubs, and other plants for the Atlantic seashore 433
Garden flowers: annuals, biennials, perennials.

CONTENTS

Bulbous plants. Plants for rock, wall, water, and bog gardens. Fragrant plants and herbs	436
Garden troubles: Pests, diseases, weeds and their controls	445
Botanical gardens and Arboretums	456
Parks and display gardens	461
Agricultural colleges and Agricultural Experiment Stations	474
Special plant societies	479
Other national organizations	481
Books for further reference	482
Bibliography	487
Index	489

LINE ILLUSTRATIONS

BY VIRGINIA HOWIE

Garden plan	21
Measure for tree shade	25
pH scale	34
Double digging	36
How to install drainage tile	37
Compost heap	43
How to take soil samples for testing	46
Plant anatomy	53

LIFE CYCLES OF:

annuals; biennials;	55
perennials; tubers;	56
bulbs	57
Methods of asexual reproduction	60
Details of air layering	74
"Scaling" a lily bulb	75
Preparing different types of cuttings	76
Propagation box	80
Whip and tongue graft	82
Wedge and cleft graft	82
Budding	83
Measure for watering	90
Pruning objectives	102
Espaliered fruits	107
Pruning tools	110
Method of securing coldframe sash	116
Hand tools for the garden	124-125
Trellises and arbors	130
Spraying and dusting equipment	131
Lawn tools	133
Operation planting	149
A dry well to save a tree where grade is changed	155
"Chocolate layer" preparation of lawn soil	157
Cutting garden plan	173
How to thin seedlings	177
Supports for tall plants	178
Plan for mixed herbaceous border with lilies	181
Division of perennials	182

BUILDING THE ROCK GARDEN:

Plan for a herb garden	190
Rock garden	195
Make it three dimensional	196
Placing largest stones	197
Setting large rocks in soil	198
Rock garden with steps	198

xii LINE ILLUSTRATIONS

Making retaining wall	198
A wall garden	202
Small garden pool	206
Patio with "plunging" bed for potted plants	212
Patio with garden plan	214
How to construct a self-watering window box	216
Self-watering system for rose garden	222
Post-and-chain support for roses	225
Removing rose suckers	227
Pruning roses	228
Vegetable garden plan	237
Trellis for tomatoes	244
Pinching out new growth on tomatoes	245
Supports for pole beans	247
Hilling up corn	247
"Heeling in" nursery stock	255
Dwarf fruit trees	259
Pruning apple trees	260
Pruning peach trees	261
Grape supports	262
Pruning grape vines	263
Raspberry culture	266
Strawberry plants	268
Rooting strawberry runners	269
Even-span and lean-to greenhouses	273
Potting shed with storage space	275
Portable potting bench	275
"Crocking" for potted plants	281

CALENDAR HEADINGS:

January	295
February	303
March	311
April	318
May	326
June	333
July	341
August	347
September	352
October	358
November	365
December	370

PHOTOGRAPHIC ILLUSTRATIONS
BY THE AUTHORS, EXCEPT AS NOTED

GARDEN WITH ROCKS *(Paul E. Genereux)*	1
INCREASE IN TULIP BULBS	2
HORIZONTAL ROSE CANE SHOWING VERTICAL GROWTH	2
HORIZONTAL LANDSCAPE DESIGN IN HARMONY WITH HOUSE *(Paul E. Genereux)*	3
FLOWERING DOGWOOD	3
CLIMBING ROSE ON POST-AND-RAIL FENCE	4
PERENNIAL BORDER	4
SOIL MAP	6–7
AREA MAP	8–9
SPRING ROCK-GARDEN BLOOM IN SHADE *(Paul E. Genereux)*	11
GARDEN WITH POOL *(Paul E. Genereux)*	12
KNOT GARDEN—COURTESY OF BROOKLYN BOTANIC	12
ROCK GARDEN *(Paul E. Genereux)*	13
TERRACE WITH PLANTS IN TUBS *(Paul E. Genereux)*	13
MODERATE-SIZED ROSE GARDEN *(Paul E. Generux)*	14
ROSES WELL ARRANGED IN LIMITED SPACE *(Paul E. Genereux)*	14
HYBRID TEA ROSE	15
GRANDIFLORA ROSE	15
STRAWBERRIES READY TO SERVE	16

FOREWORD

Here is a different kind of garden book.

While designed especially to guide and aid the beginner, it will also, we believe, be valuable to the experienced gardener in enabling him to make sure that all his garden operations are attended to just when they should be done. Furthermore this is accomplished without the usual time-consuming research, sometimes in other books, for those unfamiliar details about operations that to him have not yet become routine.

In order to make this book of the widest possible use, the information concerning things to be watched for and attended to from month to month has been sectionalized in PART III, SELECTIVE, COUNTRY-WIDE MONTHLY CALENDAR. Therefore in whatever part of the country the reader may live, he will find, concentrated in one place, definite suggestions that apply to his own local climate.

These suggestions are in the form of brief reminders. As he looks them over—in a matter of fifteen or twenty minutes for each month—he will decide which of them apply to *his own particular interests and conditions.*

Then, in case he needs information as to the details of just *how* to do the jobs indicated, he will find these given in the preceding chapters of the book, which cover garden planning, planting, and maintenance. Reference page numbers, inserted in the calendar section, enable him to turn immediately to the instructions he seeks, with no time wasted in hunting through other books or magazine files to find out *how* to do any task that has been suggested. In other words, in this one book, he has a whole garden library at his fingertips, with just the information he needs, *when he needs it.*

The very great advantage of such an arrangement will at once be evident to any home gardener who, with many other matters on his mind, has so often suddenly realized that the time for doing something that he wanted to do has slipped by. Frequently this may mean a delay of an entire year!

Very often, too, it means the loss of money that might have been saved, as when one has to pay a half-dollar or more apiece for perennial plants that could just as well have been started from seed the previous summer at a cost of a few cents each. The same thing applies to shrubs, trees, evergreens, hedges, and other components of attractive home surroundings. Most of these will cost dollars where they might have cost dimes had they been purchased in small sizes and then grown on to landscape-size specimens in a home nursery —*if* the homeowner had only been reminded of it at the proper time!

At least once every month in the year, and in most cases much more frequently, the average home gardener lets some garden operation slip by that costs him money because it was not done on time. It is just such expensive omissions and mistakes that this book is planned to obviate.

In addition to these omissions there are dozens of others which, while not involving actual loss of money, result in home surroundings much less attractive than they should be— a less perfect lawn, for instance, or poorer displays in the flower borders, or vegetables or fruits that are not as fine as they might be. Such misadventures and losses often are the direct results of failure to feed, spray, or provide protection for plant material just when one or perhaps all of these things should have been done to assure best results.

The sum total of such errors of omission, even on the average small place, is the difference between well-cared-for grounds and gardens, of which the owner is justly proud, and the mediocre or ill-kept property that never commands a second look from the passer-by, and of which the owner is secretly ashamed.

More than a half-century of practical gardening experience, under widely varying conditions, is condensed in this volume. It is the hope of the authors that it may bring to others much of the same pleasure they have enjoyed in acquiring the information that has gone into its making.

PART ONE

YOUR HOME GROUNDS: HOW TO PLAN, PLANT, AND MAINTAIN THEM

> I'd leave all the hurry, the noise, and the fray
> For a house full of books, and a garden of flowers.
> *Ballade of True Wisdom* by ANDREW LANG

CHAPTER 1

Planning the New Place

At last you have a place of your own to plan! There is no thrill in the world quite like it, unless perhaps the building of your new house; and even in that case it is quite likely that the architect and the builder will not leave you as free a hand as you have in developing your grounds and gardens.

Furthermore it is not a thrill that will be finished in a few weeks or a few months. It continues for years, with each passing season bringing new projects, new changes, and new successes. It is, in more than one sense of the word, a growing entertainment and satisfaction.

Even when one is not starting from scratch but taking over a place already established, the adventure is almost as exciting. The house may be more or less permanently set in a definite pattern; but the grounds are not. Here, quite literally, the sky is the limit. There may be old trees or large shrubs which cannot readily be moved, but with few exceptions they can be worked into the planting plan.

Frequently old trees, too large to move, but occupying an undue amount of space or casting shade over too large an area, are tolerated much longer than they should be. We recall, with some amusement from this distance in time and space, a very old tulip tree that had grown up in the remains of a stone wall on land where we built a house. This tree was for several years our pride and joy. Nothing grew under it but a tangle of weeds and poorly nourished wild benzoin that had become tall and leggy. Then one night in a hurricane it blew down—falling away from the house fortunately. We heard the crash, and a flashlight revealed what had happened. We spent most of the remainder of the night lamenting our loss, but in the morning something wonderful had happened. Our study and bedroom were flooded with sunshine, where formerly they had always been filled with filtered green light. The same was true of one end of the big living room. We liked the change immensely—though we were somewhat reluctant to admit that fact even to ourselves.

After the wreckage (which incidentally revealed that our fine old tree was rotten at the heart) had been cleared away, we discovered that it had left us a perfect site for a rock garden, with stones on the spot. These, moved into proper position and supplemented by larger ones to form a ledge with water dripping in a natural manner from the crevices, formed an area that attracted more attention from visitors than anything else on the place. Best of all, most people assumed it to be not man-made but a bit of nature's handiwork with merely a few cultivated plants added.

We have told this story not to point a moral—though one might be found without digging very deeply—but to bring out two facts: one, that the homeowner should not hesitate to make radical changes about the grounds; and two, that it takes a comparatively short time to give a garden area a completely new look.

MAKE A LONG-RANGE PLAN

By far the first and most important step to be taken in developing an attractive place, and one that will provide the greatest returns in everyday satisfaction, is to make a definite long-range plan.

If the place is a fairly large one, and you feel that you are not capable of developing such a plan, by all means consult a landscape architect. By so doing you can avoid serious mistakes that in all probability would cost you more than his fee. Not only that, but he undoubtedly can make suggestions that will give you better immediate effects than you would otherwise be likely to achieve.

Lacking the services of a landscape architect or of the more modest "garden consultant," you can do your own planning by thoroughly studying one or more of the several excellent books available on the subject. (See Books for Further Reference, Appendix.) You will find these helpful in any

PLANNING THE NEW PLACE

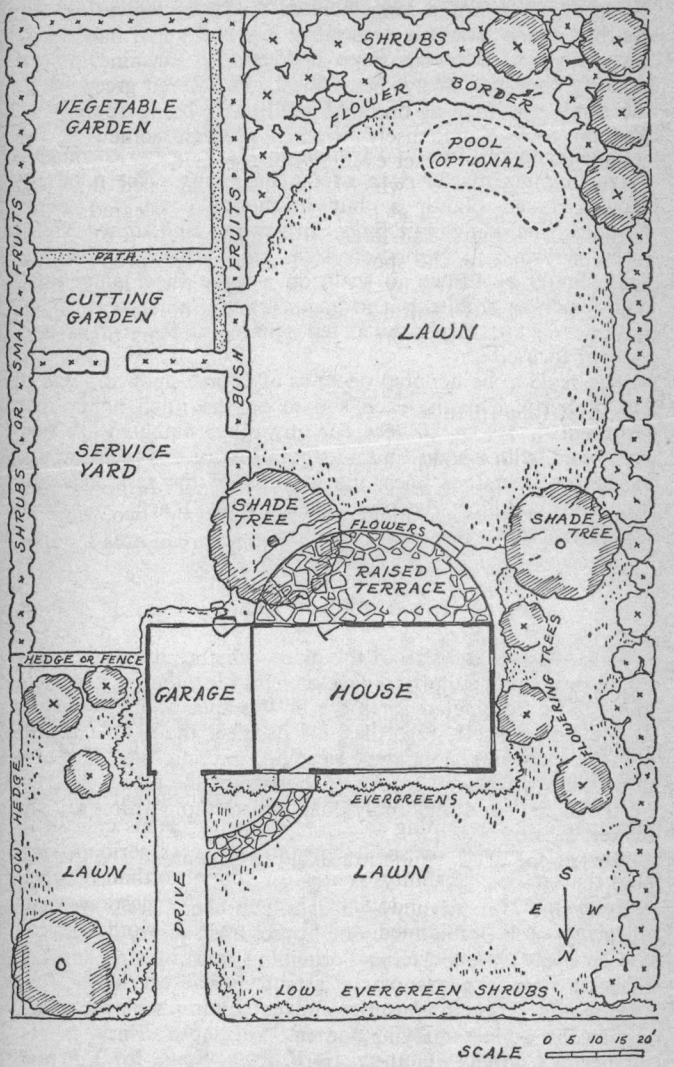

event, because you will undoubtedly be adding to your plantings for many years; that is part of the fascination of the game!

THE MASTER PLAN

It saves much time and trouble in the long run to make a very complete master plan at the beginning. This need not show detailed plantings, but it should cover the entire grounds, including buildings, driveways and other traffic lanes, service and recreation areas, and projected plantings. This should be drawn to scale on a large sheet of squared paper such as architects and engineers use, obtainable at any stationery store. Paper ruled ten squares to the inch is convenient to use.

The scale to be adopted depends of course upon the size of the property. That is, each square on the ruled paper may represent 5, 10, or 20 feet (or any other number). A two-man team, with a stake and a length of twine can measure and locate the boundary lines, the location of the residence and any other buildings, the roads, walks, walls, fences, and existing large trees.

THE IMPORTANT AREAS

Regardless of the size of the place, whether it be a country estate or a small suburban development plot, there are certain areas to be designated for more or less specific uses—just as in the house itself, regardless of its size, there are specific areas for cooking, lounging, sleeping, bathing, etc. The outdoor areas will vary because of the size of the place, the "lay of the land," and the individual interests or whims of the owner.

Among the areas which are likely to be wanted are the following:

Screening (for privacy)—hedges, shrubbery, walls, fences.
Utility—for clotheslines, dog house, trash disposal, etc.
Rest and Outdoor Living—providing areas of both sun and shade, a view of gardens or a distant vista.
Play—for grownups' games and/or children's playground.
Gardens—Flower Beds, Borders, Vegetables, Fruits
Special Gardens—Cutting, Herb, Rose, Rock, Wall, Water
Locomotion
Lawn

PLANNING THE NEW PLACE

Only the vitally interested gardener with expansive grounds should plan for all of these areas; on a small place it would not be possible. The lawn, for instance, must probably be utilized for play, and possibly (if it extends to the rear of the house) for outdoor living. There may not be space for a separate flower garden, in which event the flower borders may include flowers for cutting as well as for decoration where they grow. The vegetable and fruit areas may be combined or omitted altogether. If the owner does not wish to do this, a few vegetables may be incorporated in a wide flower border.

In one of the most interesting small places we ever saw this was done. The vegetables were not in rows, but in small groups; a few dwarf fruits and everbearing raspberries formed part of the screen planting that extended around three sides of the plot. At the rear of the house, out of sight from the road, a well-kept shaded lawn provided space for lounging, with a hammock and rocking chairs that invited complete relaxation. At one side a small, neat garden house took care of tools, mowers, and other equipment. The whole layout was one of the finest examples of *multum in parvo* that we have ever seen.

Now we are ready to begin the plan. We have to start with the given dimensions and the location of the house and other buildings, if any.

The next step is to locate on the plan any other existing features, such as big trees, rocks, banks, or other marked changes in elevation.

Next we fit into the remaining space the other special areas desired, and for which *room can be found*. One of the worst mistakes that can be made is to try to crowd in too much. If there is not sufficient space for all, then an effort should be made to *combine* some of them, as suggested previously.

Screening. If the place is a small one, and privacy is a consideration, then a fairly tall but dense-growing hedge is one solution. A strip at least three feet wide should be allowed, even if the hedge is to be kept trimmed—a task in these days of electric hedge trimmers not nearly so time-consuming as it used to be. Where space is at a premium, a stout wire or wattle fence, or a barrier of louvers covered with vines, may be a better solution.

On the somewhat larger place, a mixed border planting of trees and shrubs, or shrubs alone, provides more effective screening and at the same time makes a most attractive addition to the landscape picture. It should be kept in mind however that a planting of this type cannot be kept under such complete control as to height and breadth as can a hedge or planted fence; and that it may eventually shut out prevailing breezes, a view, or sunshine that is desirable.

With the "walls" of the outdoor living area provided for, the next step is to decide on the number of "rooms" and their locations.

Utility Area. This should include the tool house, if there is to be one, a yard for drying clothes, a sunken garbage can with heavy lid and foot pedal, etc.

In many modern houses the garage serves as the tool house. In our own home in fact, it is the tools (power mowers, power cultivator, power edger) that really are the masters of space, with barely enough room left for the car and opening the door to the driver's seat. Of course about once a month we say we are going to clear out a lot of hand tools, flats, unplanted bulbs, etc., which somehow collect in what should be free floor space, but it's always *next* month. This in spite of the fact that we have a garden house for storing hand tools and materials *and* a potting shed. By all means plan for a separate tool house if you can!

Play and Rest. For both grownups and youngsters, a large part of the summer will be spent out of doors. Where enough space is available it is well to have separate areas for active play and for peaceful relaxation, but with the decreasing size of the average home plot of ground this becomes more and more difficult. It is often possible, however, to find space for at least one play area, even if for nothing more than a spot for practicing basketball, a croquet or badminton court, a putting green, or an area for pitching horseshoes. The advantage, where teen-agers or near teen-agers are involved need not be stressed here, for it will mean children staying and playing at home instead of wandering off to find entertainment elsewhere.

If there is to be an area for rest and relaxation—and occasional outdoor entertainment of a few guests—this may be placed at the rear or to one side of the house, protected as much as possible from the street. The ideal thing is to have it connected with the porch (in an old-fashioned house) or with the terrace in a modern one. Even a slight difference in elevation helps to set it off.

Shade. This subject we have touched upon, but it should be given a bit more consideration. Most of the things that are done about the new place, or one that is being renewed, show immediate results. A hedge, for instance, may be only 18 inches or 2 feet high when it is set out, but the owner can readily visualize what it will be like in two or three years when it has attained a height of 4 to 5 feet. A flower garden, when first made, is a two-dimensional flat area; but it doesn't take much imagination to behold it in full bloom with 4- to 6-foot hollyhocks, delphinium, cosmos, lilies, and hardy asters making a background for the lower-growing bedding plants in front of them.

With a shade tree it is a very different matter. When you set out a spindly whip of an elm, oak, beech, or even a dogwood or a clump of birches, the area it will eventually shade, even after a few years, is almost unbelievable. Adequate shade, even in a very moderate-sized place, is desirable. Nothing else can contribute quite so much comfort, not to mention esthetic value, to its owners during the summer and milder months of the year.

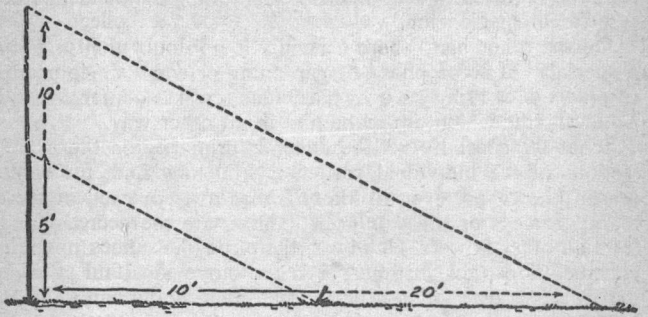

In deciding on location for tall trees, take into consideration how much dense shade they will cast as they mature. This can be estimated by measuring the shade cast by a pole of given length. If, for instance, a 5-foot pole casts a 10-foot shadow, a 25-foot tree will throw a 50-foot shadow.

There is a present trend among nurserymen, as a result of the shrinking size of average rural and suburban homes, to develop lower-growing forms of our popular shade trees, and the small place owner will be well repaid for hunting them up.

To measure how far the shade of a tree will reach in 5 to 8 years, hold an old-fashioned bamboo fishing pole erect at the location of planting, check where the shadow falls, and use a little simple arithmetic.

The Foundation Planting is less important than it was when houses were constructed on stone or cement foundations extending several feet above the ground level. One still sees the dire results of planting tall-growing evergreens or shrubs against such houses in order to get an immediate effect. Lists of plants on pages 400 and 402 include many low-growing species suitable for planting close to house walls and under windows.

SPECIAL GARDENS

Whether or not special gardens of any sort may be desirable depends upon three factors: the size of the place; the character of the location; *and* the zeal and stick-to-itiveness of the gardener! In any event the beginning will do well not to attempt too much at first. Only after he has acquired some of the techniques of gardening, and has gained some idea of the time required to accomplish certain things, should he venture far in specializing.

On the other hand there certainly is no doubt that making a specialty of some phase of gardening or some single group of plants does bring its own particular rewards—interests and achievements which are to be had in no other way.

What the specialty will be depends primarily on the predilections of the individual gardener, who may find, for some reason known not even to himself, that roses or cacti or rock plants, azaleas or lilies or even dahlias, are more fascinating than all other flowers. However, there may be other impelling considerations; for instance, a rocky slope ideal for a rock garden; a sandy spot in a hot climate that would suit cacti to a "T"; or boggy low land that could readily be converted into a water garden. If such is the case, by all means make the most of it.

The Hardy Border. The mixed border (a long, comparatively narrow bed) containing a varied assortment of perennials, with or without annuals and biennials added, is generally the most satisfactory single garden feature. In it one may enjoy almost unlimited varieties of plant forms, flower forms, and colors. Most important of all, a continuous succession of bloom may be achieved from the time the snow melts in spring (with such early bulbs as snowdrops and crocus and spring perennials like arabis, iberis, and creeping phlox) until the first snow in autumn, when the last hardy chrysanthemums and asters, monkshood and late-blooming annuals finally succumb.

Flower Beds, or special areas for some particular type of flower, or for cutting, serve a somewhat different purpose. Some plants, because of special requirements in culture, do best when given a space to themselves. Roses—with the possible exception of the climbers and some shrub roses—do much better in a bed of their own, as do dahlias, most lilies, chrysanthemums, and species requiring support, such as sweet peas and snapdragons.

Rock, Wall, and Water Gardens. Any of these, properly incorporated in the landscape scheme, add immensely to the charm and beauty of a place. But they are not to be stuck haphazardly into the garden picture. To be really effective they must have, at least to a passable degree, the appearance of having been placed there by nature.

Often a mound, a steep slope, or a gully which at first seems to present a serious problem may be developed into a distinctive special feature. Anything that can be done to add the third dimension of *height* to a level plot greatly adds to its attractiveness. *Where such a possibility exists, the area in question should be considered when planning the landscaping,* even though development of the area must be left until later.

Vegetable and Fruit Gardens. One of the unfortunate things about the shrinking size of ground plots for suburban homes in most sections of the country is that there is less room for home vegetable and fruit growing. Even more regrettable is the fact that this is only half the story. There are millions of places where vegetables and possibly some fruit could be grown, with both profit and pleasure to the owners, but where never a seed is planted or a tree set out.

This indifference to home food growing is on the increase even though most home-grown vegetables and fruits are infinitely more flavorful and tender than those that have been developed by the plant breeders particularly for "eye appeal" and shipping quality rather than for flavor. Shipped thousands of miles to the chain-store outlets which dispense them, most vegetables today are either withered by the time they're sold or kept plump by constant syringing or by storage in cellophane bags. Many fruits that are likely to spoil in transit are shipped so green that they reach the table still unripe, even though artificial skin coloring may make them appear appetizing. More concerning this is said in chapters 17 and 18. It is suggested that, before the complete plan of the development of the home place is decided upon, a space for vegetables and or fruits be allotted to this use. It is always easier to eliminate projects on the plan than to find space for them afterward.

TAKE TIME IN PLANNING YOUR PLACE

One final word on making your planting plan:

Don't be in too great a hurry. You can move a tree, even a big one, or transplant a whole hedge *on your planting plan* in just a couple of minutes. The actual operation, once a mistake has been made, may take hours or even days.

When you have prepared the plot plan do not at once begin to fill in the different areas—lawn, play and rest areas, garden plots—directly upon it. Instead use a tissue or tracing-paper overlay and mark the areas, drives, walks, and paths on this. Then try a different arrangement, and if unsatisfied with it, still another. Only after comparing several possibilities can you be certain that you have the one which will best suit your purposes. The same is true of placement of each flower bed, border, and any other landscape feature.

Leaf after leaf drops off, flower after flower,
Some in the chill, some in the warmer hour:
Alike they flourish and alike they fall,
And earth who nourished them receives them all.
                                    WALTER SAVAGE LANDOR

CHAPTER 2

The Soil and How to Manage It

No matter how much or how little gardening the owner of a small country place or a suburban home may plan to do, his basic problem—after the planning is done—is the *soil*. The soil is the home in which his plants have to live, and it is the major factor in determining whether they prosper vigorously, merely manage to exist, or fail utterly. In fact his soil—next to climate (temperature, moisture, and wind)—will determine *what* he can grow successfully.

The character of the soil depends upon two factors; its *physical* structure and its *chemical* content. Both of these, fortunately, can to a considerable extent be altered by the way the soil is handled, what is done in its mechanical treatment, and what is added to it. While this is true, the fact remains that much less work and care is involved when the owner uses plant material that is naturally adapted to the type of soil he happens to possess.

This of course is not always possible. The soil, for instance, upon which the authors have established their present garden was about as unproductive as any that could well be imagined, boasting only scrub pine, barren areas of wild tuft grasses that could establish themselves on bare sandy spots, and, where the best "soil" was, wild black locusts and an impenetrable tangle of cat brier and the Cape's famous "trippin' briers." There was also a bumper crop of poison ivy to add to our problem.

Friends, especially those who had seen our former home, thought we were bemused to select such a location. It suited our requirements, however, in every other respect and it was a challenge to our skill as gardeners, which we rather welcomed. The results we have achieved make a very good demonstration of what can be done in the way of soil alteration, even from a very unpromising beginning.

TYPES OF SOIL

Almost everyone, even the apartment-house dweller, knows that there are different types of soil, though his experience with them may be limited to having to clean mud off his shoes or shake sand out of them.

The two best known and the two extremes of texture are found in *sandy* soils and *clay* soils. Within these two types there are again marked differences. If the sand particles are sufficiently coarse we have a gravel which is really not a soil at all, as the individual particles merely fall apart if one attempts to move it. If, on the other hand, clay particles are sufficiently fine, we have a plastic, monolithic mass like modeling clay which, if dried out, forms a stonelike substance or, if sufficiently wet, may be smeared like paint.

When sand and clay (or silt, which contains clay as a rule) are mixed together they blend to form what we know as *loam*. This may be a sandy or a clay loam but differs from its component parts in that it will hold water instead of letting it all drain through as does sand. Unlike clay, it does not remain in sodden lumps and masses, which when they do dry out become as hard as bricks.

To grow good crops or good turf, or to support vigorous shrubs and trees, the soil must be in such physical condition as to absorb and hold a large amount of moisture, but at the same time be open enough to let *surplus* water drain down through it without creating a muddy mass. The ideal soil should hold approximately equal amounts of air and of water; for roots of plants, in order to function normally, must have both.

This knowledge takes us the first step on our way to understanding what type of soil is needed to grow plants successfully. Two other steps, however, remain. One of these is to know the function of organic materials in soil building; the other is to learn the part played by various chemical elements.

ORGANIC MATERIALS IN SOIL BUILDING

Let's look first at the role played by organic materials—animal and vegetable matter undergoing the process of decomposition. It is part of nature's scheme of things that every living plant or animal, when it dies, shall contribute something to the lives of the plants or animals that come after it. This holds true whether the plant or animal is returned directly to the soil, or whether, after having served as food, it is transformed into the waste materials we call manures.

Organic materials when mixed into the soil improve it in many ways. They provide small amounts of the chemicals required by plants in their growth; they add humus to the soil structure; and they provide food for the soil bacteria, which, in turn, releases those chemicals in the soil that are otherwise unavailable to the plants.

Humus (decaying animal and vegetable matter) is an all-important factor in soil fertility. It makes an open, porous soil which allows both air and water to penetrate freely; and also, acting in the soil like millions of tiny sponges, absorbs and holds the water and *the chemical food elements that are in solution in it*. These chemical food elements *must* be in solution before the roots of plants can take them up.

On the other hand humus permits free drainage of *surplus* water down to lower levels. Most forms of plant life, including all the trees, shrubs, flowers, grasses, fruits, and vegetables usually found around a home, cannot long survive in a sodden soil.

One further benefit provided by humus is that, as it forms no provoking clods, it is easy to work. A humusy soil warms up quickly in the spring, making possible earlier preparation and more successful planting. It is in fact a "friable" soil—one that you love to touch!

PLANT FOODS: CHEMICAL ELEMENTS IN THE SOIL

So far we have discussed the physical aspects of soils—the materials which go to make them up, and their various characteristics. We can have all of these in favorable amounts and combinations and still have a soil that is not fertile, that will not make plants *grow*.

There are a number of elements essential to the successful growth of plants. First of all they must have oxygen, carbon, and hydrogen, all of which they obtain from the air and from water.

Next come the three chief nutrients: nitrogen, phosphorus, and potassium. One or often all of these must be supplied or supplemented in the form of fertilizers.

Calcium, magnesium, iron, and sulfur are other important elements that must be present, but most soils contain these in sufficient quantities so that they need not be added. Desert and other alkaline soils are among the few exceptions to this rule. Most of them lack sulfur, and sometimes other elements such as boron.

The so-called trace elements: manganese, boron, copper, zinc, and molybdenum contribute to plant growth, but are needed in such infinitesimal quantities that they seldom have to be added. Many complete fertilizers today, however, do contain these trace elements.

Not only must all of these elements be present in the soil, air, and water, but they must be in forms that are soluble or that will readily become so through soil acids and bacterial action.

The three elements contained in all "complete" fertilizers are nitrogen, phosphorus, and potassium. The percentage of each which commercial fertilizers contain must, by law, be marked on each bag or package. A 5–10–10 formula for example contains 5 per cent nitrogen, 10 per cent phosphorus, and 10 per cent potassium. If boron is present, that is expressed by a fourth figure. The numerals representing the percentages of the several elements are always given in the order mentioned above.

Often, too, the material or materials used in the mixture to provide the given amounts of nitrogen, phosphorus, and potassium are stated. For instance nitrogen may come from sodium nitrate (nitrate of soda) or from tankage or blood and bone (slaughterhouse by-products); phosphorus from superphosphate (processed phosphate rock); and potassium from potassium chloride or wood ashes (potash).

CHEMICAL *vs.* ORGANIC SOURCES

It will be noted that some of these sources of plant-food elements are chemical, others organic. In theory this should make no difference; in actual practice it does.

In the first place, the rapidity with which the chemical is

released and can be taken up by the plant roots is an important factor. The nitrogen from nitrate of soda, for instance, is available almost instantly, while that from bone meal is released very slowly.

As a rule the chemical elements in organic matter become available more quickly than those from mineral sources. The latter take longer to break down in the soil and release the chemical elements in forms that can go into solution and be taken up by the plant roots.

The great big plus in favor of organic sources is that they add not only essential chemical elements to the soil, but also organic matter—and how vitally important that is we have already seen in the discussion on humus earlier in this chapter.

Acid and Alkaline Soils. There is still another respect in which soils differ from one another. They may be acid, sweet, (alkaline), or neutral.

The great majority of plants thrive in soil that is neutral to slightly or moderately acid; a few demand an acid soil; and still fewer a really sweet or alkaline soil.

Soil acidity or alkalinity is measured by what is known as the pH scale, arranged like a thermometer, with 1 representing maximum acidity and 7 as the neutral point (see diagram, page 34).

The question of soil acidity, while important, does not cause as much concern as formerly. More gardeners have come to realize that *a soil in which the humus content is maintained at a high level* greatly decreases the likelihood of injury to plant growth from too great a degree of acidity. It should be noted, however, that the key word here is *maintained,* for soil humus, like an unfed fire, is quickly consumed unless kept replenished.

The Subsoil and Its Importance. The subsoil is, as the word implies, the soil beneath the surface layer. Unlike the surface soil, it has remained for hundreds of years with little or no alteration, other than gaining the nutrients and humus leached down into it by rainfall. In some places the subsoil may be only a few inches below the surface, in others a foot to 20 inches. In our Midwestern states, for instance, where for centuries the prairie grasses grew and rotted down, the topsoil is often up to two feet deep.

Subsoils, like topsoils, vary greatly in composition. They may be sandy or gravelly, allowing rain or applied water to drain away so quickly that plant roots are only temporarily benefited by nutrients in the topsoil above; or they may be

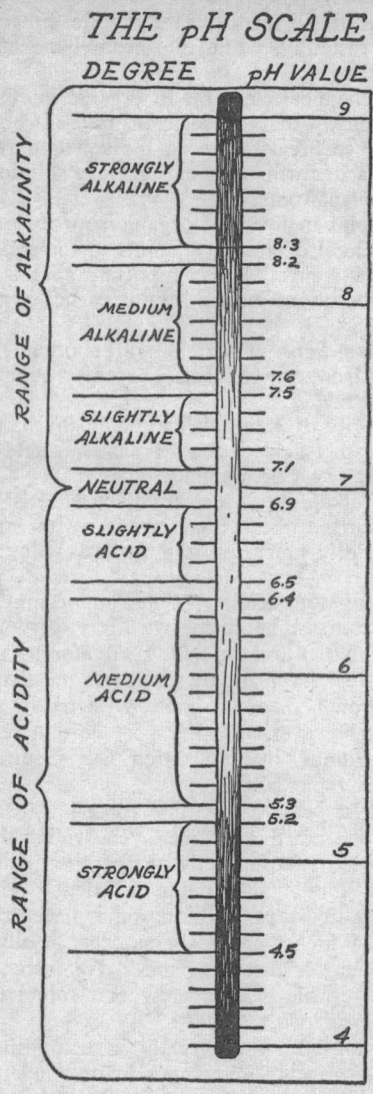

clay or "hard pan," an impervious cementlike layer that holds surplus water so long that air is excluded and plants are quite literally drowned, just as they are in areas that are flooded by the construction of dams.

Some years ago, in landscaping a new home, we had two American elms, each some 25 feet in height, put in for our client. The nurseryman, for a small additional cost, gave a two-year guarantee that they would live. Late the following summer, which was excessively rainy, one tree turned yellow and finally dropped its leaves and died. Examination showed that it had been planted in a pocket of clay subsoil, and for lack of drainage had literally drowned, though no water had collected on the surface. The replacement tree, put in with proper tile drainage to a lower level, grew lustily.

Where the topsoil is very shallow, only 3 to 5 inches, it may be made deeper by turning up, whenever the garden is dug or plowed, 2 to 3 inches of subsoil to be mixed with the surface soil. Or the English system of double digging may be employed.

In extreme cases, where a tenacious clay subsoil exists not far below the surface, the only solution is to put in a drainage system that will carry off the surplus water. While this may be made a do-it-yourself job, it is usually better to have it done professionally.

The first step is to establish a grade from the high point on the area to be drained to some low point such as a roadside gutter or a drainage ditch. The drains should be sufficiently below the surface to escape accidental breakage or disturbance, usually a minimum of 8 to 12 inches. Either ceramic drain pipes (which are 24 inches long, with an open collar at one end that permits soil water freely to enter the joints), or the newer composition drain pipe (which has perforations along its entire length) may be used. The latter has the advantage that it can be laid in a continuous strip to a more even slope, thus saving much time. Also there is less chance of accidental breakage after it is laid.

If some coarse, nonpacking material such as small stones, crushed stone, very coarse gravel, or brick and mortar rubble is filled in around and over the drain tile or pipe, the effectiveness of the drainage system is greatly increased. The sketch on page 37 shows the layout for a drainage system for a moderate-sized area.

A most important point in installing a drainage system is that there shall be no sags or low spots. If there are, the whole purpose is defeated, for water that has drained *into*

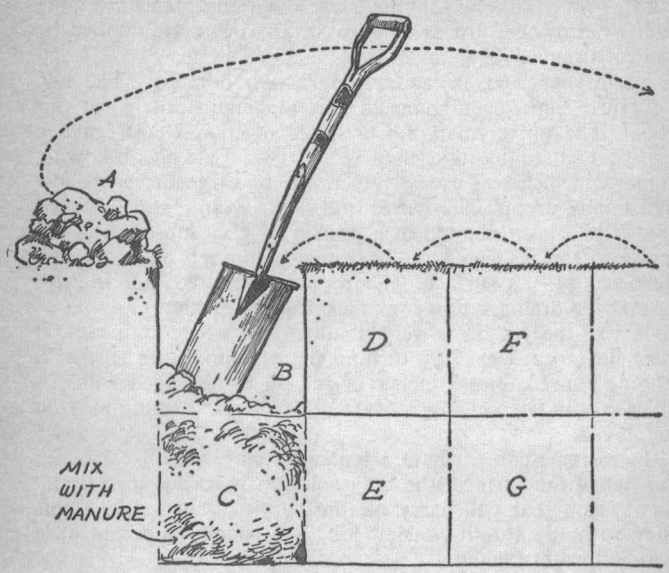

DOUBLE DIGGING. A—*Soil is removed from area B, making an open trench.*
C—*Subsoil in area C is forked over and mixed with manure or peatmoss and compost.*
D—*Topsoil from this area is forked over, mixed with compost and fertilizer, and placed in trench C.*
E—*This area is forked over and treated as area C.*
F—*Is treated as area D, the enriched soil being placed in area D. This operation is repeated over the entire area to be dug.*
A—*Topsoil A is enriched and carried across at the end of the digging operation to fill in the remaining open trench at the far side of the garden.*

the system from a higher elevation will, at such places, drain *out* of it, back into the soil.

Too porous subsoil, so sandy or gravelly that little or no moisture is retained, creates a very serious condition. The only remedy here is to build up the amount of humus in the surface soil by every means available—such as adding manure, peatmoss, and other forms of organic matter; using mulching materials wherever possible; and growing "green manure" crops such as rye, ryegrass, oats, clover, and vetch (see pages 41-42).

Where heavy (clay) soil does not dry out promptly after rain, it is necessary to install drainage tile, with open joints to admit water. This greatly increases the range of plants which may be grown.

SPECIAL AREA SOIL TYPES

While our discussion so far has covered average soils such as are encountered over most of the United States, there are areas where nontypical soils present special problems. In some instances such soil types are almost state-wide, in others less than the size of a county, or even of a township.

Though we cannot go into complete details about such soils, we can guide the reader in recognizing them, and tell him how to set about making them better fitted for growing the average run of trees, shrubs, and other plants.

Clay and Sandy Soils. These, as we have seen, are the two extreme types of average soils found everywhere. The way to improve the structure of either is to add the other, *plus humus.*

Peat Soils. These are composed basically of vegetable matter that has started to decay but has been arrested in the process by being covered with water or with soil. (Under some conditions the process continued to eventually form coal.)

If the vegetable material happened to be sphagnum moss, it was converted to what we know as moss-peat: or more generally, but incorrectly, as peatmoss, for it is peat formed from moss, *not* moss formed from peat.

If the vegetable matter was made up of sedges and other

bog plants, the eventual product became peat—or sedge peat —quite different in its physical make-up from moss-peat. This is true particularly of its more limited capacity to absorb and hold water.

Both types of peat are extremely valuable for horticultural uses—but to home gardeners especially so in their processed commercial forms, added to other soils.

Muck Soils, found in drained or dried-up bog and marsh areas, also contain much decayed or semidecayed vegetable matter and serve for the extensive growing of special crops such as celery, lettuce, onions, and cranberries, which are suited to the conditions they provide.

Frequently such muck soils, partially dried, are dug and sold or peddled locally to inexperienced homeowners and gardeners who are misled, by their nice crumbly structure and black-as-your-hat color, into thinking that they are necessarily "rich." They may be; but there is an equal or better chance that they may be next to worthless. The novice is well advised to consult his local county agent before buying. He is likely to have some knowledge of such materials offered for local sale.

Adobe and Gumbo Soils cover extensive areas of low rainfall in the West and Southwest. Often they are naturally well supplied with plant-food elements but these are unavailable because there is not enough moisture to release them and because of the soil's physical properties. For their treatment and improvement see page 49.

A BRIEF LOOK AT THE SOILS OF THE UNITED STATES
(See insert for map.)

Roughly, the soils of this country are divided in half by an imaginary line running north and south in the vicinity of Lincoln, Nebraska.

West of this line, soils are largely unleached (except in areas of high rainfall along the Pacific coast and in a few fertile valleys and river basins). That is to say there is so little rainfall that the soluble salts of potassium and sodium and the less soluble calcium and magnesium salts remain near the soil surface, unleached and unavailable to plant roots, thus contributing in varying degrees to aridity.

East of this line, rainfall gradually increases, and as it does so, salts, mineral nutrients, and humus are increasingly leached down below the surface to varying depths, but usually not beyond the reach of plant roots. In the east and central parts of the United States, a great variety of ornamental and food plants may be grown, not because the soil is more fertile than much of that farther west, but because of the long growing season, and because the high rainfall makes readily available to plant roots the nutrients from the topsoil. *The Alkaline Soils,* some of which are so saline that they cannot be made fertile until their salt content has been artificially leached away, occur in those parts of the country where rainfall is very low, for fertility is closely related to humidity, since, to be available for plant growth, nutrients must be in solution.

In the driest regions we find pale *desert soils (adobe),* practically without humus, where the surface salts contribute to their gray color; or very dark, fine-grained, silty *gumbo* soils which, when wet, become soapy, waxy, or sticky, and are completely unworkable in that condition. Often desert areas are so strongly alkaline that only alkaline-resistant plants can survive except where conditions have been improved through irrigation and when necessary, also by leaching of the surface salts (page 50).

East of the desert areas, *grayish-brown soils* occur which contain some humus and a considerable content of soluble salts. Instead of accumulating on the surface, as in the desert itself, calcium carbonates are here leached down by a little more rainfall (5 to 18 inches annually) to a depth of 12 to 15 inches. On these unimproved soils, low, sparse grass and wild shrubs are found. With irrigation other things may be grown, but commercially these lands are used largely for grazing.

Chestnut soils occur east of the grayish-brown, in areas where rainfall is 15 to 22 inches per annum. Here calcium salts are leached down 14 to 24 inches below the surface. There is more humus content, enough to give it a chestnut-brown color, and on it cereal grains can be grown where artificial irrigation is used. Providing adequate water makes this land highly productive.

East of this again, we find the Great Plains of the central United States, the soil containing little potassium or sodium but a heavy content of calcium salts 24 to 36 inches below the surface. In the thick humus layer, 15 inches or more in depth, formed by the prairie grasses that originally grew there, there exists ample nitrogen and mineral nutrients, released only by moisture.

The true *prairie soils,* very dark or almost black in color, are to be found still farther east, in the area of which the present Iowa corn belt is the heart. Here, where rainfall is heavy, the wild prairie grasses originally grew to the height of a man, and created a humus layer of 20 inches or more. This humus layer retains large quantities of nutrients and moisture, providing the richest soil in the country for the commercial growing of corn, oats, wheat, and fodders.

Eastward from the prairie lands, the country was originally timbered. Rainfall is high—30 to 50 inches—and humus considerable, though, except in northern forest sections, it has been carried well below the surface together with calcium salts, iron, and aluminum. Because of favorable climate and plentiful rainfall, however, these soils become highly productive when well fertilized and regularly supplied with supplementary humus.

In the far northern lands, which are both cold and wet, more of the ample humus, salts, and other nutrients remain near the surface because of the natural mulch on the forest floor, but for many plants the growing season is too short.

Along the border states from Minnesota to New York, on the Atlantic Seaboard and along the Gulf coast, areas of rainfall and humidity have created soils largely made up of decomposed organic matter and therefore called *organic soils*. These, when drained and correctly handled, are highly fertile.

REMAKING AND MAINTAINING SOILS

So now we come to the all-important part of this chapter: how to improve unsatisfactory soils and how to maintain good ones. For even a good soil has to be *kept* good. Otherwise it will run down—and in time run out!

Every homeowner or gardener has, of course, to start with the soil he has, but unless it is a *very* exceptional soil, he can within the course of two or three years change it to the type that will support most of the plants he desires to grow. In most instances this development need not involve any very great expense.

The one thing he should *not* expect to do, if his soil is lacking in humus, is to convert it into a productive loam merely by adding large quantities of chemical fertilizers. Yet, as a result of ignorance and exaggerated and misleading claims made by some unscrupulous advertisers, this is exactly what hundreds of thousands of gullible new homeowners annually do expect to accomplish.

Here is a safe and sane program for creating productive soil in areas where there are no *acute* soil problems of alkalinity, salinity, alkali-salinity, or acidity. First, determine the character of the soil you have to start with.

One need not be a chemist to determine if he has sandy soil or a clay soil. If decidedly of either type, it may be improved by adding, if it is procurable, soil of the opposite type. A one- to two-inch layer of either type will usually work wonders, especially if supplemented by a dressing of lime (see page 48) and by humus.

A heavy application of *manure*—a layer two to three inches thick, is the quickest method of improving both the physical condition of the soil and providing immediately available plant foods. It should be partly rotted; and a mixture of horse and cow manure is better than either one alone.

Hen manure and sheep manure are very strong, and best used only after they have been mixed with compost, dead leaves, or other organic roughage and have begun to decay.

All animal manures are becoming, in most sections, more and more difficult to get. Therefore, to add sufficient amounts of humus to build up a soil in such areas, it becomes increasingly necessary to use substitutes for them.

The two most useful substitutes are *peatmoss* and *green manures*. The latter is made up of crops which are grown for the purpose of digging or plowing under before they mature, to decay in the soil, and thus add to it large amounts of humus (see also page 93).

Peatmoss has the advantage of being immediately effective, furnishing humus in an ideal form. Green manures have the advantage of being very much less expensive—just the cost of the seed and sufficient fertilizer to give them a good start—but they require several months to a year from the time of sowing until they have been turned under and have decayed in the soil. Some of them, such as rye, ryegrass, and winter vetch, may be sown in the fall to make winter growth and be turned under the following spring. Other good, green manure crops are vetch, sweet clover, crimson clover, alsike clover, and hairy vetch. All the clovers and vetches are legumes and so have the extra advantage of adding nitrogen to the soil.

A procedure which we have used successfully in bringing much of our barren soil into a high degree of productivity is that of sowing winter rye on flower beds or vegetable plots as soon as they are cleared in late summer or fall, adding a high nitrogen fertilizer to give them a quick start, and turning them under as the ground is needed in spring. No patch of soil, at any time of year, is left long without a cover crop on it to manufacture humus.

The Compost Heap is another most valuable source of humus

to the home gardener. In an efficiently run garden there is always one mature heap ready for use, plus a more recently made pile in the process of decomposition.

If one heap is built each autumn, using vegetable wastes stored for the purpose during the summer in a rough pile, plus undiseased, pest-free plants which have completed their growth cycle, and weeds which have not gone to seed, the gardener will at all times have compost available when needed.

To build an ideal compost heap, the following materials should be at hand:

1. Coarse dead stalks and stems such as those of corn, zinnia, or marigold for the bottom layer.
2. Grass cuttings, dead leaves, young weeds, and other vegetable wastes and garbage such as rotting or overmature fruits and vegetables, and peelings.
3. Garden soil.
4. Peatmoss and/or well-rotted leafmold.
5. Agricultural lime.
6. Manure, if available.
7. Complete fertilizer.

Location should be in part shade, where water is available, and in a position screened from flower gardens and the outdoor living areas.

Size can be as desired; 4 to 8 feet by 4 feet is convenient. After measuring off the area, a shallow pit one foot deep is dug; or a bin, built of cement blocks or boards, may be used as a base.

First layer. Fill the pit with coarse stems and stalks and with any large lumps of undecomposed compost left over from siftings of older, mature heap.

Second layer, 6 inches deep, is of grass cuttings, weeds, garbage, etc., from rough storage pile. Sprinkle this with complete fertilizer and lime, and wet down.

Third layer, 3 inches deep, is of garden soil.

Fourth layer, 3 to 6 inches deep, should be of manure if available, or peatmoss mixed with dry commercial manure such as Bovung or Driconure.

Repeat sequence, beginning with the second layer, until heap is 4 to 6 feet high.

The heap should be built with the sides sloping gently inward, and the top left with a saucerlike depression to hold water. When completed, enough water is given to saturate all materials in the heap without leaching.

The entire heap may be turned "inside out" with a spading fork at the end of one and a half months to hasten decompo-

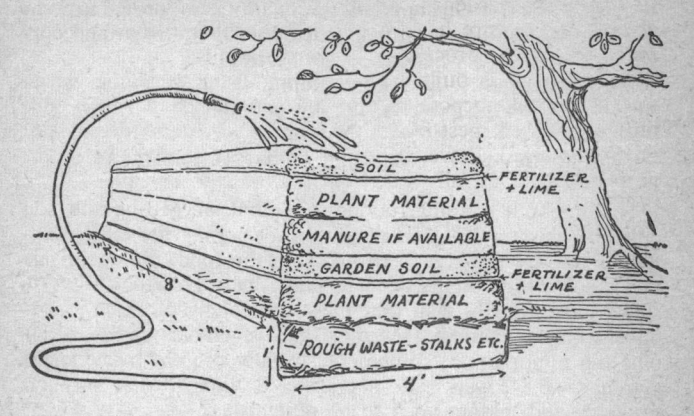

One of the greatest aids in growing plants of all kinds is the maintenance of a well-made compost heap, sprinkled occasionally to keep it moist. It may not look as neat as our artist's sketch, but if it can be placed near the garden itself, much time will be saved as the rotted, sifted compost is transported to beds and borders.

sition; and again a month later. We seldom turn our compost but depend on the varied contents of the heaps, including manure, fertilizer, lime and peatmoss, to complete decomposition in 4 to 6 months.

In climates subject to extended dry spells the heap should be watered frequently to facilitate rapid rotting; it must be moist at all times.

In from three to six months, depending on how well it has been built and the materials it contains, the compost is ready for use. It may be sifted through an inch-mesh screen for potting up seedlings or setting out young plants, or to place in rows and beds for outdoor seed sowing; or may be used unsifted in perennial beds and borders and in the bottoms of holes when planting trees and shrubs. The product should be very dark in color, light in texture, but rich, easily sifted, and crumbly.

Martin E. Weeks, of the College of Agriculture, University of Massachusetts, in his booklet *Composts for the Home Grounds* states that well-made compost is the equivalent of the best grade of animal manures, *plus* its added content of chemical fertilizers and lime.

Many State Experiment Stations issue bulletins on compost making, stressing the use of locally available materials.

So much for the first step in building up productive soils

—getting them well supplied with humus in order to keep them open, to hold moisture, provide good drainage and conditions favorable for beneficial soil bacteria.

Now we come to the second step.

PROVIDING THE ESSENTIAL CHEMICAL ELEMENTS

Having built a solid foundation—that of getting the soil into first class *mechanical* condition, or setting the table so to speak—we are now ready to bring on the food, the chemicals in the soil which plants need to make lusty growth.

We have already seen that these are chiefly nitrogen, phosphorus, and potassium (the meat and vegetables of the meal) plus the minor or trace elements usually present in sufficient amounts—the sugar, salt, pepper, and vinegar that stay on the table and seldom need to be replenished.

Nitrogen. There are many materials which provide nitrogen: organic sources such as animal manures and processed animal and vegetable materials like tankage, cottonseed meal, and a number of others, seldom in these days used by the amateur gardener. Chemical sources include ammonium nitrate and sodium nitrate (nitrate of soda) ranging from 5 to 15 or 20 per cent of nitrogen in very quickly available but not long-lasting forms. The effect of nitrate of soda, for instance, can often be seen within two or three days after it is applied. Newly developed types of nitrogen-bearing chemicals —such as urea—release the nitrogen slowly and so are much more effective as season-long fertilizers. Nitrate of soda and similar quick-acting forms are excellent for giving plants a strong, quick start, but should be used with judgment and caution. Otherwise their use may result in too luxuriant, soft growth, or may even "burn" the roots. The chief function of nitrogen in nature's plan is to assure luxuriant growth of foliage of good color and substance.

Phosphorus, second of the big-three plant-food elements, is effective in vigorous root, tuber, and seed development, and so complements or balances nitrogen.

Many soils are low in phosphorus, particularly in forms that can be taken up by plant roots. Fortunately this element, in forms readily available as plant food, is to be had in superphosphate, and in triplephosphate. The former contains 20 per cent and the latter 45 per cent phosphorus. Both are commonly used in commercial fertilizers as a source of phosphorus. Bone meal contains 20 to 25 per cent phosphorus, plus some nitrogen, and is a very safe (nonburning) fertilizer to use, *especially in transplanting.*

Potassium, third of the big three, is important because it contributes to vigorous root growth and strong, sturdy stems. It is present in ample quantity in most soils but, unfortunately for gardeners, in forms that cannot be taken up by plant roots until abundant humus in the soil and the action of soil bacteria have made it so.

In most soils that are well supplied with humus, potassium in available forms will be ample. Where a soil analysis shows that it is deficient, it may be added by applying sulfate or muriate of potash. Where wood ashes are to be had, either homemade or purchased, they provide an excellent organic source of potash.

"COMPLETE" FERTILIZERS

Few homeowners these days attempt to mix their own fertilizers, but some knowledge of their ingredients is essential to those who wish to procure the best types and use them to the best advantage. Millions of dollars are wasted annually on "special" fertilizers for this, that, and the other purpose, which can accomplish no more than standard mixtures.

Every fertilizer must carry an analysis showing how much of each of the three important plant-food elements—nitrogen, phosphorus, and potassium—it contains. The best give information as to the sources from which these are derived. If the fertilizer mixture is an honest one, and carries the ingredients your particular soil needs, it will grow roses just as well as it will grow potatoes. No special formula is needed for "special" purposes, with the exception of such special groups as azaleas, rhododendrons, and other acid-loving plants which thrive best on acid-forming plant foods or those supplemented by acids.

It is infinitely more important to find out what your soil *needs, and procure a fertilizer that will provide it, than to buy special fertilizers for the* plants *you intend to grow.*

SOIL TESTS AND ADVICE ON SOIL IMPROVEMENT

For the gardener whose land is in an area where lack of fertility, extreme alkalinity, salinity, alkali-salinity, or acidity is a general problem, the first act should be to take soil samples from various spots on his grounds and have these analyzed by the nearest Agricultural Experiment Station.

The results of these tests then determine what must be done to improve each particular soil and to maintain it in a state of fertility. Specific advice on his soil problem is what each gardener needs in such areas, and it is what he will get if he submits soil samples to his county agent or Experiment Station.

Soil tests should be taken in the following manner:

In a 10-quart pail 5 to 10 samples are taken from each area to be planted—the number of samples depending on the size

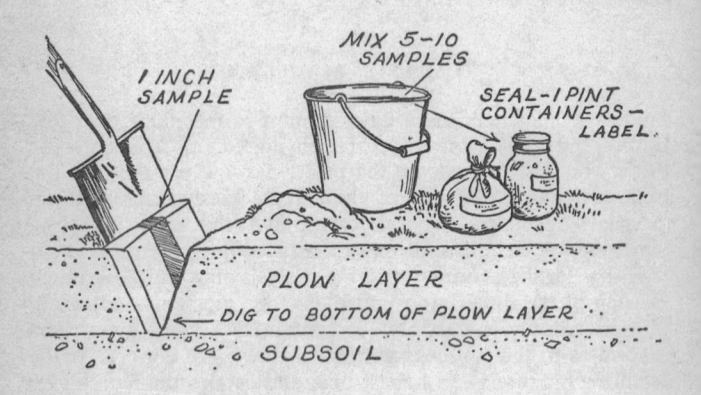

How to take soil samples for testing.

of each plot. Each sample is taken to the full depth of a transplanting spade, but need be only an inch in width and one in thickness. The various samples for one plot are then mixed thoroughly together in a pail, and a pint of each mixture is packed in glass or in a heavy plastic bag. Seal each container to prevent contamination and label each so that it can be identified as to the part of the garden from which it came. A sample of subsoil taken at 18 to 24 inches in depth may also help, especially in muck or peat soils.

Other information that will assist the analyst in determining what should be done is:

When the plot was last limed, manured, green manured,

THE SOIL AND HOW TO MANAGE IT 47

and fertilized, with rates of application. Any other amendment that may have been used should be mentioned, giving, if possible, date and quantity applied per 100 square feet.

Drainage conditions and what, if anything, has been done to improve them if they are unsatisfactory.

When the report comes back it should include specific recommendations for improvement and how often these corrective measures are to be repeated. In dealing with problem soils, new tests should be made every 2 to 5 years.

Does this seem like too much trouble? It may take you an hour at most to prepare such samples. The result is likely to save you many hours of labor that will not yield maximum results, to say nothing of wasted expenditures for seed, plants, and fertilizers. *Think it over!*

Pretty much every county in these widespread United States—including ice-locked Alaska and sun-flooded Hawaii—has a man waiting to help you with your particular soil problems. He is your local county agent. Your taxes help to support him; do not hesitate to ask for the assistance he is glad to provide.

SPECIAL SOIL PROBLEMS AND THEIR SOLUTIONS
ACID SOILS AND THEIR IMPROVEMENT

In the eastern part of the United States, soils which have proved unsatisfactory for growing most plants are frequently too acid for all but a comparatively small group of acid-lovers.

Acid soils may be improved and their pH raised to a point where most plants readily grow by:

1. A regular program of *green manuring* (pages 41; 93) which, by adding humus, reduces acidity while improving the soil's mechanical condition.

2. The application of *raw ground limestone*, the material most commonly used to correct moderate soil acidity. This can be applied in fall or spring at the rate of 10 pounds to 150 square feet; or as directed by the county agent after soil samples have been analyzed.

3. *Wood ashes*, which contain large percentages of lime as well as potash, may be used at the rate of six pecks per 100 square feet.

A pH between 5.5 and 6.5 or 7 (neutral) is suitable for most flowers and vegetables.

TABLE

POUNDS OF RAW GROUND LIMESTONE PER 1000 SQUARE FEET TO RAISE pH TO 6

Original soil acidity	Light sandy soil	Medium sandy	Loam and Silt	Clay
pH 4.0	90 lbs.	120 lbs.	172 lbs.	217 lbs.
4.5	82	112	157	202
5.0	67	90	127	150
5.5	52	67	97	120

AMOUNTS OF SULFUR REQUIRED TO CHANGE pH OF A SILT-LOAM SOIL

from pH	to	lbs. sulfur per 100 sq. ft.
8	6.5	3.0
8	6.0	4.0
8	5.5	5.5
7.5	6.5	2.0
7.5	6.0	3.5
7.5	5.5	5.0
7.5	5.0	6.5

ACIDIFYING AND FERTILIZING NEUTRAL OR NEAR-NEUTRAL SOILS IN ORDER TO GROW *ACID-LOVING PLANTS*

Azaleas and rhododendrons prefer a pH of 4.5 to 5.5; hollies and camellias 5 to 5.5. Special treatment must be given neutral or near-neutral soils to attain the needed pH. For this purpose the following mixture may be used:

Equal parts by weight of aluminum sulfate
iron sulfate
ammonium sulfate

Sulfur (325 mesh) or superfine, can be worked into the soil before planting, or added to acid mulches such as hardwood leaves, pine needles, or acid peatmoss, before applying these to established plantings.

An acid fertilizer (4–6–8 formula) suitable for feeding acid-loving plants consists of a mixture of:

10 lbs. ammonium sulfate
35 lbs. 16% superphosphate
17 lbs. 50% sulfate of potash
28 lbs. cottonseed meal
10 lbs. aluminum sulfate

This is applied at the rate of *not more than* 1 to 1½ lbs. per 100 square feet, acid leafmold and/or acid peatmoss being applied at the same time.

For clay soils which need acidifying, cottonseed meal alone makes an effective acid fertilizer.

ALKALINE AND SALINE SOILS AND THEIR IMPROVEMENT

Much can be done to improve highly *alkaline* soils where excessive sodium is present; *saline* soils which contain high percentages of salts, but not sodium; and those *alkaline-saline* soils which are plagued by too much sodium and also large amounts of saline salts.

ALKALINE SOILS

Should be tested by the nearest Agricultural Experiment Station to determine just what corrective measures are needed.

Such soils exist in arid regions of very low rainfall and also in some parts of the West (as in Washington State) where a high water table and impervious soil texture cause surface accumulations of salts.

Symptoms of alkalinity are: light gray color (exceptions are gumbo soils, which are almost black but of a sticky or waxy texture that cannot be worked when wet); excessive washing (erosion); and the characteristic of forming hard, brick-like or fragile clods or crumbs when dry.

Correctly amended these soils release their calcium—a most important plant nutrient—which is unavailable in their natural state. When improved many such soils can be made highly productive. In dry regions, irrigation is necessary for reclamation.

Amendments applied commonly contain sulfur:
Gypsum (calcium sulfate) contains 19.5 to 21 per cent calcium and 16 to 18 per cent sulfur. It dissolves quickly and easily in irrigated soils and releases its calcium at once, so it is the fastest acting amendment.
Iron sulfate must be carefully handled, because when wet it is converted into sulfuric acid. It works fast in moist soil to form gypsum.
99 per cent dry sulfur, if ground very fine (40 mesh or finer), forms sulfuric acid quickly and converts to gypsum. Lower grades and coarser grinds require greater quantities —up to 3 times as much as the 99 per cent fine ground—to give comparable results.

Lime-sulfur (calcium polysulfide) and *Blue Chip Sulfur* are other forms often used.

The county agent or nearest Agricultural Experiment Station should be consulted as to the best material to use in any specific area, and the quantity needed per 1000 square feet.

SALINE SOILS

Where salinity occurs without excessive alkali, leaching is the only solution. It is impossible to remove or change these salts by the application of any chemical or other soil amendment. In irrigated land (as in the California desert regions) and where the water table is high (as in some parts of Washington State), excessive soluble salts are often deposited in the surface soil and must be washed away.

Sometimes a temporary pond is created on saline land until enough salt has been leached down to a lower level to make the land usable. The area is then permitted to dry out, is fertilized, and planted. Where much irrigation must be resorted to, the salts may reform in time. In this case, leaching is repeated at intervals, as needed.

Where salinity is present but less pronounced, beds may be built on a slant so that, when irrigated, the salts can drain off.

In the case of salinity, as in that of alkalinity, tests of the soil should be taken and recommendations of the State Agricultural Station followed.

ALKALINE-SALINE SOILS

When both problems discussed above occur in conjunction, leaching *and* amendments containing sulfur must be resorted to. Here the advice of a government soil expert is essential to success and no time should be wasted in seeking his help through the nearest State Agricultural Experiment Station.

Drainage. Alkaline and/or saline soils which are poorly drained, with a water table a minimum of 3 feet below the surface, must be made porous enough so that the water is lowered to at least 5 feet.

Wind erosion may also be a problem both in dry land areas and in such sections as the Columbia River Basin. Dust bowl conditions develop in windy country where unplanted soil is very finely pulverized and does not contain enough clay and humus to hold it in a wind.

THE SOIL AND HOW TO MANAGE IT

Such soils should be rough-dug or tilled *when wet,* leaving the clods that form until planting time, to prevent blowing of the fine particles. As little time as possible is left between the operations of cultivating and planting. When watered, fragile clods or crumbs such as are formed by many of these soils break up or dissolve very readily.

Humus, HUMUS, HUMUS. In preparing new beds and borders in these soils, the wild growth is dug under to decay and form humus. Under no circumstances should it be removed! The more humus in the soil, the less danger of soil erosion. As soon as matured plants have been removed from beds and borders in autumn, a cover crop should be planted to hold the soil. Summer cover crops are also planted on fallow land. *Windbreaks* are helpful in preventing erosion from excessive blowing.

FERTILITY AND FERTILIZERS FOR ARID SOILS

In arid soils ample *potassium, calcium,* and needed trace elements are often present and can be made available by means of irrigation, which puts them in solution.

Where *potassium* and *nitrogen* are lacking in slightly alkaline soils, potassium sulfate and ammonium sulfate are good sources, both reducing alkalinity and providing major nutrients. Phosphoric oxide is recommended to supply phosphorus where needed.

Boron is a trace element sometimes found to be lacking in arid lands, and where it is not present certain plants will not thrive (walnuts, clover, and strawberries are examples). Borax can be used to supply this deficiency, 4 to 6 pounds being applied to the soil around each mature tree; beds and borders in similar proportion.

Through the dear intercourse of sun and dew
Of thrilling root, and folding earth, anew
They come, in beauty.
> The Buds by JAMES STEPHENS

CHAPTER 3

The Plant and How It Grows

This is not a book about botany—"the branch of biology dealing with plant life," according to Mr. Webster.

There are many successful gardeners—that is, people who succeed in making plants grow—who know next to nothing about botany. However a certain amount of information about plant anatomy and growth helps both in selecting plants which will give the results we wish to attain and in achieving success in their culture.

THE PLANT'S ANATOMY

A plant, like an animal, is a wonderful combination of specialized parts or organs which work together in their own mysterious ways to maintain a living entity capable both of supporting itself and of creating offspring in its own image.

The most significant difference between animals and plants is that the former can move about at will to search for and find their food and drink. They can even leave their environment if it becomes too hostile and seek another. A plant is anchored to one spot and either lives upon what nature provides or perishes.

Without being technical it may be said that the plant is made up of these several distinct parts.

THE PLANT AND HOW IT GROWS 53

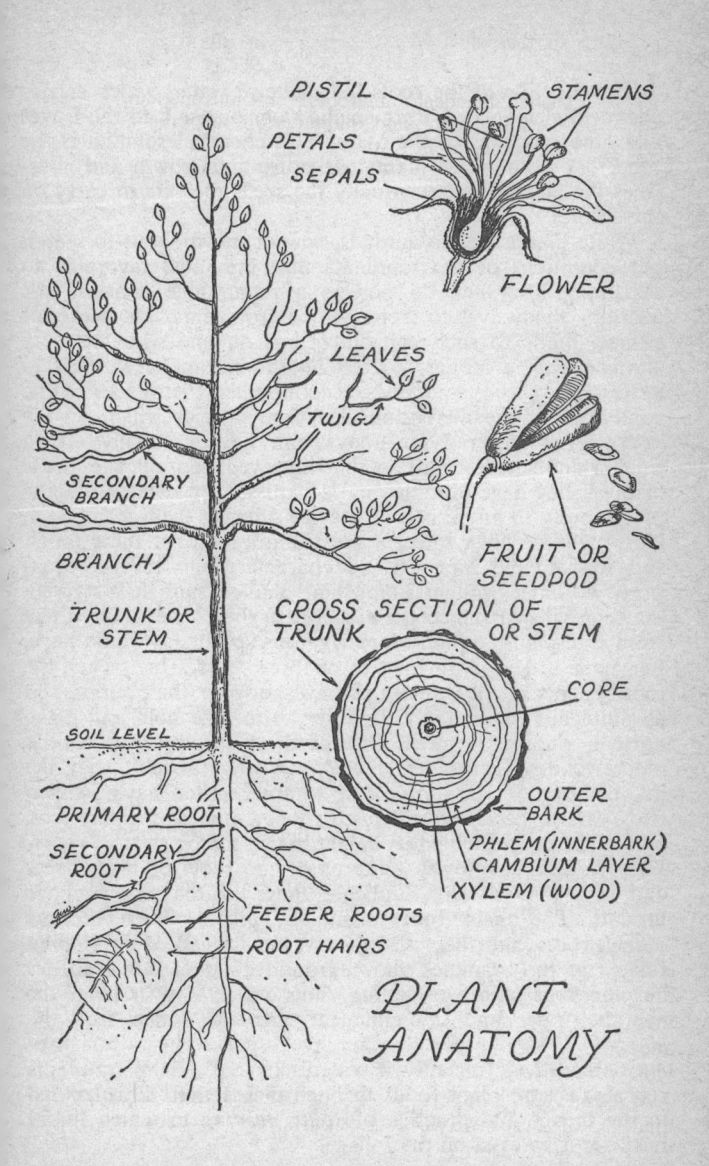

Roots
Stems or trunks
Foliage
Flowers
Fruits
Seeds

The function of the roots is to take in water, which carries chemical elements up through the stem or trunk to the leaves and other portions of the plant. This chemical solution is the food that sustains the plants' structure and growth and nourishes the flowers and eventually the seeds that are to carry on the species.

While plants, unlike animals, cannot move about to search out conditions or environments that are most favorable to sustaining life, they do possess a remarkable capacity for adapting themselves to their own environments. There are, of course, limits to such capacities; but no one who has ever climbed even a moderate-sized mountain can have failed to notice how shrubs and trees accommodate themselves to the conditions of the increasing elevation. Species which on the lower levels towered far above him have gradually grown smaller and smaller until, at the windswept summit, the giants of the valley have become gnarled, misshapen dwarfs clinging precariously to any crack or crevice offering them a toe hold. Personally we always feel a great admiration for these tough and indomitable high-altitude characters. On several occasions we have brought home and planted such half-starved, under-privileged subjects. In each case they have suffered less from transplanting than more vigorous specimens would have, but made little growth for two or three years. Then, when the root systems seemed finally to have got over their surprise at an abundant food supply, they began to take hold and make normal, vigorous growth. One of these specimens is a little moosewood (*Acer pennsylvanicum*) which came from the hill country of Vermont. Last summer, after having taken two years to decide that it liked its new home, it finally took hold and nearly doubled its height in one season.

The Roots. The growth patterns of the roots of many trees and shrubs in a way duplicate those of the plants above ground. The main roots send out others which become branch roots, and these still others; but instead of developing foliage as the branches above ground do, the root branches develop root hairs or feeding roots which absorb from the soil the water and the chemical nutrients which feed the plant.

Comparatively recently it was discovered that many plants can also absorb plant foods through their leaves. This has led to the theory and practice of *foliar feeding* in which liquid fertilizer is sprayed on the foliage.

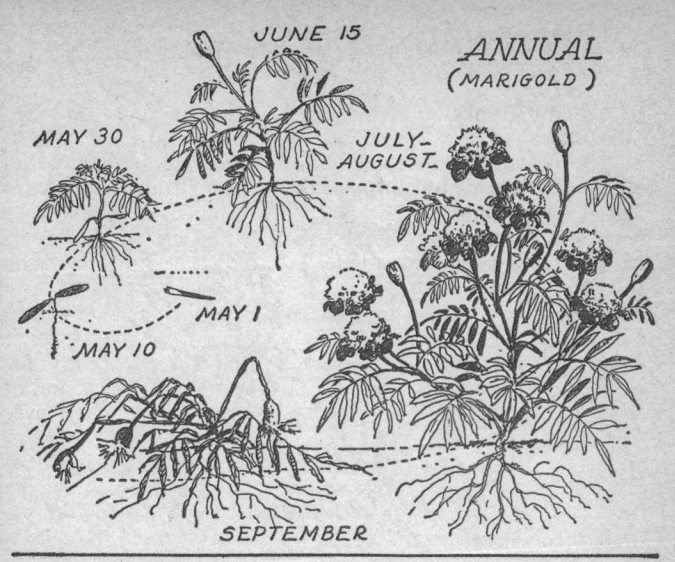

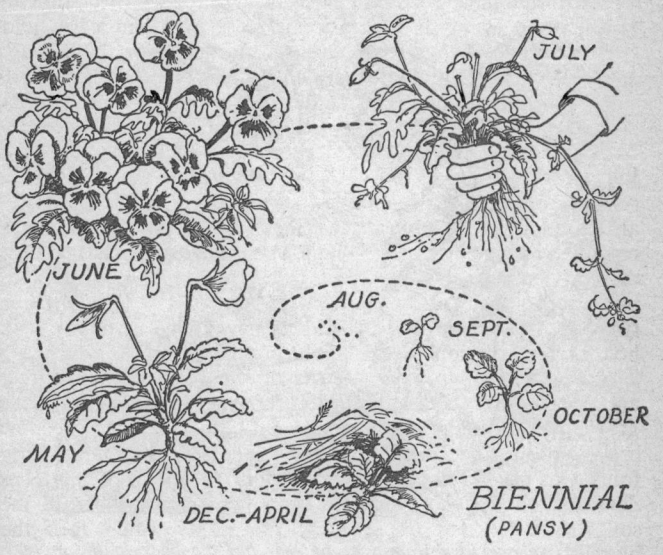

The life cycle of a plant may extend for a few weeks or months, or may continue for several hundred years. It is important that the gardener know the growth habit of any plant which he attempts to grow. Annuals (above) live but a single growing season. Biennials (below) take two growing seasons to reach maturity, bloom, seed, and die.

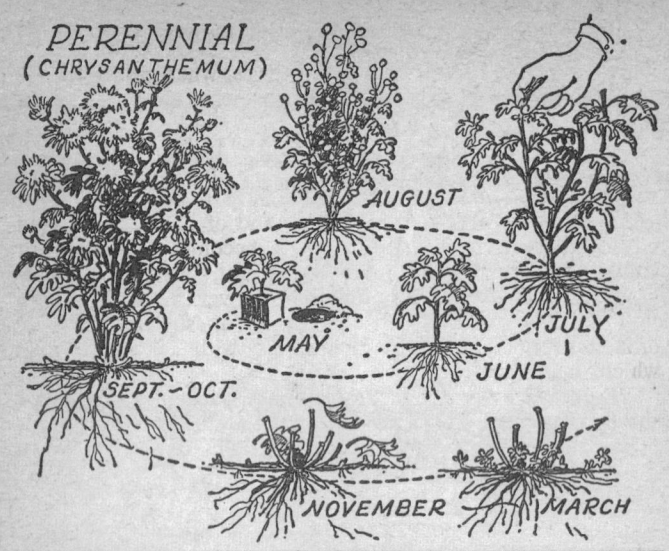

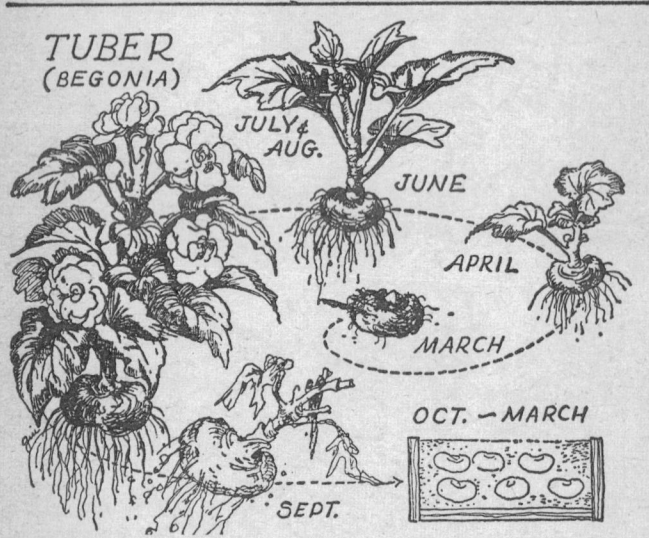

Perennials *(above)* live from year to year but die back to the ground each winter where freezing occurs. Hardy roots throw up new growth each spring. Tubers *(below)*, as well as corms, are like true bulbs in that they live on from year to year. Many are frost-tender and must be given frost-free storage in winter. Started into new growth in spring, they produce summer flowers and are dug and dried off for storage each autumn.

THE PLANT AND HOW IT GROWS

Often the main roots of very old trees, where they join the trunk, gradually become more like branches than like roots, as in the case of ancient elms, oaks, and some evergreens.

Stems and Trunks. As a seed sprouts and begins to grow, that portion above ground pushes up into the air "reaching for the sun." It develops leaves and eventually a central stem or group of stems. In the case of trees and of many shrubs and vines, this central, permanent growth becomes the trunk (or trunks) which, like the main or taproot, branches and re-branches. Just as the terminal roots cover themselves with fine hairlike roots which absorb food, so the terminal branches or twigs clothe themselves with leaves through which they "breathe."

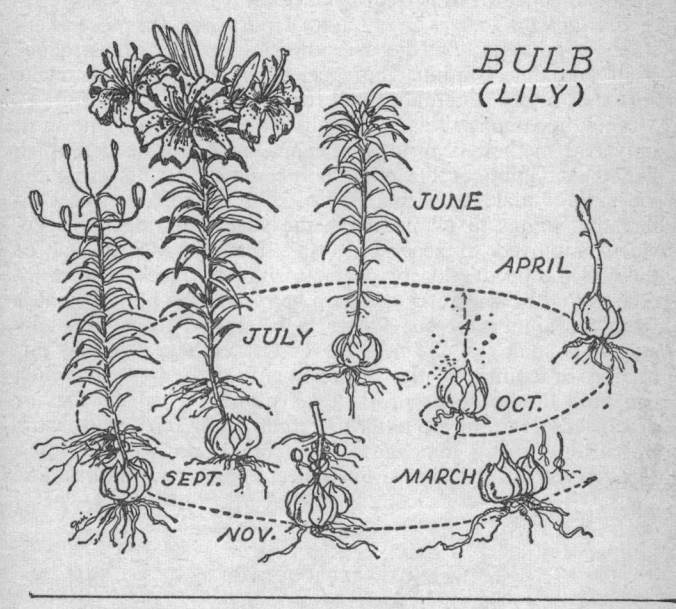

While the description above applies particularly to trees, shrubs, and perennial vines, it is true also, in modified forms, of annuals, biennials, perennials, and bulbs that die back to

Many true bulbs such as lilies, daffodils, tulips, and other spring-flowering sorts are winter-hardy in the north. Once planted, they live and bloom for some years. Most hardy bulbs are fall-planted for bloom the following spring or summer. Tender bulbs like amaryllis or veltheimia are grown in pots in the north and wintered indoors, but remain in the garden year-round in warm climates.

the ground each year. The growth cycle of a number of different types of plants are shown in the accompanying sketches.

Here the miracle of growth begins. The soil, water, and chemicals combine to be transformed into life-giving sap which is carried onward and upward, defying the law of gravity, to the very tips of every branch and leaf.

This pipeline system of trunk or stem, with its branches, continues growth until the plant is mature—which may be a matter of a few weeks or of several centuries!

The *leaves* of the plant (or in some species the scales, bracts, or skin surfaces that take the place of leaves) form the breathing apparatus through which it gets the oxygen that, like any living thing, it must have in order to exist.

This combination of roots, stem structure, and leaves continues to function in perfect balance until the plant dies.

Reproduction. Just as every animal possesses, or more accurately is possessed by, the overpowering instinct to reproduce itself and thus continue the species, so also do plants make sure that future generations will follow them.

They accomplish this in various ways but by far the most universal method is through the production of seeds, which like the creation of the embryo in animals results from the merging of male and female germ cells. One of the most interesting things in all nature is the variety of ingenious devices employed to accomplish this mating. Most usual of these is the production of nectar to lure the bee or other insect so that he will carry away on hairy legs the pollen (male) from the anthers of one flower to be dusted over the sticky stigma (female) of the next flower visited. The result of this mating of course, is the development of seed—seed which can hold life suspended for weeks, months, even decades or (reportedly) centuries until the right conditions trigger the mysterious spring that starts it ticking again when, with a force out of all proportion to its size, it bursts its imprisoning shell.

ASEXUAL REPRODUCTION

There are also other methods of reproduction, some accomplished by nature, others by the ingenuity of man. Nature, for instance, equips some plants such as strawberries or the strawberry-begonia (*Saxifraga sarmentosa*) with "runners" at the tips of which new plants are formed. Blackberries and some shrubs and vines whose canes or branches bend

THE PLANT AND HOW IT GROWS 59

over and touch the ground root at the point of contact or self-layer as the gardener puts it. Then, like Antaeus, son of Terra, the earth goddess, they spring up from contact with the soil, full of renewed energy, to form new plants.

Asexual reproduction stimulated by man includes artificial layering, which occurs when a branch is partially cut through and then buried in soil or wrapped in sphagnum moss to encourage rooting, and the simpler method of rooting stem or leaf cuttings described in Chapter 4.

All plants produced by any of these methods are exact replicas of those from which they were obtained.

In contrast to this uniformity, plants produced from *seed* may "come true" or may vary widely. Seedlings from a natural species will be like their ancestors, although occasionally a "break" or "sport" occurs—one chance in a thousand or million. Plants resulting from a "cross" between two different species or forms are likely to vary greatly, and thus we get new varieties.

Books have been written on the science and the techniques of plant breeding, but that does not concern us here. We are interested in how best to keep the plant we have growing satisfactorily.

HOW PLANTS GROW

The more we know about a plant, the better we can care for it. As we have seen, the root system gathers food, in solution, from the soil. This is passed up through the trunk or stem and branches to the foliage, new growth, flowers, and, eventually, to the seed containers (fruits, nuts, pods, etc.) and into the seeds themselves. This is greatly oversimplifying an extremely complicated and mysterious process, but it may help the beginner to get an idea of the plant machine and how it works.

To keep this living mechanism, the plant, in operation, there must be available air, water, food, light, and a suitable range of temperature. To provide these is the function of the gardener—YOU. Of course you will have a very capable assistant—nature. Without a garden and without you, she would attend to all these matters in her own way—*the survival of the fittest!* But since, in having a garden at all, you have elected to take over from nature, the responsibility becomes yours. You can't lick the old gal, but you can join her, or, more accurately, coax and persuade her to join you.

Air, the first of the elements with which you are concerned,

Methods of asexual reproduction.

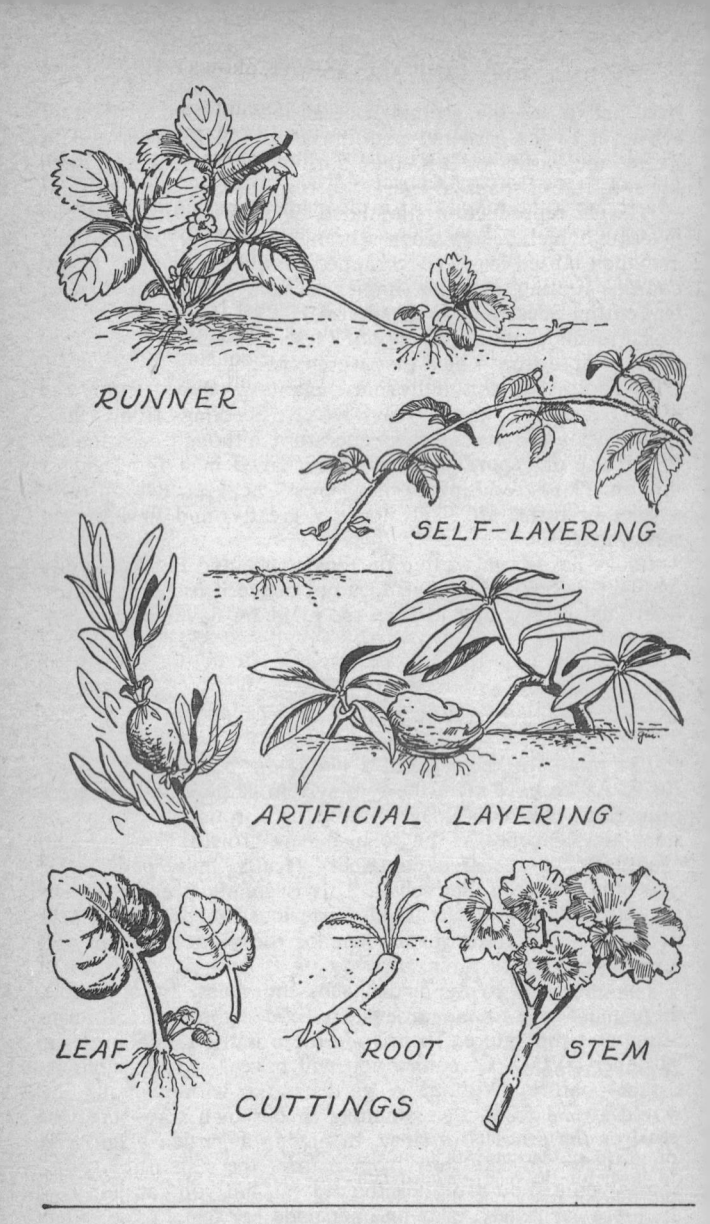

THE PLANT AND HOW IT GROWS 61

is always available. But pure, nonstagnant air is best for plants, as it is for humans. Plants can't be expected to thrive as well in the smoke-laden, dusty atmosphere of a city or in the smog of a factory district as they do in open country. If adverse air conditions exist in the gardener's locality, he can, unfortunately, do little about it unless the entire community cooperates. He can, however, keep his plants uncrowded and provide adequate air circulation.

Water, if plants are to do their best, must be available when they require it. If it is lacking, their food supply is also cut down, as all plant nutrients are taken in solution. Certain types of plants, such as those in deserts and other low-rainfall areas, go "dead" for weeks or months, and revive almost overnight when the dry season ends. Most of our garden plants suffer quickly and severely when the water supply gets much below normal. They may survive but they are stunted or otherwise injured, and during the dry spell are anything but ornamental. *The money spent on an adequate watering system (Chapter 5) is likely to be the most rewarding of any investment the garden-minded homeowner can make.*

Food. As with all living things, a plant must have food if it is to continue to live. The three most important items in its diet are nitrogen, phosphorus, and potash. In addition to these, there are several others, called trace elements, less important but still essential. All of these and the relative parts they play in plant nutrition are also discussed in Chapter 5. The essential point here is that these elements must *all* be present: the lack of any one may check or even completely halt normal growth and development.

Light is another essential for practically all living things. Many, to make normal or maximum growth, require direct sunshine. Even the shade-lovers do not tolerate darkness. One of the tests of skill of a gardener is that of choosing locations for the various trees, shrubs, perennials, and bulbs he wishes to grow; and vice versa, of selecting species and varieties of plants that will be happy in the locations he has available. Fortunately for beginners, catalogs of the most reliable firms provide, in their descriptions of plants, information on these important points.*

---

* *One for the book:* This note is for believe-it-or-not Ripley. As the senior partner in this co-author team was correcting the typescript of this page, dealing with *light,* the junior partner (who had just been to town for the mail) handed him a letter from Canada from which the following is a quotation: We are also gardening in our basement, under fluorescent lights, during winter months and with quite satisfactory results. . . . This morning I found in *Illuminating Engineering* an

Temperature. One need not be a gardener to realize that temperatures—high, low, and averages for the year—are a major factor in determining what may be grown where. Few persons, however, realize to what extent temperatures may vary as a result of local conditions, either natural or man-made. Elevation is one very important factor. One friend of ours, for instance, has part of his garden at water level by a stream that runs through his grounds. The temperature here is occasionally ten degrees lower than it is at his home on a hilltop less than three hundred feet away. Ten degrees makes a big difference in what can and cannot be grown.

We have fig trees and camellias that have lived through several successive winters without covering except for a heavy mulch about the roots. They are in sunny locations, sheltered from wind. Moved a hundred feet in any direction they would certainly have perished during one of the winters they have gone through.

Micro-climate areas may be created on most places. A suitably placed wall or even a tight board fence screened with vines or shrubs to make it less obtrusive may move one section of your garden at least one and possibly two zones south! Leave one side open to leeward, however, so that in severe weather cold air cannot be bottled up inside the wall or fence and possibly kill borderline subjects. We once saw hundreds of rare specimens killed or injured inside such a protective barrier on the eastern shore of Maryland after a very severe winter.

DETERRENTS TO GROWTH

Having looked at one side of the coin, let us for the sake of emphasis turn it over and for a moment examine the other side—conditions that may deter or interfere with normal growth.

Lack or Excess of Light and Air. Avoid placing sun-loving plants in shady spots on the north sides of buildings, or in the shade of trees or shrubs, or *where trees or shrubs now small may in a few years be casting dense shade.* Vegetables and

---

article (copy enclosed) on Experimental Gardening on a Polaris submarine. The article described plant culture in horticultural vermiculite plus water and chemical plant foods, by members of the submarine crew. A number of crops were successfully grown but lettuce proved to be the most satisfactory and the most popular.

Thank you again very much for the opportunity you gave us last summer to visit you at your very lovely place.

many plants that require full sun show a difference in growth if they are in shade for even two or three hours a day. Conversely, shade-lovers soon wither and dry up if subjected to full sun.

Avoid planting shrubs or even vigorous-growing perennials too close together. They may shade and crowd each other when they attain full growth as well as shutting off the air circulation so important to their well-being. It is equally dangerous to subject doubtfully hardy species to rough, prevailing winds.

Cold. Make sure that the tree or shrub you would like to have will be hardy in your section of the country. If in doubt, consult your county agent. If he doesn't know from personal experience he can find out for you; that's part of his job. But keep in mind what has been said above about micro-climates. There is often a good deal of satisfaction in growing something that is out of the ordinary for your locality.

Heat. High temperatures, in themselves, are less likely to prove fatal or even injurious to plants than are low temperatures. High readings however, are frequently accompanied by severe drought—a devil's tandem of black funeral horses for the gardener! Under such conditions those who have made good use of mulching have much to be thankful for. Mulches keep the ground cooler and also decrease the loss of moisture by evaporation.

Dryness. Even in cool weather the ground may get excessively dry. High winds, especially dry ones, suck moisture from the soil as rapidly as do excessively high temperatures. Moisture is an absolute essential for plant growth, and once it is gone there is only one remedy: to replace it. Water is the cheapest "fertilizer" one can buy, but few gardeners fully realize its importance.

Pests and Diseases. Despite improved controls, insects and other plant pests are still a serious factor in damaging plant growth and—equally important to the home gardener—the appearance of plants. Fortunately materials for control have been tremendously improved. All-purpose sprays and dusts containing chemicals to control sucking and chewing insects as well as fungicides to keep diseases in check are particularly helpful to the home gardener. To assure normal, healthy growth of such plants as roses, for instance, regular applications of all-purpose sprays or dusts are essential. With less susceptible subjects, an application should be made *as soon as* trouble appears; or in advance as a preventive in cases where it can be anticipated, as for mildew on phlox or lilacs, or thrip on gladiolus. Remember the old adage about an ounce of prevention? It still goes—double!

Old Age, for which there is no known cure in spite of the advances science is making these days. However, old age in some types of plants may be postponed almost indefinitely. The lilac that once in the dooryard bloomed just goes on indefinitely. We have a clump on our river bank where, reportedly, a tidewater mill once stood some two hundred years ago. This specimen, the main trunk recumbent like a sleeping giant, has now spread into a colony and apparently is ready to go on till doomsday. Even the oldest portion, we suppose, is not literally the original plant. The death of most shrubs, even those which do not sucker and form colonies, is most often due to failure to cut out old wood—thus admitting more light, air, and moisture. An azalea which we have had for over twenty years (and so far as we could find out was around fifty when we bought it) has been moved three times and was once nearly lost due to mishandling in a long-distance truck ride in the wind. It has finally decided to make one more comeback, however, and presented us again last spring with a few flowers on new wood sprouting from the roots! Neglect, resulting in overcrowding and slow starvation, kills many more trees and shrubs than old age.

Let here no seed of a season that the winter
But once assails, take root and for a time endure;
But only such as harbor at the frozen centre
The germ secure.

EDNA ST. VINCENT MILLAY

CHAPTER 4

New Plants from Old: Methods of Propagation

GROWING PLANTS FROM SEEDS AND CUTTINGS,
AND BY BUDDING AND GRAFTING

Everyone who gardens, no matter on how modest a scale, sooner or later becomes a plant propagator. An unscientific but perhaps sufficiently comprehensive definition of propagation might be: *The growing of new plants from parts of old plants.* These "parts" may be seeds; pieces of stems, roots, or leaves, single buds or eyes.

One usually starts gardening with plants growing in pots or other containers, which someone else (usually the nurseryman) has propagated. There is of course much pleasure to be had from nurturing such plants, but nothing to be compared to the exciting thrills that come when the gardener begins to grow his own plants from their very start in life.

The several methods of propagating plants include growing them from seed; from bulbs, corms, or tubers; from cuttings; by budding and grafting. The first two of these methods are nature's way of doing the job; the others are man's. The skillful gardener employs them all.

GROWING FROM SEED

The simplest method of propagating plants is from seed.

Seeds are among the most intricate of all the many marvels of nature. They vary in size from the fine dustlike particles of the begonias to the near football dimensions of the coconut. Yet each individual seed is a time bomb so delicately adjusted that, although many of them will withstand extreme degrees of heat, cold, and even moisture, it will, when just the right combination of conditions prevail, explode into a living organism. It is the gardener's province to provide these conditions; and to do so at a time, and under such circumstances, that the baby plantlet may prosper.

In growing plants from seed there are three things of vital importance to be considered. They are:

The quality of the seed itself
Correct timing
Control of conditions

The question of quality is not merely a matter of having fresh, live seed that will sprout. Of equal importance is having seed that are *well bred*. It's the old truism that one cannot make a silk purse out of a sow's ear.

The beginning gardener will do well, before ordering seeds, to make some inquiry among friends more experienced in gardening as to which firms have the best reputations. Usually a concern that specializes in some flower—such as pansies, primulas, delphinium, sweet peas, or even zinnias—will have first-quality seed bred from selected strains. Some firms state on each package the per cent of germination, based on recent tests.

Price is a matter of very secondary consideration. A single superior plant from a packet of seed is worth several times the difference in cost between just good seed and really superior seed.

Timing in seed sowing is important because upon it depends to a large degree the prospect of ultimate success. Some seeds, for instance, germinate better at low temperatures than at high; others just the opposite. Some germinate within a few days, others require a considerable time; some, indeed, need a period of stratification or prolonged burial in soil before they will sprout. Some make very rapid growth after they come up; others require more time to develop strong root growth and "crowns" before they send up flowering stalks. Others such as many of the lilies germinate but for a long period make growth only underground, developing root strength before sending up slender green spears into the sunlight.

The control of conditions under which seeds are sown is, within limits imposed by nature, up to the gardener. He can provide almost any type of soil by making special mixtures for the small amounts that will be required. He can control the amount of moisture they get during the germination period. With modern, inexpensive equipment such as automatically regulated heating cables, he can provide the desired temperature. Fluorescent lights take care of the requirements of timing seed sowing even where they must be started in cellar or basement.

The beginner who may not wish to bother with all, or even with any, of these contrivances, may still start all the plants he is likely to require with no other equipment than a small frame made of a few boards and covered with an old window sash or two.

THE MECHANICS OF SOWING

Each one of the several factors involved in starting plants from seed contributes its part to ultimate success. If any one of them goes far wrong, the result may be total failure. Let's briefly consider each in order.

Equipment. First item here is a *place* in which to start seed. For outdoor sowing this may be a simple frame or seed bed located where it gets full sun and all the protection possible from prevailing early spring winds. A typical frame, with glass sash to cover, is shown on page 116. Temporary sash may be made of light wooden frames covered with plastic, but glass sash are more satisfactory in the long run.

Drainage is very important, as a single flash flood can ruin a whole crop of seedlings. Provision should be made for shading the glass when necessary. Light, slatted shutters giving shifting shade are ideal; old burlap bags fastened together provide dense shade and also protection from severe frosts.

Soil for the frame should be both rich and porous. We use a mixture of two thirds compost, which contains plenty of humus, and one third peatmoss. Seeds are sown in a thin layer of sharp sand, vermiculite, or pulverized sphagnum moss sifted over the surface.

Some strong-growing seedlings such as calendulas, zinnias, and large marigolds may be started directly in the frame, sown in rows 3 to 6 inches apart. Most, however, are started in small flats of wood or pressed fiber, and later transplanted to the frame. These may also be potted up in plastic, clay, or fertile peat pots which are then plunged to their rims in the frame. If peat pots are used, seedlings root through into the rich frame soil, and carry much of it with them when transferred to the garden.

In addition to the frame, a supply of containers should be on hand. These will include flats, pots, and bulb pans (shallow flower pots). The old clay flower pots and pans have now been almost completely replaced by plastic ones (which for most purposes are decidedly superior), and by pots made of compressed peat with plant nutrients added, which are planted out "pot and all."

The standard flat is a shallow (2½- to 3½-inch-deep) wooden box with a slatted bottom that provides ready drainage—and makes possible *watering from the bottom* by placing the flat in an inch or so of water until moisture shows on the surface, a method which we swear by. Standard florists' flats are usually 20 or 22 inches long by 14 or 15 inches wide, but smaller ones are often more convenient for the gardener. The small wooden or fiber boxes in which seedlings are grown, and sold by retailers in the spring, are of a convenient size for small plantings.

Seed Sowing Mixtures. Success in starting plants from seed depends *very largely* upon the medium in which the seeds are started. In the old days a 50–50 mixture of garden loam and sifted leafmold or "woods soil" or "chip dirt," gathered in the forest or from the half-rotted debris around the chopping block by the wood pile, answered well. Now these are no longer available, and probably would not serve if they were, for certain diseases which cause tiny seedlings to damp-off (decay at the soil line or before they emerge) have become so prevalent that, without some defense against them, failure is more likely than success.

Certain soil mixtures have been developed which help to assure success. Best known of these are the famous John Innes mixtures in England and the University of California soil mixes developed in this country. The seed mixture recommended by John Innes is made up of 7 parts composted medium loam, 3½ parts peatmoss, and 3½ parts coarse sand, all measured by volume. To this is added 2 pounds of superphosphate and 1 pound of chalk. For use in this country the above materials might be translated as follows: 7 parts good loam, 3½ parts peatmoss, and 3½ parts sharp sand. Add 2 pounds of superphosphate and 1 pound agricultural lime.

The U. C. Soil Mix B, recommended for seed sowing, is composed of 75 per cent by volume of fine sand and 25 per cent by volume of pulverized peatmoss, to each cubic yard of which is added 6 ounces potassium nitrate, 4 ounces potassium sulfate, 2½ pounds single superphosphate, 4½ pounds dolomite lime, 1¼ pounds carbonate lime, and 1¼ pounds gypsum. The pH of this mixture with fertilizers added should be 6.8.

For years we have used in our own seed flats one third by weight of sifted compost, one third pulverized peatmoss, and one third sharp sand, well mixed and covered with a surface layer of sterile vermiculite, perlite, or milled sphagnum moss.

Even with these special mixtures, however, success is not assured, for the worst of the damping-off diseases, Rhizoctonia, (Rhizoc. for short), is so contagious and persistent and has become so widely disseminated, that unless all containers, equipment, and soil are kept sterilized, good results can by no means be assured.

Most amateurs are finding that the use of new or sterilized containers and an absolutely sterile material in which to sow the seeds gives the greatest assurance of success. *Composition planter trays, plus either milled sphagnum moss or vermiculite (an expanded mineral product) provide these conditions.*

The standard trays are about 6 by 4 inches, with holes in the bottoms to provide drainage. Even when filled with either material, and thoroughly moistened, they are light and easy to handle. Roots of seedlings develop marvelously and can be lifted out for transplanting with little or no breakage. Naturally, planted in such a sterile medium without nutrients, seedlings must be transplanted very young to a richer mixture or, if this operation must be delayed, plant nutrients must be supplied when watering.

Watering Devices. Maintaining the correct degree of moisture at all times is another most important factor in starting seedlings. Too much water, or serious lack of it for even a few hours, may cause failure.

The ordinary hose nozzle and the usual watering-can sprinkler head apply water with too much force and in too large droplets to be ideal for very small seedlings. A shallow pan or tray of galvanized sheet iron 2 inches deep (which a tinsmith can make up) will permit moistening the soil from the bottom up. A mist nozzle, to replace the ordinary hose nozzle, moistens the surface without knocking over or washing out even the tiniest seedling.

Trays, pots, or boxes in which seeds are planted may be kept moist for days without watering by covering them tightly with a pane of glass, or with a sheet of cellophane of suitable size held in place by a rubber band.

Labels are an important part of garden records. It is well to have several sizes (say 4-, 8-, and 12-inch) available. Painted labels, being weather-resistant, are well worth the slight additional cost.

Seed sowing is something of an art. Even distribution of the seed is essential because the less the tiny roots—often more extensive than the top growth at this stage of development—are tangled together, the better. Very fine seed such as that of begonias and large-flowered petunias may be mixed with fine sand to aid in securing even distribution. Never sow all the seed in a packet just to use it up. Extra seedlings that mean overcrowding *are just weeds,* often very harmful ones. Two dozen good, strong seedlings in a pot or flat often make more of an ultimate show in the garden than a hundred or more overcrowded, spindly ones.

Some gardeners like to sow seed directly from the packet, but we get better results with a 6-inch piece of plastic hose cut at an angle to a sharp point and plugged at the other end with a cork. By tapping this with the forefinger, it is possible to distribute sizable seeds almost one by one, and even very small ones with some degree of accuracy. Gadgets similar to the home-made one described above are available at seed stores.

Inoculants. Disinfectants. The seed sower also makes it easy to apply inoculants such as Legume Aid, Nod-O-Gen, and Nitricin; and disinfectants such as Spergon, Semesan, or Rootone, to the seeds being sown. These materials are advantageous (1) in introducing nitrogen-gathering bacteria into the soil where legumes (peas, beans, etc.) are being sown; and (2) in protecting seeds against harmful bacteria which cause seed-borne disease. A pinch of powder or a few drops of liquid is placed with the seed in the sower, which is then closed with the thumb and shaken thoroughly.

Correct temperature is essential in securing good seed germination. Optimum temperatures vary with different plants. Peas (including sweet peas), for instance, will germinate and grow in soil that is little above freezing; while others, such as tomato and torenia or portulaca, prefer 70 to 80 degrees. Most seeds will germinate satisfactorily at 70 to 80 degrees, but should be given 5 to 10 degrees less soon after they are up.

Moisture can be maintained to and through the germination period by the means already described above.

Light is not essential while seeds are germinating, but once they have begun to show above the surface soil they should be brought *immediately* to full light. Otherwise they grow spindly, on weak stems, straining toward whatever source of light may be available.

STARTING THE SEEDLINGS

Seeds may be sown in the open ground, where they are to grow. This is the method used with most vegetables and many flowers. The thing here is to prepare the seedbed, or at least the surface inch or two, so that the soil is finely pulverized and smooth, also making sure that it contains plenty of humus. The latter may be provided by a light layer of compost or of peatmoss, sifted or pulverized, and raked into the surface soil. There should also be provision for watering with a very fine spray, such as that from a "mist" or "fog" nozzle.

Much more certain results, especially with difficult subjects, may be had by starting seeds in a frame, no matter how crude a one, as described in Chapter 7.

Until the seeds have germinated their first true leaves, usually quite different from the seedling leaves or cotyledons, the soil should never be allowed to dry out completely on the surface.

Thinning out the seedlings where germination has been good is vitally important. To neglect it for even a week or so may mean very serious injury to the remaining plants. This operation is just as essential where seedlings are to be transplanted later or where they have attained considerable size. Give each plant room to grow freely.

Transplanting is the next step in growing plants from seed. As a general rule, the earlier this is done the better. It consists of removing the tiny seedlings from the pot, flat, or seedbed in which they have been started, and replanting them, either in the open ground, in well-prepared and enriched soil where they will grow to maturity, or in flats or small pots in soil containing enough nutrients to bring them to a size where they can hold their own in the open garden or in the spot where they are to grow.

The soil to be used in transplanting to flats or pots will depend upon the type of planting. A soil mixture suitable for the great majority of plants is made up of sifted material from the well-rotted compost heap (page 42) to which may be added peatmoss, loam, and/or sand in varying proportions, according to the character of the plants to be grown. Lime (a half cup per bushel) may be added for plants requiring an especially "sweet" soil, and a complete, organic plant food at the rate of 1 pint per bushel if loam must be substituted for sifted compost or if the compost available has no fertilizer or manure in its composition.

For transplanting into flats, we like to use a layer of old, well-decomposed manure (or if this is not available, of peatmoss plus a generous sprinkling of commercial dried manure) in the bottom of each flat before filling it with the soil mixture. This has the triple advantage of providing a sponge which holds moisture, of supplying extra plant food, and of providing a fibrous mass into which the seedling roots will pass and hold together in a dense root ball when the plants are cut out of the flat for transplanting or setting out in their permanent positions.

Repotting. As the plants in small pots, which are usually placed side by side, begin to crowd, repotting is in order. According to the type of plant, this will take place anywhere from a few weeks to several months.

When clay or plastic pots are used, a look at the root ball indicates if repotting is needed. Invert a pot, secure plant and root ball with the fingers of one hand, and with the other rap the pot against the edge of bench or table. A close network of roots around the ball means that more soil, and hence a larger pot, is needed. With the root-through type of peat or fiber pot, repotting should be done as soon as roots have thoroughly penetrated the pot's walls and before they begin to form a tangled mass.

After repotting, plants should be well watered and provided with moderate shade to prevent excessive wilting. An occasional misting or fogging may be needed, but usually this is not required.

ASEXUAL PROPAGATION

While the propagation of plants by means of seed is the method most generally employed by amateur gardeners, obtaining new plants by other means is not too difficult.

To begin with, many plants, and especially man-made varieties (*cultivars,* as the botanists call them) will not come true from seed, and can only be propagated by means of growing new plants from sections (cuttings, buds, or pieces of root or bulb) of the parent plant.

Dividing. The simplest and quickest of these methods is the use of sections of the parent plant that are provided with both tops and roots. These we acquire when we take up and "divide" such plants as irises, chrysanthemums, and phlox; such clump-forming bulbs as daffodils; shrubs like forsythia, spirea, and Rugosa roses; or when we cut off and replant a young lilac that has come up several feet from its parent bush; or transplant the "runners" of strawberries.

The rankest amateur can scarcely fail to succeed with this method of propagation. It is desirable to damage roots as little as possible in dividing clumps or in removing offshoots of parent plants; and also to do the job while the parent is dormant, in early spring or sometime after bloom is over in the case of bulbs and such perennials as iris and Oriental poppies. Where plants form "crowns," like chrysanthemums for example, the old woody centers are discarded and root cuttings, with stems and leaves attached, are taken from around the outer edge where growth is vigorous. It may be desirable to cut back the top growth of shrub divisions, but this is more for the purpose of encouraging compact new growth than to assure the success of the operation. Naturally we take care to provide good soil, plenty of water, and a mulch, if the weather is dry, to keep the soil moist.

Layering is actually a modified form of division. All that the gardener does, actually, is to lend a helping hand to nature in order to produce new plants, still attached to their parents, until sturdy root systems have been developed. It is an easy method of obtaining new plants of azaleas and shrubs like forsythia and old-fashioned shrub roses, to name but a few. New, half-hardened growths of these plants may be induced to form roots by fastening them down in loose, friable soil and covering them with a suitable rooting medium as shown in the accompanying sketch. At a point where a branch of comparatively young, but well-hardened growth may be bent down to the ground, a slanting cut is made, on the lower side, half to two thirds of its thickness. This is held open with a small pebble or twig. A forked stick, brick, or stone serves to hold it in place. Success can be made more certain by preparing the soil at the point of contact with the ground with a pocket of peatmoss or a peatmoss-sand mixture, and treating the cut with a root stimulant such as Rootone. Some shrubs form roots naturally along branches which come in contact with the ground and in propagating these no cut need be made though otherwise the process is the same.

The rooting medium should be maintained in a moist condition by the mulch and by watering as frequently as necessary, especially during the first few weeks. After rooting—which may take anywhere from a few weeks to a year according to the subject and to conditions—the new plant is severed from its parent and transplanted to a permanent position.

Air layering differs from ordinary layering in that the job is done above ground instead of in it. It is used principally in the propagation of greenhouse plants such as rubber-plant (ficus), dieffenbachia, philodendron, and gardenia, but also with some hardy subjects.

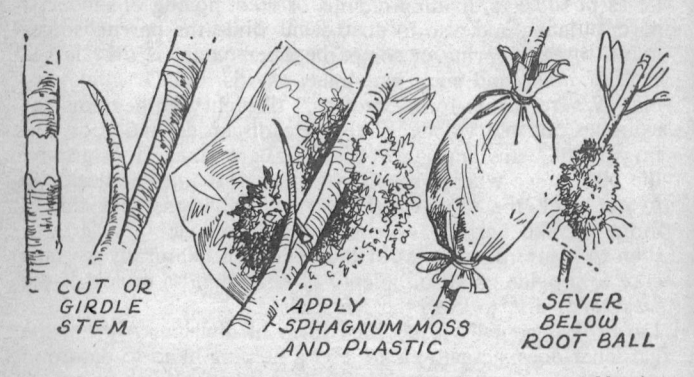

Details of air layering. Especially prepared kits are available for doing this work. The rooting material must remain moist until rooting occurs.

In air layering, the top of a plant, or the tip of a branch the wood and bark of which have not yet become really hardened, is selected for the operation. At the point determined, a short cut is made a half to two thirds through the stem. This cut—which should be made cleanly with a sharp blade, leaving no frayed edges—is then held open with a bit of wood. Or the bark may be "ringed" or "notched" (see sketch above). The cut parts are then dusted with a root stimulant such as Hormodin or Rootone, and firmly wrapped in sphagnum moss that has been thoroughly moistened by dipping it in water and squeezing it to remove the surplus.

The ball of moss is then wrapped in a sheet of polyethylene of suitable size, and tied securely at top and bottom to make it as nearly airtight as possible. A special propagating kit, by the name of Airwrap, may be purchased, which makes the operation a very simple one.

The ball of moss is left on, in its wrapping, until roots

NEW PLANTS FROM OLD: METHODS OF PROPAGATION 75

have begun to penetrate it—a period which varies with the subject and conditions from several weeks to several months. The rooted tip, with root-filled moss intact, is then severed just below the root mass, and potted up. It should be kept in a moist, sheltered place or in a glass-covered frame until new growth indicates its recovery from the operation. The number of plants with which this method is successful is limited. Before trying it, the amateur would do well to consult his State Experiment Station or a book on propagation as to which plants, in his area, are likely to root under these conditions.

Bulbous, Cormous, and Tuberous-rooted plants are propagated largely by natural or artificial division, though some species such as tuberous-rooted begonias come readily from seed.

Daffodils and many other bulbous plants produce bulbs which become double and finally split and separate, forming dense clumps with interlaced feeding roots. When these clumps become so dense that they stop blooming, they are dug, the bulbs in each clump are separated, and replanted to grow on.

Tender bulbs like amaryllis, veltheimia, and ismene also in-

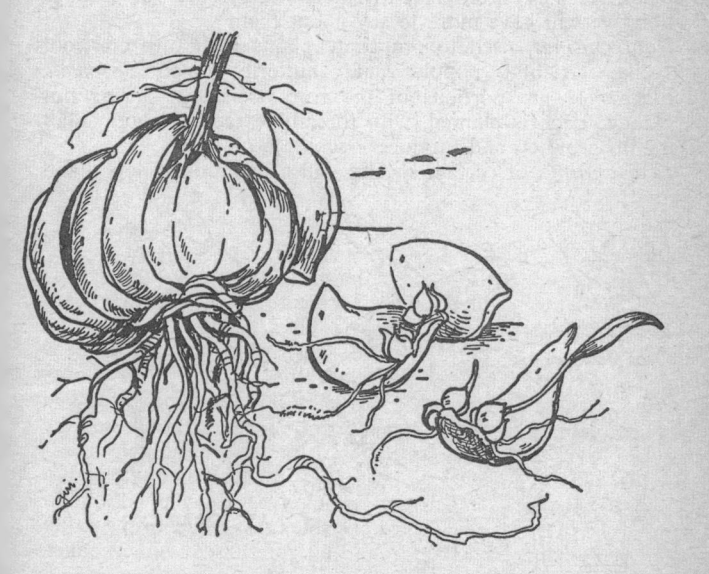

"Scaling" a lily bulb to promote the growth of bulblets. A rapid method of increase where it can be used.

crease naturally by producing small side bulbs or offsets above or below ground. When these are ready to split off, they may be removed and planted separately. This is increase by natural division.

Lilies increase naturally by bulbils formed at the stem nodes above ground in some varieties, or by bulblets which develop underground in others. Gladiolus cormlets form around the parent corm underground in much the same way.

To increase lilies asexually by artificial methods, individual scales are removed from a parent bulb and each of these is rooted like a cutting to form a separate plant.

Many tubers can be cut into several pieces, each containing one or more "eyes," and each of these pieces, planted and grown on, will produce a separate plant. Examples are dahlias, potatoes, and tuberous begonias.

CUTTINGS

A cutting, as the name implies, is a severed portion of a plant. *Stem cuttings* are made from portions of the stem of a plant. As these are by far the most widely used for propagation, we will have more to say about them.

Root cuttings, used to propagate plants with tuberous roots —like Oriental poppies and butterfly weed (*Asclepias tuberosa*)—are portions of the root itself, cut during dormancy. Each is planted, with threadlike feeding roots adhering, to grow on and produce a separate plant.

Leaf cuttings of certain species will also produce new plants.

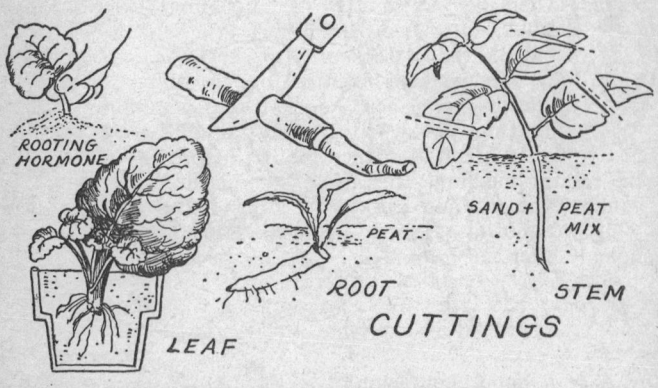

Details of preparing different types of cuttings.

Gesneriads like African violets and *episcias* are propagated by taking mature leaves with one-inch stems, treating the base of the stems with a rooting stimulant and sinking the stems in a rooting medium until new plants form at the soil line.

The leaves of Rex and other large-leaved begonias, cut at the veins, and laid flat on a bed of moist sand, will produce roots at the cuts which may be developed into new plants.

Some greenhouse subjects such as piggyback plant (*Tolmiea*), twelve apostles (*Marica*), and Bryophyllum (*Kalanchoe verticillata*), and some other succulents, produce plantlets on the leaves which may be detached and potted up. Others, like the *Echeverias* and other sedums propagate new plants readily from individual leaves. The bases of these are sunk in the rooting medium which, in this case, may be pure sand.

Softwood stem cuttings of a great many annuals, biennials, and perennials, many shrubs (including roses, azaleas and camellias), and not a few trees, may be rooted by the amateur. They provide a quick, easy, and fairly sure way of increasing one's supply of a great many favorite plants, both to extend one's own garden material and to supply extras to give to friends or to "swap," a good old-fashioned custom that adds much to the pleasure of gardening.

Such cuttings are made of terminal new growth which has hardened sufficiently to be "firm" but which is still pliable or crisp like a fresh snapbean, and capable of reviving quickly after being cut. They may vary in length from 3 to 6 inches, and usually at least two eyes or leaf joints are left above the surface when they are inserted in the rooting medium. Large leaves should be trimmed back a third to a half.

If cuttings must be transported or held for any length of time, they may be kept from wilting by rolling them in a damp cloth or newspaper. For instance, geraniums (which root easily from soft-wood cuttings) are left lying on the bench for 24 hours after they are cut before being placed in the rooting medium. This gives time for the stems to dry or callus at the cuts and, as they are grown and even propagated with less moisture than most other plants, they root more quickly after this treatment.

ROOTING MEDIA

A very important factor of success is the selection of the material in which the cuttings are to be rooted. In former days the standard rooting medium was clean, sharp (gritty), medium-coarse sand. For many plants (including geraniums, *Impatiens holsti,* and *Daphne cneorum*) this is still a perfectly satisfactory material. Other materials have come into use, however, and whether by themselves or in combinations are now more generally employed.

Among these are vermiculite (expanded mica); perlite, a volcanic mineral; milled sphagnum moss, and pulverized peatmoss. All of these are sterile when used fresh from the package or bag. A mixture of one half sterilized sand and one half pulverized peatmoss is perhaps the safest and most foolproof medium for the beginner.

After the base of each cutting is cleanly recut just where the stem is firm and crisp, it is dipped in a root stimulant such as Rootone or Hormodin and set *firmly* in the moist rooting medium. Do not try to root cuttings in water. This method is slower and less efficient.

If many cuttings of one variety or one species are to be rooted, an ordinary flat may be used as the container. For outdoor propagation, one section of a frame may be filled with the selected rooting medium, and the cuttings set in in rows.

Where only a few each of different plants are to be propagated, bulb pans or flower pots serve well because they can be given individual treatment if required, as concerns temperature, moisture, and light. Moreover, some cuttings root vigorously in a few weeks, while others may require months. With practically all, however, rooting is hastened by maintaining moist air around the *tops* as well as keeping the rooting medium moist.

The nurseryman accomplishes this by using a propagating frame or box, which can be kept closed to hold the moisture. In greenhouses an automatic "misting" system is often employed to keep the air saturated with moisture. The amateur can make a small propagating box by taking a wooden box of any convenient size, 5 or 6 inches deep, and constructing sides and ends of double-thick window glass, held together at the corners with waterproof tape. (Your hardware dealer will cut the glass to your specifications.) Glass should extend 6 to 10 inches above sides of box, according to the size of cuttings to be rooted. A pane of glass 1 to 2 inches longer and wider than the box forms the cover.

The method we have most frequently employed for rooting a few cuttings at a time is very simple. We merely take a bulb pan of suitable size—usually 6 or 8 inches—and cover the bottom with drainage material (broken pieces of clay

NEW PLANTS FROM OLD: METHODS OF PROPAGATION 79

Simple propagation box, with glass sides and top. Plastic bag or a plastic plant-dome, fastened over a bulb pan, is a useful device for rooting a few cuttings of one kind.

pots), add a half-inch layer of coarse peatmoss or sphagnum, and then fill to within a half inch of the rim with the rooting medium. After the cuttings have been inserted, the bulb pan is covered with a cellophane bag or a plastic dome which gives an almost airtight seal, and allows the condensation to run back into the edge of the pot. The pot is placed in a saucer which serves as a sub-irrigating device whenever lack of moisture on the inside of the cover indicates that the rooting medium is getting dry.

Whatever method of rooting is used, the cuttings, as soon as well rooted, should be transferred to individual pots in a soil mixture well supplied with nutrients. If roots get more than an inch or so long, many of them are likely to be injured in the operation.

Hardwood cuttings are made from firm, stout stems of woody plants, usually taken in autumn from the oldest of the current year's growth. Generally 4 to 12 inches are the best lengths to root, though with easy subjects such as willow and mulberry, they may be as long as 3 or 4 feet. Often they are taken with a "heel" or piece of the main stem of older wood attached at the base. Autumn-cut hardwood cuttings are tied in bundles and buried, laid horizontally in moist soil in a frame so that the cut ends may callus. In early spring they are separated and planted in rows in a moist rooting medium in an outdoor propagation bed to develop roots and grow. Many shrubs, trees, and small fruits may be increased in this

GRAFTING AND BUDDING

Grafting and budding are methods of propagation in which a piece of one plant is transferred to another and eventually becomes a part of it. They may be used to provide a stronger growing root system; to obtain several varieties of fruits or flowers on one plant, as is often done with apples; or to create a special type or form of plant, as when a bush or trailing rose is grown on a stout cane of another type to produce a small tree or a trailing effect.

In *grafting,* a section of stem or branch is used which has several "eyes" or leaf joints. *Budding* is really a type of grafting in which a single bud or eye is employed instead of a cutting containing several eyes.

In both operations the essential thing to keep in mind is that the union must first be effected by bringing together sections of the cambium layer or *bark* of both plants. In the bark alone can this new growth be initiated, just as all new growth of any plant develops.

In simple or whip grafting, a section of year-old growth, usually—in the case of fruits or flowering trees—about the thickness of a pencil, is cut into sections each of which contains three to five eyes. These are known as scions. A long, sloping cut is then made at the lower end with a razor-sharp blade, so as to leave the bark uninjured and the cambium layer firmly attached to the wood itself. A branch or trunk of a young tree of the same thickness (the understock) is similarly cut at its top with a long slope. Then the scion is closely bound to the understock, the cadmium layer of bark of the two pieces meeting at all possible points (see sketch). The graft may then be covered with grafting wax until it "takes."

In whip and tongue grafting, after the sloping cuts are made, the grafting knife is driven straight down, first into the scion and then into the understock near the points of the cuts, to form a "tongue" in each (see sketch). Scion and understock are fitted closely, the two tongues interlocking, and the cambium layers of bark of each neatly meeting the other. The graft is then wrapped with cotton cord and covered with grafting wax.

In wedge or cleft grafting, a large branch of understock may be used. This is cut straight off (see sketch) and a cleft made down its center with a grafting chisel or heavy knife driven to the desired depth with a wooden mallet. One or two scions are then trimmed at the lower ends to tapering wedges and fitted snugly down into the cleft at the outer edges so that the cadmium bark of the scions meets that of the understock on the outside. The graft is then bound and covered with wax.

There are many other more complicated types of grafting, such as bark, rind, saddle and veneer, but for readers who wish to try these, we recommend one of the books on propagation listed in the Appendix.

While grafting is usually done early in spring—February to April, according to climate and the species to be grafted—the scions may be prepared any time during the winter if they are afterward buried in moist soil or kept in damp peatmoss wrapped in plastic, at a temperature close to freezing.

In budding, a T-shaped cut is made in the bark of a young branch of a tree or shrub of another variety of the same species as the bud. The vertical portion of the T may vary from half an inch to an inch, or according to the size of the bud. The buds are taken from young stems of the current year's growth, each bud being sliced off the stem with about half an inch of rind above and below it (see sketch). The wood inside is best removed, leaving only the bud and bark on each side of it—including of course the precious cambium layer. Great care must be exercised, however, not to remove the base of the bud with the inner wood. The upper corners of the T-cut on the understock are now carefully turned back with the end of the budding knife (designed for this purpose) and the bud is slipped into place so that the bark of bud and understock are in close contact. If the operation is carefully done, there will be no rough or torn edges. The bud is then securely held in place by bandaging the wound with a rubber band under slight tension, the end slipped under the last two or three turns (see sketch, page 83).

If conditions are right, the inserted bud will begin to grow normally and in a surprisingly short time the wood will have callused over. After the wound has completely healed and the bud has developed into a vigorous shoot or branch, the top of the original or root-stock plant is severed. Usually this is done early in the spring following the operation.

The best time to attempt budding is when sap is beginning to flow and when the bark is soft, plastic, and least likely to tear during the operation. For most plants these conditions exist early in spring, just as growth is being renewed.

In either budding or grafting the amateur will do well, if it is at all possible, to watch the operation actually performed before attempting it himself. If he belongs to a garden club,

WHIP & TONGUE GRAFT

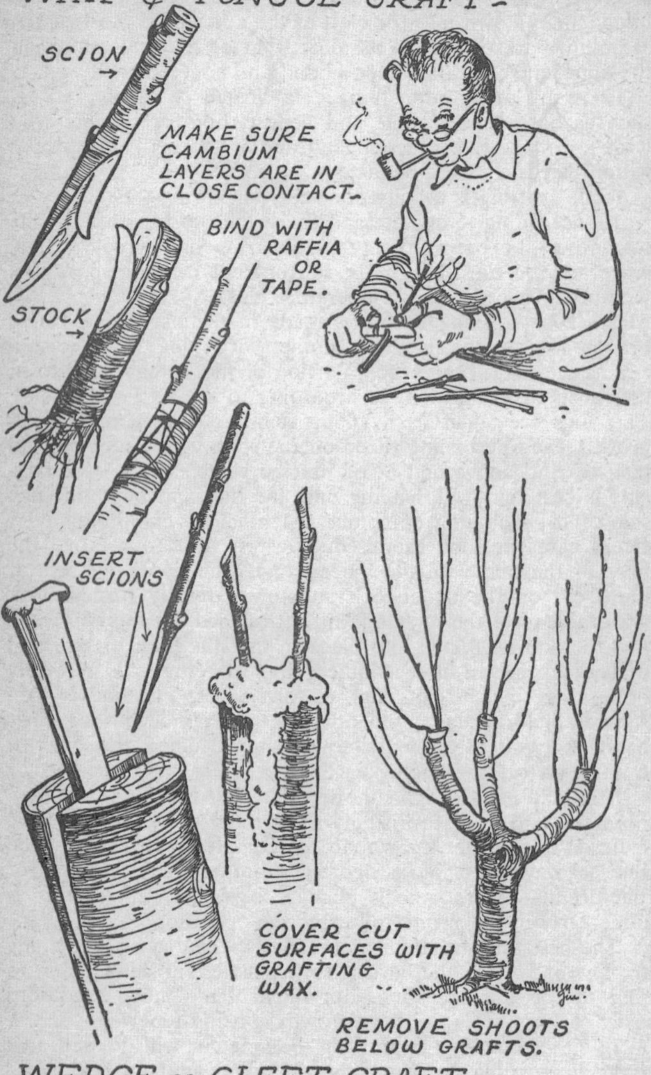

WEDGE OR CLEFT GRAFT

BUDDING

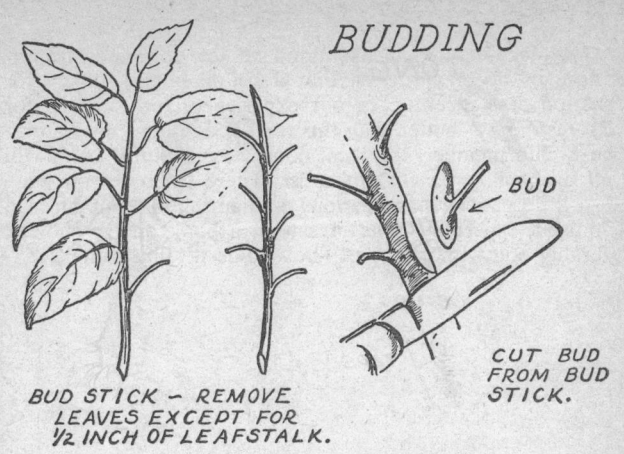

BUD STICK — REMOVE LEAVES EXCEPT FOR ½ INCH OF LEAFSTALK.

CUT BUD FROM BUD STICK.

a. CUT MADE IN BARK.
b. BUD INSERTED.
c. BIND WITH RUBBER BAND.

REMOVE LOWER LEAVES FROM ROOT STALK.

FOLLOWING SPRING — CUT JUST ABOVE BUD.

some member may in all likelihood be able to demonstrate it for him; or he may suggest that it be made the subject for discussion at a meeting. In our experience, few subjects for programs "draw" better than this one. If one does not happen to be a club member, the local county agricultural agent will in all probability be glad to assist. There is no reason why, with a little patience, any serious amateur should not succeed by himself, especially if he invests in a book on the subject, preferably one with plenty of "how-to-do-it" illustrations.

> Thy gardens and thy gallant walks
> Continually are green.
> There grows such sweet and pleasant flowers
> As nowhere else are seen.
> The New Jerusalem. ANONYMOUS

CHAPTER 5

Keeping Plants Vigorous and Healthy

Gardening is the technique and the science of keeping plants growing vigorously. Landscaping is the art of employing plant material to produce effects which are esthetically pleasing. The two are often confused. In this chapter we are concerned only with what makes plants tick—and how to keep them ticking happily.

The beginning gardener must learn to realize that plants are living organisms which, if they are to prosper, must breathe, eat, drink, sleep, and have periods of rest, all in a congenial environment. The old proverb that one man's meat is another man's poison applies equally to plants. One grows lustily where another would perish.

It is the gardener's job, first of all, to select plants which prosper in the environment which he can provide. This includes temperature; light, sun, and shade; moisture; the physical character of the soil; and the chemical elements it contains, as discussed in Chapter 3.

Next he must make sure that his plants receive adequate amounts of such foods as they demand. In many instances nature provides all that is needed in this department. Giant trees, some of them centuries old, survive to remind humanity that plants can get along without man better than he can without them!

However, the gardener is not content to let plants exist

where *they* choose to grow, and so in many cases—and in fact in more and more as man continues to alter and ravish the face of the earth—he must provide plants with foods that will enable them to live, let alone to thrive and multiply. Water, of course, as well as food, is essential.

In the third place, the gardener must protect his plants from their enemies, both insects and diseases. Here again the gardener has provided himself with an ever-increasing amount of work since he has destroyed the natural enemies of plant enemies—birds for instance, who live largely on insects. Furthermore, many of the fruits, flowers, and ornamentals which he himself has developed are much more susceptible than were their original forms in nature. Fortunately, science is constantly producing materials which simplify the process of protecting plants from their enemies.

With this over-all glance at the picture, let us now take a closer look at some of the details.

TEMPERATURE

One need not be a gardener to realize that not all plants grow in all climates. The chief factor determining what will grow where is temperature. That is why planting zones—such as those indicated on the endpaper map—are based on average temperatures, and especially on "first frost" and "last frost" dates.

Altitude is another factor to be considered. Hence many gardens in any particular zone are either much warmer or much colder than the average for most gardens in that zone. The gardener must ascertain where his property fits into the picture. This he can do by consulting his local county agent and experienced gardeners in his local garden club, which, incidentally, he should join if he would like to have friendly assistance in meeting many of his garden problems.

Micro-climates, as the word implies, are variations, within limited areas, from the normal conditions surrounding them. Protection against prevailing winter winds, too strong sunshine, and heavy storms can make a big difference in the kind of plants that can be grown successfully. A hill, a house, or even a hedge can provide the necessary protection.

A wall may dam up the flow of cold air down a slope, resulting, on cold nights, in a difference in temperature of a few degrees. If those few degrees have been just above or just below freezing, they may mean the end of a display of flowers that could have gone on blooming for weeks longer.

Results may often be more serious. We have seen the loss of several beds of rare plants, including many fine shrubs, due to just such a condition. Our house is near the edge of a steep bank running down to a salt-water river; there frost often strikes, or ice forms, at times when we escape it. The difference in the growth of plants, in areas only a few hundred feet apart, is often very perceptible.

A coldframe is the outstanding example of a micro-climate reduced to the nth degree. Within its boundaries of a few boards and a frail cover of glass, a tiny bit of your garden is moved one to two hundred miles to the south!

Water features, either natural or artificial, can be used to create micro-climates—most desirable in climates where summer heat is a problem. A wide, shallow pool which throws off moisture just as a pan of water does on an old-fashioned steam radiator, creates a cool little oasis in a hot, dry landscape. Running streams and fountains are even more helpful in reducing dry heat, for the water is constantly in motion and so is more readily absorbed into the air.

The forming of micro-climates, by utilizing natural variations in topography, building walls, planting windbreaks or hedges, is of practical help to any gardener who wishes to extend the range of the plants he can grow. On larger places, a planting of evergreens or a wide border of mixed shrubs provides shelter from prevailing winter and spring winds that will advance the flowering of perennials and bulbs by as much as two weeks, and in addition lessens the danger of injury from summer storms.

Shade. While the majority of our cultivated ornamentals like full sun, there are many that are happier in partial shade, and some that demand it (see list, Appendix). Shade may readily be provided for these plants by a few quick-growing, leafy trees such as birches, Chinese elms, and pin oaks. For this purpose, greedy and shallow-rooting trees such as maples, poplars, and magnolias are to be avoided.

MOISTURE

The country over, season after season and year after year, more plants are injured or lost for lack of sufficient moisture than from any other one cause. Yet the average gardener spends many times as much per annum on plant foods and gadgets as he does on providing an adequate watering system.

The reason? It's simple: No one makes any money selling *water*. No company puts on a multithousand-dollar advertising campaign to convince the home gardener that he needs it to make his plants grow successfully.

The homeowner who can have his own water supply is fortunate; for if it is adequate he will not be faced with an ordinance forbidding him to use it just when his plants and his garden most need it. Unfortunately the privately owned water supply is a vanishing luxury. What then?

Well, there are many ways of making such water as is available count to the last drop.

First: keep the soil in which your plants grow well supplied with *humus*. This holds water like a sponge and keeps it from leaching down into the lower layers of soil out of reach of thirsty roots—and incidentally carrying with it essential plant foods.

Second: keep bare surfaces *mulched*. This not only greatly decreases the amount of moisture lost through evaporation from the soil surface (which in dry windy weather can be tremendous) but it also keeps the soil surface many degrees cooler than when it is fully exposed to the sun. Mulching also saves a great deal of labor in controlling weeds. Under a mulch many weeds fail to germinate; or if they do, and succeed in pushing up through it, they are weak, leggy, and easy to remove, roots and all. Mulching does not actually provide moisture, but it does work wonders in conserving it once it has been provided.

A mulch is any material spread around and between plants to cover the soil and thus prevent, or at least curtail, the loss of soil moisture through surface evaporation. Nature's own mulch is the matrix of decayed and decaying vegetable matter—leaves, twigs, needles of coniferous evergreens, surface roots, and plants to be found in any forest, or even under a group of shrubs or trees, unmolested by the hand of man.

As man, at an ever-accelerating pace, takes over the surface of the earth from nature and strips it of its natural mulch mantle, it becomes increasingly important that he should replace it wherever he can.

For this purpose almost any material that will decay may be used, but some are better than others. Half-decomposed material from the compost heap is excellent. Grass clippings, if not applied so thickly as to ferment or pack and keep out air circulation, are good. Dry hardwood leaves, pine needles, or other materials locally available, such as cranberry vines, seaweed from the shore, sawdust, wood chips, and the chopped stalks of sugar cane or corn, redwood or fir bark can be utilized. Among the numerous commercial products available are peatmoss, buckwheat hulls, chicken litter made

KEEPING PLANTS VIGOROUS AND HEALTHY

from ground peanut shells, bagasse, shavings, and well-rotted strawy manure, where it may be obtained. Even flat stones, pebbles, or coarse pebbly sand will serve in a pinch, conserving moisture in the soil beneath, though of course they add no humus.

Mulches are applied in a layer from 2 to 4 inches thick, according to the material and the purpose for which they are used. Some types, notably sawdust and wood chips, may, in the process of decomposition, temporarily reduce the available nitrogen in the soil, due to its use by the bacteria affecting the decay. This is the reason that sawdust is often condemned as a mulch. Although this "loan" of nitrogen is later repaid to the soil bank, it is well, in using mulches of this type, to supplement them with an application of nitrogen, raked in before applying the mulch at the rate of 1 pound of sulfate of ammonia or 1½ pounds of nitrate of soda per 100 square feet.

Third: if, for any reason, a mulch cannot be used, *cultivate frequently,* even if no weeds are in evidence. The best tool for this purpose is a scuffle hoe, which has a thin, double-edged blade on a long handle and is worked by "scuffling" it back and forth. With it one can clean ground of small weeds almost as fast as walking, and the soil surface is left in a nice, loose mulch. Our two scuffle hoes—one 6, the other 8 inches wide—get more constant use than any other hand tools we have.

Watering. If despite everything that can be done to conserve moisture—by the use of humus, windbreaks, mulches—the soil still dries out to a degree that interferes with normal growth, then plants must be watered.

The average home gardener wastes a large percentage of the water he uses for his plants by "sprinkling." The first thing to learn about watering is that a sufficient amount should be given at each application to penetrate the soil well down into the root zone of the plant, crop, or bed being watered. If the surface only is made moist, to a depth of a fraction of an inch (or a few inches in the case of trees or large shrubs) it never reaches the *feeding* roots.

The depth to which water penetrates depends upon the character of the soil. In sandy or gravelly soils deficient in humus, it goes down immediately—and keeps going! (Much of the soil in our grounds on Cape Cod is the type of which natives say, "Rain goes faster after it hits the ground than it does coming down; fog's a lot better!") On a heavy clay soil, water penetrates very slowly, and if applied too rapidly accu-

Use a coffee-can measure when watering. After watering, measure depth accumulated in can. Then dig nearby to see how deep moisture has penetrated soil. You now know, when water is X inches deep in can, just how deep it will have moistened the soil.

mulates on the surface and is lost by running off or by evaporation.

On a loamy soil (which is a mixture of sand and clay) it will penetrate readily, and if enough humus is also present is then absorbed and held.

Each gardener must determine for himself the method of watering best suited to his needs. If he has more than one type of soil, or grows a wide variety of plants, he will get best results by employing several methods.

Until he becomes familiar with the moisture requirements of his soil and his crops, he should do a little experimenting. A simple method of determining how much water is required to moisten any particular soil to a depth of 4 inches (the minimum for any but very shallow-rooting crops) is as follows: Take a fairly wide-mouthed, straight-sided can and mark the inside to indicate inches and half inches. Place the tin—being careful to have it level—where it will get the average "rainfall" from a sprinkler or other watering device. When it indicates that ½ inch of "rain" has fallen, shut off the water. Then take a trowel and dig down into the soil, making a straight-sided hole that will clearly show just how deep the moisture has penetrated.

A few trials will indicate how much water you should apply to moisten the soil to the depth desired, and the coffee-can measure, left in place, will show when it has been applied. This, of course, is a rule of thumb rather than a

KEEPING PLANTS VIGOROUS AND HEALTHY

scientific way of estimating your soil's moisture requirements, but serves all practical purposes.

Watering Equipment. There are all kinds of devices for applying water, from the time-honored one of holding the thumb over the end of a hose to get a fanlike spread, to automatic oscillating devices that throw very realistic raindrops in alternating waves from side to side, so that they have a chance to soak in without forming puddles on the surface. In our experience such rain machines are far superior to the various revolving sprinklers which apply water much too rapidly and much less uniformly.

Plants of varying sizes and under varying conditions make it desirable to have available different methods of applying water. For watering freshly sown seeds and small transplants, a mistlike spray is the most desirable. The misting or "fog" nozzle applies water in a floating mist that does not knock over or "lodge" the finest seedlings. Similar to this in effect are the perforated plastic hoses which may be attached to the regular hose. Laid along the length of a bed or border, one of these will deliver fine mistlike sprays from a number of small openings. Where only small areas are to be watered, these are more practical than the oscillators, which cover quite large areas.

Other nozzles we find very useful are the water-breaker, which gives a gentle flow of water in tiny streams like a heavy but gentle rain, and the general-purpose spray nozzle, which applies water rapidly and with considerable force.

For vegetable or other large gardens, a permanent irrigation system, controlled from a central valve, is the most convenient—and also the most expensive. These are usually installed by professional concerns and are a bit too complicated for the average do-it-yourself gardener.

Wind Barriers. The rate of evaporation of moisture from the soil is controlled to a large degree by its exposure to wind passing over it. Anything that protects an area from strong air currents materially helps to conserve moisture. In the case of new plantings in beds or borders, or of individual plants, a temporary screen of any sort is of assistance. Small plants may be covered with newspapers or strips of plastic held in place by stones, berry baskets, plastic domes, or Hotkaps.

THE FEEDING OF PLANTS

We have already discussed (in Chapter 2) the fact that plant growth is dependent upon the presence of certain chemicals in the soil; and that those chemicals must be in available form, i.e. readily soluble, because plants can take up their foods only when it is in solution.

Of the three principal plant foods—nitrogen, phosphorus, and potassium—the first is the one likely to be soonest exhausted; and the third, potassium, the least likely. A superabundance of one type of food does not make up for the shortage of another. The gardener therefore should so arrange his plant-feeding program that *all three* are available in adequate supply.

Nitrogen may be obtained in a number of materials. Quickest acting of these are nitrate of soda and sulfate of ammonia. The former, applied in small pellets or crystals, followed by rain or a thorough watering, may noticeably stimulate new growth of foliage in a few days. By the same token, its beneficial effect is soonest exhausted. Recently, forms of nitrogen that are much slower acting have been developed. Such synthetic organic nitrogen carriers as calcium cyanamide and urea take a little longer than nitrate of soda but are still quick-acting. The new combination nitrogenous fertilizers, using several nitrogen-bearing materials, continue to provide this vital nutrient throughout the season. These have proved particularly valuable in fertilizing lawns, but are equally important for other long-season crops.

The *fertilizers* most commonly used about the home grounds—and for commercial crops, too—are termed "complete" fertilizers. That is, they contain all three of the principal elements, nitrogen, phosphorus, and potassium, and minor trace elements as well.

It is mistaken economy to purchase fertilizers on the basis of the price per bag. The lower the percentage of nutrients present, the more you pay for useless "fillers" that are combined with these to make up the total weight. As a rule the total percentage of the complete plant foods should be at least 20, as in a 5–10–5 or 10–6–4 mixture. (See also Chapter 2.)

It is seldom necessary to apply any one of the three main nutrients separately, except in the case of nitrogen for lawns. With the other two elements, phosphorus and potassium, a complete fertilizer can be used, with a formula high in the elements most needed and low in the others.

The beginning gardener should learn to distinguish between organic and inorganic (chemical) fertilizers.

The former are made up of processed animal and vegetable materials: bone, dried blood, slaughter-house wastes (tankage), cottonseed meal, and the like. The chemical fertil-

KEEPING PLANTS VIGOROUS AND HEALTHY

izers are derived from inanimate substances such as nitrate and potash salts, phosphate rock, and various manufacturing by-products.

The *organic fertilizers* are safer to use, that is, there is less danger of "burning" or otherwise injuring plants in case of an accidental overdose. In *transplanting* especially it is better to avoid the use of chemicals; in fact many instructions for transplanting or setting out even sizable trees or shrubs advise using no fertilizer in the planting holes. We have never observed any injury from this practice, however, but have had good results from the reasonable use of *organic* fertilizers in such operations.

In using fertilizers, best results are usually obtained by making two or more moderate applications rather than one large one.

A satisfactory system is to make the first application just before sowing seeds or setting out plants, and a second one considerably later; with vegetables and annuals, when they are half grown. Most perennials and shrubs may be fertilized just as growth starts in the spring, and again just before or after the flowering period. Usual amounts to be used are suggested in connection with different types of plants, throughout this volume.

Humus (discussed in Chapter 2), in addition to its other advantages, acts as a sponge to absorb and hold plant nutrients that have gone into solution, thus preventing their loss through leaching from excessive rain or watering.

Manures and composts have the double advantage of adding both plant foods and humus to the soil. In fact the most effective—as well as the pleasantest—way to utilize animal manures is to incorporate them with organic materials in the compost heap. This is like starting a bank account, and requires some planning ahead—but it pays excellent dividends. We keep a series of heaps going. (See Chapter 2 for details of constructing the compost heap.)

Green manures are crops sown to be plowed or dug under, usually in an immature state, where they are grown. The growing roots penetrate the soil and improve its friability, and also gather food elements which are brought nearer the surface.

Crops used for this purpose include several of the legumes, such as cowpeas, vetch, and clover, that add to the nitrogen in the soil. Others, such as winter rye and oats, produce a mass of green material, while the soil is not otherwise occupied, to provide humus when it is turned under. (See also Chapter 2.)

PREPARATION FOR PLANTING

The information given so far in this chapter will be of no use in providing a green lawn, bigger roses, or more vigorous trees and shrubs—*unless it is put to use*. In most instances nine tenths of the successful growth of a plant depends upon what is done to the soil *before* it is planted.

England is famous for its beautiful gardens. The climate, with its abundant moisture and the absence of the extremes of winter cold and scorching summer heat which we experience, may be credited with a great deal of this horticultural success, but much is due to the extreme thoroughness practiced in preparing the soil for planting. No one who reads English books on gardening can fail to be impressed by this. In connection with our editorial work we read many of these volumes, and the constant emphasis on what should be done *before* planting stands out like a bandaged thumb at a bridge party.

Too often American gardeners sow their seeds or set out their plants in soil that is completely *un*prepared. This is especially true of beginning gardeners, but by no means limited to them. Misled by blatantly extravagant, if not patently false claims in advertising—which go unchallenged in most editorial columns—they plant with little or no real preparation of the soil, depending upon wonder-working "miracle" chemicals to give them Jack-and-the-beanstalk results. Recently we saw a full-page ad in one of the country's leading —and in many ways most reliable—newspapers, devoted to a new method of lawn making purporting to provide a perfect, weed-free turf. Supposedly this could be achieved in a few weeks merely by spreading over the ground a combination of three layers of especially prepared fabric, carrying seed, and fertilizer contents. This might be possible, but how long would such a lawn last? Its remains, of course, might be rooted up to make a good, but rather expensive, addition to the compost heap.

As we have seen, the soil factors involved in obtaining and maintaining good plant growth are:

        its physical condition,
        its capacity for retaining moisture,
        its nutrient content.

Our problem, therefore, is to provide, as far as is practical, the maximum in each of these factors for the plant or crop to be grown.

KEEPING PLANTS VIGOROUS AND HEALTHY

Physical condition. The soil should be "worked up"—by hand digging, plowing, or rototilling—to a depth adequate for the plants or crops to be grown. Where there is a hard subsoil this may be broken up with a pickax or a crowbar to improve drainage. Usually it is left in place, but if too close to the surface it may be advantageous to remove some of it entirely to make possible a larger prepared planting hole or a deeper bed.

If the subsoil is sandy or gravelly, usually the best course is to leave it undisturbed, or to mix with it clay soil and peatmoss or other humusy material to increase its water-holding capacity.

Either of these treatments is more readily employed in preparing planting holes for trees or shrubs than in the case of a lawn, a large flower garden, or a vegetable plot. For such extensive areas, poor drainage may be improved by extra-deep digging or by subsoil plowing. Too rapid draining may be slowed up by the incorporation of humusy materials such as manure, green manures, sod turned under (either broken up in small pieces or grass side down), peatmoss, or compost.

The *depth* to which ground should be prepared varies with different types of plants. But as we stress throughout this book *the deeper the better*. The following figures should be taken as minimum:

Flower borders:

annuals	5 to 6 inches
perennials	6 to 8 inches
Lawn	4 to 6 inches
Roses	18 to 24 inches
Shrubs (holes)	18 to 24 inches; 24 inches in diameter
Trees (holes)	24 to 36 inches; 36 inches in diameter

In the preparation of planting holes it is advisable to remove soil from holes completely (placing it on burlap or in a wheelbarrow) and then refill with prepared compost.

The *nutrient content* of any soil is determined by the amounts of the several elements in *available form* which it contains, as discussed earlier in this chapter. Different plants, in growing, use up these elements in different amounts, foliage plants like lawn grass demanding more nitrogen than others, some more potash, etc.

In commercial farming and vegetable growing, special formulas, designed to provide these plant food elements in just the right proportions for the crop being grown, are employed. Special formulas are also put out, in fancy packages and at fancy prices, for the home gardener's use. He can get them for lawns, for roses, for this and that special purpose, but they are by no means essential. We have grown just as good roses with potato fertilizer as with any other, though of course if we were growing roses by the acre we would try to get a formula especially suited to the crop *and* the soil in which they were grown.

For the amateur's garden, the most important distinction is between plants that demand or prefer an acid soil—such as rhododendrons, azaleas, kalmias, and camellias—and plants which particularly demand neutral or alkaline soil. In the former case, a fertilizer with an acid reaction should be used, and in the latter, lime may be applied if needed. See the table at the close of this chapter.

Final preparation for planting then includes these three steps:

First: digging or plowing the area and, if necessary, improving the drainage and removing large stones or roots.

Second: applying and *digging in* peatmoss, compost, and/or other humus-forming material, and lime if required.

Third: applying and raking in fertilizers, either inorganic (chemical) or processed (pulverized) organic materials.

Just before planting, it is advantageous to go over, with an iron rake, the area where seeds are to be sown.

ORGANIC GARDENING

We are often asked what stand we take on organic gardening—as though it were a challenge to our religion or our politics!

We make a practice of using all of the organic material, of whatever sort, that we can get. In addition to this, every fall and spring we plant cover crops of winter rye, vetch, clover, or some other fast-growing ground cover for turning under as "green manure" (pages 41; 93).

We do not, however, eschew the use of all chemical fertilizers, insecticides, and fungicides as do the dedicated organic gardeners. As a matter of fact, we would have had great difficulty in growing green manure crops (to provide the humus so badly needed on our sandy, porous soil) without the assistance of chemical fertilizers to give them a start.

We have never seen convincing evidence that organically grown vegetables and flowers can be made immune to insect and disease attacks, and we have encountered numerous instances of evidence to the contrary. When possible, we use

KEEPING PLANTS VIGOROUS AND HEALTHY 97

natural organic materials such as rotenone or pyrethrum for spraying and dusting, but in an emergency we resort to chemical materials. We do agree that vegetables and fruits—practically "manufactured" on vast areas with chemicals and irrigation and harvested prematurely—are lacking in flavor and probably in nutritional value.

In short, we use all the organic material we can obtain, but do not hesitate to employ chemicals where they are likely to beneficially supplement the organics, or save a diseased or insect-ridden crop from ruin.

SYMPTOMS OF NUTRIENT DEFICIENCY

Nitrogen: Light green to yellow leaves starting at bottom of plant, turning first pale green, then yellow.
> Cucumber: pointed blossom end.
> Fruit: poor set; early leaf fall.
> Corn: leaves with yellow midrib, edges green. Most likely to occur in sandy or water-logged soils.

Phosphorus: "Leaf scorch," often mistaken for drought or fire blight.
> Corn: yellows at leaf tips and along margins.
> Cucumber: small stem end.
> Potato: marginal scorch of lower leaves.

Boron: Celery: cracked stems.
> Beets: heart rot and canker (cracking of outer skin near soil surface, followed by breaking down of root tissue).

UPKEEP

The general appearance of the home and grounds depends not only upon how much thought and good care have been employed in planning it, and expense and labor in planting it; there is a third factor which too often is neglected. It may be expressed in the word "upkeep"—but that is perhaps a little too all-inclusive. What is specifically referred to here is vigorous growth and good health.

To cover the former, little need be added to the information and suggestions given in preceding chapters. Pests and diseases, however, are another matter; and the novice at gardening will not have gone far before he begins to encounter them. If he takes the trouble to learn what he can do about them *in advance*, he will save himself much trouble, disappointment, and heartbreak.

FERTILIZERS, THEIR NUTRIENT CONTENTS, REACTION AND APPLICATION

Reaction	Fertilizer	Source	Application per 100 sq. ft.
alkaline	bone meal	organic	3 to 6 pounds
acid	cottonseed meal	"	3 to 6 "
alkaline	cyanamid	inorganic	combined with others
acid	dried blood	organic	2 to 4 pounds
	manure		
	dried cow or sheep	"	1 to 2 pecks
	dried poultry	"	½ peck
none	muriate of potash	inorganic	1 to 3 pounds
alkaline	nitrate of soda	"	1 to 3 "
acid	sulfate of ammonia	"	
none	superphosphate		3 to 6 "
acid	tankage	organic	4 "
slightly acid	urea	inorganic	combined with others
alkaline	wood ashes	organic	6 pecks

GENERAL FERTILIZER FORMULAS AND THEIR RECOMMENDED USES

Applications as noted or as directed on the packages

Plant	Formula		Pounds per 100 sq. ft.
annuals	5–10–5 or 4–12–4		3 to 4
azaleas and rhododendrons	4–12–4	plus 25% organic nitrogen— or 2 parts cottonseed meal and 1 part ammonium sulfate	3 to 4 1 to 2
lawns	10–6–4 or 11–4–8		3 to 4
perennials	4–12–4 or 2–10–10		3 to 4
roses	4–12–4		3 to 4
shrubs	4–12–4 or 10–6–4		3 to 4
trees	4–12–4 or 10–6–4		3 to 4
vegetables, leafy,	4–12–4	and side dress with	3 to 4
root	2–10–10	nitrogenous fertilizer	3 to 4

KEEPING PLANTS VIGOROUS AND HEALTHY

In the first place he will learn to be *constantly on the watch* for the first sign of injury to his plants caused by pests or diseases. In fighting many of them, promptness is almost as important as it is in fighting a fire. And so the wise gardener keeps on hand, ready for instant use, one or more of the all-purpose controls, and equipment with which to apply them. (See Appendix and page 130.)

As a rule the more vigorous and healthy a plant, the less likely it is to be attacked. But exceptions to this rule are so frequent that one cannot rely upon it.

In guarding against many plant pests and diseases, sanitation is quite as essential in the garden as in the house. Plants that are kept well fed and uncrowded are less likely to be attacked by either pests or disease, and are more likely to make a recovery if they are attacked. With feeding, as with most things, it is possible to overdo. Plants forced into abnormally lush growth—as for instance by the use of an excess of nitrogen—may be unduly susceptible to trouble.

Weeds, too, are pests when growing where they are a menace to cultivated plants. A weed has been described as a plant growing where it is not wanted. (One of the worst "weeds" we had in our vegetable garden last year was a vigorous, self-sown crop of that excellent "greens" *Tetragonia expansa,* more commonly known as New Zealand spinach.)

Of recent years various chemicals have been more and more frequently employed in the control of weeds in large-scale vegetable growing and farming operations, as well as for destroying unwanted growth along highways and roadsides. In the home garden and about the home grounds these materials should be used with great caution (as in the eradication of poison-ivy) or applied by a professional operator. The control of weeds in lawns by the use of chemicals is an exception to the above statement; but in our experience and observation, these "patent medicines"—with monosyllabic names dreamed up by high-salaried advertising experts who would not know a weed from a watering can—are in general not nearly so effective as the extravagant claims made for them would imply. We suggest a small-scale test treatment under one's own conditions before making any considerable investment in any such panacea. For weeds and their control see Appendix.

INSECTICIDES, FUNGICIDES, AND HERBICIDES

New or improved insecticides, fungicides, and herbicides are constantly coming on the market in these days of rapid scientific discovery. By the time this volume reaches the reader, a number of materials may be available which were unknown at the time this was written. We can only list the best materials for home garden use known to us at this writing.

Products are offered in garden centers, seed and hardware stores, usually under trade names. The label of each package, however, bears a list of ingredients, with percentages of active and inactive content. Our recommendations in the Appendix (pages 451 and 453) for insecticides and fungicides, with but few exceptions, do not use trade names, but those of the chemicals themselves. In the table of herbicides (page 454, Appendix) trade names are used without any intention on our part of recommending a single product over all others. Commercial products manufactured by reputable companies are as represented. By consulting the list of ingredients on each package displayed in the store, the buyer can select the one best suited for his purpose.

Many products are available as dusts, concentrated liquid sprays to be diluted in water, or powders to be dissolved in water and used in spray guns. Dusts are easiest to apply. In general, sprays do a more thorough job. Directions on each package tell exactly how each material should be prepared for use, how much water is to be added to a given amount of material to make a spray, and, in cases where the material or spray mixture is to be applied to the soil or lawn surface, how much is needed to cover 100 or 1000 square feet.

Since the publication of Rachel Carson's controversial book, *Silent Spring*, and the articles, lectures, government research, and legislation resulting from the furor it caused, all gardeners are aware of the potential dangers to man, animals, birds, and even fish from the indiscriminate or careless use of many insecticides and other related materials.

The label on every product bears explicit directions and precautions if the material is toxic to man or to animals. These must be *followed to the letter* for ensurance against injury to any living thing.

Sometimes beginners increase the given dosage of an insecticide, or even of a fertilizer, on the theory that if a little is good, more is better. Nothing could be further from the

KEEPING PLANTS VIGOROUS AND HEALTHY

proven facts. Following such a course may well result in injury to plants, materials, birds, or wild creatures, or worst of all, to the operator.

The following precautions should be observed in all cases. (From Home & Garden Bulletin No. 46, U. S. Dept. of Agriculture.)

Most insecticides and fungicides are poisonous. Those that are recommended . . . can be used with safety provided these precautions are carefully followed.

Handle insecticides and fungicides with care. Follow all directions and heed all precautions on the labels.

In handling, mixing, or applying insecticides and fungicides, avoid inhaling them; keep them out of eyes, nose and mouth. Work on the windward side of the areas treated.

For detailed lists of insecticides, fungicides, and herbicides, see Appendix.

For information of dusters and sprayers, see page 130.

Good cultural practices will do much to prevent and control pests, diseases, and weeds in the home garden. The following measures should be taken:

1. Good drainage is essential.
2. Fertile soil containing a constant supply of humus.
3. Good-quality, appropriate fertilizers applied as needed.
4. Plants suited to the soil and climate should be grown.
5. Weeds should be kept under control and never permitted to go to seed.
6. Best-quality grass seed contains few weed seeds. Buy only certified seed.
7. Before sowing seeds, treat with seed protectant. See page 70.
8. Check purchased plants to be sure they are pest- and disease-free.
9. Disease-resistant varieties of many plants are available. These reduce danger of trouble.
10. When pests or diseases have been present during growing season, burn all garden trash which might harbor them through the winter, to appear again next season. A thorough garden clean-up each fall makes for a clean garden in spring.

> The lopped tree in time may grow again,
> Most naked plants renew both fruit and flower.
> ROBERT SOUTHWELL

> Just as the twig is bent, the tree's inclin'd.
> ALEXANDER POPE

CHAPTER 6

Pruning and Training Plants

Almost all trees, shrubs, and perennial vines grown about the modern home place require, at one time or another, some attention involving pruning or training.

While both these operations necessitate the removal of parts of the plants, let us at the outset make clear the distinction between the two.

Pruning is done primarily to ensure better growth, more bloom, or greater health for the specimen. *Training* may also involve such removal, but it is done for the benefit of the pruner rather than of the plant: to make the plant grow, or assume a form that, for esthetic reasons, he prefers. Often the two objectives overlap, but it should always be kept in mind that they are distinct.

Few people realize the fact that nature herself does a great deal of pruning. Forest trees, as they struggle upward in the competition for light, lose their lower branches. The same thing happens with ornamental trees if planted too close together, and with shrubs about the home grounds that are allowed to crowd each other. Storms, too, often remove branches or even tear out the tops of trees and shrubs. The results of this type of pruning are likely to be anything but desirable. In fact much of the pruning done by the gardener

ENCOURAGE MORE VIGOROUS GROWTH.

ELIMINATE COMPETITION.

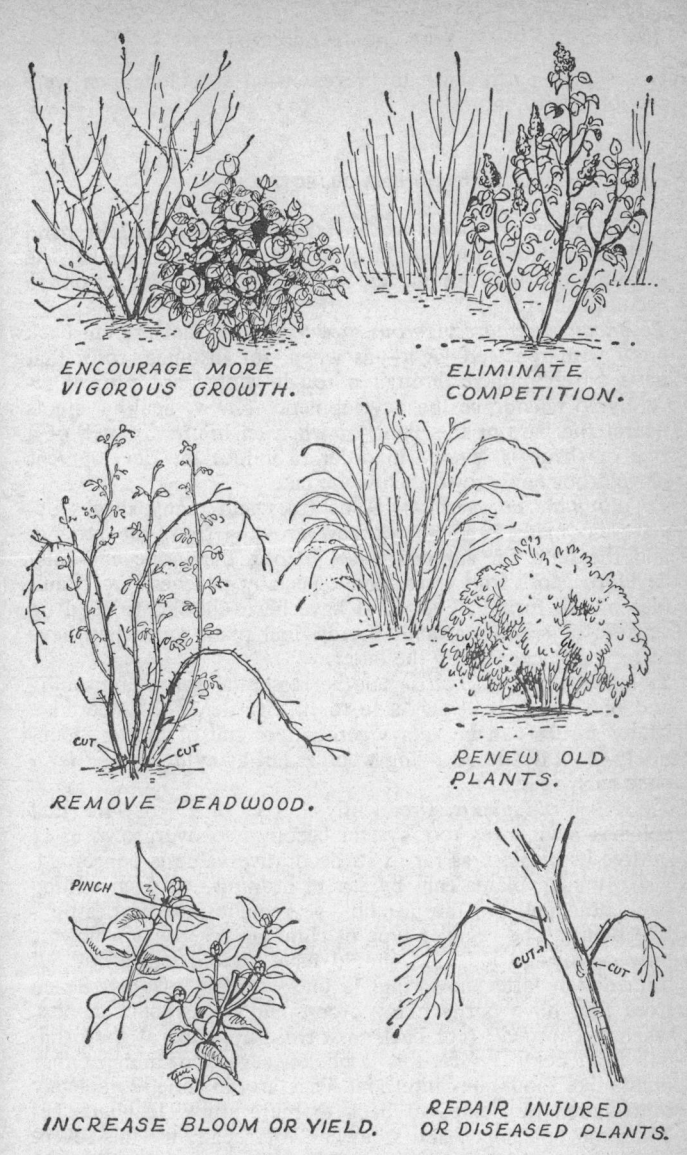

REMOVE DEADWOOD.

RENEW OLD PLANTS.

INCREASE BLOOM OR YIELD.

REPAIR INJURED OR DISEASED PLANTS.

Before you start pruning, be certain just what you wish to accomplish by it.

is designed particularly to prevent what would happen were the job left to nature!

PRUNING OBJECTIVES

The gardener should never take a pruning tool in hand without having some definite objective as to what and why he is going to prune. Among the several things he can set out to accomplish are:

To encourage more vigorous growth. Plants that are cut back grow with renewed vigor—as when, for instance, roses that have barely pulled through a tough winter are pruned severely to encourage the development of new, healthy shoots nearer the base of the plant; or when an injured branch of a tree or shrub is severed in order to induce the development of vigorous new growth below the cut.

To eliminate competition. Some trees and many shrubs develop so many branches or new growths from the ground, and the fight for survival is so intense, that none can fully develop. Most fruit trees, and especially peaches, are examples of the former; lilacs that have been allowed to send up suckers or sprouts around the original plant until they have formed a thicket typify the latter.

To remove dead wood is another essential form of pruning and one which is always safe for the gardener to undertake. Many shrubs can be kept vigorous and full of bloom indefinitely if all dead and dying wood is cut away *at ground level* once each year.

To renew old plants. Frequently a tree, shrub, or vine that still has a vigorous root system becomes so overgrown as to outlive its purpose as far as its decorative value is concerned. Usually such plants can, by severe pruning—or even cutting back practically to the ground—be remade into new, attractive plants. The rambler type of climbing rose, which flowers only on new wood, and should have all old canes cut out immediately after flowering, is one example of this. Peach trees that have borne many crops, and occasionally apples, when "dehorned" (cut back to leave only stubs of the original branches), typify this kind of severe pruning. Other plants like mountain-laurel and lilacs are, in time, completely rejuvenated by being cut back to mere stubs. If plants become too tall, leggy, and sprawling for repair, try this severe pruning before rooting them out altogether.

To increase bloom or yield. Many fruits, if left to grow naturally, are almost sure to set more flowers or fruit than can be properly matured or ripened. Nature is not interested in the size or perfection of blossoms or fruit set. And so, even though she removes part of the crop by letting it fall off while immature, if the pruning is left to nature alone, it is not likely to be well done.

The pruning away of dead flower stalks or branches, as with roses, lilacs, and other flowering shrubs, with perennials like delphinium and lupine, and even with most annuals, is calculated to produce more or higher quality bloom later on. Disbudding of dahlias and chrysanthemums is really a form of this type of pruning.

To repair injured and diseased plants. Pruning often plays an important part in the restoration of injured plants, as after storm or ice-breakage, and also in the cure of diseased specimens. Here on Cape Cod, where we have so many hurricanes and northeast storms, we often find it necessary to perform such repair operations. A fine young tulip tree, brought with us from New York, lost 15 feet of its top two years ago, and the unsightly stub seemed hardly worth rehabilitating. However, we cut the main trunk neatly just above a strong branch, and fastened the branch in an upright position by attaching it to a long bamboo stake bound to it and to the tree trunk. After a few months it had formed a vigorous new leader and the support was removed. Today the tree is handsomer than ever, more dense, but not so tall as it would have been if uninjured.

Where disease has begun to attack a plant, as in the case of rose cancer for instance, cutting back to clean, live wood before the trouble has gone too far may save the plant.

Equally important is the use of pruning to *forestall* injury, by eliminating weak crotches, poorly placed limbs, entangled boughs or roots and the like.

TRAINING OBJECTIVES

When pruning is to be undertaken to change or modify the shape or habit of a plant in order to make it more beautiful, or to induce it to fit better into a certain space or garden picture, the gardener should be perfectly clear in his mind just what he is going to do before starting to use the pruning shears.

To control size and habit of growth. It often happens that a tree or shrub is planted where it fits in all right for a few years, but later completely outgrows its surroundings. Who, for instance, has not seen, under low windows, foundation plantings of evergreens that have been allowed to grow until they nearly obliterate the front of the house? Often a maple or other shade tree or evergreen almost completely occupies a front yard until no space is left for a lawn or for any other use.

There is a limit to the control of size by pruning, but if taken in time, and faithfully continued, the results which can be accomplished are almost unbelievable.

The same holds true for the control of *habit of growth*. Many years ago when the famous Seabrook Farms in New Jersey undertook an extensive orchard operation, I complimented—in the column of a Seabrook house organ which I edited at the time—the little German who had charge of the pruning, stating that he could do anything with an apple tree except make it jump through a hoop. Instead of being flattered, he burst into my office in a very irate mood, with the statement that his skill had been greatly underestimated. A year later he stopped in again and asked me to take a ride in his jeep. We ended up in the yard of his neat little home, where, with pride, he showed me a young apple, growing lustily, topped by three perfect hoops formed by the willowy branches. "Ja," he exclaimed triumphantly. "You see, I *can* make heem jump through a hoop!"

The extreme example of controlling growth habit is to be found in topiary work in which dense-growing shrubs, especially box, are trained, trimmed, and tortured into the forms of urns, roosters, animals, or what-have-you. Fortunately this garden "art" is now seldom encountered in this country, although still to be seen in famous old gardens in Great Britain and Europe.

Espaliered fruits or vinelike shrubs such as *Pyracantha coccinea* or *Hydrangea petiolaris* (climbing hydrangea) represent another extreme example of training plants to desired forms by means of pruning away unneeded branches or tops and guiding the remainder by tying the young, pliable branches to a frame or fastening them to a wall in exactly the positions in which the gardener wishes them to grow.

Hedge pruning, when sheared to shape, is simply a less difficult and less tortuous form of topiary work. To be successful this must be begun when the plants are small—whether they are privet, barberry, or trees such as hemlock or arborvitae. Shaping, topping, and shortening of side branches must be done frequently to assure dense growth over each entire plant. A season of neglect may result in bare spots which fail to fill in after the too large, neglected branches have finally been removed.

ESPALIER FORMS

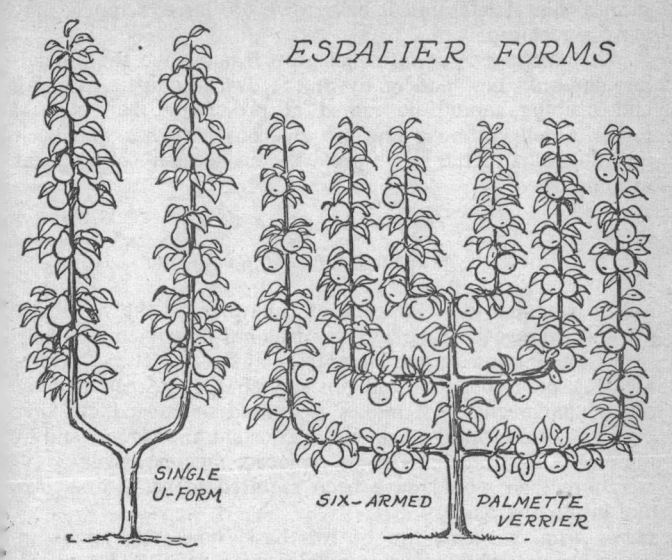

SINGLE U-FORM   SIX-ARMED   PALMETTE VERRIER

In formal gardens, or against a sunny wall, espaliered fruits or certain types of flowering shrubs may be used effectively.

Informal hedges, where plants are permitted to retain their natural habit of growth, must still be shaped frequently by pruning, to keep "wild" branches in check and to remove all dead or dying wood back to the main stems.

Shrubs. The training or shaping of shrubs need not be confined to chopping graceful flowering specimens like spirea and forsythia into ball or club-shaped atrocities, though one too often sees these on places where untrained help is brought in by the day to mow and "prune."

The correct way to prune and train all flowering shrubs of fountainlike growth is to preserve and assure the continuance of their natural, graceful forms. Remove wood too old to bloom or any that is dying, throwing out only a few live side branches; also shorten or remove straight, suckerlike branches which shoot up vertically; and preserve all young, vigorous, curving branches.

Evergreens of formal shapes like the columnar Chinese or Irish junipers; the vase-shaped yews and globular mugo pine, and some of the compact arborvitaes as well as boxwood, may need judicious pruning to preserve their forms. Removing a maverick branch or shoot as soon as it appears accomplishes this. If left until it has grown too large, removal may leave a bare gap.

With evergreens of informal growth habit like the Spreading Japanese Yew and many of the dwarf junipers, pruning and training should be aimed at preserving their *natural* forms. Often cutting a few too vigorous branches well back into the heart of the shrub prevents the necessity of frequent pruning.

PRUNING EQUIPMENT

When buying tools for pruning it pays to get the very best. On the average home place any pruning implement is likely to be, barring loss, a very long-term, if not a lifetime, investment. A poor tool that will not stay sharp, that gets slightly out of alignment, that makes a bruised or ragged cut that does not heal properly, becomes a constant annoyance, and in the end is likely to have to be replaced, thus eventually costing more than would have been required to get a first-class tool in the first place.

Hand pruning shears are of two basic types: the anvil, in which the cutting blade comes down upon a flat bed; and the two-bladed, or scissor type, in which the two cutting edges shear past each other. The anvil type has the advantage that even in the toughest use, the tool remains in alignment; while in the scissor type the blades may be forced apart, resulting in a ragged cut and in injury to the tool. The anvil type of shears, however, is more likely to crush the bark if it is soft than is the scissor type with its two cutting blades that pass each other as they shear a twig or branch. Even the scissor type, unless of excellent quality, and kept very sharp, is likely to spread apart slightly as the blades are pressed together, resulting in a badly bruised cut. Where much pruning is to be done, it is advisable to have both types.

Pole pruning shears are similar to hand shears except that they are operated at the end of a pole, making it possible to reach very high branches. The better types, equipped with levers, easily cut off quite large branches.

Pruning knife, made with an extra-strong blade, terminates in a curved point. It can be used in many places difficult to get at with shears, and is in general very useful about the garden.

Lopping shears, with two long handles, are designed to cut larger branches than hand shears. They are especially useful in caring for shrubs and hedges, and quite an essential tool on a large place or one that is wooded.

Pruning saw. The blade may be straight or crescent-shaped, and used either in the hand or at the end of a pole. A *pole saw* is effective for making neat, clean cuts of branches too heavy or too high to be handled with shears. The straight-bladed type with teeth on both sides is likely, in the amateur's hands, to do more harm than good!

No pruning tool is better than its edge. The use of a dull pair of shears or saw may, by bruising or tearing bark and wood, initiate decay or disease, and so do much harm. Kept on hand, for frequent use along with one's pruning tools, should be a good sharpening stone. We find the small type to be most useful. Occasionally—once every year or two according to the amount of use—it pays well to have all pruning tools professionally sharpened. This is an early winter job, so that they will be ready for late winter, spring, and summer use.

THE TECHNIQUES OF PRUNING

To employ the art of pruning effectively it is essential to know something of the growth habits of plants in general; and then—from observation or study—of the plant being pruned, in particular.

If you observe the growth of a tree, shrub, or vine in your garden, you cannot fail to note that the *terminal* bud of a main stem, or of any lateral, usually makes the most vigorous growth. If this bud is injured or removed, then the one next below it takes its place as the leader. In the case of a tree such as a pine or spruce, if the terminal growth—the "leader"—is broken or removed, then *one* of the cluster of branches just beneath it will outgrow the others, turn upright, and take its place just as in the illustration of the tulip tree which had its top torn out in a hurricane.

What is not so commonly known—although examples of it may be observed in almost any garden—is that if a branch or cane of any plant is bent down, then the buds that remain highest up will tend to take the lead in new growth.

Furthermore, if part of a plant (the cane of a vigorous climbing rose, for instance) is trained horizontally or in an arch, then the buds in the *upper* surface are those to grow most vigorously (see photograph above).

It is essential to keep these three points in mind in pruning to control or direct plant growth.

Select your pruning tool to do the job required; and keep all cutting edges razor-sharp to avoid leaving bruised bark and thus inviting disease.

PRUNING AND TRAINING PLANTS

Another most important fact for the beginning pruner to realize is that any pruning cut should be made close to a growing part of the plant, or to an "eye" that will make new growth. Any "stub" that is left beyond growing wood is very likely to die back and eventually may decay and result in serious injury. This is the reason for removing entire branches of trees or shrubs as close as possible to the main trunk of the plant.

Nature tends to cover up wounds left by pruning with new bark. It is often surprising how quickly and how thoroughly she can do this. But pruning wounds of more than an inch or two in diameter are best treated with tree-wound paint immediately after they have been made. If this special paint is not available, any ordinary outside paint will serve.

It is best, wherever possible, to *anticipate* in pruning. A forefinger and thumbnail pinch in spring may save fifteen minutes' work in autumn or next spring. Much light pruning can be done with a pruning knife (see sketch, page 124), which takes up less pocket space than a penknife. I always carry one about the garden and grounds. It is kept—along with folding rule, garden gloves, hand weeder, pruning shears, and other frequently used and easily mislaid small items—on the "snatch" shelf by our garage door, where it can be picked up or put down on the way to or from the garden.

> Framed in the prodigality of nature.
> SHAKESPEARE

CHAPTER 7

Coldframes and Hotbeds

Perhaps the most exciting day that can come to the novice at gardening is the one when he finally resolves no longer calmly to accept the verdict of gray-bearded Old Man Winter when he snarls, *"This is where we stop!"*

Oddly enough the gardener's most helpful assistant at rebelling against this age-old command is glass. Glass, one of the frailest of all materials; glass made of sand!

The simplest of structures employed in growing things out of season is the coldframe—a small rectangular pit covered with removable glass sash. When temperatures in the frame get too high the sash may be taken off entirely or partly raised to admit only the desired amount of cooler air.

A hotbed is similar to a coldframe, but there is the essential difference that some means of *artificial* heating is provided. Thus the operator ceases to be entirely dependent upon the vagaries of the weather. If, in addition to artificial heat within the frame, the glass sash is also covered with some form of insulation, then frost may be kept out even in sections where long periods of very cold weather are experienced. Hotbeds originally were heated by fermenting manure —hence the name. Nowadays electric heating cable provides the heat.

The greenhouse differs basically from a cold frame or hotbed in that it is designed to be not merely an accessory to outdoor growing, but to serve as an indoor garden with a succession of flowering and foliage plants from one end of the year to the

COLDFRAMES AND HOTBEDS

other. For this reason the greenhouse, in this book, is discussed separately (see Chapter 18).

What type of frame? The amateur gardener will do well to start moderately for a season or two when he decides to tackle the adventure of gardening under glass. Success in this field depends very largely upon the gardener's being able—as well as willing—to give regular attention to it. The flower garden or the vegetable garden may be left to itself for a week or even longer; but a hotbed or even a coldframe, for most of the season for which it is in use, requires daily attention, particularly in the matter of ventilation. A few hours of bright sunshine, even if the temperature is down to freezing or below, may run the temperature in the frame up to 80 or 90 degrees or even more, and quickly dry out and severely injure any plants in it, especially any that are in flats or pots. Opening the sash to provide ventilation is easily done, but there must be someone available who will attend to it.

Frames may be bought, ready-made, complete with sash. These can be set in place quickly and with very little work. The do-it-yourself-er, however, may get more space for his money by purchasing only the sash, and then constructing his own frame.

Sash is available in three sizes: the standard 3×6 feet; half-sash 3×3 feet; and the zephyr or home garden type 2×4 feet. Standard-size sash are too heavy for a woman—or for many white-collar men these days—to handle. Of the two smaller sizes, we must prefer the 2×4 foot as it provides more direct sunshine in proportion to the area covered inside of the frame. This is important during late fall, winter, and early spring, when sunshine strikes the frame at a very low angle—just the period when it is of most use.

The 2×4 sash, weighing but 14 to 20 pounds, is easily handled. In case of breakage it is readily repaired, as the glass, instead of being held in place by putty, is merely slipped into grooves. For general-purpose gardening, two frames of small or moderate size are much more useful than one larger one. The only additional material required will be that needed to make two more ends.

Where two frames are used, one may well be placed in semishade or where it will be shaded at least during midsummer. We have one long frame under an old cherry tree trimmed up to form a huge umbrella. This frame gets filtered sunshine during late autumn and early spring, but just the right amount of "high" shade during late spring, summer, and early fall. It makes an excellent spot for growing tuberous begonias and other plants, after they have been taken out of the greenhouse, to develop until they are set out in beds, flower boxes, or planters for the summer.

Another method of providing conditions for plants that do not like full, direct sunshine, is to make a board 12 or 15 inches wide and the exact length of the frame, and to nail to this two or more pairs of 1×2-inch cleats 3 or 4 feet apart. These are placed so that they extend 4 inches or so below one edge of the board. When the board is placed on top of the lower side of the frame, the cleats hold it in place, thus converting what was the lower side into the high side. Consequently when sash are put on they slant in just the opposite direction from which they formerly did, and the sun's rays are deflected, thus keeping the frame cooler.

A removable divider for the frame often proves useful. This is a piece of ¼- or ½-inch plywood cut at an angle to match the slant of the sash, and sufficiently wide to penetrate a couple of inches into the soil. Two pointed pieces of 1×2 extending 6 inches below the lower (straight) edge and nailed to it are pushed down into the soil in the frame to hold the divider firmly in place. In use it is, of course, so located as to match the edge of a sash. This makes it possible to maintain two different temperatures within the frame.

LOCATION

The location of the frame will have much to do with its contribution to the success of the garden. Its two chief requirements are full exposure to direct sunshine and protection from prevailing cold winds. If you have a pet cat or a dog, turn it out of doors on a sunny winter day and it will pick out the spot for you! If there is no location against the sunny side of a wall, there may be a hedge that will serve the purpose. In warmer climates, one of the fast-growing evergreen privets or any other evergreen shrub may be used. In the north, hemlock, pine, yew, or red-cedar, all of which may be kept sheared or pruned to any desired height, will answer. A tight board or picket fence—which later can be "planted out" with vines or evergreens—may be utilized.

Drainage. Equally important in selecting a location for the frame is the matter of drainage. There must be provision for any surplus water within the frame to be absorbed or to drain away quickly. In locations where natural drainage is poor, the quickest way to improve this condition may be to dig out the soil to a depth of 2 to 3 feet and fill in gravel or cinders to provide drainage for any surplus water within the frame.

Allowance should be made for at least 6 to 8 inches of soil over the drainage material.

BUILDING THE FRAME

The frame itself may be built with 2×4-inch stakes and 1-inch rough boards, preferably 12 inches wide. As a result of many, many years of experience with frames, we would recommend the use of 2-inch planks. These will last not only twice, but many times as long as 1-inch material. Top board for each end of frame may be cut (see sketch, page 116) on an angle, 9 inches at one end and 3 at the other. End posts to hold the sides and ends in place may be made of 2×4s. A 3×3, sawed diagonally, is stronger and will prove more convenient when flats are being placed in the frame. As the dimensions of hotbed sash of different makes vary somewhat, the sash should be on hand before the frame is constructed so that all measurements can be carefully checked. After the top sides and the ends of the frame are in place, the additional boards or planks can be fitted beneath them to extend the frame any desired depth into the ground. It is advisable to batten the cracks where the top boards and those placed beneath them come together as there will be some expansion and contraction according to the season and the weather. Also a piece of 3×1, nailed along the back of the frame and projecting an inch or so above it, helps to hold the sash steadily in position and also to check any leakage of warm air.

In many years of experience we have found that it pays well to treat very thoroughly, with creosote or some similar preservative such as Conservo, all wood to be used in building a frame. Also we have learned to take the precaution of placing on the outside (near the top of each end of the frame) two stout screw eyes. To one of these is secured a piece of plastic clothesline, which is then run the length of the frame *over* the sash, passed through the screw eyes at the other end of the frame, and then back over the sash again to the fourth screw eye at the end from which the line started. Here it is securely tied. This makes the quickest and most permanent method we have ever found for protecting the sash from being blown off during gale winds or freak storms. When not in use the plastic cord is laid along the outside of the frame or coiled up at one end. A further use for this cord is to hold securely in place any burlap or mat covering that may be put on over the glass (to keep out frost, or to prevent deep freezing inside the frame) in winter.

FRAME CONSTRUCTION
FOR FIVE 2×4' SASH

2×4"
3×3" CORNER POSTS
1½" SIDES & ENDS

Method of holding sash (also burlap or other covering used over glass to keep out extreme cold) securely in place with plastic clothesline.

SOIL FOR FRAMES

Under some conditions the soil where the frame is built is suitable for use as is, but in the great majority of cases it is much better to remove it and replace it with a mixture prepared for the purpose. This is especially true if existing soil is either heavy clay or very sandy. Usually some of the original soil removed from the frame can be used in making up the mix to be put back into it.

Soil for a general-purpose frame should be such as will drain rapidly, but at the same time should contain sufficient humus to retain moisture, when the surplus has drained through, so that too frequent watering is not required.

The mix we use is made up of sifted compost to which peatmoss is added if necessary. In any event, about one third coarse peatmoss is mixed into the bottom layer of 3 inches or so. This provides an additional reservoir for moisture, beneficial not only to plants grown directly in the frame but also to pots plunged to their rims; and even to flats or trays placed on the surface. If the only available soil for the frame is of clay, sand and peatmoss should be added to the mix. If very sandy, add more peatmoss.

FRAME MANAGEMENT

No matter how well the frame may be constructed, the attempt to grow plants in it is likely to result in failure unless the gardener understands at the outset that *it is not a garden area,* and that it cannot be treated as such. Even when, during frost-free periods, the sash is left off entirely, the frame needs careful attention in regard to watering; and flats and even pots plunged into the soil should be moved frequently to prevent overcrowding and rooting through the soil.

Temperature. The greatest problem in handling plants in frames is the control of temperature. Even on a very cold winter day a few hours of bright sunshine may skyrocket the temperature up to a dangerous point. If for any reason a frame must be left untended for a considerable period, it is much better to leave the sash partly open. The risk that the temperature may drop lower than is desired is less serious than that it may go too high if it remains closed. Plants are much more likely to recover from a severe chill than from dehydration.

In moderate sections plants in large pots, tubs, or planters are sometimes wintered over in extra-deep frames or pits. They are best placed on a layer of pebbles or turkey gravel to assure good drainage. If there is danger of frost penetrating the frame, most large plants may be left for days on end with the sash covered with mats made for the purpose or with heavy burlap bags.

Plants in peat pots that are scheduled to be transplanted later to the open are sunk part way into a layer of sifted compost or a sand-peat mixture so that roots that have penetrated the pot walls will suffer minimum injury when they are moved out.

Plants in clay or plastic pots are best sunk half their depth and should be moved often enough to prevent their rooting through into the soil below, which they are prone to do very quickly.

Cuttings in peat pots should be sunk to the rims as they are much more likely to be injured by having their roots disturbed than are seedling plants. Roots growing out through the sides of the pots form wonderful root balls for transplanting as they do not have to undergo a recovery period before renewing growth in their new environment.

Spacing. Plants in frames require elbow room and air just as much as they do if growing in the open. This is especially true of young plants in flats, pots, and multiple peat pots or "strips." As soon as plants begin to crowd they should be moved further apart or every other row of strip pots may be removed and placed elsewhere. Hardy vegetables—such as cabbage, broccoli, and lettuce—and hardy annuals and perennials may be removed from the frame as soon as danger of hard freezing is past and placed in a sheltered location until they can be planted out, thus leaving more space for the really tender things.

Watering. The inexperienced gardener very soon will learn that he cannot trust to nature to do this job for him. Plantings in flats and in pots and even those planted directly in the soil of the frame, and particularly in a hotbed, dry out in an astonishingly short time. This is especially true in bright, sunny, or windy weather. A spigot near the frame, or a length of hose extending to it and left permanently in place during the growing season, is a great time and labor saver. A good nozzle for this purpose is a type with an adjustable spray and an automatic shut off (see page 277).

Feeding. Plants placed temporarily in frames usually require no additional feeding before they are moved out to their permanent locations. Plants being *grown* in a frame, even if the soil has been well enriched, benefit from an occasional feeding with a general-purpose fertilizer. Materials with an extra-high nitrogen content are best avoided however. "Little and often" is the rule to follow.

Keep frames clean! Litter such as dead and possibly diseased leaves or plants, weeds, empty flats, and pots all encourage pests and diseases. An occasional spraying with an all-purpose pesticide and fungicide, even when no trouble shows itself, is good practice.

Shading. Plants in a frame, cut off from ordinary air circulation, are much more likely to suffer in hot weather than those in the open. One way of compensating for this is to provide some method of shading. The good gardener, instead of depending on sheets of last Sunday's newspaper, will have on hand substantial slatted sash. These are of the same size or very slightly larger than the glass sash and are made up of two pieces of 2×2 the length of the sash, with cross slats of ¼-inch wood ¾ of an inch wide spaced at intervals of 1 inch. Either redwood, white pine, or cypress, all light and decay resistant, are excellent for this purpose. While providing shifting shade, the slat sash do not interfere with full ventilation.

THE HOTBED

Hotbeds, as has already been explained, are merely coldframes provided with some artificial means of heating. The most satisfactory and most easily regulated kind of heating is an electric cable. Heating kits including thermostatic controls are available in a wide range of sizes.

To give good results without exorbitant expense for heating, the hotbed must be of substantial construction and very thoroughly insulated. It may very well be sunk deeper into the ground than a coldframe—provided of course that adequate drainage is maintained. Or it may have soil mounded up against the outside. Also, if a choice is available, it is well to have it so located that it will get full, direct morning sun from November on, as midwinter afternoon sunshine has no more strength than a twice watered-down highball.

Further protection during the winter in the form of mats, Fiberglas bats, burlap, old quilts, or what-have-you, will not only cut down the cost of heating but provide assurance against possible loss of plants from too low temperatures.

Another method of providing additional insulation is to erect a temporary frame of rough boards or of chicken wire outside the hotbed, leaving a space of 4 to 6 inches between it and the walls of the frame. This is stuffed with marsh hay, straw, dry leaves, or peatmoss. The latter material is much the best and really costs nothing as it can be used in the garden after it has served to protect the frame. Lining the walls with heavy building paper held in place by lath strips affords still further insulation.

BULBS FOR INDOORS

One of the most rewarding of all uses for the coldframe is in connection with "forcing" bulbs for bloom indoors in the winter, or in the greenhouse. In our opinion, and based on long experience, there is no gardening operation that brings more certain and satisfactory returns in proportion to the effort involved.

Although the term used for this particular method of growing hardy bulbs is "forcing," it is a misleading one. To get the best results the plant must be grown *cool*—just as when Mother Nature takes charge of the job in the garden.

The bulbs best adapted to this method of growing are the so-called Dutch bulbs—tulips, daffodils, hyacinths, crocuses, and the like. To get the best results it is important to use first-quality or top-size bulbs. While they may be grown in pots, it is much better to get bulb pans—which are merely more squatty flower pots—as these are both more sightly and less tippy. Soil from the compost heap—or garden soil with about one fourth each of sand and peatmoss added to it—gives good results.

Bulbs are placed in the pots or pans, and these are sunk to the rims in the frame and covered with leaves or straw. No attempt is made to prevent freezing; in fact sash is best left off until soil begins to freeze and then opened or removed during any prolonged mild or sunny spell during October to mid-December. (We once had a number of pans of bulbs buried in a trench which filled with water during a midwinter thaw and then froze into a solid cake of ice, locking them tight until late February. But when we finally were able to extricate them and bring them indoors, they bloomed perfectly.)

Any time after mid-December the pots may be brought in, a few at a time, and placed where they will receive light but only moderate temperatures (40 to 50 degrees if possible) until they have made a few inches of growth, after which they will be happy in a sunny window sill. Once the flowers have opened, they should be kept as cool as possible—*espe-*

cially at night—until they fade. After that the pots are returned to the frame, or covered with soil or mulch out of doors to complete growth. They may be planted, deep, in a permanent location in the garden as soon as the ground can be worked. Many bulbs, after possibly skipping one year of flowering, re-establish themselves satisfactorily after forcing and become permanent occupants of the garden. (For discussion of spring-flowering bulbs, see Chapter 11.)

> ... There is always work,
> And tools to work withal, for those who will;
> JAMES RUSSELL LOWELL

> There is no jesting with edge tools.
> BEAUMONT AND FLETCHER

CHAPTER 8

Tools and Equipment

No owner of a new home can go far before realizing that he will need adequate equipment—in addition to big ideas and willing hands—to create the little paradise he envisions in his mind's eye.

Unless he has someone to guide him, he is quite likely to make costly mistakes in the tools he buys. The amount and type of equipment he should eventually possess depends upon both the size of the place and how he expects to develop it. The sign above his tool-house door should read GO SLOW.

To begin with, the tools required to maintain home grounds in good condition are of two types: those used for many different tasks, such as digging, cultivating, raking; and the more specialized ones, employed for mowing, hedge trimming, pruning, and the like.

With tools that are to be kept in more or less constant use —such as hoes, rakes, pruning shears, spades, trowels, and lawn mower—it is good policy, and in the end least expensive, to get the very best, which does not necessarily mean the highest in price. With those used less constantly—such as shovels, a crowbar, a wheelbarrow—it may be advisable, if funds are limited, to settle for a less expensive grade; but even here, in the long run, this is doubtful economy.

HAND TOOLS FOR MANY TASKS

One of the first operations in gardening is preparation of the soil. With the ever-increasing use of power tools, real digging has become almost a lost art, but even so the modern gardener must occasionally dabble a bit in the dirt and get his fingers soiled.

Spades. The one tool most useful for preparing soil for planting, and for general use around the place, is a round-pointed, long-handled shovel. It may well be supplemented by a square-pointed, short-handled digging spade.

If much transplanting is to be done, a transplanting spade with a narrower blade, rounded at the tip, will prove extremely useful, as it does a neater, more efficient job, with less effort. In fact we find the transplanting spade our favorite for many jobs other than actual transplanting.

Spading fork. In ground that is already in good tilth, and for turning under cover crops or other humus such as peatmoss or manure, our preference is the spading fork, with its broad, flat tines. This is an ideal tool for breaking up clods of soil, leaving a fairly smooth surface ready for raking. It is also our preferred digging tool in preparing beds or borders for planting and transplanting.

Power tools. The investment of a considerable sum of money in a tractor, or other power-driven equipment, does not make good sense unless one is certain that there will be sufficient work to be done to make it pay off. Many inexperienced homeowners find out too late that they might better have hired the tractor work done, and expended the money saved on hand tools and plants. Many garden centers, seed stores, and hardware stores rent small power equipment for the do-it-yourself gardener.

For transplanting. Back through the ages the trowel has been the symbol of gardening, yet only recently have there been any changes to improve it. Modern trowels are made from one piece of metal so the head no longer keeps separating from the handle. The blade has been curved so that a rounded, firm ball of roots is taken up with the plant, and in some types the handle has been curved to fit the operator's hand. We find most generally useful a long-shanked type with a wooden handle that fits into the metal ferrule. These are heavy-duty hand tools which never bend or break under pressure. For taking up seedlings or separating young plants grown in a flat, we like a small-sized mason's trowel with a flat,

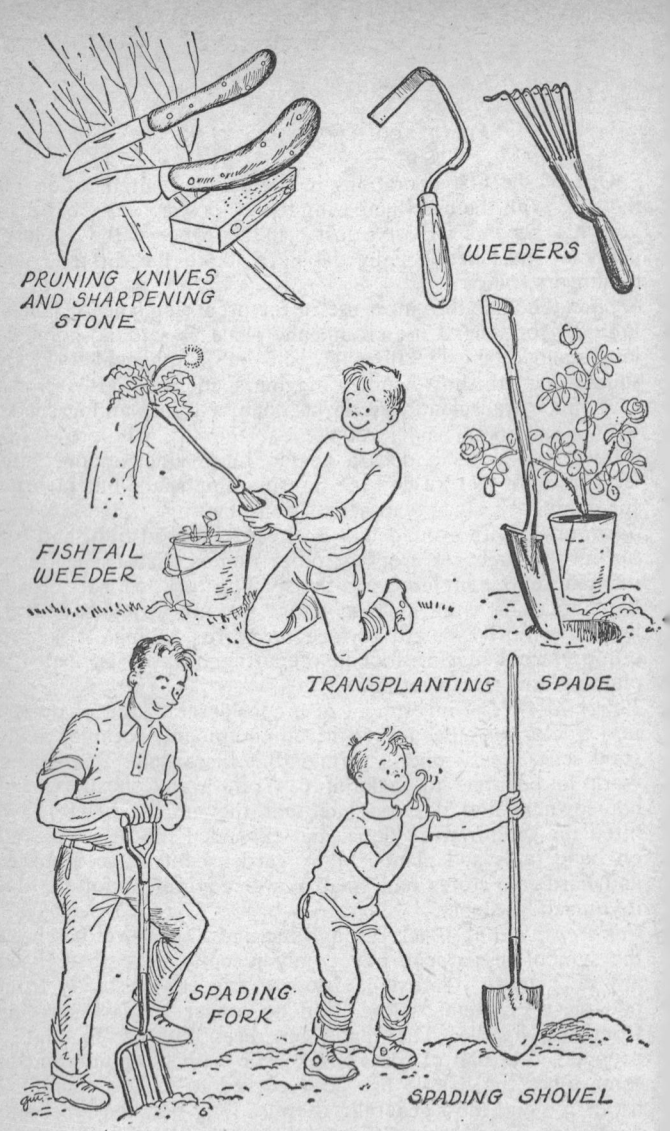

It is poor economy and time-wasting to skimp on essential hand tools.
Keeping them clean and sharp saves time, temper, and money.

MODERN-
ONE PIECE
TROWEL
STRAIGHT
SHANK
MASON'S TROWEL
TULIP
DIBBLE
STEEL
BOW
RAKE
LAWN
RAKE
ONION HOE
ALL-PURPOSE
HOE
SCUFFLE HOE

diamond-shaped blade, which makes it possible to cut out plants with minimum injury to the roots. It is also convenient for many other garden operations on young plants and is indispensable in the greenhouse.

Two other hand tools useful in setting out plants in the garden are the dibble and the holemaker. The former is merely a development of the pointed stick, used to make holes to receive the roots of small plants—such as those from a seed flat, or strawberry runners—for transplanting. The holemaker is a device for *removing* the soil to leave a hole to receive larger plants, especially those from pots or from seed or nursery rows or bulbs. Both tools are used quite frequently on a place of any size but can scarcely be classed as essential, since the trowel and the spade will accomplish the same jobs, even if not quite so neatly and rapidly.

For cultivating. Cultivating, as has been explained, is necessary not only to control weeds but also to conserve moisture in the soil. Usually both operations are accomplished at the same time. The ideal method is to stir the soil around plants or between rows of plants so frequently that weeds never get beyond the seedling stage. This keeps the surface soil in a condition known as a dust mulch, so dried out that few, if any, weeds will start in it. This surface soil, although completely dry, oddly enough forms a blanket that helps to keep the soil beneath it moist, just as it is to be found under a flat stone or a piece of plank.

The oldest and simplest tool for cultivating is a hoe, and to this day it remains the most useful for home garden areas. The beginning gardener often makes the mistake of purchasing the largest hoe he can find, the type known as a field hoe. Much more useful for the average home garden is the small-bladed or "onion" hoe. In fact the one hoe that we use more than any other is an old field hoe so worn down that it is even smaller than an onion hoe. It was half gone when we acquired it, out of sentiment, at an auction some forty years ago. The original hickory handle, long since worn satin smooth, is still tight in its ferrule. It serves excellently for taking out weeds close to a row or between plants, although no longer of use for cutting out big plants or hilling up potatoes or roses. Equally useful is the modern, "all-purpose" hoe, which has a small, sharp triangular blade attached to a curved steel shank. This tool is favored by the distaff side of the family. See sketch, page 125.

The scuffle or push-hoe has a very narrow blade sharpened at both the front and the rear edge. Pushed along the ground just beneath the surface, it cuts off all weed seedlings and leaves a good soil mulch. The blade cuts on both the push and the backward pull and so can be used as the operator walks backward. This has the decided advantage that the newly cut weeds and the soil are not trampled and pushed back into the soil after the ground is worked over. Some weeds, purslane and chickweed, two of the worst garden pests, for instance, reroot quickly if trodden into the soil. In rainy weather they may be even worse in a few days than they were before being hoed.

Rakes. Both in handling the soil and in caring for the lawn, the rake is an essential tool. For the former job an iron rake is best. For all-round general use, a "bow" rake with slightly curved teeth proves most useful. Where there is much lawn raking to be done, a rake with straight teeth, either metal or wood, proves a worthwhile addition. For raking up cut grass or leaves or any extensive area, a fan-shaped, larger capacity but lightweight rake with spring teeth is a great time and labor saver. Originally this type of rake was made of bamboo and these are still available, but the modern metal ones do a better job and are much more durable.

Hand weeders. Where vegetables or annual flowers are grown in beds or garden rows, a hand weeder is one of the most useful of all tools. These are of various types and sizes. The one we like best has a flat blade turned at right angles to the shaft. This may be held in different positions to cut off weeds, to destroy sprouting weed seedlings, or, turned vertically, to root out larger ones. Another has seven stiff wire fingers and is especially good for cultivating crusted clay soil. The "fish tail" weeder with a V-shaped blade like an asparagus knife is the kind to use for going well below the surface for deep-rooted weeds like dandelions, dock, or poke seedlings. It is available with either a short or a long handle. We find rather inefficient the cuplike hand weeder of cast aluminum with three broad teeth at the edge of the cup; and even more exasperating, the claw weeder made of soft metal with broad teeth, which often bends or comes out of its wooden handle before it gets the weed out. Long-handled spring types for dandelions and similar garden weeds are fine as long as they work, but the springs are often short-lived.

Knives. Anyone who does much gardening has use for at least two knives: a small one for light pruning and cutting flowers and a much heavier one for real pruning jobs and for heavy cutting. For the former, we use a flat-handled, one-bladed knife which is very light; and for the latter, a heavy, hook-bladed pruning knife. To make work easy, and what is more important to leave smooth, clean cuts that heal evenly, any knife used about the garden should be kept *very* sharp. For this purpose it is well to have on hand a sharpening stone *kept with the edged tools,* in addition to the usual whetstone for grass clippers, scythes, sickles, and other equipment.

For protecting plants. Throughout the year there is almost no season when some plant or crop is not in danger of injury from one source or another, in addition to those caused by pests and diseases. Protecting plants from such potential threats is possible *if* one acts quickly.

MECHANICAL PROTECTORS

Hotkaps made of treated paper or domes made of plastic, placed over plants threatened by frost or by too hot sun or drying winds, lessen the danger of injury or total loss. The plastic domes cost more but are less expensive in the end since they can be used repeatedly, season after season. Some of ours have been in constant use for more than fifteen years and are still doing duty. These miniature, transparent tents not only keep off light frosts but also protect plants from pest injury.

Box protectors. A homemade plant protector that we have found most useful in our gardening (especially for covering young vine crops) consists of a box 12×16 inches and 6 inches deep, covered with fine mesh copper wire. The boxes are made of 6-inch wide ship lap, or ¼-inch white pine, cedar, or cypress nailed to pointed corner posts that extend 3 inches below the bottoms of the boxes and are pushed down into the soil to hold them in place. They are set over newly planted or set-out hills or groups of flowers or vegetables particularly subject to attack by insects, birds, or small animals. They also afford some protection against low temperatures and wind. We often place them over plants or hills which have been covered with Hotkaps when the plants have grown so large that the Hotkaps must be removed. Some of these boxes are still in use after fifteen years, though careful storage is essential if the screening is to be kept intact.

Treewrap is a weatherproof, stretchable paper 3 to 6 inches in width, that comes in 50-yard rolls. It is used to wrap up the trunks and branches of newly or recently set trees as a protection against sun scald, rabbits, field mice, and other pests. It is wrapped from the top down. In areas where deep snow may be expected, the wrap should be started high enough to ensure protection above the snow level.

Wilt-Pruf is a liquid to be sprayed on shrubs, trees, and other woody plants to provide a thin coating that prevents excessive evaporation, which may cause dehydration of plants just after transplanting or during transportation.

PLANT SUPPORTS

Supporting plants and training them often go hand in hand. Let us consider available supports on which the training can be done, for if inadequate equipment is chosen for this purpose, it will be both expensive and time consuming to correct later on.

Fences, gates, trellises, and arbors sold at garden centers and chain stores, although neat-looking, are constructed of lightweight material and often do not remain erect or plumb for longer than the second or third year. Often they are too small to support a vigorous climbing rose or a trumpet creeper through more than a couple of seasons' growth.

The do-it-yourself gardener can find no more rewarding garden feature to construct than a well-designed and *substantial* trellis or arbor. If this is beyond his skill or takes more time than he has to spare, he may have it made to order *to his own specifications*. If of good material and well constructed, such equipment will last for many years. If the cost is too great, he may use a post-and-chain support (page 223) or a substantial aluminum chain-link trellis that may be secured to a wall or to a vertical post.

Whatever type is employed, if it is to be held in place at the ground level, it should have its foot posts or anchor blocks *set in concrete*. If only a small job is to be done, a ready-mixed concrete will answer. This material need have only water added to it to be ready for use.

There are a number of strong, decorative fences and gates on the market which look well, are sturdy and long-lasting—but not cheap! If a fence is to support climbing roses or perennial vines, the cheapest and sturdiest permanent type is post-and-rail. Frail fencing of lightweight wood, like the arbors and trellises, is hardly worth erecting. If time is not important, it may be less expensive to plant a young hedge instead of a fence, using sheared evergreens, barberry, Korean box, box-leaved holly, or one of the hedge materials listed in the Appendix. Time and reasonable care will create a beautiful, impenetrable barrier.

Trellises and arbors are both useful and ornamental, but most of those put up have to be replaced in a few years. They should always be of substantial construction. It requires little more work to place the bases in concrete, and at least trebles their life expectancy.

DUSTING AND SPRAYING EQUIPMENT

Dusters. Though spraying has largely replaced dusting in the control of insects and diseases in the home garden, there are many occasions when "spot" dusting saves time and is effective. In the last few years several small hand dusters of the ball-bearing type have come on the market, sold frequently by rose companies and others that offer rose dusts for sale.

Those illustrated in the sketch on page 131 are effective and not likely to get out of order. The old-fashioned puff-gun type, formerly sold, is almost useless as it is practically impossible to deliver from it a fine, even distribution of dust. The best obtainable is none too good, for dusting is hard work at best.

Sprayers. The application of insecticides and fungicides has been revolutionized by the development of devices which screw onto the end of a garden hose and automatically mix spray materials with water as it is applied. While dusts tend to lodge on the upper surfaces of leaves—and, with any hand duster, more or less unevenly—a fine mistlike spray covers all

TOOLS AND EQUIPMENT 131

The effectiveness of any spray or dust depends upon getting thorough, even coverage. Inadequate equipment means constant waste of money. The type that automatically mixes spray material with water as it comes from the hose is easy to use and effective, as is the slide-type sprayer. Pressure cans are expensive for use on large areas. The hand duster (second from top) is short-lived and not very efficient while the rotary duster (center) does a really good job. Keep equipment clean!

parts of the plant uniformly, and where necessary, the soil mulch beneath it. The material to be sprayed on is placed in a small container in the specified quantity, and then sucked up into and mixed with the water from the hose. This equipment may also be used for applying fertilizers in liquid form as in lawn or other foliar feeding.

Pressure-tank sprayers of various types are used extensively in commercial growing, and smaller models are available for the home gardener. Tank sprayers have two advantages: they give more accurate control of the exact spray formula to be used; and they can be carried about wherever needed, without having any hose to be bothered with. However, they must frequently be pumped up to maintain pressure and must be thoroughly cleaned after each use. Sometimes it is difficult to get parts when needed, such as new leather washers which must be renewed occasionally, especially if oily materials are used.

Our own choice is a so-called "trombone" sprayer, a development from the crude bucket sprayer, which came into use in the First World War. The spray material is placed in a pail and mixed with water according to directions. The "trombone," attached to a long rubber hose, sucks up the spray at each stroke and then expels it forcibly, either in a mistlike spray or in coarse droplets through the adjustable nozzle. We find it much easier to clean than a tank sprayer and have little trouble in getting sufficient pressure as long as the leather washers remain soft and pliable. Here again the best available type should be purchased if efficiency is wanted, and *extra washers* should be bought or ordered at the same time.

For house plants, and for spot spraying in the greenhouse or coldframe, one of the all-purpose pressurized can sprays is invaluable, though expensive. Read the directions carefully before buying, to make sure the spray material is suitable for your purposes.

LAWN EQUIPMENT

On many modern suburban grounds, the lawn receives more attention than any other feature. In fact it becomes a sort of status symbol, not quite in the class with a swimming pool, but a lawn that is better than that of the Smiths' or the Jones' is something worth striving for!

Unless one's lawn is fairly extensive, an old-fashioned hand mower may be a much better investment than a power mower. The term "old-fashioned" does not apply to the efficiency of the machine, for modern, manpower-propelled mowers are very great improvements over the much heavier out-dated ones of the past. And they leave less hand trimming to be done than does a power mower.

A riding power mower will, of course, make you feel like a king—or at least a major general on horseback. A walking-type power mower, however, costs only a fraction of the price of a riding type and requires less storage space and less expense for upkeep. In fact many small power mowers cost little more than hand mowers, though they need repairs and tuning up more often, as well as the expensive "white gas" on which many run.

When purchasing a power mower it is always a good idea to get an extra blade *at the same time*. It is just as important to keep the blade sharp on a power type as on a hand mower. With an extra blade on hand, the machine will never be laid up just when it is most needed. The size and type to be purchased depends largely on the area and type of turf to

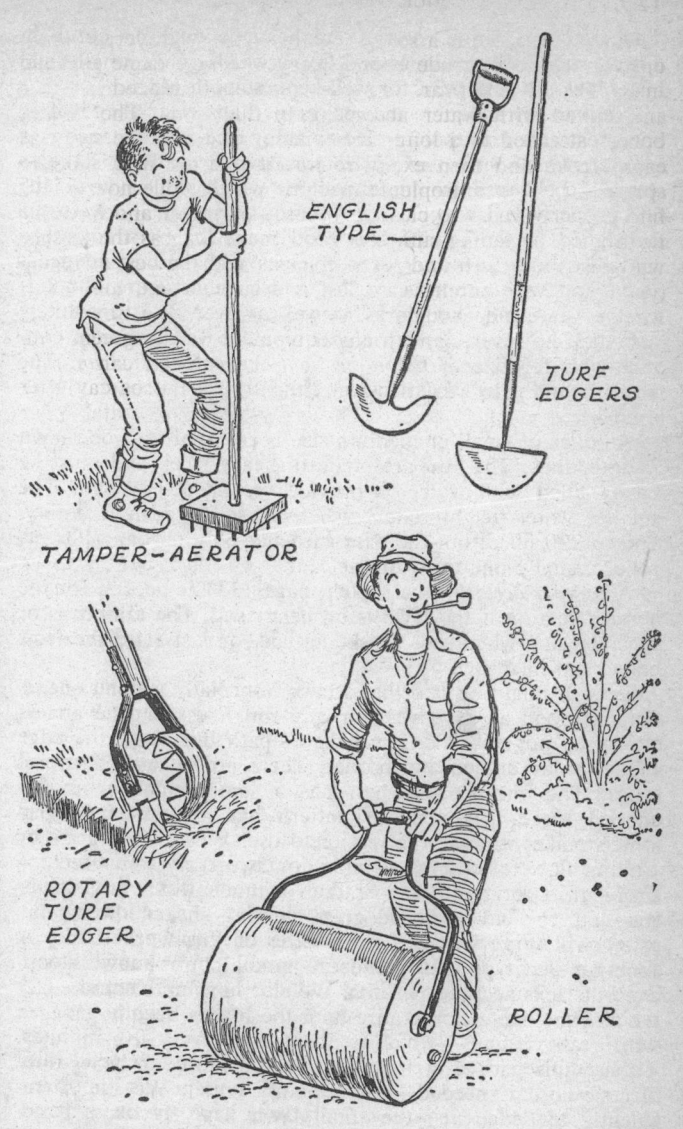

Very important tools for making and maintaining an attractive lawn are the turf edger, the tamper-aerator, and the water-ballast roller.

be cared for. Some rotaries are heavy enough to cut light brush, such as berry vines and heavy weeds, while small, light machines are just right for well-kept, smooth lawns.

Next to an adequate mower, or perhaps even ahead of it, the most essential tool for lawnmaking and maintenance is a good *fertilizer and seed distributor*. It is a costly mistake to get a too cheap, inadequate machine which will never do the job properly and which, after a season or two, will have to be consigned to the dump. The good machines both sow seed and distribute fertilizers or herbicides with speed and accuracy, and with proper care last a decade or more. Ours is twelve years old and works as well as ever. It is absolutely essential, however, as with any equipment that comes in contact with fertilizers, *that it be kept scrupulously clean*. The best method is to *wash* it out and then dry it thoroughly after each use.

A *roller* of small or medium size is essential for good lawn maintenance. The best are made of heavy steel, and must be partly filled with water to provide the needed weight. The smaller water-weight rollers weigh 40 to 60 pounds empty, 160 to 220 filled; but the wise gardener only partially fills his roller, usually one third to one half.

A *tamper-aerator* (see sketch, page 133) is needed for the aerator feature if the lawn is on heavy soil. The tamper is of special value when sods are being laid, or just after the frost comes out in spring.

Edgers. It might be said that a lawn, especially a small one, is only as good as its edges, for any roughness or unevenness shows up not only along a drive or path but along the edge of every flower bed and border. There are edgers of several types. The one we like best has a semicircular or moon-shaped blade. The English pattern has a fork-handle-grip which makes it somewhat easier to use. Where long grass or trailing flowers such as petunias or sweet alyssum create a problem, a rotary turf edger does a much faster and neater job than the old-fashioned grass clipping shears, though the latter will serve where there is little of this work to do. A long-handled type with a squeeze-handle control saves stooping but lacks accuracy of aim. We also have an electric edger which runs like a house afire until the blades become clogged with grass cuttings—which is about once every five minutes. To use this gadget, a hundred feet or more of heavy-duty electric cord is needed—and a handy outlet. We use it frequently to "edge up" the small lawn near the front door, which is completely surrounded by beds, a holly border on one side and a bank rock garden on the other.

PART TWO

SPECIAL GARDENS, AREAS, AND PLANT MATERIALS

Go then, and plant a tree, lovely in sun and shadow.
MARION C. SMITH

CHAPTER 9

Trees, Shrubs, and Vines

Let us begin by emphasizing again that the owner of a new home should give first consideration to the location and planting of trees, shrubs, and perennial vines.

This is contrary to the usual procedure. Naturally the new owner of a piece of property is anxious to beautify it as quickly as possible. By the time the house is finished and the last throes of moving in are over, the bank balance is likely to be at a very low ebb. Small wonder then that the prospect of colorful flowers and a green lawn seems much more appealing than plantings like trees and shrubs that make so little show the first year and, with many trees, not for several years. Nevertheless there are cogent reasons for planting *trees, shrubs, and vines first:*

Relating them to other features of the landscape is of primary importance.

They will form the most striking and the most permanent part of the plantings around the home, and give it more character than any others.

Since they require more time to mature and to form an effective part of the landscape, the sooner they are started, the sooner the grounds will have a finished look.

They will add greatly to the value and salability of the property, especially after the first few years—and this added value increases year after year.

Finally, if one wishes to plant a few fairly large trees to obtain immediate effects, they should be put in before anything else. Moving and planting operations, if delayed until after other parts of the landscaping have been done, are likely to cause damage to lawns and gardens, and possibly even to walks or driveways.

Second Choice. If you are the owner of an established home and grounds but want to change or add to the existing plantings, you have another choice. By purchasing trees, shrubs, and even vines in small sizes one can start a little home nursery, which will save considerable money—possibly even make some!—and assure excellent results. The inexperienced home gardener should not be afraid to attempt this even though it sounds overambitious for a beginner.

As a matter of fact, young trees and shrubs can be planted and "grown on" for a few years, till ready for transplanting to their permanent locations, with greater assurance of success than the beginner can expect with most flowers. Set out a foot or two apart, in rows two to three feet apart to permit easy cultivation, shrubs and most trees will, in two to four years, have made husky small specimens that may be transplanted in late autumn or early spring to their permanent positions.

This system has the further advantage that transplanting may be done under the most favorable conditions. When we moved to our present home we nursery-planted many small trees and shrubs, most of them young seedlings from our former place. In six years, many of these have become tall, vigorous young trees. An elm (brought here in the back seat of our car, the roots wrapped in damp sphagnum) now has a typical vase-shaped top 22 feet tall. A similar "baby" tulip tree now measures 18 feet in spite of having lost nearly half its top in a hurricane. If they do not suffer for want of food and water, the growth made by many small trees is almost incredible.

One of our favorite trees is the White Pine (*Pinus strobus*), but only the Pitch Pine that is common on the Cape today grew on our acreage. We procured several hundred 2-year seedlings and planted them about one foot apart in nursery rows. For the first year they had to shift for themselves as we had not yet moved in. We had some losses but most of them grew vigorously to transplanting size and we now have several groups of fine specimens 9 to 12 feet tall, in addition to an extensive White Pine hedge planting—all at an initial cost of pennies per tree!

What Trees for You? Before purchasing trees, the homeowner should have two kinds of information:

First, what species thrive in his locality.

Careful observation of the surrounding countryside is a

pretty safe guide, but don't be entirely limited by this. Consultation with a local nurseryman or with the county agricultural agent will help further and perhaps give you added ideas. Marked distinction and beauty in the home landscape are often achieved by obtaining species and varieties of trees and shrubs that succeed in the local climate and soil, but which are seldom or never used in the area. Most homeowners are content to "follow the leader" when it comes to selecting plant materials, and automatically plant the same things they see on other places around them. In certain parts of Pennsylvania and Connecticut for instance, magnificent specimens of Copper or Purple Beech are to be seen on many old estates and even in modest gardens. At the time these were planted, they were probably a novelty in these sections, but today their dignity and beauty characterize the countryside.

Don't be afraid to venture a bit! Here on Cape Cod and on the Islands, one frequently finds fine old specimens of unusual trees that have survived the years, because the sea captains who brought them home from the Orient did not realize they were not supposed to be hardy here! Micro-climates very often make a great difference in what may be grown.

Second, how the species chosen will fit into his particular landscape scheme, *when they approach their full size.*

One constantly sees examples of what happens when cute little evergreens of the wrong varieties are set out in foundation plantings under windows. If left there, as frequently happens, the windows are blocked and the flower borders beneath them rendered useless.

Even more serious is the result of planting a potentially large tree such as a maple, oak, horse-chestnut, fir, or spruce in a space that will be much too small long before the tree reaches maturity. The owner cannot bring himself to cut it down; the lawn beneath it gradually goes to pot; and if the place is a small one, all chance of achieving an attractive, comprehensive planting is lost.

HOW TO SELECT TREES

The great importance of our former warning must now be apparent: an over-all plan for the planting of grounds should be prepared before *any* purchasing or planting is done. It is so easy to shift trees and shrubs around on paper, and so difficult and expensive to do it with the actual living materials!

Before a decision can be made as to the types and varieties to be planted, it is essential to know just where each is to be placed. It is important to visualize, as nearly as possible, how the plantings will appear ten years or so hence, and this is not easy. On occasion we have tried to help an inexperienced client to "get the picture" by placing trimmed branches or wood strips of various heights where trees were to be planted. The result shows roughly how much sunshine will be shut out, or how much of a distant view may be obliterated when trees in such locations begin to approach maturity. Results are sometimes startling. The proper time to move big trees, very definitely, is before planting them!

What Trees for Me? That is a puzzling question. You can get a fairly good idea of the various sizes, shapes, and characters by borrowing a book on trees from your library. It will be more rewarding, however, to visit a park or a botanical garden, where mature specimens may be seen and studied.

The most noticeable difference is that between evergreens, which are green throughout the years, and deciduous trees, which drop their foliage during the winter. There are even a few needled, cone-bearing trees that drop their foliage during the winter. The larches are typical of this group.

Especially on small places it often makes a big difference whether or not a tree retains its foliage throughout the year. Shade that is welcome in summer may be exactly what is *not* wanted during the winter. On the other hand, an evergreen hedge which shuts out street noises and provides a degree of privacy may be just as desirable in December as in July.

The following list includes a number of the most desirable trees for home landscaping in Areas II, III, and IV. Trees especially adapted to the South, Southwest, and other special areas or conditions will be found listed in the Appendix.

Although trees may be bought by mail, it is usually much better (except in the case of seedlings or very young specimens) to purchase at a nursery where they may be personally selected. Even at a young age they have begun to show some individuality in size, shape, and, in the case of certain evergreens, in color. The nurseryman tries to grow his stock to be as uniform as possible, but often an irregular specimen gives the homeowner a much more interesting and artistic effect if good judgment is used in placing it. At almost any big flower show one may find displays that illustrate this point. Such offbeat plants can usually be obtained at considerably reduced prices.

TREES, SHRUBS, AND VINES

SHADE TREES

Deciduous	Evergreen	Ornamental
** Beech, American	Arborvitaes	Cherries,
** Purple	in variety	Flowering
Birch, Canoe or	** Fir, Balsam	Crabs, Flowering
Paper	** Hemlock, American	Dogwood,
** Elm, American	** Canadian	Flowering
Chinese	Carolina	Dogwood, Kousa
Siberian	Junipers,	Hawthorns
** Larch, American	in variety	** Horse-chestnut
** European	Pine, Japanese	Laburnum
** Linden, American	Scotch	Magnolias,
European	** White	in variety
** Locust, Honey	** Spruce, Blue	Maple, Japanese
Maple, Amur	** Norway	Mountain-ash
** Norway	** Red	(Sorbus)
Red	** White	Oxydendron
Scarlet	** Umbrella-pine	** Paulownia
** Sugar	(*Sciadopitys*	Silver Bell
** Oak, Pin	*verticillata*)	(Halesia)
Red	Yews,	Witch-hazel
Black	in variety	(*Hamamelis*
Scarlet		*japonica;*
** White		*virginiana*)
Sassafras		
Sweet Gum		
** Tulip		
Willows		

** Very tall—over 60 ft.

SHRUBS

While the use of trees, except in very small numbers, is limited to the fairly extensive property, shrubs may be employed freely on all but the smallest of places. Judiciously placed, they help to make an area appear considerably larger than it actually is. Many of the taller shrubs give much the effect of trees, and to that extent increase the *apparent* size of their surroundings.

Types of Shrubs. As with trees, the shrubs, once established, are usually lifetime fixtures and therefore should be selected with consideration for the size they are likely to attain at maturity.

Catalog illustrations are often misleading. First of all, they are usually close-ups of small specimens in full bloom. The inexperienced gardener is quite likely to visualize them as pictured, in strategic locations around his grounds. He may forget that many of them will be in flower for only two or three weeks out of the entire season and may be quite lacking in decorative effect when not in flower. Then, too, in the course of three or four years, they may become entirely too large for the locations in which they have been placed.

Again, as was true in choosing trees, the best way for the inexperienced homeowner to procure a really satisfactory selection of shrubs is to make a few visits to a neighboring botanic garden, arboretum, or genuine nursery (not merely a sales center). Even though such a trip may take the best part of a day, it will pay off handsomely in the long run.

Shrubs for color. On either the large or the small place, shrubs are more effective than any other plants in providing masses of color above the ground or flower bed level. For really striking mass color effects, the two may be combined, as they often are in public or private show gardens. For the average home grounds, however, where a pleasing prospect is desirable week after week through the season, something less spectacular but more continuous is to be preferred.

In most cases, therefore, it is important to plan for a long succession of bloom in selecting flowering shrubs. Especially in northern latitudes, the great majority of shrubs flower in the spring, but one should try to plan for color during the summer and autumn also. There are several not-too-large trees that flower in summer or autumn and where space permits these may well be included in planning the shrub planting. Following is a list of some of the most satisfactory flowering shrubs. Fragrance and fall coloring in foliage or fruit is also noted.

For a list of hardy evergreen and flowering shrubs, with the zones in which they are at home, see Appendix.

Shrubs for Screens. One of the most practical uses for shrubs, especially in suburban development areas, is to secure some degree of privacy or to shut out undesirable views.

Here the ultimate height required for the screen should be carefully calculated. Left to itself, such a screen often grows taller than is necessary and consequently shuts out much wanted sunshine or light. Of course, it may be kept within bounds by pruning and trimming, but this takes time and labor—more each season as the hedge grows older.

Privet, widely used as a tall screen as well as for trimmed hedges, will attain a height of from 10 to 15 feet. Most deciduous types hardy in northern climates are not too attractive

TREES, SHRUBS, AND VINES

DECIDUOUS FLOWERING SHRUBS

Early spring	Late spring and early summer	Late summer	Autumn and winter
Azaleas F	Callicarpa B AC	Albizzia	Baccheris halimifolia
Almond, Flowering F	Calycanthus F	Buddlei F	Gordonia AC (*Franklinia alatamaha*)
Cydonias	Carnelian-cherry B	Buckeye	
Forsythia F	Deutzias	Clethra F	
Jasmine F nudiflorum	Dogwood shrubs B	Hibiscus	Tamarix hispida
Kerria japonica	Eleagnus F	Hydrangea	Witch-hazels F
Lilacs F	*Euonymus alatus* AC	Hypericum	
Mockorange F (Philadelphus)	Kolkwitzia	Sorbaria	
Peony, Tree	Lilacs F	Stewartia June to Aug.	
Spireas	Potentilla	Vitex macrophylla	
Snowberry B	Roses, Shrub F		
Symplocos B	Stephanandra AC		
Tamarix tetrandrus	Viburnums B AC F		
Wintersweet			

AC—autumn color
B—autumn fruit
F—fragrant

HARDY SHRUBS AND EVERGREENS SUITABLE FOR SCREENS AND HEDGES

Deciduous	Height with some pruning	Evergreen * Must be kept well-pruned
Azaleas, in variety	2–6	Arborvitae Tom Thumb
Barberries, in variety	3–4	Little Gem
Bayberry	2–9	Chinese
		Rosedale
Cornus (Dogwood)		Compacta
Gray	6–15	Golden
Mas	6–15	
Tatarian	6–10	
		Boxwood, English*
Cotoneaster lucida	3–10	Korean
Cydonias	3–10	Hemlock, Japanese*
Deutzias	6	Hollies, American*
		Chinese
Euonymus	6	English*
Dwarf Burningbush	6	Japanese

Winged	6–8	Juniper Andorra	
Hawthorn, Cockspur	6–25		Hill Japanese
English	6–15		Hillbush
Washington	6–25		Meyer
			Needle
Hibiscus, Chinese	6–20		Savin
Shrub Althea	6–12		
Lilacs	6–20	Pine, Mugo	
			Waterer
Maple, Hedge	6		
Mockorange	6–10	Yew, Brown's*	
			Intermedia*
			Hicks'*
Ninebark, Yellow	6		Hatfield*
			Dwarf Japanese*
Osage-orange	6–20		Spreading "
Privets, improved varieties	4–12		

Rosa multiflora
  rugosa & hybrids
  Red Robin } 4–6
  setigera

Evergreen-Flowering

Russian-olive	6	*Abelia grandiflora*	
Sea-buckthorn	6	Firethorns (Pyracanthas)*	
		Hollygrape, Oregon	
		Laurel, Mountain (Shade)*	
		Leucothoe	
		catesbaei	
		racemosa	
Spireas	3–10	*Pieris floribunda*	
		japonica*	
Viburnums	6–12	Rhododendrons*	

in winter—especially when littered up with bits of newspaper and other wind-blown debris.

In selecting plants for a screen, it is best to procure something that will provide the desired height *with a minimum of pruning*. A low-growing evergreen such as Hicks' Yew or Mugo Pine is more decorative and requires less constant care than hedge material such as barberry. These are, however, more expensive to start with.

Lists of hedge and screen material for the South, California, and the cold areas of the northern United States appear in the Appendix.

Shrubs for Hedges. Many of the considerations which apply

TREES, SHRUBS, AND VINES 145

to the selection of plants for screens apply also to hedges. It might be said that the screen begins where the hedge leaves off. There is a difference, however, for the *bottom* of the hedge is as important as the upper growth, and many plants cannot be kept green and dense down to ground level.

The various privets and barberries are the plants most widely used for hedges. Of the privets, the fastest growing is the ubiquitous California Privet (*Ligustrum lucidum*), which under favorable conditions attains a height of 3 to 4 feet the first season. This, however, is not reliably hardy in northern sections and at best it lends no distinction to a planting. The hardier Amur River Privet (*L. amurense*), more upright and compact, is well worth the extra cost.

Many improved forms of barberry are now available, including *Berberis mentoriensis,* one of the best, which requires very little pruning and holds its foliage well into midwinter as far north as southern New England and Chicago. *Crimson Pygmy* is a new dwarf barberry only a foot or so in height, suitable for a very low hedge or border.

In considering the cost of a hedge or a border planting one should remember that one is dealing not only with a long-term investment, but with probably the most conspicuous feature of the landscaping. Summer and winter it is there for every passer-by to see and to appraise—even without any conscious effort on his part to do so. It seems only common sense then to give extra thought—and if necessary an extra generous allowance—to this item in the landscaping budget.

VINES AND OTHER CLIMBERS

The third general group of plants used in making the home grounds more interesting and attractive includes those that climb, either of their own accord or if provided with suitable support. Virginia creeper (*Parthenocissus quinquefolia*) and wisteria are examples of the former, though one clings by tendrils, and the other by twisting stems. Climbing roses on the other hand, do not really climb but can be tied to supports such as a trellis or post. There are also many shrubs with long, arching or trailing branches that, with suitable encouragement, give a vinelike effect. *Forsythia suspensa, Cotoneaster horizontalis,* and *Pyracantha c. lalandi* are examples.

Correctly placed, vines and climbers, by the very habit of their growth, form highlights in the general picture, and take up little ground space. Many of them, however, grow vigorously and may take over if not kept well pruned. Therefore it is necessary to give some of them an occasional, severe cutting back in order to keep them within the allotted spaces. Wisteria, trumpet creeper, akebia, and honeysuckle are examples of this type.

Some of the annual vines are so vigorous as to make an almost unbelievable amount of growth during their single season. Typical of these are moonflower (*Ipomaea bona-nox*), balloon-vine (*Cardiospermum halicacabum*), and cup-and-saucer vine (*Cobaea scandens*)—semitropicals that, in northern climates, are treated as annuals. They are started in greenhouse or frame and set out after all danger of late frost. We have had Cobaeas so handled, grow thirty-five feet up a house wall of rough stucco, with no other support, reaching the peak of the second-story roof by August. We always plant moonflowers (started under glass) where we can enjoy the great, white, morning-glory-like blooms as they open, very slowly at first, and then with an almost explosive burst. A favorite game when guests are present, is to bet which unfolding bud will be next to open—something not easy to predict.

As the methods by which vines climb vary, it is important to know what type of support should be provided for each. Some, such as wisteria and passion vine, are twiners, often hugging their supports so tightly that only with great difficulty can they be torn off. They coil around twigs or branches, while the tip of the growing plant actually waves slowly about in a circle, seeking to find the next support to be encircled. They move clockwise or counterclockwise, but *always* in the same direction for any one species. And they just cannot be made to turn the other way!

Another type sends out tendrils that grasp and cling tightly to twigs or branches, other plants, or similar supports. Typical of this group are springlike tendrils issuing—like those of smilax—from the leaf stems or from the main stem of the plant, as with Virginia creeper. Still others are wall climbers such as ampelopsis, and have tendrils ending in tiny suction discs that cling tightly to a flat (but not to a polished) surface. A few, of which English ivy (*Hedera helix*) and creeping fig (*Ficus pumila*) are examples, have aerial roots that penetrate the slightest crack, fissure, or unevenness, thus holding the main stems securely.

Types of Supports. The differences to be found among climbing plants are not merely of botanical interest. They are definitely to be considered when it comes to selecting a vine or a climber for some specific location. A disregard for the manner in which a species supports itself may result in its failure to give the desired effect, no matter how much care may be lavished upon it in the way of feeding, watering, and spraying.

The mistake most commonly made in providing supports for vines is that of not having them substantial enough or ready soon enough. This is especially true in the case of climbing roses, and of such heavy vines as wisteria, trumpet-vine, and bougainvillea. Most of the neat-looking but all too flimsy arches and arbors sold by garden centers and hardware stores will scarcely stand up by themselves for more than four or five seasons, especially if the wooden posts supporting them are buried directly in soil instead of with concrete footings as they should be. How can they be expected to stand up under the weight of heavily foliaged growth in heavy winds? Little wonder one so frequently sees sagging or half-fallen specimens that completely destroy the attractiveness of an otherwise well-cared-for garden!

In planning supports for vines or climbers of any sort, it is essential that they be of types that will fulfill their purpose. A rough wall, well suited to provide support for ivy, climbing hydrangea (*H. petiolaris*) or creeping fig would be useless for wisteria, moonflower, or passion-flower. A trellis, suitable for the latter, would be shunned by the ivy or climbing hydrangea (see page 129).

Cultural pointers. As a class, vines require less care than most other types of plants. Nevertheless one cannot expect satisfactory results from a plant that has merely been stuck into the ground, watered a couple of times until it "takes hold," and then left to shift for itself. Yet this happens frequently. Of all groups of plants, vines are the most likely to be neglected. The wonder is that as many succeed as well as they do.

The majority of vines are not particular as to soil. The clematis group are happiest in a "sweet" soil (see page 47). Ordinary garden loam in good tilth suits most of the others. Planting holes should be large, deep, and well prepared, as most vines are likely to be pretty much "on their own" after the first year's growth.

As the majority of established vines are more likely to be too vigorous than too weak and spindling, often little or no annual feeding is required unless the soil is very poor. Pruning, however, is needed, though often neglected or altogether omitted. Most vigorous-growing vines should be pruned annually, especially during the first few years of growth. This is especially true of such rampant growers as wisteria and trumpet creeper.

Along with the pruning should go training of the main

148 SPECIAL GARDENS, AREAS, AND PLANT MATERIALS

stems, securing them in position if need be until they have taken the permanent form which is planned for them. (Lists of vines will be found in the Appendix.)

Espaliered plants are particularly attractive in formal surroundings. These are fruits, shrubs, or even suitable vines that are trained into more or less geometrical designs by the nurseryman or the gardener. They are especially effective against a house or a sunny wall surrounding a patio. Consistent pruning is required to maintain these attractive designs, and unless one is prepared to provide this, they are best not attempted.

POINTERS ON PLANTING

Trees, shrubs, and vines, the most expensive landscape features, are often planted with less care than are perennials and even annuals. To do a really good job of planting, it is important to have all preparations made before receiving the stock. Once received, the earlier they are put into the ground, the better start they will get.

The first step is to mark, with fairly substantial stakes, the exact locations where they are to go. In placing the stakes, careful thought should be given to their ultimate height and diameter. It is easy to shift stakes around until one is satisfied that the best locations have been selected, but very difficult and sometimes fatal to trees or shrubs once they have been planted.

All planting holes should be made *large* and *deep*. Eighteen inches in depth and at least that much in diameter is none too much for bareroot stock. For "B and B" (balled and burlapped) stock the holes should be at least 6 inches deeper and 12 inches larger in diameter than the root balls themselves.

Unless the holes are being made in excellent soil, all earth removed from them should be discarded. (It is well to shovel it into a wheelbarrow and remove it at once if the holes are being dug in turf areas.) Holes made where a clay subsoil is encountered should be pierced at the bottom with a crowbar to improve the drainage.

Into the bottom of each hole put 6 inches or so of the best soil available, or of good compost mixed with a peck or two of peatmoss. Instructions for planting trees and shrubs usually advise against using any fertilizers in the planting holes. We go along with this so far as *chemical* fertilizers are concerned; but personally we always use a mixture of one

① MEASURE ROOT BALL.

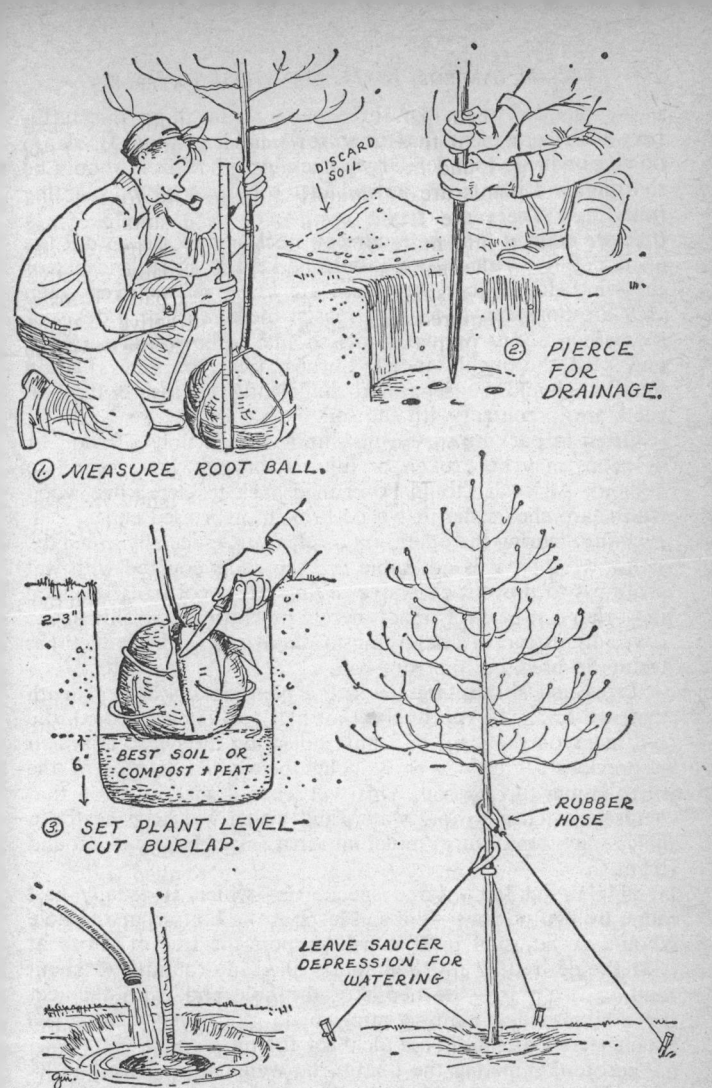

② PIERCE FOR DRAINAGE.

③ SET PLANT LEVEL — CUT BURLAP.

④ TAMP SOIL ⅔ FULL — WATER THOROUGHLY.

⑤ FILL HOLE — BRACE WITH 3 GUY WIRES.

OPERATION PLANTING. *Measure root ball and dig hole 6 to 10 inches wider and deeper. Loosen or punch holes in subsoil if it is clay or hardpan. Put prepared soil or compost in bottom of hole. Cut slits in burlap around root ball, but do not remove it if soil is loose around roots. Partly fill hole, after setting tree; firm soil around roots and water. Then fill hole, leaving saucerlike depression, and water again. If tree or shrub is large, brace in three directions—especially important with evergreens.*

part bonemeal to two or three parts of an all-organic fertilizer, at the rate of a quart or so for a small (15-inch) hole, to double or triple that for larger ones. Any fertilizers should be thoroughly mixed with the soil in the bottom of the planting hole.

Care of plant material. If nursery stock cannot be set out the same day it is received, it should be kept in shade and out of the wind. Remember that these are *living* plants, even when they are dormant. If for any reason there must be a delay of more than a day or two, roots should be buried in a trench and kept thoroughly moist. Shrubs, trees, or vines tied in bundles should be separated sufficiently to assure that all roots are in contact with the soil.

Often in packing or during shipments, portions of roots or branches may be broken or injured, or may have begun to dry out. All such should be pruned back to clean, live wood with sharp shears that leave no broken or bruised ends.

Planting. During the operation of planting, especially in windy, sunny weather, it is advisable to keep roots covered with wet peatmoss to prevent excessive drying out. Root balls wrapped in burlap can be kept intact merely by cutting long slits in the covering instead of attempting to remove it, as this sometimes results in breaking the root ball.

Trees and shrubs are set in the planting holes at a depth that will bring the top of the root ball (or, if bare-rooted, the soil mark on the stem or trunk indicating the depth at which it previously grew) 2 to 3 inches below the surface of the surrounding turf or soil. This will leave a shallow basin that tends to catch and hold water, and which will keep neatly in place any temporary mulching that may be used around them.

In planting fairly large specimens—which is usually best done by two persons—the soil level at the bottom of the hole should be adjusted until it will support the tree or shrub at just the desired level. Then soil is filled in around it to about half to two thirds the depth of the hole and, with the feet or a blunt-ended tamping stick made moderately firm. (The youngsters' baseball bat is ideal for the purpose!)

Before completing the filling, run water in the hole and let it soak in, repeating this operation two or three times if necessary, until no more water is readily absorbed. Then complete the filling, treading the soil until it is well firmed.

For the next few weeks, until new growth indicates that the tree, shrub, or vine has actually begun to grow in its new quarters, water frequently enough to make certain that the soil about the roots never dries out. Mulching helps greatly in keeping the soil moist. If weather is dry and windy it is well to sprinkle the tops occasionally.

In the case of tall trees, especially of evergreens in windy areas, bracing in three directions with well-secured guy wires (see sketch, page 149) is essential. Where any wire touches the tree, it is passed through a piece of old hose to prevent its cutting into the bark. Rope is of no use for bracing as it will sketch too much to provide lasting support.

Valuable specimens are often given still further protection by wrapping the trunks in Treewrap, by mist spraying the tops, if in foliage, frequently for a few weeks after transplanting, or by spraying the foliage with Wilt-Pruf.

> Grass is the forgiveness of nature ...
> Forests decay, harvests perish, flowers vanish,
> but grass is immortal.
>
> JOHN JAMES INGALLS

CHAPTER 10

Lawns and Turf Areas

There is an old saying that "the lawn makes the place." Like most old sayings, this is an overstatement. The fact remains, however, that poor turf will ruin the general effect and attractiveness of any home grounds, no matter how good the rest of the landscaping may be.

The lawn is usually the first work to be undertaken when a place is being improved. This is not always the most desirable method of procedure, for new turf can easily be damaged in the process of bringing in and planting trees and shrubs, laying out permanent walks, making a pool, or getting other outdoor operations under way.

The owner has to decide when the lawn is to be made—or remade. In reaching a decision he should keep in mind not only the considerations suggested above, but also *when* it is best to undertake lawnmaking or remaking in his particular region. In general, in short-season sections of the country (Areas I, II, III, and IV) first choice would be autumn and second choice the earliest possible moment in spring. In long-season sections (Areas V and VI) the recommended time varies with the *type* of lawn, the grasses (or other plants) to be used, and the rainy season. In some very warm climates both a summer lawn and a winter lawn are employed, one overplanted on the other, to keep a green turf the year around.

Materials and equipment required to make a new lawn or

remake an old one are: lime, peatmoss or humus, fertilizer, and—if required—excellent topsoil for the surface layer. Tools needed are: a spading fork, a rake, and a roller. In dry weather, especially on light soil, adequate facilities for watering are essential.

What type of lawn? Before any work on lawnmaking is undertaken, the homeowner should consider the uses to which the turf will be put—whether principally as an important part of the all-over landscape plan, "for to admire and for to see," a play area, or just ordinary lawn requiring no special care and expensive upkeep, but both usable and attractive (page 20).

It must be admitted that the show (or perhaps we would be justified in saying the "show-off") lawn, if adequately maintained, contributes greatly to the over-all appearance of a place—but the IF is a very big one. We have made such lawns for ourselves and for others. Our present "lawn," which attracts much favorable comment here on Cape Cod, where fine turf is difficult to maintain, is the result of merely cooperating with nature. After clearing from about an acre of wild land a tangle of poison ivy, catbriers, and woodbine, we began to mow regularly with a rotary mower and to root out clumps of coarse tuft-forming grasses such as witch, crab, and orchardgrass, filling in the resulting holes with compost, and encouraging natural turf-type grasses to spread. A top-quality lawn grass mixture containing Merion Bluegrass was sown where the fill-ins were extensive.

This lawn was made under the light, partial shade of a grove of native black locust trees, well thinned out and trimmed high up. Although rather light and sandy, the soil is well supplied with humus, and also with nitrogen (provided by the nodules on the roots of the locust trees). Such a lawn could not be made so readily just anywhere. But it frequently happens that areas around new homes are torn up and remade at great expense, when a very good turf could have been developed at a fraction of the expense merely by surface dressing, oversowing, and regular mowing.

By an odd freak of circumstance, our smaller lawn, along the front of the house, illustrates the other extreme of lawnmaking. Here we started with an excavation over 5 feet deep, resulting from the fact that, when building our home, we removed a pocket of coarse, gritty sand ideal for mixing our concrete and mortar. The gaping hole that was left—some 20 feet long by 6 wide—was filled with a mixture of poor soil, plus the "chocolate icing" layer described on page 156. On this was sown a top-quality, general-purpose lawn seed—plus white Dutch clover as a "seek-no-further" device to keep young rabbits from investigating the flower beds on the bank and the terraces above the lawn.

This strip of lawn, made six years ago, and maintained by our standard treatment (as explained in the following pages) has remained in excellent condition with no remaking or reseeding, although the traffic over it is heavier than normal.

PRELIMINARY PREPARATIONS

Most beginners fail to realize that using good seed is only half, and much the smaller half, of making a good lawn. The preliminary preparation of the soil is what really counts, but except in very rare instances, this is not to be accomplished merely by using a large dose of a high-power, quick-action fertilizer.

On most moderate-sized places the lawn is both the most conspicuous and the most permanent feature of the landscape. Why then does it not merit the best that can be put into it?

What use? A quick glance at the over-all landscape plan for a small place (Chapter 1) will show that there are likely to be several lawn areas. In the average place these may all be treated in the same way, but sometimes it is worthwhile to consider them separately, at least to the extent of having a "show" or front lawn, and a play and work area. For these, different types of grasses are desirable. But in both cases, thorough preliminary preparation of the soil is the same.

Grading is the first step if the house is new. After building is completed, grading of the entire area should be undertaken. This must not be neglected. Before any soil is moved, all refuse left from building—empty cans, scraps of metal, bits of paper, pieces of wood, and bottles—should be cleared away. Frequently the builder uses these as part of the back-fill against the house foundations, with the result that they cause future trouble, starving and stunting struggling plant material.

The next step is to have topsoil—for future lawn and prospective flower beds—pushed to one side, in one or more heaps. Otherwise, when grading is being done, good soil in certain areas is almost certain to be buried. When this happens, the lawn is more than likely to have poor spots, or areas that quickly turn brown at the first touch of hot, dry weather, no matter how much water or fertilizer is applied. (The removed topsoil is used in preparing the "chocolate icing" layer later described.)

LAWNS AND TURF AREAS 155

In establishing the over-all grading for the property, it is advisable to have the surface slope away from the house at an angle sufficient to carry off heavy rains. Where the property lies considerably above street or road level, the creation of a steep bank should by all means be avoided—even if it is necessary to build a wall of suitable height instead of carrying the turf down to the sidewalk level. Banks or steep slopes are not only very difficult to mow, but also difficult to maintain in good turf.

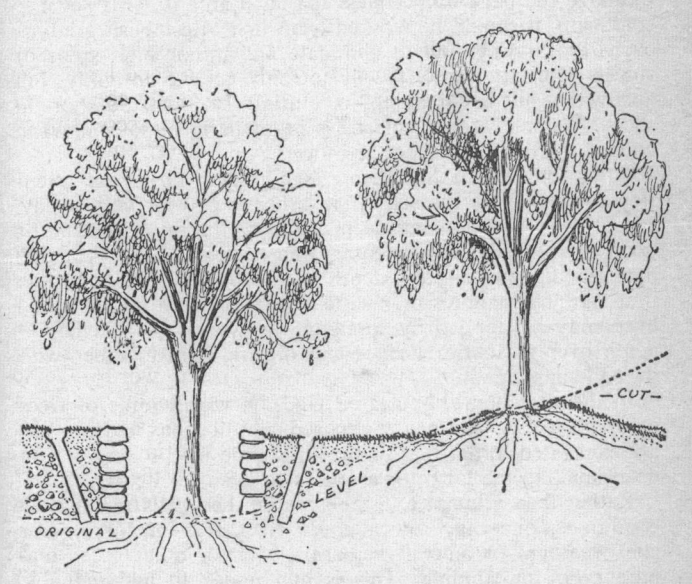

Where soil level must be raised around trees, making a dry well may save it.

If existing trees present a problem in establishing a grade this difficulty may be overcome either by building "wells" of suitable size around the trunks, or by sloping the surface up to them.

The next step is to *mark off* definitely the area or areas that are to be put into turf. This should be done even if the lawns are not to be finished until after other planting (trees, shrubs, etc.) has been done. In laying out lawn areas we find it convenient to use ¾-inch rope or a flexible hose that may readily be adjusted to curves until both the size and the shape of the areas desired for grass can be definitely determined. Such lines may then be marked permanently by driving in short stakes at intervals.

Drainage. To produce and maintain good turf, uniform even in appearance, and permanent, the lawn area must be well drained. Low areas where water may collect and stand after rain or during winter and early spring result in poor or even dead turf. If drainage is needed, installing it is the very first step toward satisfactory results. (For a general discussion of drainage see page 35.) Unless the lawn area is fairly level to start with, it should be worked over, first to establish gradual, even slopes, and then to eliminate any minor high spots or ridges. The latter, if left, will not only appear unsightly, but also will result in "scalping" or cutting the grass too short in spots. A smooth, even surface is particularly important when cutting is done with a power mower.

After the surface has been rough-graded, turn your attention to improving the soil. If it is heavy clay or very sandy, add a layer 2 to 4 inches deep of soil of the opposite type or good loam. This supplementary material is then thoroughly dug, or cultivated in, to a depth of 4 to 6 inches. At the same time, animal manures or unsifted compost from a well-rotted heap may be applied by spreading a layer 2 to 4 inches in depth over the entire surface and digging it in together with the soil supplement.

In the case of newly cleared land, on which roots of trees or brush, rocks, and newly exposed subsoil areas and the like are excavated, often it actually *saves* time in the long run to delay making the lawn for a season or even for a year.

Rather than attempt to establish a finished lawn under such conditions, one may sow a cover crop of winter rye, (for cold weather) or annual ryegrass, clover, or other green manure crop for summer. This is dug under to add valuable humus and to help break up a stiff soil before the area is prepared for seeding lawn grass.

SURFACE SOIL—THE "CHOCOLATE ICING" LAYER

Having made lawns in many localities and on many types of soil, we are convinced that the surest and quickest results are to be attained by applying, *after* the ground has been prepared as described above, a 2- to 3-inch top dressing of especially prepared compost and fertilizer—a chocolate icing layer to the lawn cake.

Such a specially prepared seedbed offers the most favora-

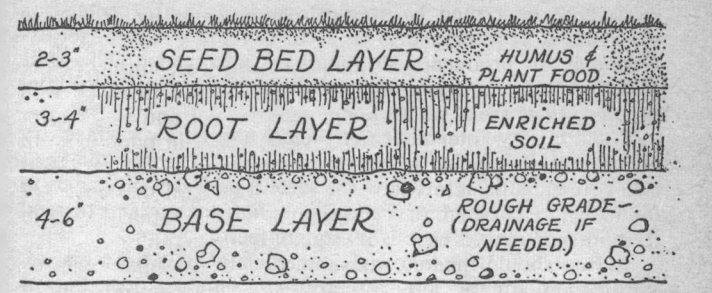

```
2-3"   SEED BED LAYER      HUMUS &
                           PLANT FOOD
3-4"   ROOT LAYER          ENRICHED
                           SOIL

4-6"   BASE LAYER          ROUGH GRADE—
                           (DRAINAGE IF
                           NEEDED.)
```

Thorough preparation in making a lawn means better turf, minimum upkeep.

ble conditions for quick and even germination, and a vigorous start for the tiny grass seedlings, particularly the finer grasses where a mixture is used.

The making of this compost does not involve a great deal of additional labor. Any extra time spent in preparing it is more than made up for in getting the turf well established. The compost is made up of two parts (by bulk) compost-heap soil (or clean, rich loam) and one part peatmoss (preferably sphagnum peat). To this add, for each bushel, 2 to 3 quarts of dried organic manure (such as Bovung, Driconure, or Milorganite) and 1 quart of bonemeal. The ingredients are thoroughly mixed by being sifted in alternate shovelfuls through a ½-inch mesh screen. The fertilizer may be added either during the process of sifting the soil and peat or after it has been spread. The former method is preferable as it helps start immediate bacterial action in the heap. If it is applied after spreading, rake in thoroughly.

A pre-emergence weed killer or a combination weed killer and fertilizer may be applied at this time. This precaution is well worthwhile unless one is sure he has weed-seed-free compost. If any weed killer is used, be sure to *follow directions to the letter,* allowing the full time stipulated between its application and seed sowing.

Seed. In order to decide wisely what grass or grass mixture is best suited to *your* climate and soil, see the discussion on *What Grass for You?* in this chapter, or consult your county agent or nearest State Agricultural Experiment Station.

Sowing. While small, hand-operated gadgets are available for sowing grass seed, it is much better, except for very small areas, to use a combination fertilizer and seed sower. One of these may be rented from most garden supply centers or hardware stores that sell grass seed. For the owner of an extensive lawn it is better to purchase a spreader. This will prove useful at all seasons in fertilizing flower beds and borders as well as the lawn itself.

If soil is very dry, water *thoroughly* and let the surface dry off before sowing. To assure an even stand, divide the seed into two equal parts and sow the second part at right angles to the first. Use for each operation, only *half* the amount of seed recommended per 100 or 1000 square feet.

Sowing should be followed immediately by a light raking. We like best for this job a generous-size bamboo rake, but an ordinary garden rake, wooden or iron, will serve. This raking must be done with a light hand, merely to cover the seed, or most of it, from sight. Any ridges or furrows formed will result in an uneven stand of grass.

Follow the raking with rolling, using a roller with just enough water in it to compact the soil so that it is firm but not hard. For small areas it is easier to use an iron tamper, or one made of a 12- to 18-inch piece of 2×8-inch plank, with a vertical handle.

Keep surface moist! After rolling, water the soil again, slowly but thoroughly enough so that no puddles stand on the surface. A "mist" nozzle on the hose is ideal for this purpose as it is for many others. A perforated hose or an oscillating sprinkler may be used instead. Do *not* apply water so rapidly that it cannot be immediately absorbed. Many a lawn has been badly damaged even before seed germinates by such careless watering that seed has been washed out or dried out in spots.

Surface must be *kept* moist, constantly, until the grass is well up, if an even stand is to be obtained. In very dry or windy weather this may mean watering twice or even three times daily for the first week or two. Some of the best lawn grasses—such as bluegrass, especially Merion and other selected strains—appear in 14 to 28 days, while fescues require 5 to 10 days to germinate. In exposed, windy, or extremely sunny places, a temporary light surface covering of straw, light brush, or something similar, if coarse in texture, may be placed on the surface. (One bale of straw will cover up to 1000 square feet.) Any such covering, however, must be removed *immediately* after germination has taken place.

Banks and Slopes. If, after grading, it is still necessary to establish grass on a sharp slope, two courses are open. The first, and best, is to cover with sods; the second is to use sods

LAWNS AND TURF AREAS

in strips or panels to hold the soil in place, and sow seed on the soil between these, keeping the seed in place with Erosionet or some similar porous ground covering.

SODDING, STRIPPING, PLUGGING, SPRIGGING

Sometimes, for one reason or another, methods other than seed sowing are used for making or renewing lawns. Some of these methods are quicker, others slower, than using seed. In all cases, however, the soil must be thoroughly prepared in advance—as outlined previously—if success is to be attained. *Sodding,* as the term implies, involves the use of growing turf to establish the new lawn. It is the surest, quickest, and most expensive method.

Sods, usually 12 inches wide and 12 to 18 inches long and about 2 to 4 inches thick, are cut from an old lawn, a pasture, or from new turf grown for the purpose. The latter cost more, but are by far the most satisfactory as they are uniform in quality and in the grasses they contain. They should be laid close together, breaking joints in alternate strips, rolled or tamped down evenly, and given light but very frequent watering—at least daily in hot, sunny weather until new roots have been established.

Stripping is similar to sodding except that narrow sods, usually 4 or 6 inches wide, are handled in rolls and set in strips about 3 to 6 inches apart. These are left to spread until the intervening soil strips are covered. The strips are rather conspicuous at first, but usually disappear by the middle of the first season if a good job of planting has been done.

Plugging. This is simply a modification of sodding, used chiefly in the case of warm climate grasses, seed of which is not available. Instead of sods, the turf to be used is cut up into small pieces, 2 to 4 inches square. In cutting, as much soil as possible is left on the roots, which should be kept moist. In planting, the plugs are set firmly, 12 to 18 inches apart each way, in holes or in furrows. On slopes, furrows should follow contours, to prevent washing in heavy rains. If soil is poor, use compost in holes or furrows. Soil must be kept moist until new growth starts. With plugging, it usually takes a season, or even a full year, before lawn develops a uniform appearance. During this time of course the surface between plugs must be kept clear of weeds.

Sprigging is a modification of plugging in which individual root clusters (stolons) are used. These are readily shipped by mail or express. They are set a foot or so apart each way except in the case of Zoysia grasses. Care must be taken not to cover the growing tips, to have the soil moist, and to keep it so until new growth starts.

LAWN RENOVATION

It often happens that the lawn problem is not that of making a new lawn, but what to do with a lawn that, either through neglect or having been improperly made in the first place—as in many subdivisions and developments—has become hopelessly run down. Possibly attempts have been made to renovate it with special seed mixtures, certain-death weed eradicators, and magic fertilizers. But unless the *soil* conditions are corrected, all of these efforts are likely to produce only temporary improvement.

This does not necessarily involve digging or plowing up the entire area. The following procedure will usually put the area back into good condition provided proper care is maintained afterward. However, if there is not proper drainage, or if the soil is so porous (sandy or gravelly) that water passes through it as through a sieve, then completely remaking is required.

Assuming fairly good soil, the following method should provide a good turf that, with continued maintenance, will *stay* good.

First, mow the old lawn, setting the blades as low as possible. Next dig up bare spots and weedy or poor areas and dig and work in a heavy application of compost. Use a weed eradicator (following directions carefully) where these are prevalent in turf otherwise fairly good. Top-dress and rake these areas over evenly with compost. Water *thoroughly*. When dry on the surface, sow seed, using full amount recommended for a new lawn on bare spots, less where some turf remains. Rake seed in and roll. Keep surface *constantly* moist by light watering for at least two weeks.

The best time to carry out this operation is *very* early spring or early fall for cool-climate grasses and according to local practice and State Agricultural Experiment Station advice for warm sections.

LAWN MAINTENANCE

Even the best of lawns is not an investment that is made and then forgotten, to go on paying rich dividends without further attention. In fact, the more perfect the lawn is, the more constant will be the attention required to keep it in A-1 condition.

Mowing, of course, is the first consideration. Mowing should begin when the new grass, if of a cool-climate type, is 2 to 3 inches tall. The mower blades—or blade, if a rotary mower is used—should be set at least 2 inches high. Mowing is best done on a cloudy day, to avoid possible injury from hot sun, and should be followed by watering if the soil is dry. Do not attempt mowing when grass is wet.

Subsequent mowings may be somewhat closer, but it should be remembered that this will mean mowing more frequently, and also that the closer grass is cut, the more likely it is that crabgrass—which loves full, direct sunshine and does not grow in even moderately heavy shade—will get a start. Never let the grass get so long between mowings that it is necessary to rake up and remove the clippings. Left where they fall they form a beneficial mulch and eventually work back into the soil, *thus returning most of the plant food elements that they have removed.*

Feeding is best done in early spring and again in late summer for cool-climate grasses; for hot-climate grasses, at the *beginning* of most active growth, and then at two-month intervals. This can be continued through the year if an overplanting is made to give a green winter carpet.

While the market is flooded with all sorts of special lawn fertilizers, the most important point in getting good turf is taking care that the *soil* is well supplied with the plant nutrients it requires—plus lime if needed, as in most cases it is —*before* the seed is sown. If that is done, a general-purpose fertilizer with a generous nitrogen content such as 10–6–4, will give satisfactory results, especially if the nitrogen is in a form in which it is released slowly, over a long period.

Some of the modern lawn fertilizers are designed both to provide nourishment for the grass and to kill weeds at the same time. While these are constantly being improved, they should be applied strictly in accordance with directions; and without depending too much on the claims made for them. Practically all advertising these days is given over to more and more extravagant claims, and lawn advertising is no exception to the rule.

For *Pest, Disease, and Weed Control,* see Appendix.

WHAT GRASS FOR YOU?

When it comes to the point of deciding just what grass to sow, there are two main points to consider:

What grasses grow best in your particular area?

What *type* of lawn will best suit your needs?

In the majority of cases—especially in the northern and cool-climate Areas (I, II, and III)—a good mixture with Merion Bluegrass, the chief ingredient, is likely to give the most satisfactory results. In the South, each general area has its most suitable warm-climate grass, Bermudagrass being used over the largest area, with one or more of the Zoysias rapidly increasing in popularity. In many parts of the Midwest and on the Great Plains, the question is one of moisture. Where irrigation or ample water is available, the cool-climate grasses are successfully grown; but without water, one of the native dryland grasses must be used. Many State Experiment Stations carry on extensive tests with various species and mixtures of grass. Anyone putting in a large lawn will do well to consult his Agricultural Experiment Station, or better still visit it and see for himself the results of its tests.

When buying grass seed do not be influenced by price. The cost of seed, compared with other construction costs *and upkeep*, is such a minor figure that, in the long run, the best *is* the cheapest. Bargain mixtures contain large quantities of short-lived "nurse" grasses, which soon disappear. If there is an insufficient quantity of the more expensive, permanent grass seed, an open turf is left which encourages the germination of unwanted weeds.

Here are some of the most widely used and most satisfactory grasses:

FOR COOL CLIMATES

BENTS include such special strains as Astoria, Colonial, Highland, and Rhode Island, and comprise the finest and most beautiful turf grasses. When correctly handled they produce fine, dense, handsome carpets such as are generally seen only on large estates and well-kept golf courses. A pH of 5.5 to 6.5 is required on extra-well prepared soil. Full sun, close cutting, brushing, ample watering, regular fertilization and top dressing, and a rigid program of pest and disease control are essential to success. Northeast; North Central; East Coast; Northwest Coast.

Creeping Bents include many strains—Arlington, Pennlu, Penncross, Old Orchard, Seaside, and Toronto being some of the best known. These fine bentgrasses are used almost exclusively for putting greens and estate lawns near the seashore, for they resist salt spray. Like the other bents these produce an extremely fine turf when meticulously cared for. Northeast; East Coast; Northwest Coast.

Redtop, also a bentgrass, is a quick germinating, short-lived "nurse" grass often used in mixture to give a temporary turf until the permanent grasses become established; or for overplanting Bermudagrass or other summer lawns for winter color in the South. Northeast; North Central; East Coast; Northwest Coast.

Velvet Bent produces the densest and most finely textured turf of all. It is used for show lawns and putting greens in areas that suit its growing requirements. It is heat, cold, shade, drought, and disease-resistant and is suited to the same climatic conditions as the other bentgrasses. It would be wise, however, to get local advice from an authority as to the advisability of using it in a locality where one lacks previous experience.

BLUEGRASSES are generally considered the best of the cool-climate lawn grasses. Kentucky or Merion Blue dominate most mixtures of high quality for the northern and central parts of the country and for other areas as well. Northeast; North Central; East Coast; Midwest; South Central; parts of the Southeast; Northwest Coast; all cool and cold areas north (including Alaska) and west where irrigation or ample water is available; 2–3 pounds per 1000 square feet.

Kentucky Bluegrass is a fine-bladed, blue-green perennial grass, long-lived and producing—when grown in full sun —a rather open turf of good, deep texture. Preferred pH 6–7. Cut at 2 inches.

Merion Bluegrass is deeper rooted, more dense, darker in color, more vigorous, and resistant to heat, drought, and fungus disease, but not to rust. As rust is less likely to attack it when it is planted with Kentucky Bluegrass, a mixture is often used of 30 to 50 per cent Merion, the balance or most of it Kentucky Blue. Merion can be cut closer than Kentucky Blue—½ to 1½ inches.

Canada Bluegrass is coarse, deep-rooted, tolerates poor soil and shade, if it has plenty of moisture, is used for athletic fields and playgrounds where it can be cut high (3–4 inches) and infrequently.

Rough Bluegrass (*Poa trivialis*) or *Meadowgrass,* prefers damp, cool weather, moisture, and partial shade but must have a fertile soil. It produces a low-growing, light green carpet not unlike Kentucky Blue except in color. This grass is almost sure to be included in any shady seed mixture for cool climates. Sometimes as much as 80 per cent is used in such mixtures. Northeast and North Central only.

FESCUES take rough treatment, endure sun or shade, moist or dry soil, and low fertility, but cannot stand the broiling summer heat of the South. They are slow-growing, producing a wiry but fine-textured turf of deep green; are mowed high; 2–3 inches; 2–3 pounds per 1000 square feet.

Red Fescue, or one of its improved strains—such as Chewings, Illahue, Pennlawn, and Ranier—are included in most cool-climate mixtures in the proportion of from 15 to 40 per cent, depending on the area where it is to be used and the use to be made of the finished lawn. Northeast; North Central; Northwest Coast.

Tall Fescue (and its strains Alta and Kentucky 31) are best suited for use on play areas, athletic fields, and airports. They are tall-growing, perennial pasture grasses producing dense leaf systems and heavy roots. Northeast; North Central; Midwest; Northwest Coast.

RYEGRASSES

Domestic or *Italian Ryegrass* is an annual used as a "nurse" grass in cool-climate mixtures to make a show of green before the permanent grasses establish themselves. By then the short-lived annual ryegrass has disappeared. It is also much used for overplanting Bermuda and Centipedegrass lawns in the South to give a green winter color; 2 pounds per 1000 square feet. Northeast; North Central; East Coast; Midwest; South Central; Southeast; Southwest; West Coast.

Perennial Ryegrass makes a permanent, coarse, tough turf though generally it is supposed to be a short-lived grass. It is often planted temporarily to form a quick green ground cover around a new house, to be turned under as green manure when the owner is ready to prepare the area thoroughly and seed a permanent lawn. Northeast; North Central; East Coast; Southeast; South Central; West Coast.

CLOVER, (White Dutch variety) though not a grass at all, is

used in many grass seed mixtures. Where a homeowner wishes to include it as part of his own lawn, however, it is really better if he sows it *separately* from the grass seed, placing it in areas where he wants it. It grows almost anywhere in the United States, given enough moisture. Though it prefers a slightly alkaline soil, it endures slight acidity and grows well in full sun or part shade. It has the added advantages of adding nitrogen to the soil through the leguminous nodules on its roots, and of being so attractive to rabbits that they eat it in preference to most flowers. It may also be planted alone as a ground cover or a grass substitute.

GRASS MIXTURES

In cool climates, lawn seed is usually sold in mixture, the content depending on the use to which the lawn is to be put, and local weather conditions.

For Full Sun

Kentucky Bluegrass	50%		Merion or Kentucky Blue	40%
Merion Bluegrass	40%	OR	Red Fescue Strain	50%
Redtop	10%		Bent, Astoria, or Colonial	10%

For Moist Shade

Rough Bluegrass	40%		Ryegrass, perennial	25%
Fescue, Chewings	50%		Redtop	15%
Bent, Colonial	5%	OR	Rough Bluegrass	30%
Redtop	5%		Fescue, Chewings	25%
			Bent, Colonial	5%

2 lbs. per 1000 sq. ft.

2 lbs. per 1000 sq. ft.

For Dry Shade

Red Fescue, any variety	50%
Merion or Kentucky Bluegrass	30%
Redtop	5%
Perennial Ryegrass	15%

Grass mixtures vary considerably in different climates. If possible consult your county agent or State Agricultural Experiment Station about what mixture best suits your locality and soil.

HOT-CLIMATE GRASSES

BERMUDAGRASS and its hybrids, such as Everglades #1, Gene Tift, Ormond, Sunturf, Tift 57, 127, or 328 are the most generally satisfactory grasses for the South. Bermudagrasses need full sun, slightly acid soil; 4 to 6 fertilizations per year; frequent mowings at ¾ of an inch; and deep watering in dry weather. In general, however, these grasses are the most drought-resistant of all. They are pale- to dark-green, upright-growing, wear-resistant, the hybrids of finer texture than the species. Seed is planted from March to April at the rate of 1 pound per 1000 square feet; or it may be sprigged or sodded at any time during the growing season. Except in frost-free areas it must be overplanted for winter green with domestic ryegrass or a lawn mixture. Southeast; South Central; Gulf Coast; Southwest Coast.

CARPETGRASS is tall, coarse, broad-leaved species which spreads by creeping rootstocks. Light green in color and disease-resistant, it stands moderate wear and needs but one fertilization a year. It is adapted, however, only to low, moist, acid situations in sun or part shade. Growing 8 to 10 inches in height, it creates a mowing problem. Seed fall, winter, or early spring at the rate of 2½ pounds per 1000 square feet; or sprig or plug. Like Bermudagrass, Carpetgrass must be overplanted in winter to get year-round color. Southeast; South Central; Gulf Coast.

CENTIPEDEGRASS makes a low-growing dense sod of light green. It prefers slightly acid soil; needs little mowing as it grows to only 3 or 4 inches; is disease-resistant; endures some shade but also, if kept watered, does well in dry, sandy soils and on steep banks. Seed at the rate of 3 to 5 ounces per 1000 square feet, mixing the fine seed with a gallon of dry sand to assure even distribution; or sod, plug, or sprig. Overplant in winter with ryegrass. Southeast, especially coastal regions; Gulf Coast; South Central; Southwest Coast.

ST. AUGUSTINEGRASS, and its improved varieties such as Bitter Blue, makes coarse, deep green turf which grows in sun or shade; endures salt spray but is subject to chinch-bug injury. It prefers a pH of 6–6.5; needs 4 fertilizations a year and watering in dry periods. As it is very tender, St. Augustine should be planted only in frost-free areas where it remains green the year-round. Sod or sprig: seed is not available. Southeast coastal areas and Gulf Coast.

ZOYSIAS are rapidly becoming the most popular grasses for the South and some species are being widely planted in the North. They are low-growing, making dark green, ruglike turf which stays green over a longer period than Bermudagrass. Their slow growth at first and the fact that they must be sprigged or plugged because of lack of seed are their two major drawbacks. Two years are needed to establish a Zoysia lawn, and during that time it requires plenty of fertilizer and water. Once established, the dense growth crowds out all weeds and care is then minimal. Regular fertilization (4 per year) and watering and frequent mowings at 1½ inches maintain a dark green, handsome sod. All Zoysia grasses brown off in cold weather and the density of the turf makes it difficult to overplant as is the practice with Bermuda and other southern grasses. (Some authorities suggest *painting* the lawn green for the winter!) By sprigging end to end in rows 4 to 6 inches apart, instead of at the usual intervals, a Zoysia lawn can be established in less than the two years generally needed. If the sprigs are in good condition when planted and the area is carefully tended, a fairly good cover should be attained in 6 to 9 months. Sods should be carefully revived on delivery by "heeling in" in damp peatmoss before they are separated into sprigs. After separating, sprigs are planted at once.

Zoysia matrella or Manillagrass, is a fine-leaved, medium-dark species growing 3 to 4 inches in height. It forms a dense, ruglike turf; grows in sun or shade on a wide variety of soils; is pest-, disease-, and weed-resistant. It is green from early spring to late fall, unless temperatures drop below 40 degrees. Southeast; South Central; Southwest Coast.

Emerald Zoysia is similar to *Z. matrella* but grows faster, is a richer green in color, and is more frost-resistant.

Zoysia japonica (Korean Lawngrass) and its improved Korean variety, *Meyer Zoysia*, are those recommended for northern lawns. They are coarser than *Z. matrella* and slower-growing, but form similar, dense, dark green turfs. They prefer full sun and are drought-resistant, though they turn brown in winter. As far as hardiness goes, the Japanese *Zoysias* can be grown from Florida to Massachusetts, Ohio, and even Michigan, though *Z. matrella* is better suited to southern conditions. Northeast; North Central; East Coast; South Central; West Coast; also Southeast and Gulf Coast if desired.

DRY LAND GRASSES

BUFFALOGRASS is a native prairie species of the West which needs full sun but stands cold, heat, and drought. It spreads by runners, is low-growing so needs little mowing, and forms a dense, gray-green turf. Midwest; Great Plains; Southwest; Intermountain.

CRESTED WHEATGRASS and its variety, Fairway, are pasture grasses which grow like Buffalograss. Though it browns badly in hot weather it grows vigorously in cool temperatures. Midwest; Great Plains; Intermountain below 5000 feet.

LEMMONS ALKALIGRASS is a tufted native adapted to moist alkaline soils. It can be used where soil is too alkaline for other grasses, if water and plant food can be supplied. West Coast.

GRAMAGRASSES are pasture grasses of the western United States which can be treated like Buffalograss.

Blue Grama is recommended for dry areas in Montana, Wyoming, and the Southwest where no irrigation is available.

Black Grama, another species, grows best in the Southwest.

GROUND COVERS AS GRASS SUBSTITUTES

In areas and climates where it is difficult to establish and maintain lawns, ground-cover substitutes are often tried. Unfortunately many of these are very limited in their adaptability. It is well therefore to experiment before investing heavily in seed or plants in this category.

Arctostaphylos uva-ursi (Hog-cranberry or Bearberry) is a creeping, broad-leaved evergreen of the Heath Family, a native of northern coastal areas, where it completely covers moors and sandy slopes not far from the ocean front. It is prostrate, with small, glossy oval leaves, pink flowers, and red berries in fall. Prefers full sun, sandy and quite acid soil. It is drought-resistant but difficult to transplant.

Ajuga reptans (Bugle-weed) is a hardy perennial with rosettes of glossy, dark green or bronze leaves, and 4- to 6-inch spikes of deep blue flowers in spring. (There are also white and pink varieties.) It spreads rapidly by stolons from which new-rooted leaf rosettes develop; sun or shade; needs moisture.

Clover, White Dutch (see page 164 for description).

Cotula squalida (Camomile) is a ground cover with light-green, fernlike leaves. Good sandy loam, full sun, and water in dry weather are essential. It is especially suited to California and the Southeast.

Dichondra carolinensis is a native of our own Southeast. Small, fernlike, kidney-shaped, dark green leaves form dense mats only 1½ inches in height, spreading by runners. It requires a deep, well-drained soil but needs plenty of moisture and grows in sun or shade. Sow 1–2 pounds per 1000 square feet, in June. Tender. Southeast; South Central; Southwest Coast.

Hedera helix or English Ivy is an excellent ground cover in shade, especially under trees. One of the small-leaved varieties makes a good choice. Most of these, though sold as house ivies, are hardy as far north as New York City.

Lippia canescens is used as a substitute for lawn grass in warm climates. It is of creeping habit, with gray-green foliage and small lavender flowers; grows in sun or shade; in per 1000 square feet, in June. Tender. Southeast; South east; South Central; Southwest; Southwest Coast.

Liriope muscari, a member of the lily family, has narrow, grasslike, dark green foliage which forms a dense turf 12 inches tall. Lavender-blue flower spikes in late summer. There is an attractive variegated form. It is tolerant of many soil types and grows well in sun or quite heavy shade. Hardy. Northeast; North Central; Southeast; Northwest.

Matricaria tchihatchewi or Turfing-daisy is a mat-forming perennial with finely cut leaves and small, white daisylike flowers; 12 inches, moisture and full sun are required. Hardy. Northeast; North Central; Southeast; South Central; Northwest.

Pachysandra terminalis, or Japanese-spurge, is a fine, dense, evergreen plant for shade which grows by underground stems and throws up umbrellalike stems topped by whorls of glossy, dark leaves. Flowers white. It prefers shade, moisture, and good, humusy loam. Northeast; North Central; Northwest.

Thymus serpyllum, and others: Creeping thymes are among the best of the small-leaved, completely prostrate ground covers. A variety of these gives many shades of green and gray and red, and flowers from white through pink to deep rose. They stand traffic well and are aromatic when the leaves and stems are crushed under foot.

Vinca minor, or periwinkle, is second only to *Pachysandra* as a shade-loving, evergreen ground cover. The dark, glossy leaves are produced on vinelike, creeping stems which root at the nodes. Showy blue or white flowers cover the plants in early spring. Good drainage and moisture are a must; it responds well to rich, woodsy soil. Northeast; North Central; Southeast.

LAWN SCHEDULE

COOL-WEATHER GRASSES

December to *March*. Prepare seedbed for new lawn whenever ground can be worked. Apply pre-emergence weed killer or weed killer-fertilizer.

March to *May*. Seed spring lawn as early as possible. Apply fertilizer-insecticide to old and new lawns. Treat old lawns with pre-emergence crabgrass eradicator. Use weed-control sprays and insecticide sprays before new growth appears on garden plants.

June. Cut new grass as soon as it is 3 to 4 inches high, setting mower blades at 3-inch height. Mow weekly thereafter at 2 inches.

July. Begin regular deep watering of lawns in dry periods. Fertilize lightly. Mow weekly.

August. Prepare seedbed for fall-planted lawns. Apply weed killers well in advance.

September. Sow seed as early as possible and keep moist until established. Renovate and fertilize established lawns.

October. Mow new lawn when grass is 4 inches high, setting mower at 3 inches. Mow weekly thereafter at 2 to 3 inches. Fertilize in mild climates.

November. If weather is dry, water deeply before freeze. Stop mowing.

WARM-WEATHER GRASSES

April. Prepare seedbed and finish grade for new lawns. Treat with pre-emergence weed killer. Remove thatch from established lawn. Order seed or sod for new lawn.

May. Sow grass seed as early as possible after fertilizing and watering. Keep moist until established. Begin to mow as soon as grass is 3 to 4 inches tall. Apply weed control-fertilizer to established lawns. Sod, sprig, or plug summer grasses. Keep moist and well fertilized.

June. Apply 1 pound nitrogenous fertilizer per 1000 square feet. Mow weekly at 1 to 2 inches. Apply post-emergent crabgrass weed killers as needed.

July. Continue fertilizer, mowing, and watering weekly. Treat for pests, diseases, and weeds as needed.

August. Continue same schedule as in July.

September. Raise mower ½ inch and continue mowing until frost. Aerate area and overplant with domestic ryegrass before the middle of the month.

October. Apply 2–4–D sprays (see Appendix, page 454) for chickweed and other winter weeds. Water thoroughly before ground freezes.

November. If area has not been overplanted, try applying a winter "lawn paint" to the dead, brown grass tops.

> Where the copsewood is the greenest,
> Where the fountains glisten sheenest,
> Where the lady-fern grows strongest,
> Where the morning dew lies longest;
> SIR WALTER SCOTT

CHAPTER 11

Flower Beds and Borders

Flower beds and borders for annuals, perennials, and bulbs should be the last part of the planting to be done in landscaping a new place. If planted too early, you may find that they are not only poorly located, but are often damaged when soil and equipment has to be brought in for planting trees, making walks, grading, etc.

It is natural of course that the homeowner should want a show of color out of doors and flowers for decoration indoors at the earliest possible moment. But certainly the more permanent and important parts of the landscaping can be laid out on a permanent, over-all landscape plan (page 21) before flower beds and borders are put in.

Placement. In deciding where flower beds or borders are to go there are several essential things to consider.

Does one want them to be seen and enjoyed from the public road or street? Are there *view windows* which make it possible to have the flower beds, or at least part of them, supplement the *interior* decoration? Does the family devote much time to *outdoor living?* If so can flower beds be employed specifically to add charm and distinction to the outdoor living area? Or maybe the lady of the house is interested in flower arranging, in which case she will want a *cutting garden* for her purpose where she may grow the flowers and foliage she especially likes to use; and where she can cut mate-

FLOWER BEDS AND BORDERS

rial at will without robbing flower beds designed and located to add to the beauty of the home grounds.

With the exception of the cutting garden, which may well be placed by itself, or actually concealed from view, (as are coldframes, compost heaps, and the vegetable garden) flower beds or borders should be a definite part of the landscape design.

Backgrounds. In deciding where any flower bed is to go, one of the most important things to be considered is what sort of background it will have.

The day of the raised circular bed in the center of the front lawn, we are happy to say, is long since gone. Too often, however, one still sees free-standing beds, rectangular, or in long, narrow strips, cut into closely clipped turf. These look almost as contrived and artificial as the old-fashioned, round, canna bed.

To show to best advantage, a bed of flowers should have a background of some sort. Often this may be the wall of a building, a fence, a terraced slope, a hedge. Lacking something of this sort, evergreens or a mixed planting of shrubs add tremendously to its effectiveness.

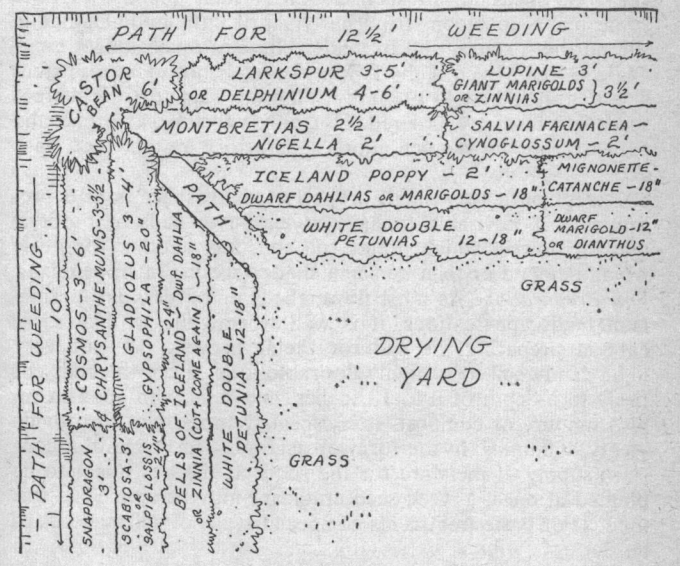

Where many flowers are wanted for cutting, plan a special garden for this purpose.

Be sure to check the growth habits of your plants so that tall-growing flowers are placed well in the rear, those of medium height in the center, and dwarf or very low-growing sorts along the front. Care must be exercised to avoid a blocked, geometric effect. This is done by placing the groups in irregular designs that tend to run together and so make a unified whole.

Usually the effect is more pleasing if the front of the border follows a curved line. This may be established by using a piece of hose or rope, adjusting it until a satisfactory curve is determined, and then cutting the turf along it with a lawn edger or a spade to leave a clean, unbroken edge. Next the turf is skimmed off and removed to the compost heap. A permanent edging of metal, wood, or brick may be put in if desired.

Long flowering season should be assured by using varieties that will flower at different times, or for exceptionally long periods (see lists, Appendix).

While flower borders may be made of either annuals or perennials, the best results for a permanent planting are to be had by using both—with some biennials and bulbs thrown in for good measure. In such a border it is possible to have some plants in bloom from early April until mid-October in the northern states, and in milder climates much longer.

Make a Plan. Even if the flower border is not to be an extensive one, it is best to prepare a planting plan *to scale,* before seeds or plants are ordered. Not only will this save time and expense, but give much more satisfactory results (see page 20).

Except on a very small property, where space is at a premium, it is advisable to have at least two beds or borders; one for flowers which prefer full sun, and another for those which demand or tolerate some shade (see list in Appendix).

Soil Preparation. As most flower beds or borders are permanent landscape features, it is well worthwhile to take *extra* care in preparing the soil for them. In very poor or very light, sandy soil, it is highly desirable to excavate the beds entirely to a depth of 8 to 12 inches, and refill with good loam, plus manure or compost. It is especially important to provide plenty of humus, in the form of peatmoss, to maintain a constant supply of moisture for the roots. If the bed is not to be planted at once, a weed seed eradicant may be applied at this time. (For basic treatments of special types of soil, see Chapter 2.)

ANNUALS

Although most of the annuals are quite tender, and a number of them are best not sown from seed or set out as plants until after the soil has really warmed up, it is advisable to prepare the beds as early in the spring as possible. In addition to this we like to use, when setting out plants, our regular "starting" mixture of bonemeal and organic manure.

There are a few annuals which germinate quickly and spring into rapid growth, producing flowers in a few weeks. These are valuable for *quick effects* needed to give color the first year in a rock garden or border where perennials will make a show the following year. For lists of such quick growers—many of which must be sown in succession to give an all-season display—see list, Appendix.

Many other annuals require a *long growing season* before beginning to flower and for these it is advisable, especially in northern climates, to start seedlings in advance of planting dates, indoors or in a frame; or else to purchase plants ready for setting out. Growing one's own plants has several advantages. By so doing the gardener can secure the exact varieties he wishes to have. He can have plants that have not been forced to maintain a production timetable; he can have them properly and gradually "hardened off" before setting out; and he can plant them a few at a time as they and conditions are ready, instead of having to do a rush job as may be the case when a large number are purchased at one time.

Annuals are usually planted in beds or borders where several species and different types of the same species are used together—marigolds and zinnias for instance are available in a wide variety of colors and in plants that range from a few inches to several feet in height—but striking landscape effects may be obtained with groups of a single variety. Even a single plant such as castor-oil bean (*Ricinus*), sunflower, or angel's-trumpet (*Datura*) can be featured as a specimen.

Some of the annual vines grow with almost incredible rapidity, reaching heights of 20 to 30 feet in time to provide weeks of bloom. Examples are morning-glory, moonflower, cup-and-saucer vine *(Cobaea scandens)*, and tall climbing nasturtiums, which, though they reach only 4 to 5 feet, make up in vigor and bloom for what they lack in height.

These fast-growing annual vines are especially important for inexpensive landscape effects in first-season plantings on a new place (see list, Appendix).

In buying annuals it is advisable to procure named varieties rather than mixtures. The seed may cost a bit more, but this cost is only a small fraction of the cost of making a garden, fertilizers, sprays, watering, etc. And in buying plants, select young, vigorous ones, in bud rather than in full bloom. This applies especially to plants in flats or other multiple containers, but holds with pot plants also.

Sowing and Planting. Success with annuals depends to a great extent upon giving them the correct *start*. Both earlier and more certain results are to be had with the majority of species by starting the plants in a greenhouse, a hotbed, or a coldframe, and then setting them out—the hardy plants after danger of hard frosts is past and the tender ones when the ground has really warmed up.

As it takes seed a week to two weeks, or even longer, to germinate in cold soil, the hardy and half-hardy sorts, if sown outdoors, may be planted a bit in advance of these dates; but tender varieties, if sown too early, are likely to rot in the soil.

With seeds sown where they are to grow, germination will be more certain if the rows or the beds in which they are to be planted are given some extra care in the way of preparation. Where they are to be sown in rows we open up a shallow trench—2 to 3 inches in depth—and fill it with a sand and peatmoss mixture. If soil is dry, the trench is flooded with water, which is allowed to soak away before the sand-peat compost is put in, after which the soaking is again repeated. Circular or rectangular beds where seed is to be broadcast are treated in the same way.

Such preparation requires a little extra work, but is well worth it. Surplus seedlings, when the "thinning out" stage is reached, come out easily, with little disturbance to those that are left, and in ideal condition to transplant elsewhere if they are wanted. Such is not the case when seedlings have to force their way up through the usual hard-packed surface soil.

Very small seeds, sown in the open, are often washed out, or badly damaged, before or after germination. Covering the surface with a light mulch, or even with newspapers, will prevent this, but such plantings must be carefully watched and any covering *immediately removed* when germination occurs. Delay for even a day may result in losing them.

Thinning out. Probably the greatest cause of poor results, or even failure, with annuals sown where they are to grow is delay in thinning them out. *Every surplus plant is a weed!* And moreover it is a weed growing in closest proximity to the plant that is wanted, and competing with it for food, moisture, and light, from the very start. Thinning should be done as soon as possible after the first true leaves develop. Very often a second thinning, and sometimes even a third, is required to provide ample space for the remaining plants to produce maximum results.

Thin out seedlings while plants are still small; the earlier the better.

Fertilizer. Even though the soil may have been well prepared, under most conditions an application of plant food, as the plants are coming into bud, proves beneficial. A general-purpose fertilizer, rather than one with an extra-high nitrogen content, is best for this, as forced plants usually have a shortened period of flowering. Growing plants should be watched carefully, and if they seem to lack healthy, dark green foliage, an application of a high-nitrogen fertilizer is indicated. A moderate application of nitrate of soda, well watered in, often shows results in a few days, as will foliar feeding. Such stimulation should not be overdone, however, or the plants, while making remarkable growth, may produce fewer than the normal number of flowers.

Mulching. When watering is a problem—for instance in suburban areas where its use is restricted during dry periods when it is most needed—mulching should by all means be employed. To be most effective it must be put on *before* the surface gets powder-dry or caked.

Supports. Many tall growing plants require supports. These include, of course, all of those which form vines—such as sweet peas, morning-glories, and *Cobaea scandens,* or cup-and-saucer vine; and also many that are not of climbing habit but—because of their height—are injured by strong winds. This includes such popular kinds as cosmos, larkspur, snapdragons, sunflowers, and tall marigolds.

Supports for the real climbers are of many types—trellises of wood, metal (of which we like best the aluminum link-chain

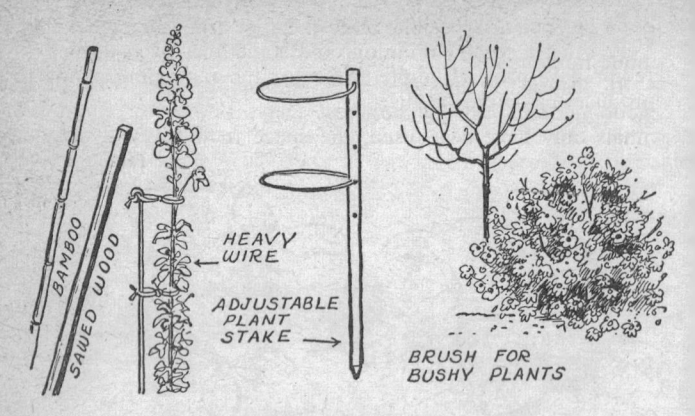

Tall plants need adequate support to prevent storm damage.

type with screw hooks to hold it at top and bottom), coarse twine, chains, and what-have-you. It is, however, plants of the second group, left unsupported, which are most likely to be injured.

For these, either of two types of support may be used. Typical of the first is the plant stake (made of bamboo, round or sawed wood or metal) to which the stem of the plant is securely tied. The effect is likely to be stiff and ungraceful but the plant is held securely.

For the other type of support, brush, wire, or netting may be employed. For garden use, brush provides the most natural-looking support, but it is becoming more and more difficult to procure, even in rural areas.

In using either type of support it should be *put in place early,* the plant being tied or trained on it as it grows. Plants that are left until nearly grown before being given support not only require much more work, but seldom can be made to look at all natural.

Pinching back. Many flowering plants that tend to send up a single, tall spike, such as dahlias and tall varieties of larkspur, snapdragon, and cosmos, may be made more branching and self-supporting by pinching out the top when they are well established. This induces the development of side growths and a more bushy, self-supporting plant. It may result also in more, though somewhat smaller, flowers.

End-of-season care. The first hard frost puts an end to most of the annuals. Too often they are left where they grew, to become an eyesore for the balance of the season—and to provide a nice winter mulch for seedlings of hardy weeds and undesirable grasses.

If, instead of this, they are removed at once, they make good material for the compost heap. Moreover, where annuals only have been used, the space they occupied may, if sown at once to winter rye or oats, look attractive throughout the winter and be benefited by the green manure, which is dug under the following spring.

BIENNIALS

Plants in this group normally require more than one season to complete their life cycle, making part of their growth the first summer and fall, going dormant through the winter, and flowering and maturing seed the following spring and summer. Some of them, if started inside early enough in the year will flower, even in cold regions, the same season they are sown. Among these are pansies, English daisies (*Bellis perennis*), forget-me-not (*Myosotis*), sweet William (*Dianthus barbatus*), and Siberian wallflower. In warmer regions they may be sown in autumn and brought through the colder months with suitable mulching to protect them from unusually heavy frosts (see list, Appendix).

PERENNIALS

Perennials are plants which, after having produced flowers and seed, live on to repeat the process from year to year. Some of them are extremely long-lived; the gas-plant (*Dictamnus*) for instance, often outlives the gardener who plants it, as do peonies. The majority of perennials, however, if left to themselves, soon form clumps of numerous offspring, becoming so overcrowded that they produce only inferior flowers, and fewer and fewer of these. So one may well realize at the start that a perennial garden is going to require more or less perennial care. Few plants in it can be left for more than two or three seasons without being taken up, divided, and replanted. And the more generously they are fed, to produce vigorous growth and extra-fine bloom, the more frequently will they require replanting (see list, Appendix).

Exceptions to this general statement are the group of ground cover plants. These are used chiefly in areas where annuals and taller perennials do not thrive. They are also excellent in rock gardens and wall gardens (see lists, Appendix).

PLANNING THE BORDER

While annuals are still used extensively in the planting of beds and borders where a formal or architectural design is followed, perennials are seldom employed for this purpose. On the contrary, they lend themselves perfectly to the permanent hardy border, their astonishing variation in habit of growth, in size, in flower, in color and season of bloom, all helping to make them ideal subjects for this purpose.

As in using annuals, so with perennials, the most pleasing result is achieved when the design for planting does not follow a set pattern but produces a natural effect. Often a group of very few plants, or occasionally even a single specimen plant of some sturdy-growing variety, used as an accent creates the most pleasing picture.

As mentioned previously, low-growing species or varieties are used at the front, tall ones at the rear, and those of intermediate height in between. Care should be exercised to avoid planting in "bands." Occasionally spreading plants of medium height should run well back into the border or be brought forward near the edge. Groups of one species, planted in uneven patterns similar to those in which a group of bulbs is placed, planted informally produce unstudied, natural effects.

Much has been written about the distribution of color in the perennial garden. Many ideas advanced are alluring in theory but seldom work out in practice. Naturally one would wish to avoid putting clashing colors such as pink and yellow, or magenta and scarlet, adjacent to each other, but very pleasing borders can be achieved without too careful color planning. Such color harmonies as are commonly used by flower arrangers in their compositions may be too complicated for the average amateur gardener. For those who are keenly color conscious, however, such color planning may prove a joy. A large perennial garden that we did some years ago for a client featured the sky blue of delphiniums, the delicate salmons of Oriental poppies, sweet William, and the feathery rose of heuchera, all tied together with plenty of white blossoms and gray foliage. It was supremely satisfying to its owner, who preferred delicate colors, softly blended. A friend who prefers pure hues uses strong reds, deep oranges, heavy purples, but blends them with foliage plants of various greens and grays.

The design for a perennial border of moderate size, in sketch shown on page 182, gives an idea of how a plan may be worked out to suit the owner.

Obtaining the plants for a perennial border may be done either by purchasing them from a nursery or growing them from seed. The new homemaker, who does not wish to wait too long for results, will find a combination of the two plans advisable.

In buying plants there is a big advantage in purchasing locally: one sees in advance what one is getting. On the other hand, unless one is within reach of a fairly large nursery where plants are actually propagated and grown as well as sold, the choice of varieties is likely to be very limited. The use of a few varieties that do not appear in every garden in the neighborhood is desirable to give the planting more individuality, and so a combination of buying some materials locally and other items by mail is often the best solution.

By whatever method the plants are obtained, unless they can be planted immediately, they should be "heeled in"—temporarily planted—sufficiently deep to cover the roots, in a shady place where they can be kept well watered. Any plants that are tied in bundles should be separated, and the roots, if long, trimmed back a bit. It is well to have in any such temporary bed a generous amount of peatmoss.

Growing from seed is entirely practical with many species of hardy perennials. No special equipment is required. In sec-

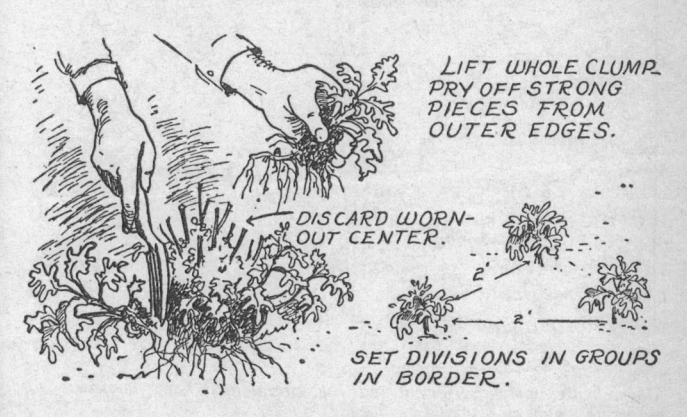

Do not let perennials "run out" through overcrowding.

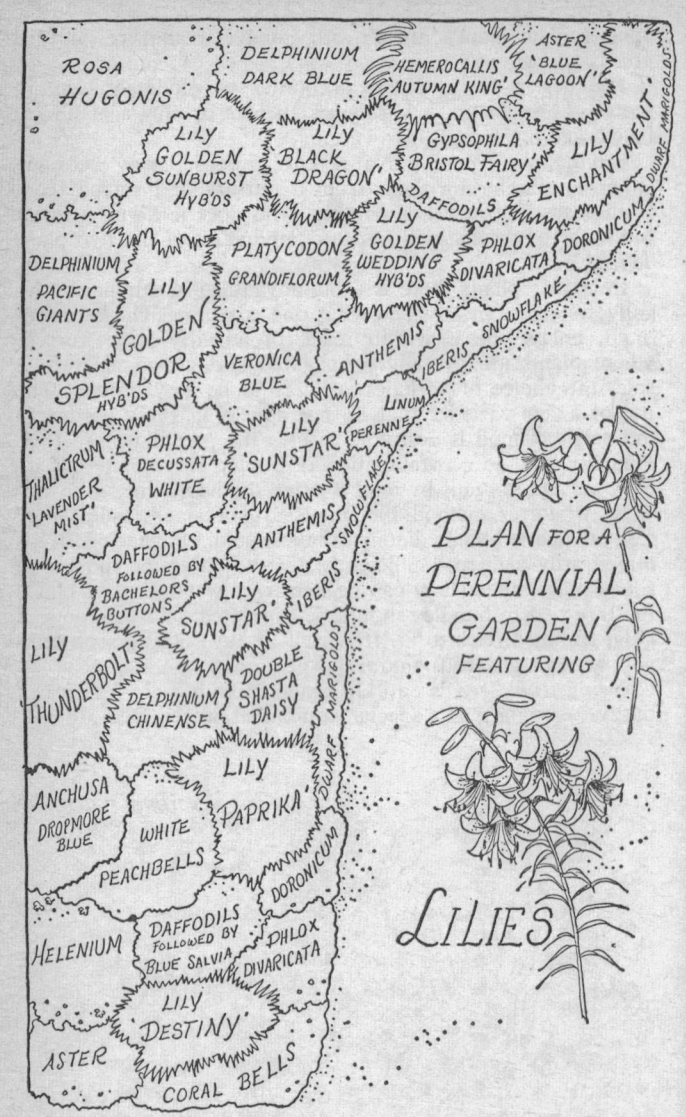

Lilies, being upright growers, may be interplanted with perennials of moderate height in a mixed herbaceous border.

tions where winters are severe, especially where there is likely to be alternate thawing and hard freezing, a coldframe will be helpful; but some of the most desirable perennials, such as day-lilies, heuchera, arabis, and rudbeckia, may be grown even without a frame.

The spacing for perennials in the border varies considerably. Some at maturity are quite large, with a spread of 2 feet or more; others require only a few inches. Some reach a height of 4, 5, or even 6 feet; others scarcely that many inches. Under favorable conditions of soil and climate, they attain much greater size than where soil, and exposure, are less favorable. The beginner is likely to make some mistakes in spacing—but these will be fewer if he takes the trouble to prepare a good-sized planting plan on a piece of heavy paper, and then marks this off, roughly to scale, on the prepared surface of the bed *before he begins planting*.

OFF TO A GOOD START

As is the case in attaining success with trees and shrubs, so in growing annuals, biennials, and bulbs, final results depend quite as much upon what is done *before* planting as upon good culture afterward. No amount of dosing the soil with high-pressure fertilizers during the summer will make up for lack of really thorough preparation of beds and borders before a seed is sown or a plant set out.

Preparation. As early in the spring as the frost is out, and the soil can be dug without a tendency to stick together in lumps that do not easily break apart, operations are begun. If coarse manure, rough compost, seaweed, or any similar bulky material is being used it is better to spread this on the surface and dig it under. Personally we much prefer a wide digging fork to a spade or a shovel for this job, but some gardeners do not.

Soils containing a considerable amount of clay should not be dug while wet, otherwise they may form bricklike clods that do not break up and disintegrate for weeks. Such soils are much benefited by the addition of any material that helps to make them more porous (see Chapter 2).

The depth to which the soil should be dug depends upon its character. If it is a shallow soil, the gardener should aim to go an inch or two deeper each time it is dug, turning some of the raw subsoil up to the surface.

After this initial digging it may be well, if a rainy spell ensues, to wait and let the area dry for a few days before proceeding with the final preparations.

In sowing flower or vegetable seeds where plants are to grow, resist the temptation to sow the entire contents of a packet in the area available. Every surplus plant is a *weed,* and must later be removed. Otherwise the result will be a tangle of weak, struggling seedlings, none of which can properly mature. The gardener can save himself a lot of tedious, backbreaking work by having the will power to throw some seed away!

Even with carefully controlled sowing there is the need to remove many seedlings, and the earlier this is done (after the second true leaf develops) the better.

After thinning, it is helpful—unless the soil is very rich—to give a light application of an organic-base fertilizer (page 98) supplemented, if soil is at all dry, by a thorough watering with a mist nozzle spray that will not beat down the remaining seedlings.

Setting out plants. Many gardeners these days procure seedling plants from local garden centers instead of attempting to grow their own. The plant breeders have achieved remarkable success in developing varieties of favorite annuals that come into flower at an early age on dwarf plants. When these are grown in individual peat pots, all the purchaser need do is to set them out pot-and-all, spaced at the recommended distances apart.

If plants are growing in flats or "trays" they should be carefully separated by cutting between them with a knife so that, in removing them, they may be lifted out with the least possible injury to the roots. Transplanting or setting out—especially in very sunny or windy weather—is best done late in the afternoon. They should, however, be set out as soon as possible, for they have been growing under ideal conditions, and will quickly show the effect of the slightest neglect. After setting each in a generous hole, the soil is filled in around the roots and made very firm, leaving a slight saucer-shaped indentation to hold water. After setting, the plants are watered carefully so that the crowns are not inundated or covered with wet soil. Protection from hot sun or wind for a few days is most helpful. Berry boxes, Hotkaps, or even folds of newspaper may be used for this purpose.

Dividing and replanting. After two or three years' growth, many perennials will have formed sodlike mats; others will have developed runners with offsets; new plants will have grown up, each with its own roots, but still attached to the parent plant; and still others will form straying, fleshy roots (rhizomes) that send up new growths similar to the original one.

Examples of the first, or mat-forming type are the common, wild white daisy and the hardy garden chrysanthemum. Strawberries and ajuga are typical runner-forming types; while bearded iris and day-lilies are rhizomatous in character.

The division of plants, and their subsequent replanting, is best done when they are dormant; in northern, cold climates, the earlier in spring, the better. Some, such as irises, Oriental poppies, and day-lilies, which go into summer dormancy, are divided when the foliage ceases growth or matures. In warmer sections, replanting may be undertaken at any time when plants are dormant, or at rest.

In taking apart plants to be divided, only strong, healthy new growths should be used. The old centers or crowns (and any diseased parts) are discarded and should be consigned to the bonfire. *Sections to be replanted are kept well separated* in order to prevent their becoming overcrowded. It is better to throw away—or still better to give away—any surplus than to replant too closely.

Peonies, since they present some peculiar problems, may be mentioned specifically here. The herbaceous peony should be planted in open ground in full sun and where there can be no competition from the roots of trees or shrubs. A wind screen at some distance is an advantage if the garden is in a windy area. Light shade thrown by such a screen or by very large trees at a safe distance is not detrimental. Plant roots 3 feet apart in a bed of well-prepared, humusy soil enriched with a complete plant food and with bonemeal. *Well-rotted* manure may be used where it is available. As ample room must be allowed for future root development, the bed should be worked to at least a foot in depth.

Set the crowns 2 inches below the soil surface and fill in around the roots with good garden loam which has *not* been enriched by the addition of fertilizer or manure. Roots will quickly seek the enriched soil below. Firm in with the feet after filling the hole, and water thoroughly. In cold climates a winter mulch is advisable on a newly planted bed, though established peonies are remarkably hardy.

BULBS

A very important feature of flower beds and borders, and one all too often given little attention or even entirely overlooked, is the adequate and imaginative use of hardy bulbs.

When bulbs are mentioned the inexperienced gardener immediately thinks of daffodils, tulips, hyacinths, and crocuses. It is true that these are the ones most extensively used. However, there are many, many others; and some of these, once suitably planted, take care of themselves and gradually establish naturalized colonies.

Moreover, the flowering season of the hardy bulbs is by no means limited to spring. In milder sections where many kinds not hardy in the north may be used, their flowering periods extend pretty much around the year.

Formal beds planted with elaborate color designs of spring-flowering bulbs, once so popular, are now pretty much limited to public parks and gardens, and even there are gradually disappearing. Home gardeners have discovered that a thoughtful selection of several species and varieties, even in very limited quantities, adds immeasurably to both the beauty and interest of the mixed border.

In northern sections the season starts in February or March with snowdrops and winter-aconite and progresses to crocuses, chionodoxas, puschkinias, species tulips, early, medium, and late daffodils, hyacinths, Single Early, Cottage, and Darwin tulips.

In summer there are the garden lilies; the hardy amaryllis, *Lycoris squamigera;* fall-blooming crocuses and colchicums; and, last of all, the bright yellow *Sternbergia lutea*, which blooms about the time the dogwood and Virginia creeper leaves are turning red.

For those who do not object to digging and storing in autumn, and replanting in spring, there are as well a whole galaxy of tender, summer-flowering bulbs, corms, and tubers (described at the end of this chapter) to brighten the border from early summer to autumn.

Culture. With plants as varied as those included under the general designation of hardy "bulbs" it is not possible in a general-purpose book such as this to give specific cultural directions. The gardener may keep in mind, however, that most of the true bulbs (and there are many more commonly called "bulbs" (that are really corms or tubers) send down very deep roots. In some species the roots are permanent, in others they die off (as does the foliage) and the bulb goes completely dormant. Typical of these last are the so-called Dutch bulbs—tulips, hyacinths, daffodils, and others (none of which, incidentally, originated in Holland).

Because of the deep roots, and the rapidity with which these develop once growth starts, it is important for best results that bulbs have a very deep, friable, and well-drained soil. Such a soil is important too in getting them down to the full depth they should go when they are planted. If they are to be planted 4, 6, or 8 inches deep, the measurement should be *from the top of the bulb to the surface.* A Slim Jim bulb-planting trowel makes the job easier.

Any garden border prepared according to the directions given on page 94 will be suitable. Our own experience, however, is that most bulbs seem to respond especially well to a generous application of bonemeal (the coarse ground, if obtainable) and so we add that when getting any area ready for bulbs. Most hardy species will benefit by an application of complete fertilizer cultivated in at the first sign of renewed growth in the spring.

The mistake most commonly made in the culture of bulbs, especially where they are grown in a mixed border, is to cut off the foliage before it has thoroughly "ripened," as indicated by its losing color and beginning to shrivel. The foliage of daffodils and similar species can be twisted or plaited and turned under, or may be fastened together with Twistems or other plant ties to get it out of the way and make it less conspicuous. The surest and easiest method, however, is to plant them just back of perennials that make spreading, early foliage growth, such as mertensia, myosotis, *Phlox divaricata,* stokesia, Oriental poppies, Shasta daisies, and lupines, or to set pot-grown annuals among and in front of them.

Replanting hardy bulbs. As previously mentioned there comes a time in the growth of most hardy bulbs when they begin to overcrowd and require digging and replanting. When this stage is reached the job should be attended to without delay. Otherwise the result will be not merely fewer and inferior flowers, but inferior bulbs to be replanted.

Most of the spring-flowering bulbs should be taken up as soon as the foliage dies down completely, *but while it is still attached.* Otherwise bulbs are difficult to locate and some may be lost. Also, if left in the ground too long, new roots (especially of daffodils) may have started and will be injured or destroyed.

After being dug, the bulbs are dried off, preferably in a cool place under cover, spread out in flats so that air can reach them freely. After drying, store in bags or boxes, away from direct sunshine, and safe from rodents, until time for replanting in autumn. Daffodils, being poisonous, are safe from the attacks of rodents. As they start new root growth early it is quite all right to replant these as soon as they have been pulled apart, if this is more convenient than to dry and store them.

TENDER BULBS

Overwintering. Tender bulbs, corms, and tubers such as dahlias, ismenes, gladiolus, tigridias, tuberous begonias, and such half-hardy subjects as montbretias, callas, etc., are taken up in fall as soon as the foliage has been touched by frost, or even before in sections where the first frost may be a "black" or hard, killing one. They are spread out in an airy, frost-free place to allow the tops to dry up somewhat before being cut off. After a week or two tops are removed and bulbs or corms cleaned of loose soil and packed, *carefully labeled,* in mesh bags, crates, or boxes.

They should be kept in a cool, frost-free atmosphere, away from too much heat. Where this is not possible, it is best to pack them in *slightly* moist peatmoss. They should be examined every month or so to make sure they are not drying out or rotting.

Most tender bulbs, corms, and tubers—such as ismenes, dahlias, cannas, and gladiolus—may be kept at comparatively low temperatures—35 to 50 degrees; but the very tender or tropical ones such as tuberous begonias and gloxinias are safer at 60 degrees, and some of the really tropical subjects, like caladiums, are safer at around 70 degrees. None should ever be allowed to get dry enough to shrivel.

Spring planting of most tender bulbs can be done directly in the border, after the soil has warmed up in late spring.

The very tender tropicals, like tuberous begonias, gloxinias, and caladiums, are started indoors in flats of peatmoss or in pots of rich, fibrous soil, and set outdoors in the beds where they are to grow in early summer after warm weather is established.

SOME TULIPS AND DAFFODILS

In a general-purpose book such as this, it is not possible to go into much detail concerning individual varieties of the various plants mentioned. With some of them, however, there are such marked differences as to time of flowering, size, and form, that these factors should be emphasized in order to guide the gardener who is really trying to get the most effective results from his time and effort.

Tulips are a case in point. By judicious selection they may be enjoyed for some six to eight weeks instead of for the usual two or three when the large-flowering late tulips, displayed in huge color cuts in sensational advertising, are the only type planted. Few gardeners, even some with considerable experience, realize that many of the species and species hybrid tulips bloom with, or even before such early shrubs as forsythia. These little fellows *remain* in flower two or three times as long as the May-flowering types.

To get a long succession of early spring color from tulips, start with some of the species and species hybrids such as Gaiety, Vivaldi, and the other Kaufmanniana hybrids, all very early, Dasystemon, Clusiana, Scarlet Elegance, and Praestans.

Following these come such varieties as Red Emperor (a very early hybrid which in a comparatively few years has become the most popular tulip in the world) and its companion, White Emperor; the Single Earlies like De Wet, Pink Beauty, and Rising Sun, many of which are delightfully fragrant; and the Double Earlies—Peach Blossom, Mareschal Niel, Murillo Maximus, and others.

In May-flowering, the first to bloom are the graceful Cottage and Lily-flowered forms such as Rosy Wings, Golden Duchess, Queen of Sheba, and White Triumph.

To wind up the tulip season come the Darwins and Breeders, typified by Clara Butt, Garden Magic, and Dom Pedro.

Daffodils. As is the case with tulips, so with daffodils; the period of bloom in most gardens is only half as long as it well might be. The gardener should take the trouble to procure a few bulbs of such tough and early-flowering varieties as February Gold and March Sunshine; such small-flowered gems as W. P. Milner, Moonshine, and Thalia; and a few not-too-double doubles like Cheerfulness and Golden Cheerfulness or Snowball. In addition he will have some of the usual "giant" varieties pushed in the catalogs, those seen in every bulb garden. More unusual varieties are of far greater interest, however. During the last few years a great many "breaks" have occurred in the daffodil family—bunch-flowered types, multicolored blooms, jonquil hybrids, and the like. The most startling are the many pink, rose, or apricot trumpets with white or cream perianths. These make real conversation pieces.

(For a discussion of forcing spring-flowering bulbs in pots for winter bloom indoors, see the closing pages of Chapter 7.)

HERBS AND FRAGRANT FLOWERS

Herbs are easy to grow, useful in the cuisine and for potpourris and sachets, and are always of special interest to visitors as well as to the feminine gardener.

Knot gardens or geometrically designed beds with paths running through them are the traditional way to plant and grow herbs. Full sun is a *must* and a moderately rich, rather sandy soil with a pH which is neutral or a little above suits most herbs.

The kitchen or culinary herb garden contains such perennials as sage, thyme, pot marjoram, chives, rosemary, mints, and tarragon; with annuals and biennials such as sweet marjoram, summer savory, borage, and parsley (see list, Appendix). An attractive evergreen edging plant for the beds is teucrium or germander, with small glossy leaves. It can be trimmed or sheared to the desired height.

HERB GARDEN

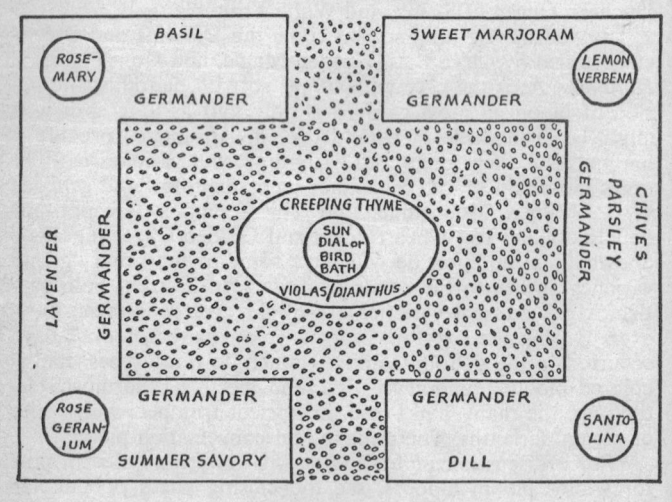

One plan for an herb garden, with suggested plantings.

The fragrant herb garden may feature true lavender, *Nepeta mussini*, scented geraniums, violas, and even lilies (see lists of Fragrant Plants in Appendix).

FRAGRANT GARDENS

Many gardeners not particularly interested in herbs enjoy specializing in fragrant flowers.

In addition to roses and lilies such perennials may be featured as dianthus, wallflowers, *Daphne cneorum, Datura arborea,* hostas, monarda, and buddleia (see list, Appendix).

Among the shrubs, clethra, English hawthorn, witch-hazel, the jasmines and magnolias are but a few (see list, Appendix).

Fragrant bulbs include many of the Single Early tulips, jonquil hybrid daffodils, hyacinths, and lily-of-the-valley.

Some summer bulbs such as ismenes (*Hymenocallis*), tuberoses, galtonia, and freesias are delightfully scented (see Appendix).

Fragrant annuals are numerous, but among the best known are sweet alyssum, candytuft, nasturtiums, petunias, nicotianas, stocks, and mignonette.

A garden or border with night fragrance, planted near the terrace, is a delight. Here nicotianas, petunias, moonflowers, lilies, and garden phlox give off delightful evening scents. Such a garden may be designed entirely in white and green for eye appeal after dusk as well as for fragrance.

> ... from the rock as if by magic grown ...
> JOHN WILLIAM BURGON
>
> Flower in the crannied wall—
> ALFRED, LORD TENNYSON

CHAPTER 12

Rock, Bank, and Wall Gardens

The general types of gardens discussed in the preceding chapter are those most commonly used. There are, however, several other specialized types which are often employed, either because a location lends itself to the cultivation of certain kinds of plants or because the owner is particularly interested in some one group of plants.

Such gardens have three distinct advantages. In the first place they make it possible to feature plants that do not succeed under ordinary conditions, and in the second, these can be used to convert areas that would otherwise be problem locations, if not actual eyesores, into unique beauty spots. Not infrequently such special gardens become the highlights of the entire landscape planting, commanding more attention and admiration than any other feature. In the third place, such gardens make it possible to display, in a way that allows their full beauty to be enjoyed, many plants which in any ordinary garden would be almost completely lost.

Typical of such specialized plantings are rock, bank, and wall gardens, and water, pool, and stream gardens. This chapter deals only with the first three of these.

THE ROCK GARDEN

First of all, the prospective builder of a rock garden should be forewarned that it must be so placed and constructed as to appear to blend in *naturally* with its surroundings. Otherwise it is almost certain to be unpleasantly conspicuous. A heap of stones and soil piled up in an open space is about as distressing a sight both esthetically and horticulturally as can well be imagined, no matter how fine a collection of plants may be wedged in the cracks. Such monstrosities are occasionally to be seen, but they are becoming rare as gardeners learn more of good design.

The immediate surroundings of the rock garden contribute quite as much to its success, as a pleasing feature of the landscape, as the plant material grown in it. A rock garden is essentially a *natural* garden; and the more its location, and the plants and trees adjacent to it, can create the effect of its having always been there the more it will add to the over-all beauty of the scene of which it is a part.

A few—even two or three—informal and picturesque evergreens such as a gnarled pine, a hemlock, a juniper, or larch; a white birch, a willow, weeping cherry, a dogwood or two will accomplish wonders in blending the rock garden into the general landscape.

Location. While a rock garden may be built almost anywhere (we have seen a very successful one on the roof of a New York skyscraper) it is certain to be easier to construct it and to maintain its plants in vigorous health if certain conditions can be assured to start with.

The first of these is good drainage. While many plants commonly designated as rock plants like plenty of moisture about their roots during their periods of early growth and flowering, they do not tolerate constantly wet soil such as is favored by bog or even wet woodland plants. In fact, during most of the year many of them exist in almost desert dry conditions. Therefore, in locating the rock garden, a slight elevation or a mound or steep slope, makes a better site than a low, poorly drained area.

It is also desirable to place the rock garden in a somewhat sheltered location. While many creeping and low-growing rock plants—such as saxifrages, thymes, and sempervivums—withstand even heavy gales without injury, there are equally desirable plants—such as anemones, aquilegias, primulas, and species narcissi—which, while the foliage itself may be low-growing, thrust their flower stems or spikes proudly aloft. These, without some protection, may be twisted and broken in wind and rain.

Shelter may be provided by a background of low evergreens and shrubs, care being taken to select those that are of natural, informal habits of growth and bearing small, inconspicuous flowers, if any. Some appropriate evergreens are:

False cypress (*Chamaecyparis*): Dwarf Hinoki; Thread Sawara; Fernspray Hinoki; Plume Sawara.
Red-cedar (*Juniperus*): Koster; Silver; Goldtip; Oldfield; Common.
Juniper: Andorra; Tamarix Savin; Sargent; Hill Japanese; Waukegan; Meyer; Coffin; Blue Coast.
Pine (*Pinus*): Swiss Stone; Waterer.
Spruce (*Picea*): Pygmy; Dwarf Alberta; Weeping Blue.
Hemlock (*Tsuga*): Japanese; Sargent's Weeping.
Yew (*Taxus*): Spreading Japanese; Dwarf Japanese; Intermedia; Brown's; Hicks'; Upright Japanese.
Good background shrubs include: *Abelia grandiflora; Buxus* (Box), in variety.
Broad-leaved evergreens: *Cotoneaster*, in variety; *Ilex* (Holly); *crenata, opaca,* and others; *Kalmia latifolia* (Laurel); *Leucothoë catesbaei; Mahonia aquifolium* (Holly-grape); *Pyracantha coccinea* (Firethorn).
Deciduous shrubs and small trees: *Callicarpa dichotoma; Calycanthus floridus; Clethra alnifolia* (Sweet Pepperbush); *Cornus florida,* (Dogwood) *kousa; Hamamelis virginiana* (Witch-hazel); *Jasminum nudiflorum; Malus,* in variety (Flowering Crab); *Prunus,* in variety (Flowering Cherry); *Stewartia ovata; Viburnums,* in variety.

Equally important protection can be afforded by so planning the rock garden area that it slopes to the south or southeast. To look at all natural it should never be built in the form of a mound, with its highest point at the center. It should occupy an irregular slope, natural in appearance; or it may include a natural outcropping of shelf rock. Either of these, backed by the shrub planting suggested, makes it possible to grow a much greater variety of plants, and also to keep them all healthier and happier than would otherwise be possible.

While most plants ordinarily used in the rock garden are sun-loving, others enjoy partial shade; so it is desirable to have part of the area receive high shade to accommodate subjects such as terrestrial orchids, hardy cyclamens, ferns, ginger, galax, and other plants of the open woods—trailing arbutus, pipsissewa, hepaticas, bloodroot, twin-flower, trout-lilies, trilliums, European ginger. Many of these require more year-round moisture than sun-loving rock plants but have a shy charm which makes it well worthwhile to cater to their needs.

Even on a moderate-sized place a rock garden makes possible the growing of many intriguing plants; but to be attractive, it must have a really natural appearance.

First a Plan. The location for the rock garden having been selected, the next step is construction. It is advisable to have this begin on paper, for changes are sure to be made as the plan is developed. Several of the principles to be followed are illustrated in the accompanying sketches.

First of all it must be kept in mind that a rock garden is *three dimensional*. Irregularly alternating and nicely balanced elevations and depressions are vital elements in its design.

This same principle of planned irregularity applies also to the ground plan of the rock garden if it is to blend into its background and surroundings without any distinctly definite boundaries. Where ground space is limited, greater height—and therefore more room for planting—may be attained by digging out part of the area to form paths and steps, the soil removed being used to build up the slopes, as indicated by the accompanying sketch.

To attain these ends it may be necessary to sketch and resketch the plan several times—not a difficult task on paper, but a truly herculean one if attempted in actual construction.

Construction. Once the location of the rock garden and the area to be occupied by it have been decided upon the next step is to assemble the materials to be used in building it.

Such a garden implies the use of rocks, but the fact that it is to be a *garden* must never be lost sight of. Hence the first consideration must be the soil to be used.

Most alpines and other plants suited to the sunny rock garden require excellent drainage, but also a soil that retains moisture well after surplus water has drained off. Both heavy

In building the rock garden one must keep in mind that it is three dimensional. It must have height as well as length and depth.

clay soils and light sandy soils are unsuited for this purpose. Alpine plants growing in the wild are usually found in what might be termed a shaly soil—one in which rock debris, in various degrees of decomposition, is present together with a considerable amount of organic matter. A satisfactory mixture for the purpose consists of:

- 1 part gritty, coarse sand
- 1 part stone chips, or very coarse gravel
- 1 part peatmoss (or screened leafmold)
- 2 parts sifted compost or
- 1 part garden loam and 1 part old, spent manure

To this should be added, for lime-loving plants such as cyclamen, edelweiss, gentians, dianthus, alpine primulas, and wallflowers, a generous sprinkling of ground raw limestone. If you are planting peat or acid-lovers such as our native woodland wildlings, acid peatmoss and well-rotted acid leafmold should be used in the mixture. It is well to have a separate area for the lime-lovers.

Loam or compost should be free of weed seeds. The best way to assure this is to treat it with one of the pre-emergence weed seed destroyers before adding it to the mixture. This should be done well in advance.

The Rocks. Both the appearance of the rock garden and the way plants grow in it depend much upon the type of stone used. If native rocks must be employed, there may be little choice in the matter, except to select, as far as possible, flat stones of irregular shapes and rough surfaces rather than rounded, smooth ones. The more absorbent the character of the rock, the better. Limestone and tuffa are the best in this respect, and granite the worst. Porous sandstone and natural outcroppings of ledge rock, cracked and split by erosion to admit pockets of soil and space for root-runs for the plants are also satisfactory. Round fieldstone boulders and cut granite should never be used, as they are unsuited both in appearance and texture.

If a natural ledge is not present, long, rather flat but irregular pieces may be laid and partially buried to create the effect of a natural ledge, especially if some with mosses or lichens growing upon them can be obtained. Wide variation in size of the individual pieces is desirable.

Building. With the materials assembled, the actual construction is begun. First step, under average conditions, is to mark out the area, and excavate it to a depth of a foot or so. Some of the larger stones can be used around the perimeter, but many should be saved for placement higher up or even near the top; otherwise the result will look like a poor attempt at masonry.

When beginning construction, place a number of the largest stones first, to determine the general design. Avoid setting in regular rows, as at left above.

After the ground layer or foundation stones are in place—buried deep enough so that they do not *look* like foundation stones but assume as natural an appearance as possible—"fill" soil is placed in back of them. Then the next tier of rocks is added, with the special soil mixture placed under and around

198   SPECIAL GARDENS, AREAS, AND PLANT MATERIALS

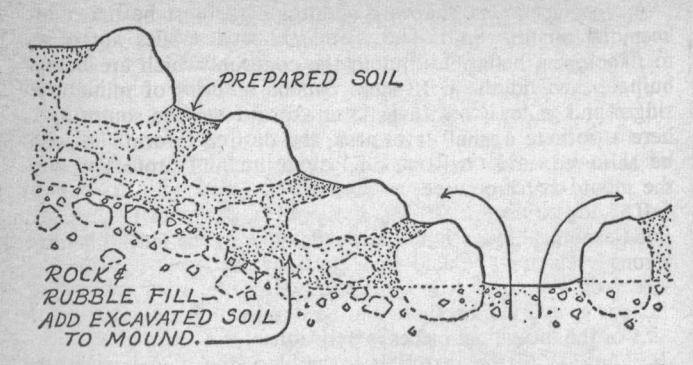

In placing the larger stones in a rock garden, a third to a half of each is covered with soil, and upper surfaces are sloped back to carry water into the soil.

these in deep pockets which run back to the fill. Most of the stones should be placed so that their surfaces slope slightly *down* into the soil behind them. Then any water striking their surfaces will drain back into the soil and be conserved for future use by the deep-penetrating roots of the plants, some of which are many, many times as long as the plants are high.

If the garden is built on a slight slope, the effect of height may be considerably increased by using steps. If each is sloped slightly down *at the back, the effect of height is increased.*

As the work proceeds, the greatest care must be taken to keep the architectural effect *irregular*. This applies not only to the stones themselves but to the contours which are being built up around them. If there can be a series of miniature ridges and valleys, with a general exposure to the south, and here and there a small level area, the desired informality will be achieved; and *also* the ideal exposure and protection for the plants that are to occupy them.

The top of the rock garden should not run up to a peak, but terminate in a series of fairly flat areas or ledges at different levels.

SELECTING THE PLANTS

In deciding what is to be grown in the rock garden, the all important matter of *scale* is most vital. A few plants which are too large, or which in a few years may grow too large, can spoil the whole effect. *The smaller the rock garden is, the more meticulously must this matter of scale be worked out and adhered to.*

Lists of plants especially suited to various types of rock gardens are to be found in Appendix. Some of these are available wherever plants are sold; others are obtainable only from firms which specialize in plants of this type (see Appendix for suggested firms). Anyone who seriously considers attempting a fair-sized rock garden should by all means visit such an establishment, or a botanical garden where rock plants are featured. The visits should preferably be made quite early in the spring as that is when most rock plants flower. Such an inspection will give the prospective rock gardener a much more definite idea of what he can grow successfully on his terrain, and of the appearance and merits of the different species and varieties than he can possibly glean from catalogs.

A great many alpine and other rock plants may easily be grown from seed. This means some delay. However it not only cuts down the expense involved, but provides plants that can be transferred to their permanent locations with minimum shock and under the most favorable conditions.

Culture. The rock garden differs from most other gardens in one important way. It is, in general, desirable to keep the plants within it *small* rather than to encourage them to reach maximum size. This begins with the selection of species and varieties to be planted. It is continued by doing more than the ordinary amount of pruning and cutting back; and by withholding nitrogenous and other plant foods that encourage extra-strong vegetative growth. This does not mean neglecting them.

Keep dead and old wood cut out of all plants which make woody, permanent stems or branches. Recover roots whenever soil is washed away from them or they are bared by frost action or extra-heavy rains. A top dressing made up of one part each of coarse sand, compost, and peatmoss answers for most plants. Where an acid soil is required, add acid leafmold (from beneath evergreens or oaks). For lime-lovers, add ground limestone—enough to thoroughly powder the surface of the soil. Rake in lightly. Wood ashes, scattered and raked in like limestone, may also be used for lime-loving plants. Do not apply too heavy a dose at one time as it may cake and form a crust fatal to the small plants.

Mulching conserves moisture, especially near the surface, and it also helps to keep down the temperature of the surface soil—a result greatly appreciated by the true alpines. For this type of plant material, a mulch of stone chips keeps down weeds, conserves moisture, keeps the soil cool, and adds to the permanent stone-chip content of the soil.

For partly shaded areas where small woodland wildlings are grown, a mulch of peatmoss, acid leafmold, or a mixture of the two is beneficial.

Watering. The rock garden, even when constructed with soil that is high in its capacity to absorb and hold water, is so exposed to wind and sun that it has a tendency to dry out quickly. While many rock plants are toughies that withstand drought, they do better if not subjected to extreme conditions in this direction. An occasional very thorough soaking in dry periods will be much appreciated by the plants. They well repay the extra work when their flowering season recurs.

Winter care of the rock garden involves not so much protecting the plants from cold—most of them are extra hardy—as it does preventing repeated freezing and thawing, and toward spring, the too early renewal of growth. Where the garden is well sheltered and exposed to full sun from mid-winter on, use a cover of evergreen boughs, marsh hay, or pine needles to keep the plants from getting their pretty little pink noses nipped prematurely.

THE BANK GARDEN

The "bank" garden may be merely a variation of the rock garden in which advantage is taken of an existing steep slope or bank or a "problem area" too rough or too steep to be converted into lawn or flower border. A planting of shrubs or low evergreens or of trailing roses or vines would take the curse off it; but the use of a little imagination and ingenuity and a modest collection of rock plants adapted to dry, sunny conditions, may convert it into one of the show spots of the home grounds.

Here a few large rocks, if available, may be used as the setting for a planting of azaleas and other flowering shrubs, with a background of suitable evergreens. Smaller stones and low-growing, spreading rock plants form the foreground.

THE WALL GARDEN

A great many of the rock plants may be enjoyed without building a real rock garden by growing them in a wall.

If it is a retaining wall—that is one built against a bank—the problem is a very simple one, provided the proper type of rocks are available.

In the construction of such a wall, the best effect is achieved when the stones are of the type recommended for the rock garden; rough, varying in size, and porous; preferably with some large ones that may be run well back into the soil behind the wall to give it increased stability (see sketch). Faced, cut stone, cobble stones, and large, rounded boulders are *not* suited to this type of wall as they are completely out of character with the plants to be grown.

The wall, anchored on a solid foundation, should slope back into the bank at a considerable angle, both for stability and the better to display the plants growing in it. The more robust species should be given places near the bottom, with trailing, tufted, and rosette-foliaged types above. Many flowers show off to surprising advantage in a wall garden. For instance, we discovered quite by accident how stunning coral bells (heuchera) are in such a location, the rather tall stems turning sharply upright from the rosettes of glossy leaves and giving somewhat the effect of miniature Roman candles exploding. These and short-spurred columbines, including our native eastern species, also provide irresistible targets for humming birds. Mosses, ferns, sempervivums, creeping phloxes, arabis, iberis, rock garden dianthus, *Campanula muralis,* and many more flourish in such a situation (see list in Appendix).

The free-standing, double-faced wall is another possibility. This can be used to wall in a patio, rose or herb garden, or

202 SPECIAL GARDENS, AREAS, AND PLANT MATERIALS

other area where greater protection or privacy is desired within.

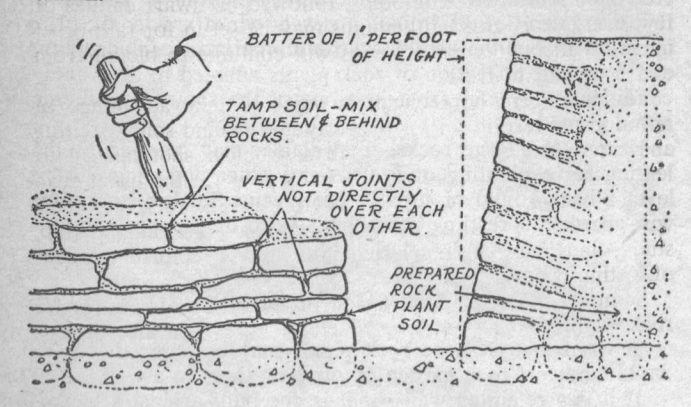

On small places where a steep slope presents a problem, often a rock-garden effect may be achieved by employing a retaining wall for planting. The more it can be sloped back the better.

Such a wall is best built 18 to 24 inches wide—or even wider where large stones are available—with a trench along the top 8 to 12 inches in depth. Plants set in deep soil pockets in the sides of the wall should not be planted too close together. The trench on top, if desired, may be filled with fi-

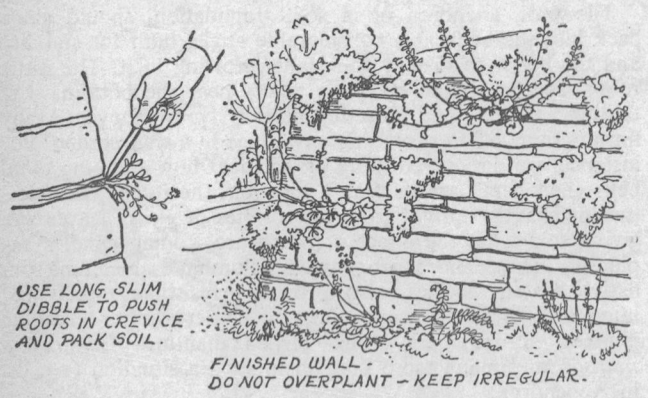

The wall garden should never be overplanted. The most pleasing effect results when most of the stonework is visible.

brous soil and used for a succession of flowers such as low-growing, spring-flowering bulbs, followed by dwarf dahlias or fuchsias. Dwarf chrysanthemums may be set in for fall; or, if in semishade, tuberous begonias will continue to bloom from early summer to frost.

The intelligent homeowner is quick to take advantage of any unusual terrain on his property and to find some exciting and interesting solution for such a problem spot instead of letting the contractor bulldoze a bank down to the usual dead level, cover or remove natural outcroppings of rock, or otherwise destroy areas which may, with a little imagination, study, and labor, be converted into unique, colorful gardens of lasting beauty.

Some of the conditions which provide natural settings for rock, wall, or bank gardens which we have seen are: a large outcropping of ledge rock, split and checked by erosion; an old, abandoned quarry; the ruined cellar hole of a house; the foundation of a bank barn with the rock work partially intact.

> Fringed pool,
> Ferned grot—
> The veriest school
> of Peace; . . .
> *My Garden* by
> THOMAS EDWARD BROWN

CHAPTER 13

Pools, Streams, and Water Gardens

Without question there is no single feature in the home landscape that is quite so effective, in proportion to the space which it occupies, as a pool, a stream or a water garden. Yet the number of places where any of these is to be found is very small.*

At our former home we had a steep, rocky slope that lent itself perfectly to the making of a miniature waterfall, fed by a little stream that trickled down, over, and through rough rocks to an ivy-bordered pool. The result was so natural in appearance that most visitors had to be "shown" before being convinced that it was not natural. After seeing rose gardens, bulb plantings, flower borders, vegetable garden, and whatever else they happened to find most interesting, it would be at this spot that visitors always congregated to rest in the shade and enjoy the sound and sight of water in motion.

At our present home, where we are perched above a tidewater river and overlook a fair-sized salt pond (it would be called a lake anywhere but on Cape Cod) our more intimate,

---

* The swimming pool will not be included in this discussion. A little imagination in planning the location of the pool, and the judicious use of shrubbery and other plant material as screening around the pool, can do much to make it fit into the over-all design. On a swimming pool project it is usually best to consult an expert.

man-made stream and pool, though planned, has been left until other projects have been completed.

To return, however, from our own problems to those of our readers, we would strongly urge that, before attempting to install any water feature of his own, the gardener first visit a public park, botanical garden, or the garden of a friend who has developed water features, where he can get ideas and study the mechanics involved in the construction of a pool or stream. The building of a *formal* pool or a damlike waterfall is comparatively simple. To get a really natural effect, however, though far more charming if successful, requires much more planning and skill.

Design is all-important in building a pool, a stream, or a bog or water garden. Where cement must be used—and in most instances it has to be—you can't make changes once it has begun to set. Usually it saves time in the end, as well as assuring much more satisfactory results, if one constructs in advance a small scale model of the project that is contemplated. Plasticine and small stones and stone chips of various sizes are the chief materials required. These, insofar as is feasible, should resemble in shape and character the rocks that will actually be used. Clippings from evergreens such as junipers, box, or box-leaved ilex may be used to give the effect of plantings. Bare twigs give the effect of deciduous trees in winter.

When it comes to the real construction, the result will by no means be an actual replica of the model; but the model will have served its purpose by saving many mistakes and much more time than was required to make it.

Location. The pool must be planned as an integral part of the general landscape scheme. Careful consideration should be given to the best location for the projected pool and the best *type* of pool for that location.

A lily pool, which requires full sun, is the best choice for grounds with few trees. A natural woodland pool, its outlet forming a wet area for bog plants is indicated on a property well shaded by large trees. On the small property it may be placed close to one of the boundary lines, with suitable evergreens or shrubs behind it. Here it may be the focal point of a private family retreat with the benefit of shifting shade.

One of the most attractive features of a pool may be its service as a mirror for the sky and for nearby plant material. This should always be taken into consideration in planning its location—another decided advantage, on a small property, in placing it as suggested above.

Often a pool and a stream may be combined without a

206 SPECIAL GARDENS, AREAS, AND PLANT MATERIALS

great deal more expense and work than would be required for either alone. Each enhances the effect of the other, and the combination adds greatly to the illusion of naturalness.

Construction. Fortunately for those who like to do their own construction jobs about the place, the making of a small stream or pool has been very much simplified by the advent of heavy plastic sheeting such as Visqueen, obtainable at any dealer in building supplies. If a layer of this tough but pliant material is placed over the foundation layer of cement—troweled smooth of course—before the surface or finish layer is put on, the result is a sort of sandwich, leakproof even though cracks may develop in the concrete.

Every homeowner who likes to be his own jack-of-all-trades should learn to use concrete. Good handbooks on the subject are available. Some of the best are put out by cement companies, and are available where cement is sold, so we do not go into the subject in our limited space here. For small jobs, ready-mixed concrete—containing the correct proportions of cement, sand, and gravel, and requiring only the addition of water—may be purchased. For any extensive work

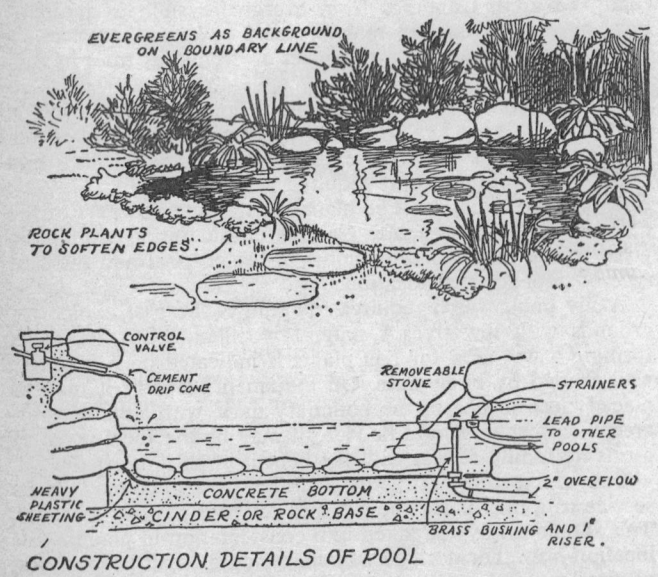

CONSTRUCTION DETAILS OF POOL

A pool, even a very small one, may make one of the most attractive features of the home landscape.

it is much less expensive to purchase the cement only and get the sand and gravel separately. Any surplus of either of these will be good for many other uses about the place.

Where there is a natural supply of water, and heavy clay soil, it may be possible to do without cement work in making a stream or a pool; but such conditions are seldom to be found. Without them, the best that can be done is to make all construction as inconspicuous as possible, and then to use creeping plants that will camouflage what cannot be concealed. Here are some of the most useful plants for this purpose:

Sun	*Shade*
ANNUALS	
Mesembryanthemums	*Bellis perennis*
Sedums	Lobelia, dwarf
Sempervivums	Myosotis
Sweet alyssum	Virginia stock
Thunbergia	
Verbena	
Vinca rosea	
PERENNIALS	
Alyssum saxatile citrinum	*Ajuga reptans*
Ajuga reptans	Arbutus, Trailing
Arabis caucasia	Campanula
Campanula carpatica	Eupatoriums
Cerastium	Ferns, dwarf
Heather	*Hedera helix*
Iberis sempervirens	Heuchera
Iris, dwarf	Hosta
Lamium maculatum	Mertensia
	Mitchella repens
	Phlox divaricata
	Primulas
	Pulmonaria saccharata
	Pulmonaria augustifolia
	Veronicas, Creeping
	Vinca minor
	Violets
	Wild ginger

Water supply. The commonly held assumption that any water feature in the garden, with the possible exception of a static pool, requires an extraordinary supply of water is quite erroneous. Little more than a trickle is needed to keep a moderate-sized pool replenished and fresh. This same trickle, dripping down the "steps" of a miniature water course, can provide an effect of naturalness and coolness out of all proportion to its size and cost.

The line supplying the water should of course be equipped with a gate valve which permits control of the amount coming through. Then, with a turn of the wrist, the trickle may be converted into a cascading freshet whenever that is desired. A ¾-inch pipe is ample for a fairly vigorous stream.

In cold climates, provision should be made for draining the system during the winter. This means the installation of drain cocks at all low points in the supply line.

THE WATER GARDEN

It is rather difficult to make plain just what the difference is between a pool which contains plants and a water garden. Perhaps it may be helpful to say that in the former it is the pool itself which is the more important while in the latter it is the *plants*—the water being merely an adjunct to their proper culture.

The ideal water garden should have areas of both sun and shade. A small stream supplying it with water may be planted with moisture-loving shrubs like our beautiful native *Clethra alnifolia* or sweet pepperbush; the swamp azalea (*Rhododendron viscosum*); *Ilex verticillata* or winterberry, with its red berries; and *I. glabra* or inkberry, which is evergreen. Nearer the stream such moisture-loving plants as cardinal-flower, foamflower, and gentians may be grown, with a ground cover of myosotis, wild ginger, or cranberry.

In the sunny portion of the pool, pickerel-weed, water arum, pond-lilies, and other water plants are at home (see list, Appendix).

The bog or marsh garden is naturally placed at the pool's outlet, where peaty soil may be provided to hold plenty of moisture. Here water irises, including our native blue flag; Japanese iris; mallows, pitcher plants, adder's tongues; the wild turk's cap lily, *L. superbum;* Jack-in-the-pulpit; marsh-marigolds and violets may be grown in wild profusion (see list, Appendix).

Water gardening is of such a specialized type that anyone planning to go into it at all extensively should procure detailed information either from one of the specialists who supply aquatic plants, or from a book devoted to this subject (see list, Appendix).

Winter care. Except in southern sections of the United States, where low temperatures are not severe enough to form thick ice, it is best to drain pools for the winter months. An alternate ensurance against ice damage to the concrete often used with small bowl-like pools with gently sloping sides is to place a small bundle of corn or sunflower stalks upright in the center. The ice, as it forms and expands, pushes up the sides of the pool, and in at the center. A log or two thrown into the water serves the same purpose. Draining, however, is much safer and more sightly.

Fish. In pools of any size it is customary to have some fish. Naturally they go with water plants. Not only do they lend interest with their color and flashing movements, but they act as scavengers. In an outdoor pool that must be drained for winter, they present the problem of being kept over until spring. They may be kept in an aquarium, but replacement with new stock each spring is not expensive, unless rare species are preferred. In a deep, natural pool where water is not drained, all but tropical varieties live comfortably in the deep water under the ice. Only a bitter winter which freezes the water in the pool to the bottom may destroy them.

> I've often wished that I had clear
> For life, six hundred pounds a year,
> A handsome house to lodge a friend,
> A river at my garden's end,
> A terrace...
>
> — ALEXANDER POPE

CHAPTER 14

The Patio Garden, Mobile Gardening, Window Boxes

The dictionary definition of a patio is: "A court or courtyard of a house ... especially an inner court ... open to the sky."

The patio garden of today, in the United States at least, may be considerably less formal. Its purpose is as often to form a connecting link between the house and the grounds as it is to shut out the world beyond. In either case the patio becomes a sort of outdoor living room, with the sky for a ceiling and the walls as nearly solid, or as completely open, as the owner desires.

The patio garden most properly goes with a Spanish or other tropical or semitropical type of dwelling. It may of course be adapted to other forms of architecture, but the design and the materials used in building a patio should harmonize with the dwelling to which it is attached—or more accurately (if the design is well thought out) *of which it forms a part*.

Often an L of the house provides two walls of the patio. A free-standing wall, vine-covered fence, or louvered barrier is used as another side and the fourth is left open. Where the patio is used chiefly in summer, its open side should face east or south, never west, unless it is well protected from late sun

THE PATIO GARDEN, MOBILE GARDENING, WINDOW BOXES 211

by large shade trees. Otherwise the broiling rays of late afternoon sun in midsummer would make it too hot and uncomfortable to use during the hours when it is most needed.

In any case, it is desirable to have trees to provide some overhead shade during the warm months. These of course can be planted (or already growing) outside the boundaries of the patio garden itself. Deciduous trees, which do not completely shut out winter sunshine, are preferable to evergreens. Fast-growing species such as Chinese or Siberian elm, tulip tree, sycamore, *Paulownia tomentosa* (or Princess tree), *Magnolia soulangeana* (our early-blooming pink or white magnolia), willow, or (in Area IV) mimosa (*Albizzia julibrissin*), or *Zelkova carpinifolia*, which is hardly as far north as New England, will soon grow large enough to begin to provide shade. Maples, though fast-growing, are undesirable because of surface roots which often force up paving, even at some distance from the tree trunk.

Year-round beauty. Even though the patio—except in very warm climates—may be used as an outdoor living room only during the summer months, it should remain attractive through the winter as well, particularly if it forms a part of the vista from a view window. To achieve this end, dwarf or semidwarf evergreens, of varied winter foliage, broad-leaved evergreen shrubs and vines, and plants like *Pyracantha coccinea lalandi* (Firethorn) and *Cotoneaster microphylia*, which can form effective silhouettes against a wall, are indispensable. Berried shrubs attract birds, an added winter dividend.

Remember that the protection afforded by the house and by the patio walls in effect moves the area at least one zone south of its actual location. As a result, many plants may be grown within the patio walls which might not survive about the grounds in the open. Among these are the less hardy types of box, evergreen azaleas; such semihardy shrubs as *Abelia grandiflora*, nandina, crape-myrtle (Lagerstroemia), and even the hardier camellias. On one of our own well-sheltered terraces we enjoy a collection of half a dozen camellias, including named varieties of both the hardier *C. sasanqua* and the more tender *C. japonica*. These get no protection except a temporary cover of a double sheet of heavy-duty pliofilm when temperatures threaten to go below 10 above zero, which seldom happens on this part of Cape Cod.

What has been said concerning evergreens and shrubs applies also to vines. The wall-clinging sorts such as the various evergreen euonymuses and the deciduous climbing hydrangea, *H. petiolaris*, appreciate the extra protection they get. Many climbers may be kept pruned to form charming traceries against a wall instead of making solid masses of greenery. Fruit trees, especially peaches, apricots, pears, and (in warmer sections) figs are suitable for espaliering. The fun of training and pruning these to the desired patterns is almost as satisfying as the lovely effects they create, silhouetted against a light-colored wall.

All hardy, permanent plants used in the patio are merely the stage setting for the many ornamentals that may be grown in pots and tubs or plant boxes, to be enjoyed while they are in flower and then removed to make way for others.

If one has a greenhouse, the display may be practically continuous from the time danger of frost is over until hard freeze in the fall. Even with a coldframe it may commence long before there is any show of color in beds and borders in the open garden.

Many flowers lend themselves particularly to display in this way. Grown in pots in a greenhouse, frame, or the open-garden cutting bed, they may readily be transferred to the patio just before they come into full bloom. If plunged into prepared holes or narrow beds filled with crushed stone or sand and peatmoss, the pots are readily kept moist through the flowering period.

A "plunging" border around the edges of a patio makes it possible to maintain a more or less constant succession of blooming plants in pots. Sink these to the rims in gravel, marble chips, or peatmoss, depending on the subjects, exposure, etc.

The large number of flowers well suited to such use include many of the new hybrid lilies, grown in large pots holding several bulbs each. A moderate assortment of varieties provides a succession of bloom over a period of two to three months and the bulbs may be used over again in succeeding years.

Other plants for the patio are forced spring-flowering bulbs and tender summer-flowering species like callas, agapanthus, amarcrinums, nerines, *Lycoris radiata*, and amaryllis. Tuberous begonias and gloxinias are ideal for shady spots, the former giving continuous bloom from May to first frosts.

Hydrangeas, roses, and tender foliage plants in tubs are a great addition if there is man-power to move them. Large nasturtium plants (grown under glass in the north) in handmade pottery containers are colorful and appropriate, and of course for the last blaze of color, chrysanthemums, even after their buds are showing color, can be moved in pots or tubs, or set directly in prepared beds.

WATER FEATURES IN THE PATIO

The ideal place for a small wall or free-standing fountain, a tiny water-fall, or a small pool, is in the patio. Its effectiveness will depend to a very great extent, on the owner's artistic sense in designing and placing it. Resist that temptation to plunk it down in the center of the area, like an old-fashioned fountain in a public square!

Much of the charm of any water feature depends upon sound as well as on motion. The exception of course is the mirror pool, but this properly belongs in a fairly large and formal setting rather than in the outdoor living-room atmosphere of the average patio.

Consider the birds. One of the reasons for having water in the patio garden is that it attracts birds. The small pool on our terrace is used constantly by our feathered tenants from earliest spring until it freezes solid in midwinter. One reason for its great popularity is the shelter afforded on two sides by a large tree and tall-growing, moisture-loving wild shrubs that thrive in the damp soil created by the overflow before it is absorbed by our thirsty, sandy subsoil.

This little pool was not included in our original landscape plan. It just happened. A quantity of mixed concrete, left over from a masonry wall had to be disposed of—but fast! We scooped out a shallow, oval depression with slanting sides, and troweled on a three-inch layer of concrete. Later, this was covered with heavy black plastic, and a second layer finished off the edge and covered the plastic from view. Of course the area was kept covered with wet bags, permitting

214 SPECIAL GARDENS, AREAS, AND PLANT MATERIALS

the concrete to dry out gradually. Around it we planted sedums, small-leaved ivies, and myrtle, which soon crept over the concrete edge toward the water, making it look completely natural.

A border for permanent planting around or near the patio may add greatly to its privacy and its attractiveness when viewed from indoors.

From the very first this miniature pool (which is within 10 feet of the nearest view window and also visible when we are at table) has been a favorite spot for song birds of all sorts. The robins use it not only for bathing, splashing, and drinking, but also as headquarters for cherry washing and tenderizing. As soon as the wild black cherries begin to turn color, they are harvested by the hundreds from the tall, old trees on our river shore some distance away and carried to the pool. At the end of the cherry season each year we have to empty the pool and sweep out the accumulated pits. (For a further discussion of water features in the garden, see Chapter 13.)

In planning the patio, one of the most important things to consider—and one very frequently overlooked—is the view from inside the house. This applies especially in cool climates, where for more than half the year it can be enjoyed only from within doors.

Especially in a modern house with glass walls, ceiling-to-floor doors of glass, or large view windows, the patio can be an integral part of the indoor living area in summer when doors are open. In winter, the patio provides an interesting near view complete with birds, if berried shrubs and evergreens form a part of its permanent planting. Therefore it should, if possible, be placed so that it can be seen from the living or dining room. Not only is it a focal center in itself, but also forms an intimate foreground to enhance more distant garden views.

A very important supplement to the patio garden is a coldframe or, still better, a greenhouse—even a *very* small one—where plants may be brought into bud or bloom before being transferred to the patio for temporary effects. Spring-flowering bulbs, such as tulips and daffodils; small flowering shrubs like azaleas or gardenias; spring- and summer-flowering perennials and annuals in variety can provide a long succession of bloom culminating in the glorious display of chrysanthemums in autumn. The smaller the space devoted to gardening *outside* the patio, the more important it is to provide a fine succession of bloom within it. This is what is known as "mobile" gardening.

WINDOW BOXES

With or without a patio, window boxes provide a neglected opportunity for effectively displaying plants. Once very popular, they gradually went out of style and only recently they have returned as decorative features in modern homes. People have discovered that they do not *have* to be planted with geraniums, vincas, and old-fashioned, scraggly "balcony" petunias. In Europe window boxes have long played an important part in gardening and their revival in this country, especially for suburban community homes where ground areas are limited, is an encouraging sign. The modern view window provides another opportunity for the effective use of window boxes. If the window goes to the floor level, a suitable box-like bed or bed-like box with adequate drainage may be made level with it. Even more effective, however, is the eye-level, or more accurately, chair-level box, attached to the house wall just below the window sill.

Window boxes also give us another opportunity for displaying plants while in flower, or at their best. When the bloom is over they are replaced by others. Plants grown in pots are of course especially well suited for such treatment. A "succession" display of early tulips (including the new species hybrids) can be followed by geraniums, begonias, or any of the compact long-flowering annuals such as petunias, marigolds, and ageratum. Trailers like coleus, thunbergia, nasturtiums, German or Kenilworth-ivy will carry through until danger of frost. These may be followed by dwarf chrysanthemums to give color until hard freeze, especially if they are given a temporary protective covering on cold nights.

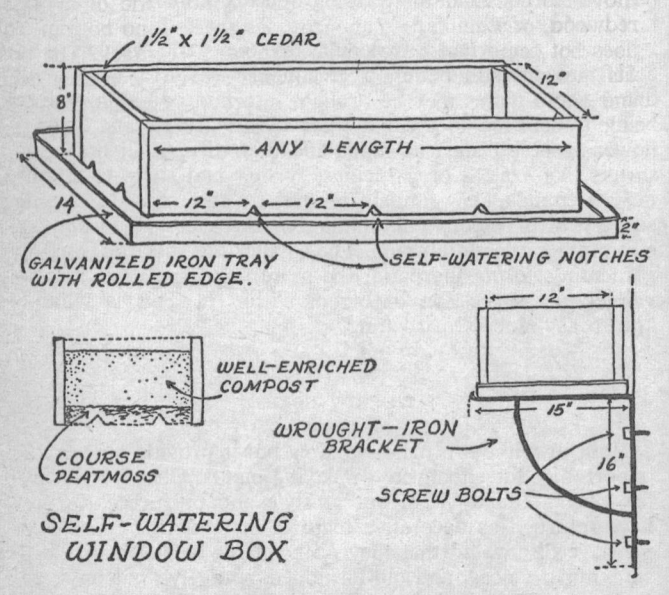

SELF-WATERING WINDOW BOX

Our own window boxes are all on the north and northeast sides of the house, where they get plenty of light but only very early morning sunshine. The only flowers we grow in these are tuberous begonias, supplemented by trailing fuchsias and a variety of vines from the greenhouse. In our moderate autumn climate the begonias continue to flower—unless it is a hurricane year!—until late in October. In winter these boxes are either removed or filled with dwarf juniper branches and black alder berries. In summer they draw more admiration and are more photographed by visitors than any other plants on the place.

In warm climates, cacti and succulents make ideal window-box subjects the year-round, as do such showy foliage plants as aucubas, dracaenas, and philodendrons. All these are suitable for modern homes. In the north they may be used during the growing season if there is a suitable place to overwinter them indoors.

We believe that poor construction is one of the reasons that window boxes are not more widely used. If a box rots out in a year or two it is a poor investment. Years ago we developed a simple "lifetime" window box. It isn't patented, so any reader can have one made. The accompanying line cut shows its construction. The box should be made of cypress, redwood, or Philippine mahogany. As there is no bottom, rot does not occur there, always its first point of attack. The box fits into a watertight pan of galvanized iron, 2 inches deep and about 3 inches wider and 3 inches longer than the outside dimension of the box. Water is run into the pan and rises up through the soil, which remains friable and open. A mulch of rough compost, added after plants have been set, helps to keep it that way. In case of heavy rains or overwatering, surplus water in the pans is siphoned off in a few minutes with a short piece of ¼-inch rubber hose. Supports for the boxes should be *very* rugged. We use 2 × ¼-inch iron brackets fastened to the wall by ¼-inch lag bolts.

> Where the petal of a rose
> Blushes in the solitude!
> *The Petal of a Rose*
> by JAMES STEPHENS

CHAPTER 15

Roses and Rose Gardens

THE ROSE GARDEN

Since gardening began, the most popular of all flowers has been the rose. The appeal of other flowers may wax and wane, but the Queen of Flowers remains unrivaled in our own and many other lands.

The beginning gardener who thinks that this popularity stems from the fact that roses are easy to grow will find himself mistaken. Although certain original species of shrub roses and their direct descendants are among the most persistent of flowering shrubs, success with modern garden roses requires some knowledge of the plant's requirements and a willingness to give it the attention it needs. Hundreds of thousands of gardeners the world over, however, are convinced that roses are worth it.

Variety is one reason for the universal appeal of the rose —variety not only in flower form, color, and size of the individual blossoms, but also in the almost unbelievable range in type of plant and habit of growth. If one requires a pot plant 6 inches tall for a window sill or miniature garden; a 20-foot climber; a flowering hedge; a cover for a bank with gravelly, poor soil; a group of weatherproof and self-sufficient flowering shrubs; or exquisite, long-stemmed, fragrant blooms for indoor decoration—and winning prizes at flower shows!—one need not venture beyond the family of "la belle rosa."

Members of this grand genus flourish from Florida to Alaska and from Mexico to Nova Scotia. Not all species and varieties range over the entire area, of course, for there are tender as well as extra-hardy types. With some winter protection, however, most of the modern, strong-growing, large-flowered hybrids can be grown satisfactorily through most of North America.

WHAT TYPE OF ROSE GARDEN?

Before ordering *any* plants, the wise beginner will learn the various types of roses available, what their requirements are, and how they may be used in the landscape. Then he should draw a plan, though it may be a rough one, and figure out how many plants, and *of what types,* he can accommodate. Only after this has been done should he allow himself to pore over the lavishly illustrated catalogs and make out an order for the roses that seem to suit his particular needs. A rundown on the types of roses follows:

I. *Garden Roses.* For a real rose garden of many varieties, planted in beds, for display and for cutting. Included are Hybrid Teas, Floribundas, Grandifloras, and—for southern gardens—Teas. EXAMPLES: Hybrid Teas: Peace, New Yorker, Hawaii. Floribundas: Fashion, Spartan, Betsy McCall, Betty Prior. Grandifloras: Queen Elizabeth, War Dance, Pink Parfait. Teas: Lady Hillington, Maman Cochet.

II. *Climbers.* While no roses actually climb, in the strict sense of the word, there are many which may readily be trained to supports such as trellises, posts, walls, and arbors. The more vigorous of these attain heights of 15 to 20 feet or more, especially in the south. EXAMPLES: Large-flowered Climbers: Blaze, New Dawn, and Climbing Hybrid Teas, which, as a class, are less hardy. Lower-growing Climbers are known as Pillars, attaining a height of 8 to 12 feet. EXAMPLES: Golden Showers, Inspiration, Coral Dawn. The old-fashioned, small-flowered Rambler type of Climber has been improved and reblooms throughout the season in varieties such as Chevy Chase and Crimson Shower.

III. *Trailers* are Climbers which make long canes that trail and spread horizontally over a bank, rock, wall, or even on level ground. This type used to be seen frequently on railroad embankments. EXAMPLES: Max Graf, Nearly Wild, Little Compton Creeper, Magic Carpet, Yellow Creeping Everbloom; also the Rambler group like Dorothy Perkins.

IV. *Hedge Roses* are quite tall-growing, thick, and bushy, and valuable not only for their profuse bloom, but primarily to serve as hedges. For this purpose, due to their thick growth and thorns, they are particularly effective. EXAMPLES: Red Robin, Hybrid 311, Robin Hood, Frensham. (Multiflora, much advertised for this purpose, is not recommended except for use on large farms or country places where extensive acreage is to be hedged in.)

V. *Edging Roses* are dwarf, or low, compact-growing roses, suitable for edging borders, rose gardens, or walks. They are chiefly in the small-flowered polyantha (many flowers in clusters) group. EXAMPLES: Pygmy—Yellow, Lavender, or Red; Margo Koster, Carroll Ann.

VI. *Miniature Roses* are quite distinct from all the above in that, although normal roses in plant habit, growth, and flowering, they are diminutive in size. The plants average 8 to 18 inches in height, and the flowers about an inch in diameter. In spite of their frail appearance, however, we have found them extremely resistant to general plant troubles and to cold. Most of them are really very small Hybrid Teas, in habit and form, though they are somewhat of a mystery in Rosedom. Their reappearance dates back to the early 1900s with the introduction of *Rosa rouletti*, which was found on a cottage window sill in the Swiss Alps; but there are records indicating importation, about 1815, to Europe from the Orient. Later they disappeared, to turn up again in Switzerland. For some years these little gems attracted attention principally as a curiosity. Recently, however, many new colors and named varieties have been introduced. Their sale has been pushed, and they have become tremendously popular, especially for indoors and for home greenhouses, where their dwarf stature and long, continued flowering period have proven great assets. EXAMPLES: Pixie, Baby Gold Star, Bo Peep.

VII. *Shrub Roses,* as the term implies, are those which in form, habit, and culture look and are treated like average ornamental shrubs. As a rule they more closely resemble the original species from which modern garden roses have been developed. While as a group they are hardier and less subject to pests and diseases than the garden roses, they are coarser in growth and much less floriferous than the modern hybrids. Many have brilliantly colored flowers and later very large or showy seed pods or "hips," which are quite as decorative as the flowers and much longer lasting. A few may well be used in any sizable planting of mixed shrubs. EXAMPLES: Harison's Yellow, an old farmyard and cemetery favorite; The Fairy; Mabelle Stearns; the Rugosas and their many hybrids; the Briers and their hybrids.

PREPARING THE ROSE GARDEN

A rose garden is one of the most rewarding horticultural projects that a homeowner can undertake—but it is not one of the simplest. You must plan and prepare it carefully, and give it care throughout the season—and this means from the time the frost leaves the ground in the spring until it freezes solid again in autumn. Otherwise, results are likely to be only mediocre.

Site. Ideal exposure for the rose garden is one to the east or south, with air drainage to a lower level, and preferably with some protection to the north and west from strong winds or storms. Soil drainage also should be excellent. In heavy, poorly drained soil, tile should be used (see page 37).

Soil. Clay soil used to be considered essential for the growing of good roses. We have seen—*and have grown*—as good roses on light sandy soil, properly handled and supplemented, as on clay. (All that is needed for success is to follow the suggestions for soil improvement given in Chapter 2.)

Soil *preparation,* however, is of the utmost importance. Roses are a long-time crop and the bed should be prepared to be adequate for many years to come. By the end of the second or third year, the roots of strong growing plants will extend down into the bed for several feet. Therefore, some of the old authorities advocated preparing the soil to a depth of 4 feet. Such an extreme is not necessary, but 18 inches, *by the ruler,* is the minimum. Most successful rose growers prepare the soil to 24 inches, and the general rule is: "the deeper the better."

Cow manure used to be considered another "must" for the rose garden, but in most localities today it can be had, if at all, only in the processed dry form. Good roses, indeed excellent roses, can be grown without it if the rose beds are well supplied with *humus,* in the form of peatmoss or other organic material, plus a goodly proportion of organic fertilizers. Roses are not overparticular about soil acidity; a pH of from 6 to nearly 7 (neutral) is agreeable to them.

Drainage, however, is another matter. Roses must have abundant moisture to provide continuous good bloom throughout the season, but water-soaked soil, even well below the surface, will prove injurious at any season of the year.

To make the best display, on the other hand, roses require

a constant supply of moisture in the soil during the entire growing season. For this reason the homeowner who wishes to make a feature of his rose garden will do well to provide an adequate watering system. For a rose garden of any size, a mere sprinkling with a hose is not only time-consuming but inadequate. Watering devices of many kinds are available (see Chapter 5), but to get uniform distribution with least work in a garden of 50 or more plants, for example, a permanent system of some sort is desirable.

Overhead watering of garden roses is to be avoided because moist foliage, particularly during hot, muggy weather,

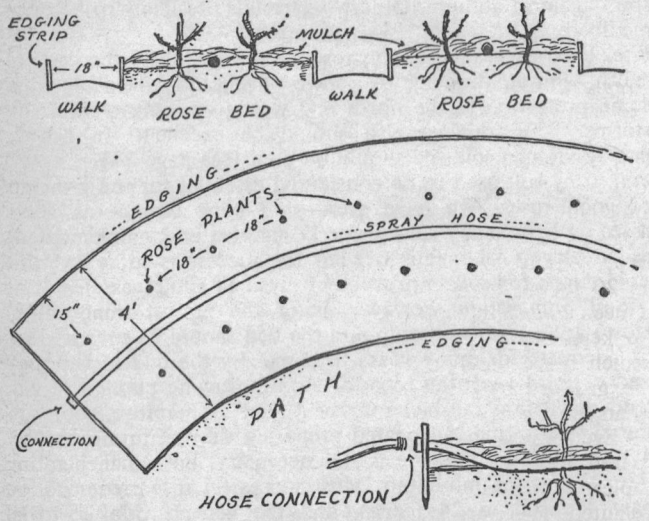

Self-watering system for rose garden. Merely connect hose and turn on spigot. No water gets on foliage to invite black spot.

encourages the development of diseases, especially black spot and mildew—the *bêtes noires* of the rose gardener in most parts of the country. Overhead watering also is likely to deceive the novice into thinking he has given his rose beds a thorough watering when in reality moisture may have penetrated the soil but little below the surface.

Having tried many different watering systems, we have worked out one which uses a perforated hose, *inverted*, left permanently in place for the season and covered with a fairly deep (2- to 3-inch) mulch. A line of hose is stretched along the center of each bed containing two rows of plants. The open end of the sprinkler hose is passed through a short, stout stake a few inches above the ground level, at the end of the bed. A regular hose, coupled to this and allowed to run for a half hour or more, gives the soil of the rose beds a slow, deep soak, with no wetting of foliage or even of the upper surface of the mulch.

At the end of the season the lengths of sprinkler hose are rolled up and stored for the winter, so that they do not interfere with any hilling or mulching that may be required for winter protection in cold climates.

PLANTING ROSES

Preparation. Before planting a rose garden, the entire area, including the paths, should be deep dug and thoroughly prepared. Roots will extend into the soil under the paths. Beds are best laid out to accommodate two or three rows only. We prefer two, since a middle row is difficult to reach for pruning, spraying, weeding, or even gathering flowers.

Plants should be set 18 to 30 inches apart according to type, variety, and culture to be given. A satisfactory average is 20 to 24, though such extra-vigorous plants as Peace or Queen Elizabeth should have all of 30. Pruning usually helps to keep the more vigorous specimens from pre-empting too much space. In a large garden, extra-vigorous varieties may be grouped by themselves and given somewhat more room than the others.

Even when the total bed area has been thoroughly prepared and fertilized, we like to make individual planting holes, marked by stakes bearing names of varieties to be planted. These are prepared by digging to a depth of 15 to 18 inches, and mixing in the bottom of each hole a quart or two of peatmoss, and about a pint mixture of ⅔ dehydrated manure and ⅓ bonemeal.

For climbing roses and shrub and bush roses which are planted individually, it is also important to prepare planting holes very thoroughly. Once established, their roots will spread far and deep, but unless they can get off to a strong start, they may never make the display expected of them. We make planting holes at least 18 inches wide and deep and set the plants 3 inches or so below the ground level (covering the "knob" or "graft" by at least an inch) to assure their getting all available moisture.

Supports for climbing roses should be substantial and permanent. The spindle-wood trellises and arbors so widely sold are next to worthless and usually have to be replaced within a few years, at considerable expense and with some damage to the roses.

Post-and-chain supports made of sturdy cedar posts 6 to 8 feet tall with two loops of sturdy chain running from post to post are ideal for vigorous growers (see sketch page 225). The posts are sunk 3 feet in the ground and placed at 8 to 10 foot intervals. A cedar post with sturdy cleats nailed across it at intervals makes a good support for pillar roses. Rambler and other small-flowered types, the canes of which are numerous but not heavy (as old canes are removed each year), may be supported on a trellis or arbor. These should be constructed of 1×3-inch strips, with sturdy uprights to hold them. Whatever type is chosen, supports should be in place before planting.

Planting. More and more, roses are being sold as growing plants, even in bud or flower, in generous-sized composition pots. Of course, these may be planted at any time, but the earlier, the better.

Fall or spring planting? Most home gardeners, however, still buy dormant, bare-root plants which are shipped either in the late fall or very early spring. In northern sections where ground may freeze hard in late September or early October, spring planting becomes a necessity. In mild climates, fall planting gives plants an early start in spring. In either case, *the earlier the plants can be set out the better.* In fact the terms "fall" and "spring" planting are misleading. "Early-winter" and "late-winter" would be more accurate, for plants (except where they may be procured locally) cannot be purchased at the tail-end of fall. If not shipped until mid-spring, they will have started into growth, despite all attempts to keep them dormant.

Unless the plants can be set out immediately upon receipt, they should at once be buried in a coldframe or trench, with damp peatmoss about the roots and covered with moist soil.

Plants are usually pruned and ready for planting before being shipped, but even so it is well to go over them carefully with *sharp* pruning shears. Long or broken roots and bruised, broken, or spindly branches should be trimmed back by cutting just above an outward-pointing bud.

Plants are set so that, when soil has been filled in and firmed down, the level is just an inch or so above the "knuckle"—the somewhat swollen section of the stem above the roots which indicates where the plant was budded. Few garden roses are grown on their own roots. For this reason plants should always be carefully watched to see if any roots originate *below* this point. These are removed at once, as they come from the rootstock. They may usually be identified by the fact that they have seven leaflets instead of the five which distinguish most hybrid varieties.

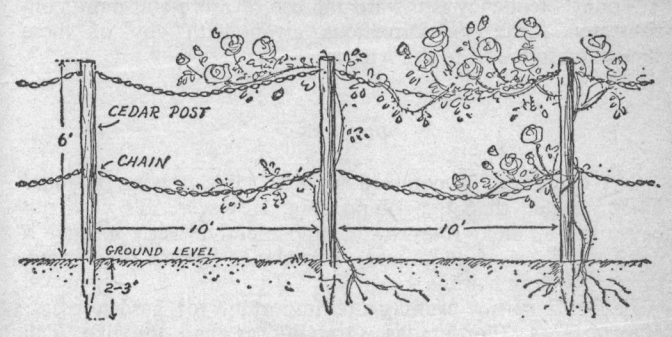

A support for climbing roses that will last a lifetime. Cedar post (set in concrete) and galvanized chain.

Feeding. No ornamental plants in the garden are hungrier than roses. When one considers the amount of new growth that is made, much of which is removed in cutting blooms and pruning, this is not surprising.

Most display rose gardens are fed repeatedly throughout the season. The average home rose garden or border will produce satisfactorily with two or three feedings. The first should take place in spring, when any winter mulch and soil protection has been removed or worked in; the second during midsummer, after the big May–June burst of bloom; and the third in autumn, when the plants have finished their September–October show and are being readied for winter. Recently, extensive experiments have demonstrated that the autumn feeding is decidedly beneficial.

What fertilizer to use? There are many special rose foods on the market—at special prices. We have never found that the brand name made much difference in the results. We use a general-purpose fertilizer with an analysis of 6–10–4 for spring and summer, and 5–10–5 for autumn. In addition to this we apply liberal amounts of wood ashes from fireplaces and brush pile in either spring or fall—a form of potash which roses seem to particularly like. An analysis lower in nitrogen would probably serve as well for the late fall application.

The fertilizers suggested above are used at the rate of 3 to

5 pounds per 100 square feet. *Do not* apply fertilizer just in a ring around each plant but spread evenly over the entire surface of the bed, placing as little as possible within 6 or 8 inches of the main stems.

Today's tendency is toward the use of more and more concentrated fertilizers. Directions given with any of these should be followed to the letter.

PRUNING

No operation in connection with rose growing is more hotly debated than that of pruning. However, this need not cause the amateur rosegrower, who merely wishes to have a good show out of doors and some choice blooms for cutting, to get any gray hairs.

Fall and spring pruning are important for garden roses: Hybrid Teas, Floribundas, Grandifloras, and the like. Tall growths should be cut back so that the plants may not whip about in high winds and loosen the roots. If not removed, such long canes are likely to kill back during the winter. Any diseased or broken wood should also be taken out, as should spreading branches inclined to tangle with neighboring plants.

The real pruning should be left until spring. Wood that has died back or has been killed back during the winter is easily recognizable long before leaves begin to develop. This should be removed, cutting to just above an outward-pointing eye, so that the bush will tend to grow to an open center. Thin, weak growths and those that are dying (with dead cores at the center) should also be removed.

How far back to cut? is an open question.

As a general rule, very severe pruning produces fewer but better flowers. Other factors involved, however, include the type and variety of rose, the individual plant, and climatic conditions. In the average garden a colorful over-all display is more desirable than a limited number of extra-fine blooms for cutting.

In the north, where winter damage is usually severe, cutting back to healthy, new wood may involve removing most of the previous year's growth. Farther south, more healthy new wood survives the winter, and may be kept, if tall, bushy plants with many medium-sized blooms are desired.

Light, moderate, or hard? Generally speaking, we may say that there are three types or degrees of pruning.

Light. These bushes are gone over and shaped up. Extra-tall or wayward branches and those that cross and rub against

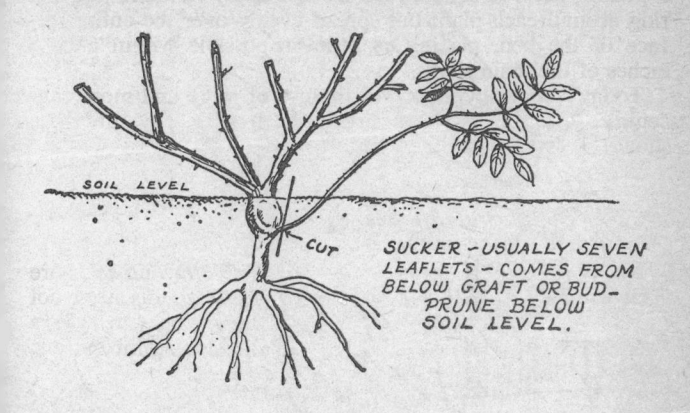

SUCKER—USUALLY SEVEN LEAFLETS—COMES FROM BELOW GRAFT OR BUD—PRUNE BELOW SOIL LEVEL.

others are trimmed back. Weak, inward-growing branches are removed. Up to about a third of the total healthy wood may be cut away.

Moderate. The main stems and the more vigorous side shoots are cut back more severely, taking care always to cut above an outward-facing bud or one that will have room to develop into a sturdy branch without crossing or crowding another vigorous cane. One aims at developing a plant with an open center. The result of such pruning is a reduction in the number of blooms, especially early in the season, but the individual flowers will be larger and of better quality. On an average, a half to two thirds of the plant is removed.

Hard. This means just what the term implies. Two thirds or even more of the body of the plant is discarded. The main canes and laterals are cut back to only two to four eyes each, which will probably mean stubs less than a foot high. The result will be fewer but larger blooms, with longer and more perfect flower stems—the kind that win blue ribbons at flower shows.

Cuts resulting from correct pruning usually self-heal very promptly, but where large canes—a half inch or more in diameter—are removed, it is advisable to apply a tree paint.

Under no circumstances should a short stub be left between a cut and a branch below it, as such stubs tend to die back. Where winter injury is common, it is safer to prune to the first outward-facing bud *below* branched growth, rather than above it, as die-back may occur at the branching point.

Pruning Climbers. The newer, large-flowered remontant or

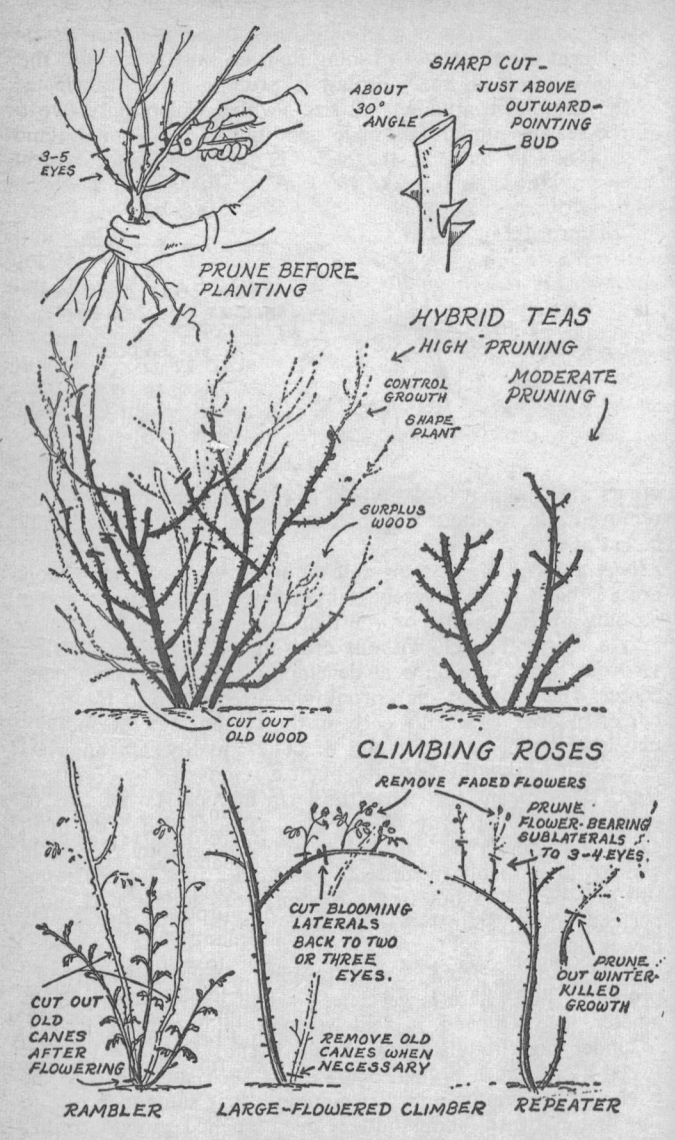

Pruning is a very important factor in growing roses. Study results carefully as a guide to future pruning.

ever-blooming types of climbing roses demand much less attention in the matter of pruning than do bush roses, but they do give a much finer display if pruning is not neglected. After they have attained full size—which will require two or three seasons under favorable conditions—the annual removal of one or more of the oldest canes encourages vigorous new growth. In taking out the old growths, it is best to cut into fairly short sections so that newer canes are not injured in the process of removal. The best time to do this pruning is just after the first big burst of bloom is over. A pair of lopping shears (see page 110) is convenient for this work, as it is a bit heavy for ordinary pruning shears.

In the case of small-flowered, old-fashioned rambler roses, *all old canes* are removed after bloom, leaving only the current year's growth, as bloom occurs each year on new wood.

The removal of dead flower heads is also important in the production of later blooms in large-flowered climbers. Blooms occur on side growths or laterals and dead blooms are snipped off with one or two buds, cutting just above a healthy bud or eye.

SPRING CARE

The first spring work in the rose garden, after all frost is out of the ground, is to remove mulching material and then rake down and incorporate in the soil of the beds the compost or loam that has been hilled up around the bases of canes. (In warm climates, of course, no hilling is necessary and this task does not present itself.)

Next comes the spring pruning—light, moderate, or hard as the gardener elects. In any event, all injured or doubtfully healthy wood, and weak, surplus, or intercrossing growths are removed. All prunings are carefully collected and burned.

The first or dormant spray follows. This may be lime-sulfur, an old but safe compound for the purpose. This spraying should be extra-thorough to give the plants a clean start. It must be applied *before* the leaves begin to unfold. If for any reason it has not been applied when this occurs, omit the dormant spray and make a thorough application of the usual all-purpose rose sprays. Spraying should be continued weekly throughout the growing season from the time the leaves begin to unfold.

The spring feeding comes next (see page 225).

After this, the application of whatever summer mulch, if any, is in order. We are firm believers in mulching for roses.

Of the many materials we have tried, we have found pine needles, tan bark, seaweed, and bagasse (chopped sugar cane stalks) satisfactory. Absorbent materials such as peatmoss may stay too wet. Buckwheat hulls and similar materials dry out and blow about.

Staking may be required for tall varieties, such as the new grandifloras, but we prefer to keep them self-supporting by pruning. Cutting long-stemmed blooms for indoor decoration helps accomplish this.

Cutting roses is really part of their culture. All blooms should be removed as soon as they begin to fade, not only for the sake of appearance, but also because fallen, decaying petals may help spread disease. Always cut just above an outfacing eye which has developed five leaflets, not three. Near the center of our rose garden we keep a large wicker basket into which spent blooms and other trimmings are tossed, then burned. We find this a great help, especially in hot weather when flowers fade quickly.

Regular spray program is essential if pests and diseases are to be fended off. A good all-purpose rose spray or dust should be applied every week or ten days without fail. The beginner who is not willing to tackle this chore regularly will do better to specialize in some less demanding flower.

Sprays are preferred to dusts both because they are more efficient if applied thoroughly and because they do not cover the leaves with residue as many dusts do. We use both a good quality trombone sprayer with a bucket to hold the spray mixture, and the glass-jar type which screws directly onto a garden hose.

Excellent, small-size ball-bearing dusters are now sold by several rose growers and purveyors of dusts. One of these is a "must" if dusting is to be used.

Winter protection. The most important step in winter care of roses is the "hilling up" around the roots in late fall, using garden loam, compost, or very well rotted, littery manure alone or mixed with loam or compost. In northern climates where temperatures go down to zero and below, hilling should be heaped as high as 12 inches. In milder areas, where below-freezing temperatures are common but less severe, 6 or even 4 inches may suffice. This work may be done well in advance of hard freeze if desired, but after the plants begin to go into dormancy.

In extremely cold locations like the Great Plains, climbers are removed from their supports, laid flat on the ground, and covered with soil for the winter. Where temperatures are not quite so low but heavy winter winds are frequent, pillars and lower-growing climbers may be protected with evergreen boughs or small Christmas trees stuck upright in the ground around the plants, bound over the canes and tied to the supports.

Near New York City, where we maintained a large rose garden for many years, we hilled moderately and then covered the beds with cut evergreen boughs which held the snow and kept the rose plants cozily cold, without alternate thawing and freezing, a condition which often results in winter injury.

In spring when danger of hard freeze is past, mulch is removed and "hills" from around the main stems of the rose plants are lightly worked into the surface soil of the beds along with an early spring application of fertilizer.

> Crown'd with the eares of corne, now come,
> And, to the Pipe, sing Harvest home.
>
> ROBERT HERRICK

> "It's Broccoli, dear."
> "I say it's Spinach,
> 'and I say the Hell with it.'"
>
> CARL ROSE.

CHAPTER 16

Vegetables for Better Eating

Why grow one's own vegetables when it is so easy to pick them up, all neatly wrapped in cellophane—cleverly colored to make them look riper or more perfect than they are!—at the nearest chain store? For those with freezers, frozen vegetables have become available in forms especially tempting to the busy housewife. Sliced carrots, chopped onions, potato balls, or even stuffed baked potatoes may be had all ready to heat up and serve.

"Why grow your own?" is a good question. And there are three good answers.

First: You can save money, a considerable amount of it during the year.

Second: You can, with a few exceptions, enjoy very much better quality and flavor.

Third: It's fun doing it!

The amount of money that may be saved depends upon two factors. First, that the home vegetable grower do all, or most, of the work involved. If he has to engage much help—assuming that he can find anyone to do it!—any possible savings will disappear. Second, that a suitable storage place is provided for vegetables to be kept for winter use. Most modern cellars with temperatures up to 60 or 70 degrees are not suitable for storing any of the root crops, though it will take care of winter squash as these require higher storage temperatures. An outdoor storage pit, however, is not difficult to construct. Those with freezers—an ever-increasing percentage of our population—may store most vegetables, frozen, with less effort than that required to winter-store root vegetables. As was mentioned above, even potatoes are frozen today.

As to *flavor*, there is no question that home-grown crops are far superior to most of the vegetables commercially available. This is especially true of leaf vegetables such as lettuce, spinach, chard, the quality of which quickly deteriorates after being cut. It is also true of many others such as peas, beans, asparagus, and corn, which must be fresh-picked to be at their best. The saying that the pot should be boiling before sweet corn is picked is not an old wives' tale. Scientific tests have proved that after picking the sugar content in the kernels decreases rapidly with every passing hour. Green peas of course are in the same category. Items, such as tomatoes, when grown for sale must be picked while still "firm"—a euphemism for "half green"—when they are to be shipped, often thousands of miles, to reach retail markets before they begin to decay. How often for instance does one get, in a market, a melon that is really sweet and luscious, as this fruit should be? Tomatoes, melons, and most other fruit should not be harvested until dead ripe if the true flavor is to be experienced.

There is another, and an even more serious factor to consider in relation to table quality in vegetables. In former days the vegetable-plant breeders' first concern was to improve flavor and tenderness. Now all that has changed. Recently, in an article in a national magazine about the achievements of a famous plant breeder, much stress was laid upon the wonders he had achieved in developing such qualities as greater "eye appeal," crops "all ripe at once" to facilitate harvesting, uniform distance shipping—*but not one word about table quality!*

Fortunately there are still some seedsmen left who cater to the home-garden trade—though their number is small compared to what it was a half century, or even a couple of decades ago.

As to our third claim, that growing one's own vegetables is really fun, we must admit that this is a matter of taste (in both senses of the word) and there is no way of proving it. It is neither a status activity such as golf nor a group sport like sitting in the bleachers watching trained athletes sweating it out while the observer eats peanuts and puts on weight.

Growing some of your own vegetables and fruits is not an activity that can be "sold" by argument. All we can suggest is that the reader try it, on a modest scale at first, to see if he is one of the many who find it worthwhile for the table, the body and the soul!

PRELIMINARIES

The site. While there is a wealth of ornamental plants that either demand or tolerate a considerable amount of shade, when it comes to vegetables and fruits an abundance of sunshine is not only desirable but essential. Usually the more the better, except under some subtropical conditions.

Good drainage is also essential. Poorly drained soils are slow to warm up in the spring, and early planting is necessary for some vegetables that do not tolerate very hot weather; and for others which require a very long period of growth. (For information concerning drainage problems, see Chapter 2.)

A vegetable plot facing south, especially if on a gentle slope, usually may be made ready for planting a week or ten days earlier than a level piece. Buildings or shrubs—especially hedges—to the north or west also afford protection, thus providing an ideal location for frames (Chapter 7) as well as for the vegetable patch.

How big? What size should the vegetable plot be? The standard answer to that silly question is the somewhat more sensible answer: "No larger than your wife can take care of."

For one's first attempt at vegetable growing, it is advisable to start moderately; and to try only those vegetables which are most easily grown—such as beans (both bush and pole), peas, radishes, onion sets, sweet corn, squash, lettuce, and tomatoes.

How much of each? That depends largely upon the family's tastes; and further than that upon the yield, which varies with different varieties, and from season to season. Last year, for instance, our bean crop was double as much as usual from the same space planted. Despite all we gave away and packed into the freezer for winter (we are still enjoying them as this is written in April) a lot went to the compost heap. There is no way of planning so accurately as to guarantee neither want nor waste.

The figures in the chart at the end of this chapter, based

VEGETABLES FOR BETTER EATING

on our own experience, may serve as a guide to the number of feet of row to supply two people. It may be multiplied by .5 for each additional member of the family; or by somewhat more for any item that is a particular favorite. Figures are for one planting, and where succession plantings are made (as in the case of bush beans, sweet corn, lettuce, and some others) they should of course be increased accordingly.

With no separate vegetable garden it is still possible to enjoy a few favorite vegetables, by making places for them in the flower borders or herb garden. A row, or several clumps of asparagus, for instance, yields stalks for the table in spring, and makes a decorative background for annuals or perennials during summer and fall. Rhubarb, after supplying succulent stems for sauce and pie, sends up tall spikes of creamy white flowers that are not only decorative in the garden, but effective and long-lasting in flower arrangements.

The most intriguing and practical use of vegetables grown in a flower border that we have encountered was at a small place were we once stopped to get photographs of a striking display of annuals that extended around two sides of a very modest plot. We were astonished to discover among the flowers, a fairly large assortment of vegetables growing not in rows, but in groups, spaced more or less casually among the flowers, but each with room enough to weed around it and harvest the crop. Tomatoes and pole beans were trained to lattice supports; beets, carrots, onions, radishes, lettuce, and others were in separate groups, carefully thinned out to give maximum yield. The owner—who did all the work herself—explained that the vegetable seeds were sown thinly wherever spring bulbs, after flowering, could have their foliage tied up, and where early annuals like candytuft had passed their prime. Spaces for root vegetables were left among the perennials, as these root deep and must have rich, open soil in which to develop. It was a sort of continuous catch-as-catch-can operation, but certainly paid off, especially as the only fertilizer used was vegetable wastes and table scraps, dug under near the flowers and vegetables in the beds, without bothering to compost them in the usual way.

This method of growing vegetables is not recommended, if one has room for even a very small vegetable garden, but it does show what can be done.

A plan comes first. One of the things most difficult to get the beginning vegetable gardener to realize is the importance of making a definite plan. What he usually does is to look through the seed catalog, select the varieties he likes—or thinks he will like—and then makes a wild guess at the amount to order. No matter how crude the plan, it will save seed, time, labor, and disappointment.

First step is to measure the space to be devoted to the vegetable garden. Next, make a list of the vegetables to be grown, and the *width* of row each will require. These widths vary from 12 inches (for such items as onions, spinach, carrots, and beets) to 4 or more feet for "spreaders" like tomatoes and bush squash. Vine crops such as cucumbers, melons, pumpkins, and winter squash require 6 feet or more. We had a volunteer Hubbard Squash last year at the edge of a garden plot, which we trained in two directions in a straight line. It attained, with no special feeding, a total length of 73 feet and produced over a hundred pounds of squash.

It is as interesting as a jigsaw puzzle to fit what one wants to grow into the space available. At the close of this chapter are some figures that will help solve the problem.

And here is a planting plan that indicates what the results of all your figuring and planning may be. The preparation of such a plan will of course take considerable time—in the long evenings of January or February when there is plenty of that commodity. But such a plan will *save* time in spring when there is something to be done about the grounds every minute. And in addition it will result in much better results for your efforts.

Preparation for planting is best begun as soon as frost is out and the soil has dried sufficiently to be dug, plowed, or rototilled. As a general rule, the earlier the better, especially if there is a heavy winter cover crop to be turned under. We do not apply manure or fertilizer until after this has been done. Then a second going-over mixes the plant foods evenly through the soil, which is left in nice condition to be given a final treatment with an iron rake to prepare a fine, smooth surface for planting.

One great advantage of preparing all the ground for planting, even if only part of it is to be used at once, is that the prompt germination of weed seeds is encouraged, and they can readily be destroyed by cultivating again before later sowings are made.

Part of the preparation for planting is to provide an ample supply of plant food. This differs little from that suggested in preparing for seeding a lawn. With many crops, however, it is beneficial to add some extra plant food in the planting holes, as described later.

If soil is extra-dry, it is advantageous to water very thoroughly before planting, preferably with a fine spray that will

20'	
ACORN SQUASH 4 HILLS — STRAIGHT NECK 1 HILL	24"
(INTERPLANTING) LEAF LETTUCE	18"
TOMATOES (8 STAKED PLANTS)	18"
(INTERPLANTING) KOHLRABI	18"
TOMATOES (8 STAKED PLANTS)	18"
(INTERPLANTING) EARLY CABBAGE PLANTS	18"
PEPPERS (10 PLANTS) EGGPLANT (3)	18"
(INTERPLANTING) SPINACH	15"
LIMA BEANS	15"
(INTERPLANTING) SPINACH	15"
LIMA BEANS	15"
SNAP BEANS SUCCEEDED BY LETTUCE	21"
SNAP BEANS SUCCEEDED BY BEETS / BEETS	12" / 6"
PEAS SUCCEEDED BY BEANS	6" / 12"
PEAS	9"
SWISS CHARD | PARSNIPS | PARSLEY	18"
BEETS SUCCEEDED BY ENDIVE	15"
BEETS	12"
CARROTS SUCCEEDED BY CHINESE CABBAGE	12"
LATE CARROTS	12"
RADISHES SUCCEEDED BY CARROTS	12"
ONION SETS " " CARROTS	12"
CORN (OPTIONAL)	36"
CORN (OPTIONAL)	36"
CORN (OPTIONAL)	36"

(Overall height: 30')

Vegetable garden plan. For those with plenty of space, an additional 15 feet has been added for sweet corn. For an ample supply, double or even triple this footage.

not make the surface muddy. One of the many oscillating or mist sprayers now available is ideal for this purpose.

PLANTING

Most vegetables are grown from seed, sown where they are to grow, but some (see page 239) do best if plants are started ahead in a greenhouse or frame. For sowing seed the surface should first be raked smooth immediately before sowing. Large-scale plantings are made with a seed drill, but in most home gardens they are sown by hand.

First step is to mark off rows the proper distance apart, with a stout garden line along which a narrow hoe or a pointed stick is drawn to make a furrow. Depth of the mark is in proportion to the size of the seed being sown. Very small seed—such as that of carrots, onions, and turnips—are covered about ⅛- to ¼-inch deep; medium sizes—beets, spinach, parsnips, etc.—½ to ¾ inches; and comparatively large seeds—peas, beans, corn—2 to 3 inches deep. In light, sandy soil or in very dry weather, planting depths may be somewhat increased.

It is important, especially in very dry weather, that the seed be firmed *in the drill* or furrow. This may be done with the back of a narrow "onion" hoe for small seeds, or an ordinary hoe for large ones. A method we have used for years, but have never seen suggested elsewhere, is to turn the wheel hoe upside down, place a light weight (such as a moderate-sized stone) on it, and run the wheel along the row. This takes very little time and nicely firms the seed into the soil. Loose soil, covered over this, serves as a mulch to hold the moisture, and delicate sprouts that would have trouble pushing up through soil firmed on the surface emerge readily.

Caution to beginners: A mistake which almost all beginners make is to sow seed—especially small seed such as that of carrots, onions, turnips, and lettuce—too thickly. *Every surplus seedling is a weed* and must be removed! Moreover, it is a weed that is growing right alongside the seedling you do want to keep, probably with roots intertangled, so that in removing it the other is sure to be loosened if not destroyed.

Much better to take an extra five or ten minutes to sow a row with seeds properly spaced (a quarter to a half inch apart for vegetables such as those mentioned above) than to have to spend half an hour or more on one's knees at the tedious job of "thinning out"—gardeners' jargon for removing surplus seedlings.

Just this past season we had a striking instance of the importance of giving individual plants in the row sufficient space to develop. Our row of parsnips germinated so poorly that we intended to replant them, but the press of other work prevented this so we finally removed all weeds, gave the plants an extra application of fertilizer, and allowed them to grow. Result: we had all of the succulent, white, sugary roots we could possibly use, and plenty to give away!

SETTING OUT

Several delicious vegetables—such as tomatoes, eggplant, peppers—require such a long season to mature that in northern sections they must be started in a greenhouse or hotbed, and later transferred to the garden as growing plants. There are others—such as cabbage and lettuce—that may be harvested much earlier in the season by starting seed early under glass and then setting out young plants. The method of doing this is described in Chapter 4. The gardener who does not possess such equipment may buy plants at any garden center. This is much easier, usually the better course for a beginner, but lacks some of the thrill of growing one's own.

Such started plants are often grown in "flats" or shallow boxes of various sizes, about 3 inches deep, but the newer method of growing them in individual pots made of peatmoss or some similar material which are planted "pot-and-all" is preferable, since by using this method there is no disturbance to the roots.

It is essential that all such started plants be "hardened off" by being exposed for several days and nights in an open frame or some other semiprotected spot before being set out in open ground. During this period they must be kept well watered as a sunny, windy day will dry them out very quickly.

In well-prepared soil, started plants may be set out with no special care in preparing the planting holes. We always feel, however, that a little extra "push" at this point is well worthwhile. Our own method is to mark out rows, and then the locations of individual plants such as tomatoes, eggplants, and peppers, and at each such point work well into the soil a shovelful of rich compost, plus half a pint of an organic fertilizer such as a mixture of Milorganite and bonemeal. This takes very little extra time and assures a fast, strong start.

CULTURE

The one great secret of success in growing vegetables is to keep ahead of the garden's greatest enemies—weeds. Unfortunately the richer the soil is made to grow fine vegetables, the more luxuriant the weeds it will produce.

In the commercial production of vegetables, chemical weed killers as well as pre-emergent treatments are now used extensively. For the small home garden we do not advocate them. Unless used with the greatest care they are likely to do more harm than good. We believe—but have no proof—that they affect the flavors of some vegetables. The methods we use to keep the weed population at a minimum are as follows:

First, *never allow a weed to go to seed*. Those that grow in corners and out-of-the-way places scatter their seeds far and wide. The first flower on any weed—and some of them, such as the chicory, wild carrot, and morning-glories, are quite lovely—should be its death warrant.

Second, *compost all fresh manure* before applying it to the garden. Very few seeds will survive the processes of decay that go on in the correctly managed compost heap (see page 43).

Third, if weeds do appear, *get them out at once*, even if other more interesting and apparently more pressing jobs have to wait. Every day's delay increases the task at compound interest, and a rainy spell may easily make it hopeless.

Tools for combatting weeds are many. It will pay well to have several types, as this not only makes the job easier but will save a considerable amount of time. Some of our favorite ones are described in Chapter 8.

Thinning is the process of removing a sufficient number of plants from a row or a hill to allow those remaining to reach maximum size. As already emphasized, every surplus plant is a weed. This should be done as soon as the second or third true leaf appears. Proper space to be left between the plants in the rows varies. Averages for some of the more important vegetables are shown in the table at the end of this chapter. Crops ordinarily grown in hills—such as cucumbers, squash, and melons—are thinned out, *before they begin to crowd*, to three or four. As thinning, even when carefully done, disturbs to some extent the plants which are left, it is well to go back over the row and draw some soil up around any that may be "wobbly."

Side-dressing is a term used for the application of plant food, along the row or around individual plants. When the soil has been properly prepared this will seldom be necessary except when one has to contend with a soil that leaches badly—such as much of our Cape Cod sand—until it has been sufficiently supplied with humus. The food element most likely to become deficient is nitrogen. To correct this, a quick-acting high-nitrogen fertilizer such as Milorganite is the standard. This is not always available locally. We now use a 20-6-4 organic fertilizer sold for lawns, but equally good for vegetables. Any high-nitrogen fertilizer will be helpful.

Mulching is less frequently employed for the vegetable plot than elsewhere about the grounds. It is, however, just as effective here, and correctly used will conserve soil moisture and save a great deal of time in cultivating and weeding.

A mulch is any material, from spent manure to strips of plastic, that may be spread over the soil, around and/or between plants. Its principal purpose is to conserve moisture by checking evaporation. In addition to this it may check or even eliminate weed growth, and also affects soil temperature. Mulches which shade the soil keep it several degrees cooler in hot, sunny weather.

The mulches we use most are seaweed and "thatch" (debris from the beach such as a mixture of dead grasses and seaweed), pine needles (we have an unlimited supply of these in our pine woods), and coarse compost, sufficiently old to contain few viable weed seeds. Mulches, which may be bought commercially in bales or bags, include peatmoss, buckwheat hulls, Stay-dry (bagasse or treated sugar cane stalks), bog or meadow hay. The one thing to guard against most carefully is any material that contains weed or grass seeds.

Harvesting and storing. Most vegetables are used, as soon as ready, directly from the garden. One of the chief reasons for having a garden at all is to make possible the enjoyment of *really* fresh vegetables. As already mentioned, sweet corn and peas lose in quality by the hour as soon as they are picked.

Any of the leaf vegetables and broccoli should (unless used at once) be wrapped in a moist cloth and placed in the refrigerator. Others should be kept in the coolest, most moist spot that can be found. Any of the root vegetables placed in damp peatmoss will remain really garden fresh for days.

Winter storage of vegetables, now that the old-fashioned dirt-floor cellar and spring or pump house are things of the past, is a different problem. Potatoes, beets, carrots, and other root crops, packed as suggested above and placed in the coolest spot available, will remain fresh for a long time if the peat is not allowed to dry out. In moderate climates (where temperatures seldom drop below 10 degrees above zero) heavy mulching with straw, pine needles, or dead leaves held in place by 10- to 12-inch wide rough lumber placed on edge, will carry any of the root crops through successfully. We use this method here on Cape Cod, as it is much easier than digging and storing.

A method sometimes used is to bury a section or two of large drain tile *vertically* in the ground in a protected, shaded location, with wooden covers to fit. With extra covering in very cold weather, all root crops may thus be kept safe even in quite severe climates.

All vegetables stored, even for a short period, should be examined frequently so that any showing the least sign of decay may be removed immediately. The old saying that "one rotten apple will spoil the barrel" applies equally to vegetables.

Freezing is a method of preserving surplus vegetables which has to a large degree supplanted canning. Freezing is so quick and easy that it is really no chore. All manufacturers of freezers send out charts and instructions for blanching, freezing, and wrapping vegetables and fruits. We simply freeze surpluses that we cannot use as they mature, and even this makes a very considerable store by the time the season is over.

THE SIX LEADERS

Where space is limited it is of course impossible to grow a great variety of vegetables. One then is faced with the problem of which to attempt.

The first factor for reaching this decision is of course one's personal taste. As that differs with the individual, no rules can be laid down. Here, however, are some half dozen, which are quite universally grown.

Lettuce. This is probably the most generally liked and most constantly used vegetable, popular at all times. Unfortunately, however, few of the present generation know what really tender, tasty lettuce is. They know only the commercially grown Iceberg type, so hard and tough that it will stand shipping thousands of miles; it is fit only to be used as a garnish for so-called salads in hotels and restaurants and by individuals who do not know better varieties. Usually it is returned, uneaten, to the kitchen and goes into the garbage pail —where it belonged in the first place. The commercial-type "head" lettuces grown in most of the United States are not even listed in French or English seed catalogs.

The loose-leaf lettuces form heads of a sort, more accurately dense clusters of leaves, all of which are tender and delicious. By utilizing a deep frame, and with some protection in winter, we find we can have lettuce here on Cape Cod for nine months of the year. (For midwinter supply we grow it in peat pots in the greenhouse.) Lettuce is much hardier than is generally supposed. In moderate climates plants set out in a coldframe in late September or October come through the winter in a semidormant condition to renew growth in March. Heavy burlap over glass prevents really hard freezing in frame during midwinter.

Our favorite varieties are Bibb, Burpeeana (an improved form of Bibb), and Oakleaf. We sow a pinch of each monthly. Big Boston is an old, semihard head type with very tender leaves which is sometimes grown for local markets. Lettuce washed in cold water, shaken semidry, wrapped in a damp cloth, and put in the refrigerator will keep crisp and fresh for more than a week.

If you want lettuce to *eat* instead of as a garnish, try two or three of the tender varieties combined and tossed in a bowl with the following dressing which we make up in quantity and keep ready in the refrigerator.

GrayRock French Dressing

1 pt. pure olive oil
2 tsp. lemon juice
  tarragon vinegar to taste
2 tsp. salt
  dash black pepper
1 clove garlic, chopped
  or pressed
½ cup chopped ripe olives

½ tsp. paprika
½ tsp. prepared mustard
½ tsp. Worcestershire sauce,
  Angostura bitters, or
  Soy sauce
1 tsp. dried salad herbs
  or fresh herbs to taste
1 tsp. celery salt

Tomatoes produce more, over a longer season, in proportion to the space they occupy than any other vegetable. They are one of the easiest to grow and most certain to yield satisfactorily; also easy to can, though in these days that is seldom done.

Seed is sown, under glass, about six weeks before the last frost date. Extra-strong, vigorous plants may be had by transplanting to 2-inch peat pots and replanting these, in their pots, to 4-inch peat pots. By spraying these with Blossom-set, when first blooms appear, it is usually possible to get them with a few small green fruits started by setting-out time. Soil used for last potting should be enriched with well-decayed rich compost, or with dehydrated commercial manure such as Bovung or Driconure. Plants are set deep—up to second or third leaf joints—as they will send out extra roots from the joints.

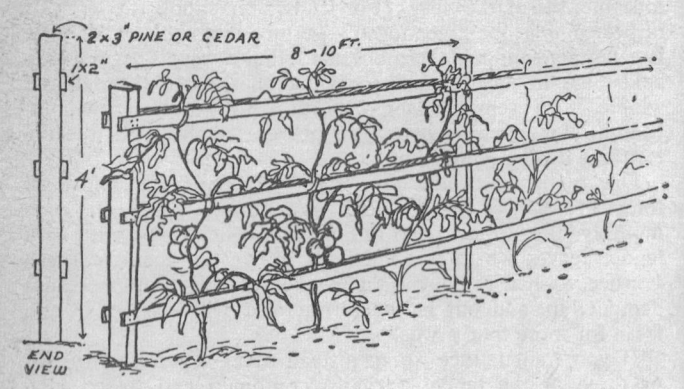

Self-supporting trellis for tomatoes. Posts may be set 8 to 10 feet apart.

While the plants are usually tied to stakes to support them, it is better, and in the end easier, to use stout "ladders' made of uprights of 2×3 pine or cedar, with four crosspieces of 1×2-inch, about 3 feet long. If taken up and stored for the winter, these will last for many years.

As the plants grow, they send out side shoots from every leaf joint. All but three or four of these should be pinched out as they appear. Those remaining are trained, and when necessary, tied to the crosspieces with soft twine or strips of discarded sheets.

We like our tomatoes dead ripe—as they are almost never found at a supermarket. We pick them when they have turned color and then place them on a window sill in full sun, using them as they ripen. As danger of frost approaches, full-sized fruits are picked green and placed on a board in a coldframe to finish ripening under glass. Some of the green fruits are used for pickles—though our aging stomachs do not allow us to partake of these delicacies as freely as we used to. For younger gardeners, green tomato pickles, piccalilli, and India relish are all well worth the trouble of making.

Well-grown plants in peat pots are available at most garden centers for those who do not care to grow their own. Hybrid

VEGETABLES FOR BETTER EATING

varieties may cost a bit more than others but are well worth the difference. Pot plants cost more than plants grown in and sold from flats, but again are worth the difference, as they suffer no transplanting set-back, and produce ripe fruits ten days to two weeks earlier.

Tomato troubles include the horned tomato worm, a big, green 4- to 5-inch long fellow not easily discovered until he has done considerable damage. Keep fruit off the ground to avoid premature rots and other soil-borne diseases.

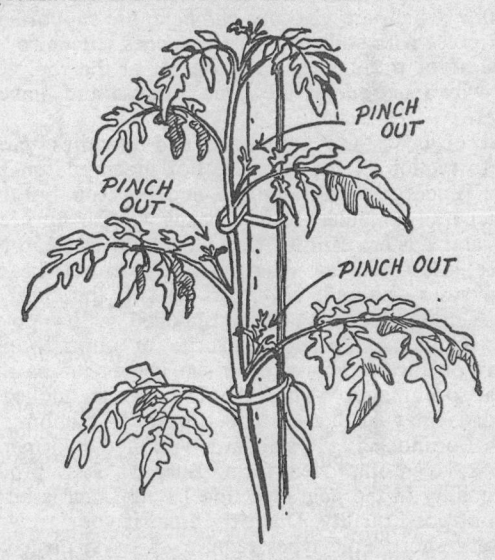

To get first-quality tomatoes, much of the new growth should be pinched out as it starts, leaving only a few main stems.

Beans. This humble legume is one of the easiest and most rewarding of all vegetables to grow. Both its types and its uses are many and varied. Largest yields, in proportion to space occupied, are from climbing or pole beans. These also have the advantages of bearing over a long season from one planting, and of serving, if supported on chicken wire in a location getting abundant sunshine, as a most effective temporary screen.

Bush beans yield for a comparatively short time, and at least three plantings should be made, at three-week intervals, to provide tender young beans for the season. As the plants bear heavily, you may have surpluses—which are readily frozen for later use. (Leftover cooked beans used in the "snap" stage are excellent in mixed salads, or simply combined with chopped white onion, chopped, hard boiled egg, and mayonnaise. Serve on crisp leaves of Bibb-type lettuce.)

As beans are killed by the slightest frost, nothing is gained by planting them until really warm weather has arrived. This is especially true of lima beans. Largest yields are obtained by thinning out the plants as soon as the second true leaves develop, to stand 3 or 4 inches apart; 4 to 5 for bush limas.

Pole beans, which are vigorous climbers, are supported by individual poles with stubs or short branches left on; or trained up "tepees" of three poles tied together at the top. A 6-foot chicken-wire fence serves the same purpose and makes picking easier.

Varieties of beans are numerous, and favorites vary from section to section of the country. For green-pod snap beans we grow Tendergreen, Tendercrop, and Topcrop, but there are others generally popular. In wax beans we like Burpee's Brittle Wax and Eastern Brittle Wax. Golden Wax (Top Notch), Cherokee, and Chocktaw Wax are others. In pole beans Kentucky Wonder—an old, old-timer—is still the most widely grown. A comparatively new, flat-podded yellow pole bean, Burpee's Golden, is a great favorite of ours. We like to "French" or slice length-wise all the above, unless they are picked at so immature a stage that they can be cooked whole. Lima beans may be had in either bush or climbing forms. Burpee's Fordhook is the standard type of the former. Fordhook 242 is an improved form. Burpee's Best produces a similar quality in the pole type. Ideal Pole Lima is large-podded and of good quality. Don't try limas if your growing season is very short. Pole types require 88 days; bush varieties about 74.

Sweet Corn is as typically American as baseball—and as universally liked. In proportion to its yield, however, it takes up more space than any of the preceding vegetables. In many sections it is widely grown for local markets, but unless it can be had, *really fresh picked,* it is worthwhile to grow your own. Some local growers today make several pickings a day so that regular customers may enjoy it at its best. If there must be some delay, keep unshucked ears in a cool place, wrapped in a damp cloth.

Corn can be grown in either hills or rows. We plant kernels 4 or 5 inches apart in short blocks 3 or 4 rows wide, to assure good fertilization. (Every individual kernel, in order to develop, must have had its grain of pollen dust, reaching it through the tube-like "silk.") We thin them out to leave the

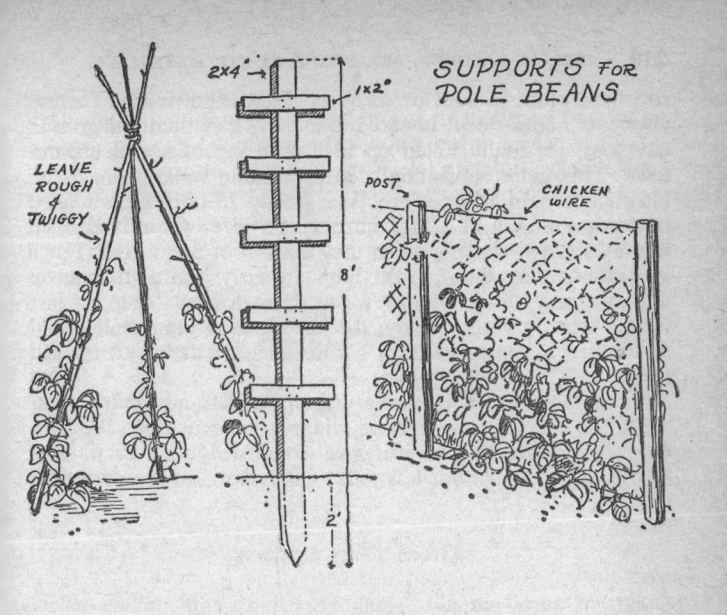

Corn that is kept hilled as it grows is less likely to be blown over in wind storms. Hilling should be started early in order to avoid damage to roots.

strongest plants a foot or so apart. Seed is sown in a furrow about 4 inches deep, covered 2 inches, and then, as growth develops, gradually hilled up to 4 or 5 inches above ground level. This helps substantially in preventing stalks from being blown down in wind. Corn is a greedy feeder, and at least one side dressing of a high-nitrogen fertilizer should be given as stalks grow, starting when they are a foot or so high. For a continuous succession, plant both an early and a main crop variety every three to four weeks from average date of last killing frost in your locality, the last planting being calculated to mature at least ten days before average date of first fall frost.

To eat off the cob, gather when kernels are in the full "milk" stage. Drop in boiling water after shucking. We boil only 3 minutes. Others prefer to extend this to 5 or 6. Mature ears (not hard but less milky) may be used for corn fritters:

Green Corn Fritters

6 ears of corn, grated	Beat egg whites stiff and set aside. Beat egg yolks until thick. To these add cream, salt, flour, baking powder and mix. Add grated corn. Fold in beaten egg whites and bake at once on a hot griddle, preferably electric so they can be served piping hot and just baked.
3 eggs, beaten separately	
1 large tbsp. flour	
3 tbsps. cream	
salt to taste	
¼ tsp. baking powder	

When we freeze corn, we either blanch perfect young ears, cut in half, and freeze on the cob, or grate older ears, heat to boiling in a double boiler, and freeze for later use in fritters.

Many varieties of sweet corn are offered in seed catalogs. There is some variation in the way they grow in different sections, and therefore the beginner will do well, when ordering, to consult a garden-minded neighbor or the local county agent.

Asparagus is given a place in this limited list for four reasons: first, it is quite universally liked; second, it may readily be grown, even if one has no vegetable garden; third, because, with very little care, it yields for a score of years, or even more; and finally because, after being cut for the table during the spring season, the stalks—which are then allowed to grow—make a most decorative, feathery hedge, 5 feet or more in height.

Asparagus may be grown from seed, but the home gardener usually procures roots. These are set out in spring, spaced 12 to 18 inches apart in a trench a foot or so deep, well enriched with rotted manure; or, if this is not obtainable, with dried commercial manure.

For the first summer no stalks are cut, the aim being to develop strong plants as quickly as possible. Growing plants should be fertilized freely, kept clear of weeds and of any pests such as the asparagus beetle (list in Appendix). The second spring some stalks may be cut for a short period. They are best taken when 8 to 10 inches high, cutting just at the soil level, and taking care not to injure younger stalks not yet above ground. Several stalks from each plant should be left to mature.

After cutting has ceased, a heavy mulch worked in between and around the plants both keeps down weeds and conserves moisture.

Melons. The only reason for attempting to grow one's own melons is that this is the surest way to have them of really top quality. Locally grown melons have disappeared from most markets; and those grown hundreds or even thousands of miles away and packed green in order to withstand shipping are seldom worth eating no matter how attractive they may look. Unless you have tasted them home-grown and sun-ripened, you really don't know how delicious melons can be. In proportion to yield, melons take up considerable space, and they are subject to injury from animals—including impatient small boys—insect pests, and diseases. But to be of really top quality, melons (especially cantaloupes) must ripen on the vine until they part from it at the slightest touch.

Melons prefer a rich soil, rather on the light side, and— especially in the north—a protected, sunny exposure that warms up quickly. As the seedlings may be killed by the slightest frost, it is desirable, in northern sections, to plant seeds under Hotkaps or plant protectors of plastic which are removed when the plants are well up.

A still better method is to sow seeds—five or six in a 4-inch peat pot—in a cold frame or in the greenhouse, about two weeks before the last frost is likely to occur. They can then be set out in the garden, pots and all, leaving only two or three plants to a "hill." In well-enriched soil they grow vigorously and should be spaced 5 to 6 feet apart each way.

We use a combination of both methods, covering the pot-grown plants, when they are set out, with plant protectors or with wire-covered frames for several days, taking care however to remove the former on hot, sunny days.

If kept well supplied with water, plants will cover the

VEGETABLE CHART

Vegetable	Number of plants or feet of row for seeding for two persons	Distance between rows or hills (in inches)	Distance between plants after thinning (in inches)	Planting
Asparagus	25 plants	36	18	Perennial
Beans, snap, bush	50 feet	24	3–4	Succession
pole	25 feet or 4 hills	36	24	Long season
Beets	20 feet	18	3	Early and late
Broccoli	8 plants	30	30	Early and late
Brussels sprouts	8 plants	30	30	Late
Cabbage, early	12 plants	24	24	Early and late
late	12 plants	30	24	
Carrots	20 feet	24	3	Early and late
Chinese-Cabbage	10 feet	18	10	Late
Corn	100 feet	36	12	Early, midseason, and late
Cucumber	4 hills	48	8*	Late; long season; plant along one edge.
Eggplant	3 plants	30	24	Late; long season.
Lettuce plants	25 plants	18	8	Early and late
seed	15 feet	18	6	Succession
Muskmelon (Cantaloupe)	4 hills	48	8*	Late; long season; plant along one edge.
Onion seed	20 feet	12	3	Early; long season.
sets	20 feet	12	3	Early
Parsley	10 feet	12	6	Early; long season.
Pea	50 feet	30	3	Early and late
Pepper	3 plants	30	24	Late; long season.
Radish	10 plants	12	3	Succession
Rhubarb	3 plants		48	Perennial
Spinach	50	18	3	Early and late
Summer Squash	4 hills	48	8*	Late; long season; plant along edge.

* between plants in each hill

VEGETABLES

Perennial

Asparagus
Artichoke (*Cynara scolymus*) Grown on West Coast.
Rhubarb

Annual

Hardy	Half-hardy	Tender
Kale	Beet	Bean
Leek	Broccoli	Corn
Lettuce	Cauliflower	Cucumber
Onion	Cabbage	Eggplant
Parsley	Carrot	Muskmelon
Parsnip	Chard, Swiss	(Cantaloupe)
Pea	Chinese-Cabbage	Pepper
Radish		Squash
Spinach		Tomato
Turnip		

NOTE: In further reference to the last column, headed Planting (opposite page).

Perennial: Indicates a permanent planting of hardy roots.
Succession: Short season crops which must be planted in succession.
Long season: Annual vegetables which remain in the rows all season.
Late; long season: Tender vegetables, set out late, which remain in the garden all the rest of the season.
Early; long season: Hardy vegetables which can be sowed early, but which take all season to develop.
Early and Late: Cool weather vegetables which can be sown early for spring crop and late for fall crop.
Plant along edge: Suggested for vine crops for the small garden so that vines can be trained away from vegetable rows.

ground quickly. A sharp eye should be kept for the first sign of injury from such enemies as cucumber beetle, melon lice, and borers (list in Appendix).

First frost will kill the foliage but any full-grown melons may be kept and ripened in a frame or a sunny window. While the flavor will not be quite perfect, it is likely to be much better than that of supermarket specimens.

Pests and diseases of vegetables and their control are listed in the Appendix.

> Thy vineyards and thy orchards are
> Most beautiful and fair,
> Full furnished with trees and fruits
> Most wonderful and rare.
> *The New Jerusalem.* ANONYMOUS

CHAPTER 17

Tree Fruits, Small Fruits, and Berries

The word "fruit" as ordinarily but not too correctly employed covers a number of quite distinct and very different plants. Consequently, their requirements and the methods employed in growing them also vary widely. Strawberries, for instance, have little in common with blueberries, peaches, or apples; yet all are commonly referred to as fruits.

As far as their culture is concerned, these several types of fruit should be considered as vines, canes, shrubs, or trees, and most of the suggestions already given in connection with those groups—as to soil preparation, planting, feeding, and general care—apply also to the fruits we are now considering.

With either fresh or frozen fruits of all kinds so generally available in the markets, why should any homeowner go to the trouble of producing his own?

The reasons are nearly the same as for growing one's own vegetables. Although the first of these is the fun of doing it, there is also the element of *quality*. Many fruits, like many vegetables, should be fully ripe before being harvested. To be handled after they have even *begun* to ripen results in bruising that develops into decay, often in an incredibly short period. Frozen fruits, *if picked and processed when fully ripe*, may be of better flavor than fresh fruits which were picked green and shipped long distances.

254 SPECIAL GARDENS, AREAS, AND PLANT MATERIALS

Here is what one of the country's leading authorities on fruit growing, commercial as well as in home gardens, has to say concerning this matter:

Home-grown fruits are as a rule much superior to market fruits. Fruits for shipment must be picked in a slightly immature condition to withstand packing and handling. They must often be harvested before the sugars and flavors are developed up to the point where the ripening process will continue. This is especially true of the more perishable fruits such as berries. . . . A fruit that is allowed to develop on the plant until it is fully ripe has quality, flavor and nutritional value that cannot be attained in fruits that must be picked for shipment. . . . Even for local handling many sorts must be picked before fully mature.

If his object is a real crop of fruit, the home gardener should attempt tree fruits, especially apples and peaches, only in localities where they are known to be successful and where spray service is available. Rainfall, frost dates, and other factors are very important in determining chances of success. Before attempting tree fruits, consult the nearest county agent and follow his advice on what *varieties* to get, as these vary with local climatic conditions.

Space is usually a determining factor in deciding what fruits, if any, are to be grown. Frequently it is *the* determining factor, since most fruits require full sun to develop and ripen properly. Overcrowded flowers will make some sort of display even if individual blooms are not up to par. Overcrowded fruits, however, will prove to be a complete waste of time and money.

The growers of tree fruits, especially of apples, have done much to make it possible for the amateur to grow his own by grafting standard varieties on dwarf-growing stocks. Fortunately, many fruits may be produced in little or no more space than is required for most shrubs or vines; and several of them, when in flower, are quite as decorative.

Location. Most of the fruits are not too particular as to soil. With the exception of blueberries, however, all prefer not to have wet feet, and even these may be grown as well on average upland ground that does not dry out excessively.

Humus in the soil, both to conserve moisture and to provide food, is as highly desirable for fruits as it is for most plants.

A rather acid soil with a pH above 5 but below 7 (the ideal is 5.5 to 6.5) best suits most fruits and is the maximum essential for blueberries, which thrive in very acid soil. In the

TREE FRUITS, SMALL FRUITS, AND BERRIES 255

preparation of soil for planting fruit trees and berries, the suggestions given in Chapters 2 and 9 apply.

To ripen properly and develop full flavor, fruits should be fully exposed to the sun for at least half of the day, preferably in the morning.

Planting. When to plant depends upon climatic conditions. In general, fall planting is best in sections where the ground freezes early in fall, and winter temperatures are severe. In areas where autumns are mild, fall planting gets the trees off to an earlier start. In either case, but especially when spring planting is preferable, the earlier the better. Any order for fruit trees should be placed well in advance to assure the arrival of the stock at an early date. Trees or bushes that have broken dormancy and begun to sprout even slightly get off to a bad start. Any fruit stock, immediately upon receipt, should be unpacked and untied, the roots soaked in water, and the plants placed in wet peatmoss or sphagnum until they can be planted.

When plants from nursery cannot be set out at once, keep roots buried in moist soil to prevent drying out.

In connection with advice on ordering early, it may be well to insert a word concerning "bearing age" trees. In our experience and that of many other gardeners we know, little or nothing is to be gained and much may be lost by trying to save two or three years in this way. Bearing age trees (unless they can be bought locally and moved with generous root balls) are sure to receive such a set-back in shipping and transplanting that they seldom bear any fruit sooner than one- or two-year-old trees; and at two or three years after planting are likely to be smaller than the others, if indeed they are alive at all.

Multiple-variety trees are also likely to prove unsatisfactory, as some branches will grow much more rapidly than others, and the pruning and spraying problems involved are enough to stump even the experts. Of course they are interesting as conversation pieces.

Newly set fruit trees of all kinds should be protected from rabbits, field mice, pine mice, and other rodents during cold weather. (See Appendix, Pests and Their Control.)

Pruning. General care after planting is much the same as for other subjects. The chief difference is that trees grown for fruit require more careful pruning. Pruning fruit trees is necessary not only for the health of the tree, but also for the quality and the amount of fruit produced.

Without going into the details of pruning all the various kinds of fruit, the guiding principles will be given in connection with the several fruits discussed in the following pages.

Mulching. In general, a mulch around fruit trees saves labor and conserves moisture in the soil. Leaves, straw, old manure, grass clippings (if not too thick), spent manure, even small stones that will pack together, may be used. With the exception of apples and pears, few fruit trees (and no small fruits) do as well in sod as in soil that is kept mulched; or kept cultivated, which provides a soil mulch. This should be borne in mind when one considers using fruit trees as lawn specimens.

Under most conditions and especially in warm climates, fruit trees benefit from summer mulching.

Spraying. If satisfactory crops are to be expected, the fruit trees, more than any other group of plants, demand frequent and meticulously timed spraying. Commercial apple orchards apply from ten to thirteen sprays during the season in order to get perfect fruit. New spray materials give promise of cutting down the number of applications required. On the other hand, many pests develop immunity to sprays being used and thus create new problems.

These facts are presented not with the idea of discouraging the homeowner from growing some of his own fruit, but to make him realize what he faces in attempting the undertaking. If he succeeds it will be a bigger feather in his cap! In any event, his fruit trees, when in bloom, will be quite as

A common mistake, especially in these days of bulldozer operations, is to fail to take advantage of the lay of the land. Here the addition and rearrangement of a few rocks have created a charmingly naturalistic setting.

Increase in tulip bulbs. The small ones require a year's growth before flowering.

In controlling the growth of a plant, one should consider training along with pruning. New growth in most plants tends upward—as that from the horizontally trained rose cane illustrated.

Here is an excellent example of keeping the landscaping in harmony with the house. The horizontal design of the planting and the spreading yews and other plant materials used achieve a very happy effect.

*Flowering Dogwood (*Cornus florida*) is a hardy, fast-growing, and trouble-free native of the eastern seaboard. Thrives in the open or in semishade. Indispensable for informal plantings. There are pink-flowered forms as well as the usual creamy white.*

A post-and-rail fence makes a sturdy support for climbing roses.

In designing a perennial border, long strips or blocks of any one species or variety of plant are to be avoided. Groups should vary in size and shape and be placed with the time of bloom of each in mind (see plan) so that the succession of color is as nearly continuous as possible. The larger the border, the easier it is to maintain constant bloom.

Daffodils, requiring little care and remaining indefinitely, are ideal for a woodland setting. Flowering tree in background is Magnolia stellata.

SOIL MAP of the

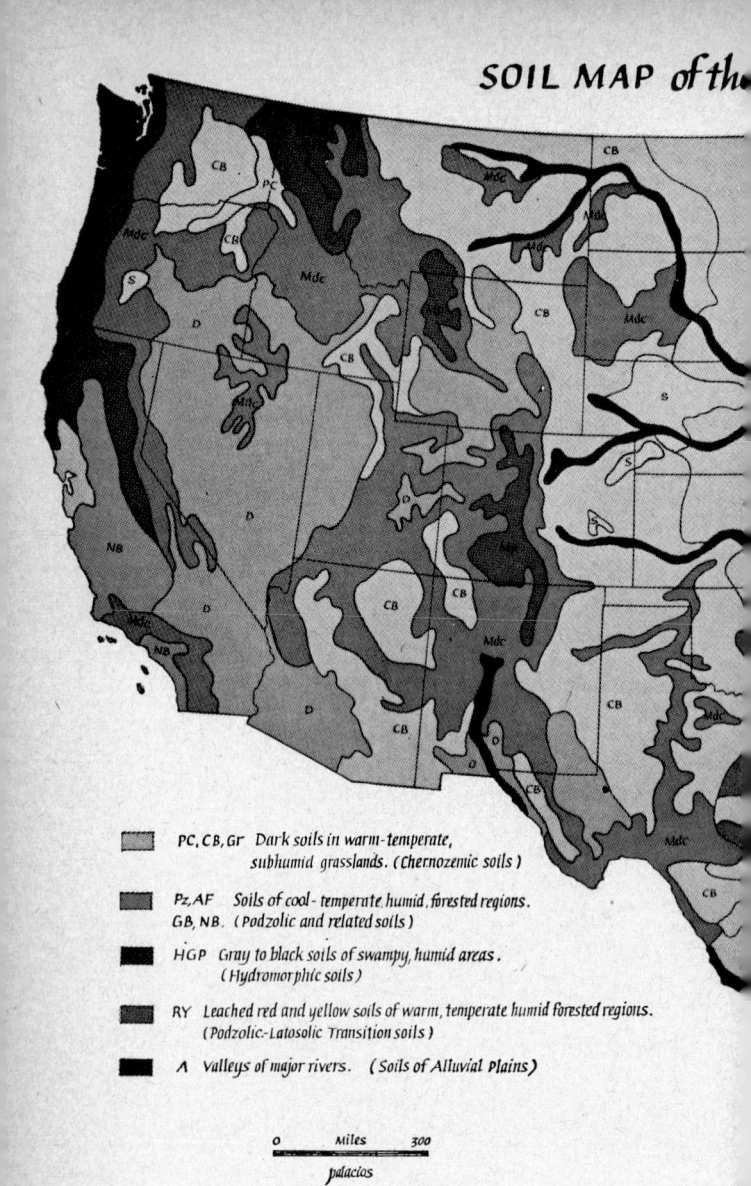

- **PC, CB, Gr** Dark soils in warm-temperate, subhumid grasslands. (Chernozemic soils)
- **Pz, AF, GB, NB** Soils of cool-temperate, humid, forested regions. (Podzolic and related soils)
- **HGP** Gray to black soils of swampy, humid areas. (Hydromorphic soils)
- **RY** Leached red and yellow soils of warm, temperate humid forested regions. (Podzolic-Latosolic Transition soils)
- **A** Valleys of major rivers. (Soils of Alluvial Plains)

0 Miles 300

palacios

NITED STATES

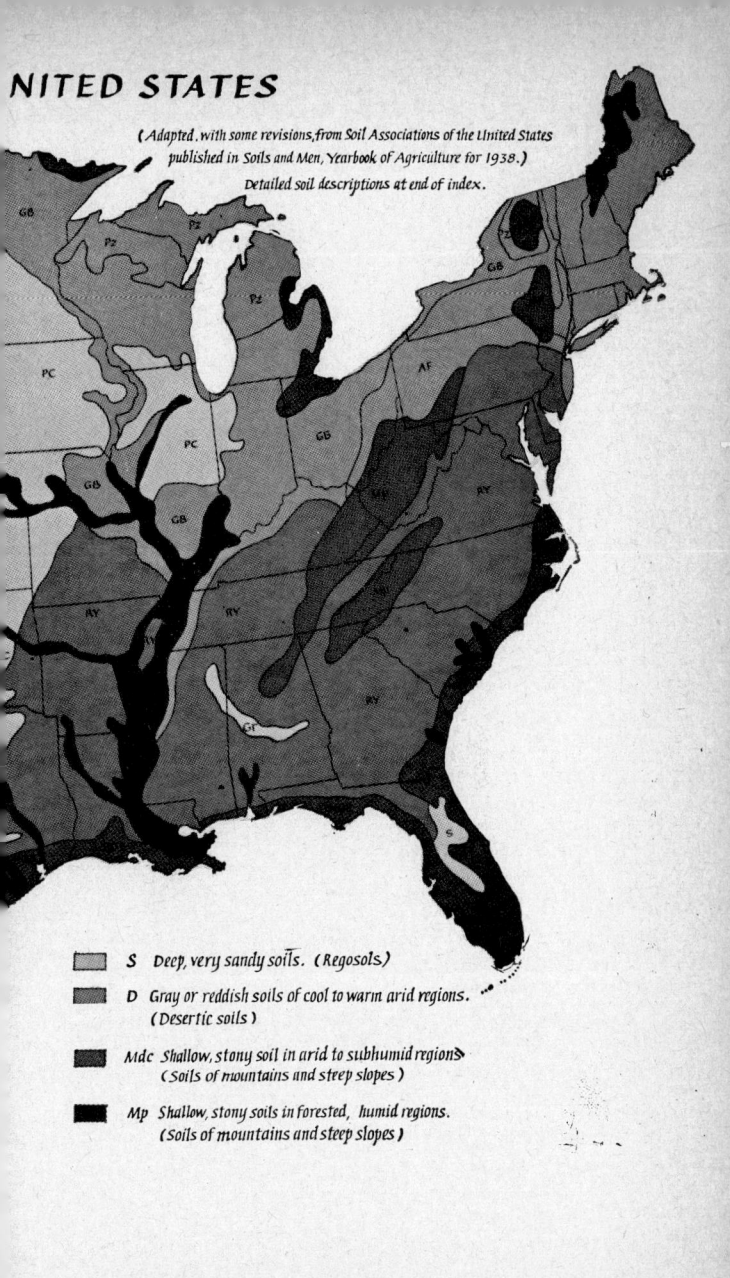

(Adapted, with some revisions, from Soil Associations of the United States published in Soils and Men, Yearbook of Agriculture for 1938.)

Detailed soil descriptions at end of index.

- **S** Deep, very sandy soils. (Regosols.)
- **D** Gray or reddish soils of cool to warm arid regions. (Desertic soils)
- **Mdc** Shallow, stony soil in arid to subhumid regions (Soils of mountains and steep slopes)
- **Mp** Shallow, stony soils in forested, humid regions. (Soils of mountains and steep slopes)

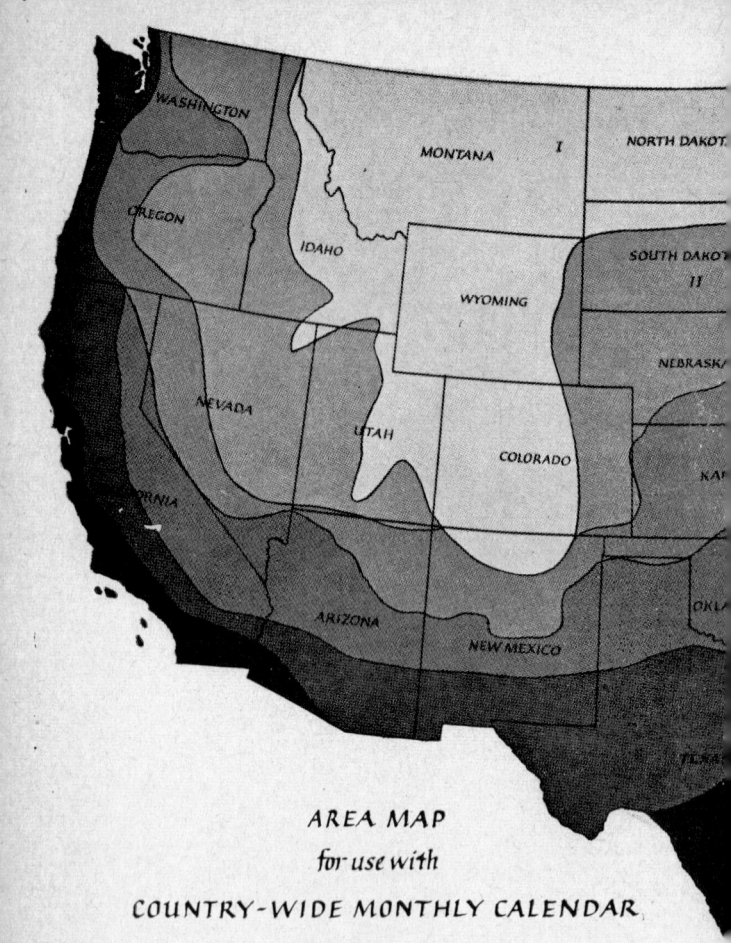

AREA MAP
for use with
COUNTRY-WIDE MONTHLY CALENDAR

See PART THREE of this book

Miles
0 — 300

Area I	Area IV
Area II	Area V
Area III	Area VI

Often money can be saved and more pleasing and original results achieved by tailoring the house to fit the building site instead of doing it the other way around. Here the use of imagination saved a mint of money.

Rocky or stony areas in shaded locations often present a special problem. In heavy shade it is advisable to concentrate on plants that bloom early, before tree foliage matures, and they should be distributed in groups or colonies which appear natural and unstudied.

In the old-fashioned knot garden, first popular in the Middle Ages, "ropes" of carefully planted and pruned herbs weave intricate patterns or knots. Low-growing plants such as dwarf lavender, germander, and santolina are used in this way, as are those culinary herbs that are not harmed by severe clipping.

A pool of water, no matter how large or how small, always becomes the mirrorlike center of interest in any garden scene. Its design and construction, however, should be in keeping with its surroundings. Skillfully placed, as in this garden, it adds greatly to the apparent length and depth of its surroundings.

A paved porch and a flagstone terrace make a natural transition to the rock outcropping in the foreground. Plants in tubs and containers used against the house may be changed as desired, while terrace and natural rock are skillfully planted with alpines, sempervivums, pinks, and creeping thyme.

This moderate-sized rose garden of semiformal design is ideal in several ways. The over-all plan makes an attractive landscape feature. The evergreens, trees, and hedge provide both privacy and effective protection against storms; the beds are so arranged as to facilitate culture and to display bloom to the best advantage; and the looking-glass pool adds charm.

A pleasing arrangement for roses in limited space. Prize-winning blooms may be grown even in a very small garden.

The Hybrid Tea roses provide the largest and loveliest individual blooms. To this type belongs Peace, the world's most popular rose. Hybrid Teas bloom intermittently throughout the season.

The new grandiflora type of rose combines the characteristics of the two named above, but is not, as yet, quite definitely established. Queen Elizabeth, growing to shoulder height and bearing masses of handsome, well-formed blooms, is a well-known variety in this class.

Pole beans require a minimum of ground space. This is Burpee's Golden — light yellow, tender, and delicious.

Strawberries are easy to grow and produce heavy crops of fruit. The secrets of success in getting lots of big berries is to set out some plants each year, and to keep soil well mulched.

TREE FRUITS, SMALL FRUITS, AND BERRIES

beautiful as any of the ornamental trees and shrubs he grows. Indeed, among plants used specifically for decorative effects, some of the most beautiful are cherries, apples, crabapples, and quinces.

The pests most likely to be encountered in growing fruit trees are aphids, borers, codling moths, curculios, fruitworms, leaf hoppers, leaf rollers, mites of various sorts, scales, and slugs. There are also diseases like fireblight and mildew. By following the spray program recommended for your locality by your county agent or nearby Agricultural Experiment Station, all troubles can be controlled *if* the sprays are applied at exactly the time specified. An all-purpose fruit-tree spray formula and schedule appear on page 456 but consultation with one of the authorities named above is emphatically advised.

Harvesting and storing. Among the tree fruits, apples, pears, quinces, and especially peaches should be gathered before they are dead ripe, but must be handled very carefully, as any bruise quickly develops into a spot of decay. Stored in a dry, cool, dark place, best spread out on shelves, they gradually ripen to eating stage. Peaches, early pears, and plums may take just a few days. Others like winter apples and pears may not ripen for many weeks. Those fine old winter apples, the Rhode Island Greening and Winter Russet, for instance, are not at their best until well after New Year's. (A good example of the many fine fruits and vegetables that have disappeared from commercial use simply because they have no "eye appeal" on chain-store counters, and can be enjoyed only by gardeners who grow their own!)

TREE FRUITS

The culture of the various tree fruits varies in detail but follows much the same general principles. The suggestions given concerning apples apply generally to the others: pears, cherries, peaches, apricots, and plums. More detailed information may be obtained from one's local Agricultural Experiment Station.

The Apple. Unless one has a fairly large place, it is advisable to use only dwarf-growing trees. These are produced by grafting standard varieties on dwarf-growing stock, known as Malling, developed in England. The type generally used is Malling No. IX. Grown on their own roots, most orchard apples produce very large trees—with trunks a foot or more in diameter and up to 25 feet in height. A dwarf tree of the same variety would be not over 8 to 10 feet in height, with side branches in proportion. No. VIII stock makes a tree somewhat larger, but still a dwarf compared to a standard. A very great advantage of the dwarf trees is that they can be pruned, sprayed, and picked with only a fraction of the effort required for standards. It should be kept in mind, however, that the *roots* as well as the tops are dwarf. It is therefore advisable, especially where high winds are likely to be encountered, to provide stakes to support the trunks until trees are well established.

In growing most fruit trees, pruning is of particular importance because *from the very start* the trees must be guided and shaped into a definite form. Left to grow normally as most ornamental trees are, they would send up strong, sky-reaching leaders with comparatively weak side branches. For this reason apples, pears, peaches, and, to a lesser degree, plums should be cut back a fourth to a third *when they are planted*. The purpose of course is to encourage as quickly as possible the development of side branches. As these increase in size, the grower must decide which ones are to be retained. The object is to keep only a few main or "scaffold" branches (four to six or eight in the case of apples) and to have these as evenly spaced as possible, but emerging fróm the trunk at different levels in order that the maximum amount of air and sunshine can reach all parts of the tree.

Once established, this scaffold of main branches is maintained for the life of the tree, but there should be sufficient annual pruning to keep an "open head"—that is, a branch structure that freely admits fresh air and light to all parts.

The pruning of apples and of other tree fruits is best done during the winter or *very* early spring before sap starts to run (see sketch, page 259).

Pears. Pear trees, once established, require less constant care in pruning and spraying than apples. Dwarf pears are standard varieties grown on quince rootstocks. They prefer a soil on the heavy side, but with good drainage.

One-year trees are cut back about a third at the time of planting and two-year trees in about the same proportion, lowest branches being removed, and all but three or four of the rest. After that, little pruning is required except to remove lowest branches (until a suitable trunk is developed) and the weakest of any that crisscross or crowd.

Plums. Plums are of two distinct types, the Japanese and the European. The former bear much larger fruits. Where soil is light or sandy, the Japanese type is usually considered to do better. In any case, overfertilizing, especially with quickly

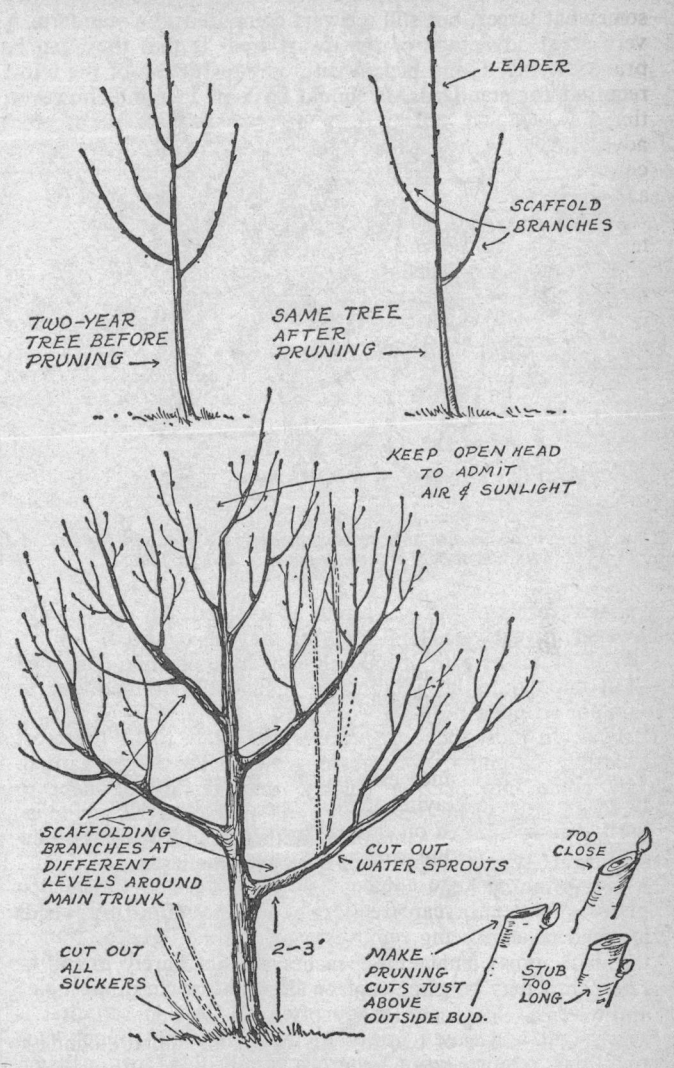

Fruit trees, in order to develop into properly proportioned producers of heavy crops, must be kept pruned from the start.

Dwarf fruit trees occupy only a fraction of space required for "standard" trees. Multiple-variety dwarfs frequently end in failure.

available forms of nitrogen, is to be avoided. On sandy soils, however, a yearly feeding in spring may be required.

With plums as with pears, only moderate pruning is needed —but enough to keep branches sufficiently thinned out to maintain an open head.

Peaches. In most sections, peaches are likely to be the most rewarding of any tree fruits to grow in the home garden. They come into bearing quickly, may readily be kept to moderate size, yield generously, and in bloom are quite as decorative as most ornamentals. With the advent of the new truly dwarf type, the owner of even the smallest place should be able to enjoy home-grown, tree-ripened peaches. The first variety of this new type grows only 4 to 5 feet tall but yields full-sized peaches.

Unlike apples and pears, peaches are not happy in sod or grass. They may be given a place along the north or west side of the vegetable garden. They often do well in soil that is rather light and sandy for other tree fruits, but under such conditions require more generous applications of fertilizer. The spraying required to control insects and diseases in much less than for apples.

TREE FRUITS, SMALL FRUITS, AND BERRIES

To bear sizable crops of good fruit, peaches need constant attention in the matter of pruning. This starts with planting. Very young trees or "whips" up to about 4 feet high are cut back a third to a half, and any side growths are stripped off. Larger sizes, up to 6 feet or so, are cut back proportionately, but three or four of the upper side branches—evenly spaced to form a head—are left, cut back to about 5 inches each.

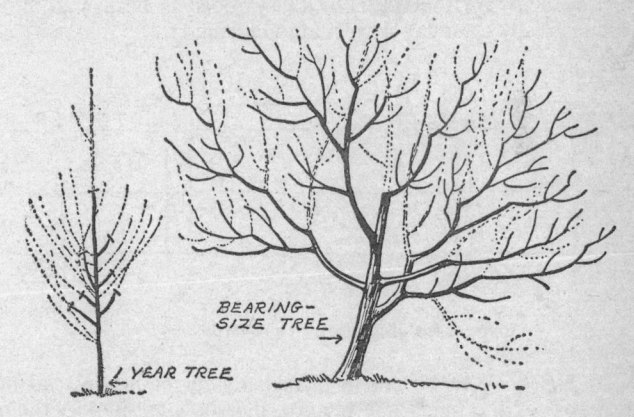

Peach trees, from the time they are planted, require annual pruning. A large part of each season's new growth becomes surplus, and if left makes a tangled, dense growth.

Peaches continue to require severe annual pruning. Branches tending to grow upright are cut back to an outside bud to encourage spreading growth; crossing or weak limbs are removed and others cut out or cut back to maintain an open head. As fruits develop, thinning may be required to keep the branches from touching each other. Heavily laden branches may require supports to prevent their breaking. In some sections the trunks need protection from rabbits, as is the case with all true fruits (see Appendix). Fruit should be gathered just before it reaches the dead-ripe stage, and handled as gently as eggs.

Apricots and nectarines require much the same culture as peaches. They are often used as espalier subjects.

Grapes, as home-grown fruit for the small place, have the great advantages that they occupy little ground area and can also serve as an important part of the landscaping. The easiest way to grow them is over an arbor, especially where shade is desired.

While grapes flourish and produce some fruit even if they

262 SPECIAL GARDENS, AREAS, AND PLANT MATERIALS

are given little or no attention, really good results are to be expected only if the vines are properly supported, trained, fed and protected from possible injury from pests and diseases.

They prefer a sunny southern exposure, a slope being preferable but not essential. Even though the vines may grow vigorously, any extreme in the way of soil, either too wet or too dry, will result in poor crops of fruit. In general, a slightly acid soil that remains fairly moist is best. Full sunshine is really essential in ripening the fruit.

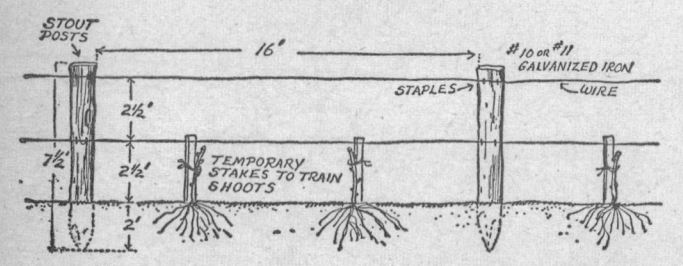

Support for grapes grown primarily for fruit.

If grapes are to be grown principally for eating instead of as a part of the landscape picture, it is best to support them on posts and wire trellises. Stout posts, extending 5 to 6 feet above the ground and 10 to 20 feet apart, carry 2 wires or plastic ropes, the first halfway up the post and the other at the top. Vines are spaced 8 to 10 feet apart and tied to wires as they grow.

Plants when set are cut back to two or three buds, and roots to 8 or 10 inches. Plant early in spring, as soon as ground can be worked. The first year the strongest cane is tied to the wires; the second year vines are trained along wires horizontally, and so on until top wires are reached. Detailed information on pruning and other phases of grape culture is obtainable from State Experiment Stations. Grapes do best with annual spring application of a high-nitrogen fertilizer. Mulching keeps down weeds, conserves moisture.

Figs can be grown much farther north than they usually are with a little extra care in the way of winter protection. The shorter the growing season, however, the smaller the crop. We secure a few ripe fruits annually even here on Cape Cod by tying down the lowest branches for the winter and covering them with heavy burlap. Another enthusiast, only a few miles away, has a hardier variety planted against a high, south-facing retaining wall, which produces a good crop an-

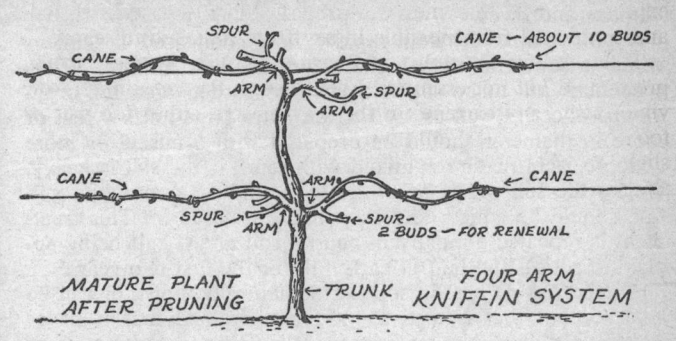

Annual pruning is required if vines are to continue to bear good crops.

nually without winter protection. Roots are much hardier than growth above ground, and new branches develop quickly when severe pruning is required after winter injury. Young plants tied up, banked with leaves, dry peatmoss, or pine needles, held in place by stakes and burlap, will stand quite severe temperatures as will larger specimens if the trunks are wrapped and the tops protected by burlap, or similar material.

In the South the fig is a decorative and valuable dooryard fruit tree. It is happiest in compact clay and wet soils that are free from nematodes, which are apt to attack the roots in rich, friable, well-drained situations. A spring feeding is advisable, followed by a summer mulch. Year-round mulching is even better as figs root shallowly and so are injured by deep cultivation. Celeste, Brown Turkey, and Brunswick are standard varieties, ripening—in the order listed—from July to September.

BUSH FRUITS

Blueberries are by far the most rewarding of the several types of berries suitable for the small home garden. They yield worthwhile crops, may easily be frozen or preserved for winter, and can be fitted into the landscape plan as they form shrubs which are very decorative from spring, when the bare stems turn crimson, to late autumn, when the foliage is a rich plum-red. Their only disadvantage is the fact that birds love the ripening fruit so much that the bushes need protection during this period unless enough are planted to supply both humans and birds.

Young plants develop rapidly into good-sized specimens which assume individual characters as they mature. When specimens are to be set in a lawn or garden area for ornamental effect as well as for berries, extra large holes 4 feet or more in diameter should be prepared with a bushel or more of loose, acid peatmoss mixed with sand, if the soil is heavy. Unless the soil pH is below 6, ¼ pound of ammonium sulfate should be added, and thoroughly watered in. This treatment is repeated annually in neutral soil areas, half being applied in spring and half in early fall for the first two years.

Blueberries do best in soil that is naturally moist, or can be kept so, but that is also so perfectly drained that it never stays soggy wet. No cultivation other than the removal of weeds is needed, but a constant mulch blanket should be maintained. Sawdust is more satisfactory than peatmoss for this purpose unless the latter can be kept moist (not wet) by frequent watering. Seaweed, bog hay, cranberry vines, or ground coconut shells are satisfactory mulching materials.

Until the plants are three or four years old, little pruning is required except to clip out weak, dying, or crisscrossing growths; or to head back any inclined to become too tall. The bushes naturally assume attractive, many-branched, spreading forms.

If there is a heavy set of flower buds on newly planted bushes it is advisable to remove most of them for the first season or two in order to establish strong plants quickly. This requires will power, but pays off well in the end.

Currants and Gooseberries used to be grown more generally than they are today. Homemade currant jelly and gooseberry jam were standard treats for special occasions as well as for everyday use.

These two bush fruits are easily grown, however, and make rather neat, well-rounded shrubs 3 or 4 feet high, which are especially attractive when in fruit. A few bushes may be fitted into a planting of shrubs where they receive much, if not full, sun. Usually they are given a place in a corner of the vegetable garden. To produce well they must not be crowded. The oldest wood should be removed right down to the ground after three or four years' growth.

Gooseberries tend to grow less erect than currants, and the lowest, spreading branches should be cut out as they start. If grown as "standards" they make quite decorative conversation pieces. Ours are planted on each side of the entrance to the vegetable garden and cause much favorable comment. We have found it necessary, however, to give the tall, bare "trunks" or stems some support. We use inconspicuous, rusted iron stakes to which the stems are loosely fastened, at intervals, with raffia ties.

In pruning gooseberry bushes, all branches over four years old should be cut out, right down to the ground. One-year-old growths produce more vigorous side shoots if cut back 4 to 6 inches.

Gooseberries and currants other than the red varieties should not be planted in areas where white pine blister rust is prevalent.

Insects which attack currants or gooseberries are: aphids; sawfly; borers, including the corn borer; fruit fly. Diseases: blister rust; leaf spot; cane blight; crown gall.

THE CANE FRUITS

This group includes raspberries, blackberries, dewberries, and loganberries. All are characterized by their vigorous, unruly, and viciously thorned canes—which bear the delectable fruits! Given half a chance, all of them increase and spread rapidly, and so they are not for the very small garden. In fact they are scarcely for the garden at all, as they are much more easily controlled in beds of their own, where they may be kept from taking over adjoining areas.

All the cane fruits prefer a loamy soil that is well drained but retains moisture. Dewberries will prosper in a somewhat sandier soil than the others. Most of them, with the exception of types recommended for the southern states, are entirely hardy and do best in the Northeast and Northwest.

Most widely grown of this group are the raspberries, which, with everbearing varieties now available, are well worth growing. Any surplus fruit at the height of the bearing season is easy to freeze or makes superb jam.

Plants received from the nursery come in the form of one-year canes with bunched roots. After tops are cut back to about 2 feet and roots trimmed, they are set out at 3-foot intervals in a row, in full sun. Planting should be done just as early as possible in spring (or in autumn in mild climates) since soil should be kept moist until they are well established. *Raspberries* tend to grow erect, but should be given some support to prevent their bending over when burdened with fruit, which tends to cluster at tips of canes. A row of 2×4 posts —or better, round posts of cedar or cypress—spaced 10 to 15 feet apart can be placed along the row. To these are fas-

266 SPECIAL GARDENS, AREAS, AND PLANT MATERIALS

tened two strands of plastic clothesline about 4 feet from the ground, one on each side of the raspberry plants. These will hold the growing canes upright and greatly facilitate both culture and picking. Old canes are removed entirely after fall fruiting, and young canes are cut back two thirds of their length.

To set out new plants, well-established suckers can be used if desired. Canes are cut back to not more than 18 inches, or to 9 inches if the grower is willing to forego any fruit the first year. In this case, the first crop will be the fall fruit of the following season, after which new canes are pruned back one third their length. Old canes are cut to the ground after fruiting. If new canes are set out every three or four years, preferably in a newly prepared location, a continuous supply is assured.

Unwanted suckers between the rows, which develop rapidly during each growing season, must be hoed out or the result will be a thick tangle of canes and little fruit.

Black Raspberries, or Blackcaps, and purple and yellow raspberries, are less satisfactory than the red varieties for the home garden. By nature they are rampant, sprawling grow-

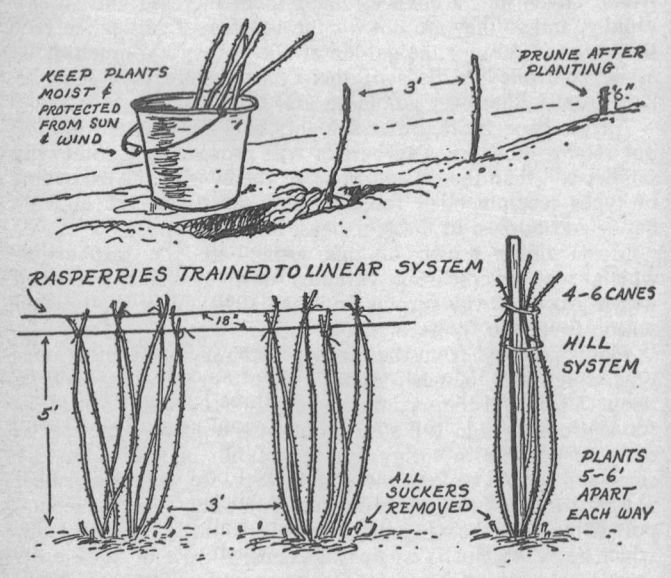

Raspberries, easily grown, are very satisfactory as a home-garden fruit crop. Old canes are cut out annually.

ers. To keep them under control, they must be pruned back while the tips are still soft to a height of 24 to 30 inches, according to the vigor of the variety being grown. Laterals also should be pinched back. For best flavor and easy picking, berries should be permitted to ripen on the vines, picked in the cool of the evening, and kept cool overnight.

Blackberries need room because the canes spread rapidly. Rows should be set 7 feet apart and, as with raspberries, all suckers or new canes appearing between the rows must be hoed out. Each year dead canes are cut to the ground and new canes reduced to 5 feet in length, only the strongest being left to bear. In general, culture is the same as for red raspberries. Bailey is a standard variety.

STRAWBERRIES

Strawberries, all things considered, are highly satisfactory for the home garden. They can be grown to perfection over a much wider range of territory than any of the others. The so-called everbearing varieties make it possible to enjoy home-ripe, fresh berries before the main crop in May or June, and in autumn until first frosts. To be at their very best, strawberries must be dead ripe before they are picked.

As few as a couple of dozen well-cared-for plants give much more than a token return; but for those who really like strawberries, a larger planting is desirable. With good culture most varieties provide at least a pint of fruit per plant, and yields up to twice that amount may reasonably be expected.

One important advantage in growing strawberries as compared to many other fruits is that every bit of the crop may be used. If at the height of the season there are more than enough to supply daily needs, the balance may be frozen or preserved for winter with less trouble than is required to keep most fruits and vegetables.

Varieties. There are two distinct types of strawberries: the one-crop-a-year June bearers, and the so-called everbearing, which produces two or occasionally three less generous crops. A more accurate term for this type would be repeat-bearing rather than everbearing.

The first everbearing varieties lacked both size and quality. These traits have been overcome in such newer varieties as Ogallala, which we consider the best of all we have tried, and Red Rich, a patented strawberry which is high-priced but worth it.

Of the numerous varieties of June-fruiting strawberries

some do better in one section, some in another. One of our favorites is an old-timer, Senator Dunlop, that does well almost everywhere.

Strawberries are not fussy about either soil or climate. They thrive in many sections, from Maine to Florida and from Oregon to California. The two things they do require are good drainage and full sun. Where there is any question concerning drainage, this can readily be provided by using a slightly raised bed. Six inches or so is sufficient as strawberries do not root deeply.

Both the size and quality of the crop depend a great deal on well-enriched soil. In sandy soil, however, humus in the form of peatmoss or compost is especially helpful because strawberries, while resenting wet feet, still require ample moisture to develop large, juicy, and flavorful berries. They do especially well where irrigation or ample watering can be provided during dry weather. Abundant moisture is most important for newly set-out plants, for unless strong crowns are formed a maximum crop of berries will never be obtained.

In addition to providing plenty of humus in the soil, a general-purpose fertilizer should be applied and well worked in —preferably two weeks or so before planting. This has the

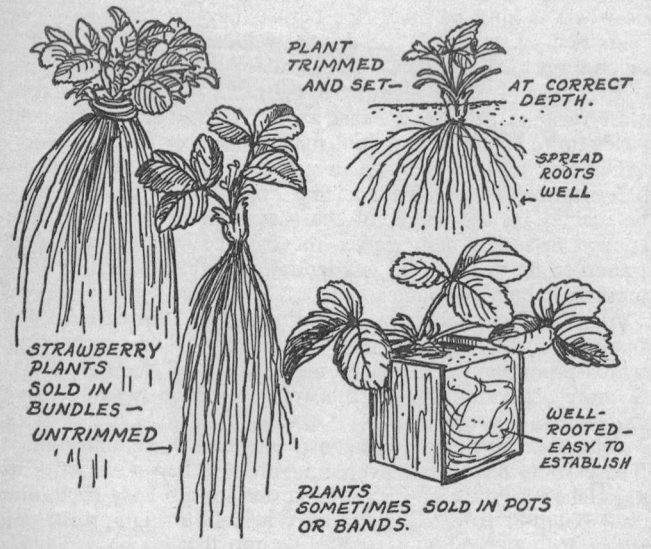

Strawberries are readily grown in the home garden. Best results are obtained when a new bed is started each year.

advantage of destroying the first crop of weeds when the surface is again raked over in preparation for planting.

Plants may be procured either with bare roots, or established in pots. Plants locally grown in peat pots, if they can be obtained, give the quickest and surest results; but either pot-grown or bare-root plants, shipped by mail, are entirely satisfactory if properly cared for.

Bare-root plants are shipped in bundles of twelve or twenty-five. Upon receipt the bundle should be opened at once, even if planting must be delayed. The roots are trimmed back to 2 to 3 inches, the plants set upright on wet peatmoss, and kept in the shade. Plant as soon as possible. Fan the roots out, cover and press them in firmly, but be careful not to get soil into the centers of the crowns. If the weather is hot and dry, keep well watered for a week or so.

Mulching is always desirable on the home strawberry bed. It not only helps to retain moisture and discourage weeds but also supports the berries, keeps them clean, and encourages all-over ripening.

While strawberries are not difficult to grow, most varieties run out quickly from overcrowding. Unless one uses the hill system, in which all runners are cut off as soon as they start, one can obtain best results and the largest berries by setting out new plants every second year or, still better, by replanting half the bed every year.

Strong new plants that receive no set-back when transplanted are grown on by rooting runners in clay or peat pots.

The very best plants for setting out are obtained by rooting the required number of runners in 3- or 4-inch peat pots filled with rich compost and sunk into the ground up to the rims. Runners are held in place with clothespins, twigs, or small stones until roots, which develop in a surprisingly short time, are established. Tips of runners beyond the pot are cut off. Plants grown in this way can be taken up and set out in their permanent positions without the slightest check.

The most common mistake made by amateurs in strawberry growing is to assume that, once established, the plants will go on bearing good crops indefinitely. New plants formed by runners quickly become overcrowded, and bear berries so small that they are scarcely worth picking, unless carefully transplanted to new beds.

Plants grown by the hill system, in which runners (except for the few needed to provide new plants) are removed as described above, may be set as close as a foot apart in good soil, though a somewhat greater distance is preferable. The rows are spaced a minimum of 18 inches apart. If kept perfectly clean and well fertilized they will give good yields for three years. But here again the very best berries are obtained by setting new plants every year. In reality, this involves little more work than weeding, cleaning, and fertilizing an old bed. Runners or pot plants set each spring, or pot plants set in late summer, with no attempt to carry them on after they have finished fruiting the following summer, provide the very biggest crops and the very best berries.

> Who loves a garden loves a greenhouse too.
> WILLIAM COWPER

CHAPTER 18

The Home Greenhouse

The day when only the wealthy could indulge in such a hobby as owning a greenhouse has long since passed. Today responsible companies all over the country sell small, home-type greenhouses, or all the materials required to assemble any size or type desired.

While inexpensive plastic ones can be bought, those made of wood, or aluminum frames glazed with heavy glass designed for greenhouse use are more reliable and substantial and in the end less expensive. Properly cared for, they will last a lifetime.

One of the most important decisions to be made when one purchases a greenhouse is whether to use it principally for growing plants, or for the enjoyment of mature plants already grown. In the latter case a conservatory rather than a greenhouse may be preferable. While a great variety of plants may be maintained and bloomed in a conservatory, it is enjoyed principally for lounging, dining, reading, possibly sun bathing.

In either case, although the construction of the house may be much the same, the floor and interior arrangement will differ greatly. In a "growing" house, a floor of dirt, gravel, or dry-laid bricks which can be freely drenched when watering, helps to maintain a moist atmosphere at all times—a great advantage in providing ideal conditions for plant growth. In the conservatory type of house such a floor would not do. Neither would the usual type of house floor. A floor of slate, tile, or terrazzo is attractive, waterproof, and can easily be kept clean. Adequate drainage should be provided.

In many situations the dual-purpose greenhouse is the answer, although such an arrangement is rare. It is entirely feasible to have a section for starting seedlings, rooting cuttings, potting and repotting plants, and other greenhouse operations along one side or end, reserving the rest of the space for decorative plants in tubs or planters, with a permanent specimen or two such as a climbing vine, palm tree, decorative orange or lemon. A hole may be left in the slate or tile floor where such a decorative feature may be planted.

Even-span or lean-to? Often one of the questions to be decided is whether the greenhouse should be of the even-span or the lean-to type. If it is to be entirely separate from the dwelling, the even-span type, unless some unusual conditions exist, is preferable. Even when this type of greenhouse is used, it is often more practical for it to be attached to the house. By doing this, you bring the under-glass garden within a step of the living quarters, where it can be entered without going out of doors.

Certain conditions, however, may make it desirable to build a greenhouse of the lean-to type, directly against the house. This has the advantage of taking up less space, of being sheltered from strong winds, and of costing considerably less to heat. The curved-eave type is also better-looking —often an architectural improvement, adding to the beauty of the house design. The lean-to's disadvantages are that it gets no cross ventilation; will be much more difficult to keep cool in hot summer weather; and, in many cases, may detract from rather than enhance the architectural appearance of the house if it is not a curved-eave type. This latter difficulty often can be overcome within a short time by suitable plantings of vines, climbing roses or shrubs.

The function of a greenhouse should determine its design. A typical layout is shown in the accompanying sketch but of course the bench plan may be altered to suit the owner's wishes. No bench should be so wide that any part of it may not readily be reached.

WORK SPACE

In planning a house one should keep in mind that many operations require some elbow room. Storage space for potting soil, fertilizers, insecticides, and so on will also be needed.

EVEN-SPAN GREENHOUSE
FREE-STANDING WITH CURVED EAVES

LEAN-TO GREENHOUSE
STRAIGHT EAVE – GLASS-TO-GROUND

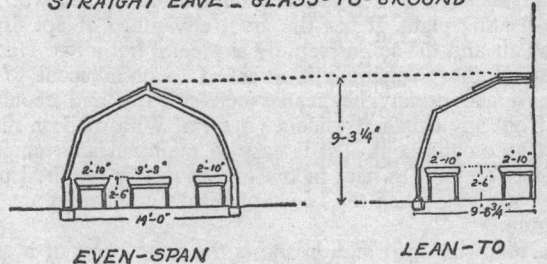

EVEN-SPAN

LEAN-TO

An even-span house is the most satisfactory for full-scale gardening under glass; gives maximum light and bench space. The lean-to type requires less space, costs less to build and heat.

Unless a potting shed is planned in connection with the greenhouse, it is desirable to leave some space at the end of a bench that can be used for this purpose. If possible, however, a potting shed should be included. Not only will it be needed for planting, transplanting, and repotting operations but also for storing compost and other soil ingredients such as peatmoss, sand, vermiculite, fertilizers.

A potting shed attached directly to the greenhouse is the most convenient, but where this is not practical, it should be placed as near by as possible. Any bins to hold soil should be made frostproof so that the contents may be available at all times.

Unlike the greenhouse, the potting shed need not receive full sun. As a considerable amount of potting, repotting, and transplanting is done during the winter and very early spring, when an unheated potting shed is not a pleasant place in which to work, a removable potting bench or board in the greenhouse will be found very useful. Cleats across the bottom to fit snugly inside the sideboards of the bench will hold it firmly in place. Upright boards are placed at the back and at one or both ends (see cut). Although our own greenhouse has an attached potting shed we find this potting board, on cold winter days, a very pleasant substitute for the sunless, chilly bench in the potting shed.

Heating. Methods of heating greenhouses vary greatly in different sections of the country. The severity and length of the winter season and the types of fuel available are factors determining the type of heating to be used. In mild areas where electricity is not too highly priced, this may be the best system to employ. Hot water will prove the most satisfactory whether installed as a separate system or connected with the house heating plant. It has the great advantage of not drying out the air and the soil as rapidly as steam, hot air or electric heating. If the greenhouse is attached to or adjacent to the house, it can usually be heated conveniently and economically from any existing residence system. With modern methods of automatic control it is easy to maintain any temperature level desired, as heat in the greenhouse is required principally at night, when the needs of residence heating are at a minimum.

The following information shows the actual cost of heating home greenhouses of varying sizes in different sections of the country, based on actual records.

A recent survey found that the fuel cost of heating small houses up to 16×32 feet (in Ohio) and 15×28 feet (in Michigan) ranged from $75 to $100 per season. Smaller

Where it is possible, there is a great advantage in having a potting shed with storage space attached to the greenhouse.

The authors' portable potting bench. Can be fitted onto greenhouse bench when wanted; saves carrying plants, cuttings, seeds to the potting shed; and provides pleasanter working space on winter days.

houses, 10×18 feet (in Illinois) and 10×21 feet (in Connecticut) ranged from $30 to $75.

In all but five of these cases, the night temperature was maintained at 60 degrees. Cost would be considerably less at 45 to 50 degrees, which is sufficient for a great many plants. Detailed information about the different types of heating systems is best obtained from the manufacturer of your greenhouse or from the county agent.

If it can be provided, a thermostat in the greenhouse helps tremendously in caring for the house and affects a considerable saving in heating costs. In most greenhouses, there are usually areas that are warmer or cooler than the average temperature of the house, but sometimes one can take advantage of this by growing cool-house subjects like snapdragons, cyclamen, and primroses in the cooler area and those which require higher temperatures where the required range is consistently maintained.

Ventilation is an important factor in the maintenance of desired temperatures in the greenhouse. Too high or too low a temperature may be equally disastrous. In fact, standard, small home greenhouses sold as "package" deals are more likely to be inadequate in providing ventilation than in the heating system.

It is possible to procure additional side ventilators and fans to blow out hot air but it is much better to make sure that there are adequate facilities for fresh air before purchasing the house. Cross ventilation provides one of the surest ways to get a flow of cool air. Doors at *both ends* of a house, for instance, are well worth the extra cost, if the model selected calls for one door only. Our own lean-to house has doors at both ends, but in addition we have installed ventilator windows above each door to carry off the trapped warm air. This is, of course, in addition to the automatic roof ventilator which runs the entire length of the house.

Shading. Almost any small greenhouse fully exposed to the sun requires some type of shading if plants are to be grown in it through the summer months. The former method of providing shade was the use of a lime whitewash, or similar material manufactured for the purpose, painted or sprayed directly on the glass. The obvious disadvantage was that, once applied, it shaded the house even during cloudy or rainy weather when all the light possible was to be desired.

Now various forms of shading that can be let down or rolled up as needed are available. We find that during certain seasons of the year—especially in spring when many young seedlings are being started—it is desirable to raise or lower the shading more than once during a day. Another great advantage of the roll-down type of shading is that one section of the bench may be shaded while the rest is left in full sun. Here on Cape Cod we also find our shading protects the glass against flying branches and other objects during heavy gales and hurricanes.

Water. The lack of adequate provision for water in most amateur greenhouses always surprises us. A single spigot can provide all the moisture the average greenhouse needs, but it requires more time to apply. We have three spigots in our moderate-sized house and another in the potting shed. We find that the time saved by not having to drag the hose around, change nozzles, and fill watering cans has repaid the cost of the extra spigots many times over.

You don't have to do much gardening under glass to realize that all types of watering cannot be done with the same nozzle. Manufacturers may claim that a nozzle can be adjusted to throw anything from a solid stream to a fine mist. In a greenhouse, however, such an all-purpose nozzle is not adequate since the tiniest seedlings and thin-stemmed transplants can easily be knocked over by a forceful spray.

We use three different nozzles and consider these the minimum for adequate greenhouse watering. The first is a "pressure breaker," which applies water freely as it flows from the hose but breaks the one solid stream into scores of tiny ones which flow out without force. The second is a "fog nozzle," which supplies water in a fine mist that settles down gently, not disturbing the soil or beating down even the most delicate seedlings. The third is an ordinary sprinkler nozzle with several adjustments which apply water evenly, either fanned out or in a heavy spray.

Another time-saver is a shut-off at the end of the hose. One type lets water flow through only while the fingers grip the shut-off tightly. The flow is stopped automatically when pressure is released. This eliminates a trip back to the spigot to turn the water off.

Other watering equipment which we find essential includes a bulb spray for moistening small trays or pots in the propagating box, and a couple of galvanized metal pans in which flats, pots, or composition planting boxes or trays may be watered from the bottom. At least one watering can should be available. We keep a second one especially for plant-food solution so that it is ready to use at a moment's notice.

GREENHOUSE OPERATIONS

The general *principles* which apply to the growing of plants under glass are much the same as those for outdoor plants. The techniques of course vary considerably. The greenhouse grower can control such factors as light, temperature, moisture, and feeding to a much greater extent than is possible in the outdoor garden. On the other hand, *unless* he controls them, troubles or even disasters are more likely to result.

Starting Seedlings. Starting plants from seed is one of the basic operations in greenhouse work. It is also one of the most fascinating and exciting. The gardener feels intimately in touch with and in control of all that goes on from the time he opens a packet of seed until the resulting plants are well on their way to maturity. Every change in the development and progress of a plant is a new thrill. Furthermore, greenhouse gardening may be indulged in all the year round.

Needless to say, it is important to procure the very best seed available—most likely those from a company specializing in varieties for underglass culture. If the seed is not used soon after it is received, it should be kept in an airtight metal container and stored in a temperature between 40 and 50 degrees, although modern methods of packaging and storing seeds have improved the vitality to a surprising degree.

Temperature is a very important factor in starting seedlings. In the open garden or even in the coldframe or hotbed, we sow according to seasonal temperatures. In the greenhouse, however, since it is desirable, in fact essential, to be able to provide different temperatures, seeds may be started at any time the gardener wishes. Time of sowing will depend largely upon when he wants the plants.

It is best to have a minimum frame or a glass-enclosed propagation box, where temperature may be controlled independently of that in the greenhouse. Such propagating kits of various types may be purchased or made at home. An extension cord with an electric light bulb placed in or under the propagating box will provide sufficient heat to maintain a temperature five to fifteen degrees higher than that outside the box. A 25- to 75-watt bulb may be used according to the size of the box. A thermometer should be left inside to check temperature. A heating cable may be used for the same purpose. Such a difference in temperature makes a marked difference not only in the time required for flower or vegetable seed to germinate but also in the number of perfect seedlings obtained.

Sowing dates, especially for annuals, biennials, and perennials that are to be flowered in the greenhouse, are determined by the dates on which one wishes to have them in bloom and the length of time it takes them to begin to flower. A further factor, of course, is the season at which different species will flower best. One would not, for instance, attempt to have sweet peas under glass in July, or chrysanthemums in April, although both feats could be accomplished with adequate control of temperature and light.

Timing. There is considerable latitude in the time when seedlings may be started for plants to be grown under glass. But especially for the beginner, it is better to be a little bit early than late. Then if anything goes wrong with the first sowing, a second one may be made.

SEED SOWING

In recent years methods of seed starting have been greatly simplified and made much more certain. Here is the method which we now use.

Disinfecting. In order to ensure success, we first take precautions against fungus that can cause seedlings to "damp off" at the soil level, a job which must be done *before* seeds are sown. There are available today concentrated materials which, diluted in water, can be used as effective sprays or drenches. One of their great advantages is that they may be applied to soil in which seeds are to be planted and *also* in soil in which seedlings, cuttings, or young transplants are growing without causing injury. The material we use is Panodrench, but others are available.

Before sowing, we spray flats, pots, benches, watering cans, and any other equipment which may infect seedlings, as well as the soil mixture in which the seeds are to be sown.

If seedlings or young transplants are obtained from an outside source, these and the pots of trays containing them should be treated *before* being placed in the greenhouse.

Soil mixes for starting seed are a vital factor in achieving success. Many mixtures are offered for sale for this purpose; or the gardener may make up his own. A generally accepted one is half fine, gritty sand and half pulverized peatmoss, by volume. We have tried most of them but now prefer plain, sifted (milled) spahgnum moss, especially for very fine seeds.

The trick in using this mixture is to get it uniformly moist *before* placing it in the containers in which seeds are to be sown. We use composition trays about 6×8 inches, 2¼ inches in depth, with drainage holes in the bottom. We prefer them because of their light weight, handy size, and maneuverability.

First a ½- to ¾-inch layer of moist, medium-coarse peatmoss is placed in the bottom of the tray, to provide drainage if needed. Over this goes the moist, milled sphagnum, pressed in firmly and evenly to within half an inch of the rim.

Sowing. Seed may be broadcast over the surface, but we usually sow in rows. Shallow troughs are made with a V-shaped marker, just the length or width of the container. The depth of these varies with the size of the seed to be sown. Except for large seed, a very shallow covering is sufficient. We use an old kitchen sieve to sift the milled sphagnum over the surface after sowing. It is pressed in firmly but gently with the flat side of a light wooden tamper. To cover large seed to a greater depth, fine vermiculite or sand may be used.

Watering. We use the misting or "fog" nozzle to moisten the newly sown containers. Moisture must be constant and uniform throughout the germination period. Drying out of the soil mix for even a few hours may prove fatal. On the other hand sogginess caused by poor drainage may rot the seeds before they sprout.

Fine seeds and those requiring a long time to germinate can best be kept moist by covering the container with clear plastic, such as Saran Wrap, held in place by a rubber band. This creates a miniature greenhouse so that the moisture, evaporating from the soil, is returned to it. *As soon as* germination takes place the covering must be removed. Small sheets of glass just a little larger than the containers are also effective, and in some instances easier to handle.

Nutrients. Peatmoss, sand, sphagnum, vermiculite, or perlite used as media for germinating seeds have the common disadvantage of lacking nutrients. As soon as the true leaves appear on seedlings started in any of these, plant food must be administered. Any of the complete liquid fertilizers is suitable for this purpose and a moderate feeding once a weeek with one of these is enough to encourage strong growth. From the time leaves begin to unfold, seedlings need all the strong sunshine they can get and fresh air, without drafts, on warm sunny days. Turn containers daily to prevent the young plants "drawing" toward the light.

Transplanting is best done as soon as the first true leaf develops. We transplant our young seedlings to peat-strip-pots, as described in Chapter 4.

Growing on. The period from the time seeds germinate until they are ready for transplanting varies greatly with different species and varieties as well as with temperature, light, and other conditions. However, as a general rule, the sooner they can be transplanted the better. It is extremely important that this shift should take place before the tops begin to crowd. Usually the roots become badly entangled before this happens and many of them are broken in the operation of transplanting.

Slow-growing seedlings started in a sterile medium such as milled sphagnum, a peatmoss-sand mixture, or vermiculite, should be given liquid fertilizer frequently enough to prevent stunted growth from starvation.

After their first transplanting, the tiny seedlings are grown on until they begin to crowd. Then they are again transplanted, this time into individual pots or into peat strips or multiple pots (fiber pots joined together at the rims so that six or eight may be handled as a unit). They remain in these until they are ready to be shifted into larger peat or other pots, to an outdoor frame, or to their permanent locations in beds or borders.

As plants develop, it may be necessary to move them about in the greenhouse in order to give the young seedlings more light and air. Any overcrowding at this period of growth quickly results in spindly, weak plants.

A layer of coarse peatmoss over crocking, in large pots, provides a moisture reservoir that checks too rapid drying out of soil.

Potting and repotting. With plants that are to be grown on in pots, repotting at more or less frequent intervals becomes an important factor in their culture, especially during the early stages of growth. Young plants may very quickly become potbound; i.e., the rapidly forming roots become a closely woven network around the inside of the pots and consequently become hardened and more or less atrophied. *Before* this stage is reached, the roots form a good ball which can readily be removed from the pot and replanted in a pot one or two sizes larger. This is accomplished by placing the fore and middle fingers on either side of the plant stem, inverting it, and then knocking the rim of the pot sharply against the edge of the bench. The plant is then repotted in a position that will leave the surface of the old ball ¼ to ½ inch—depending on the size—below the rim of the new pot.

One great advantage in using peat or composition pots for growing on young plants is that in the operation of repotting the roots are not disturbed. Roots, pot, and all are transferred to the new and larger container.

Crocking. In using 4-inch or large-sized clay or plastic pots with hard-surfaced walls, place a few pieces of broken pot or small pebbles or turkey gravel over the drainage holes to assure unclogged drainage. Over this is put about half an inch of coarse peatmoss, which serves the double purpose of preventing any soil from clogging the drainage holes, and of acting as a moisture reservoir to prevent too-rapid drying out of the soil above it. This precaution of course is not necessary where plants are to remain in the pots for only a short period as is the case with bedding or vegetable plants that are to be set out in the open ground; or with plants in peat pots, the walls of which absorb and hold moisture.

Soil used for potting should be prepared in advance and kept for this purpose. A good basic mixture is made up of three parts sifted compost from a well-rotted heap, and one part each of gritty sand and peatmoss. If no compost is available, use in place of it two parts of good loam and two parts of peatmoss. If clay predominates in the loam, increase the proportion of sand.

Sterilizing. Soil to be used for transplanting seedlings and also for potting in most commercial operations is thoroughly sterilized by elaborate and expensive equipment. The home gardener may easily sterilize the amount of soil he requires by placing a small amount at a time in a pan, a metal tray, or any convenient container, and baking it in the oven at a temperature of 185 to 200 degrees Fahrenheit, for a half hour or more. The soil should be moist but not wet. (During this operation, any member of the household with an oversensitive

THE HOME GREENHOUSE

nose should be warned to keep out!) This simple treatment eliminates weed seeds and practically all soil-born diseases.

Disinfecting. Sterile soil, however, does not guarantee the protection of seedlings from attack *after* they germinate and begin to grow. In fact it is after they have germinated and until they are large enough to be transplanted, that they are most likely to be attacked by the worst and most prevalent enemy of all—the dread damping-off disease, "rhizoc"—short for rhizoctonia. Many experienced gardeners as well as most beginners have had the bitter experience of having a flat of husky, healthy seedlings suddenly begin to topple over; and upon examination found them rotted through and shriveled just at the soil surface—with both root systems and tops still in perfect condition. Such a tragedy is enough to make even a Philadelphia Quaker use strong words!

Spores of rhizoctonia carried not only in soil but on plants, pots, tools, hands, and feet remain indefinitely viable. Fortunately it is now easy to guard against this menace, as described on page 279 in the introductory paragraph to seed sowing. In addition to general spraying with Panodrench we spot-spray pots and flats of newly planted seed, transplanted seedlings, and also cuttings. One of the nice things about this spray is that it does not have a disagreeable odor.

Once seedlings that have been transplanted into flats or trays begin to crowd, they should be given more space. In the case of annuals and vegetables which are to go into the open garden, the next step is to transfer them to a frame to harden off before they are set out in their permanent places. Those which are destined for pot culture are transplanted into small —usually 2- or 2¼-inch—pots.

Propagation by cuttings, as described in Chapter 4, may be carried on in the greenhouse under ideal conditions. In fact this is one of the great advantages of a greenhouse. The cutting bed we use consists of a frame that fits tightly into one end of a bench, extending about 4 inches above it. A second frame, equipped with two hinged panels covered with plastic, and which fits over the lower frame, gives additional depth. The panels forming the cover of the frame are equipped with counterbalanced weights supported by pulleys attached to the roof sash bars. These panels may be closed tight or raised to any degree wanted for ventilation; or they may be held upright and out of the way. A board divider through the center of the frame makes it possible to maintain two different temperatures within it merely by giving one section more ventilation than the other. When closed, the panels are level so that any moisture that collects drops back to the cutting bed and is evenly distributed. When not in use, this top section of the frame, with its hinged lids, is lifted off, leaving bench space available for plants in pots or trays.

WHY?

We debated a long time about whether or not to include a discussion of greenhouses in this book. But as so many of our friends and acquaintances get so much enjoyment from their gardening under glass, we finally decided to give at least enough informaton to guide the beginner who considers getting one.

Lack of space does not permit detailed discussion of the many intriguing plants which may be grown. We have tried, however, to point out a few things that should be considered if one is thinking of having a greenhouse, and to describe some of the basic operations in connection with operating it.

Several good books on greenhouse management for amateurs are listed in the Appendix.

PART THREE

SELECTIVE, COUNTRY-WIDE MONTHLY CALENDAR

HOW TO USE THE CALENDAR
ALPHABETICAL LIST OF STATES SHOWING AREAS
THE CALENDAR
NOTES ON COUNTRY-WIDE GARDENING PROBLEMS

How to Use the Calendar

(Based on frost dates and length of growing seasons:
not on state lines)

The Calendar section will be most helpful to you if you use it properly. It is simply arranged to tell:

WHAT TO DO

In any phase of gardening, from preparing the soil for planting to cutting flowers or harvesting vegetables or fruits, success depends upon doing the things that need to be done at just the right time.

This requires a great deal of *looking ahead*.

Even the experienced gardener often fails to think of all the things that should be done *just when it is time to do them*. To avoid such omissions, many garden-minded homeowners keep a running calendar, based on previous experience, to make sure that they attend to such things as ordering seeds and materials; starting seeds indoors or in a hotbed; sowing seeds and setting out plants in the open—some early and others late; transplanting; applying sprays; starting new plants from cuttings; renovating, feeding, or de-weeding the lawn—and so on through the list.

If even experienced gardeners find useful such a calendar of what-to-do and when-to-do-it, how much more valuable will one be to any beginner! With many of the things he hopes to accomplish, it may make all the difference between success and failure!

HOW

The Calendar section of this book is very simple to use. It differs from others in that, instead of giving condensed and inadequate information along with the reminder, or (as is more often the case) leaving the reader to try to track down such information as best he may, it gives wherever needed a direct reference, by number, to the *page* where this particular subject is discussed in one of the main sections of the book.

WHEN

The compilation of calendars to suit—as nearly as possible—all parts of the continental United States, has been a challenge. A calendar should be based on planting dates, frost dates and minimum winter temperatures because these factors determine when garden operations should be undertaken. Accordingly, in this calendar, the country is divided into six numbered areas based on spring planting dates, i.e., May 1, Area I; April 15, Area II; April 1, Area III; March, Area IV; February, Area V; and January, Area VI. Each of these areas has been given a Roman numeral as noted above, indicating that the states *or portions of states* included in it have similar frost dates, planting dates, and—with few exceptions—minimum winter temperatures.

Other cultural conditions in the United States, however, vary greatly and such factors as rainfall, amount of sunshine, and type of soil do make a difference in many aspects of garden operations. Since it is impossible to incorporate all of these factors in one calendar, we urge the reader who has special gardening conditions, unusual in his area, to read the calendar for the areas directly north and south of his own.

During the heart of the winter when much of the country is in the "deep freeze," operations in many areas are the same. Consequently, one January calendar applies to Areas I, II, III, and IV. Beginning in February, however, there is a change, for during that month residents of Area IV are preparing for March planting and sowing. In Area V, outdoor gardening begins in February, while in Area VI early planting dates are in January.

USE OF THE CALENDAR

First: At the beginning of each monthly calendar, starting on page 296 with the month of January, the reader will find a heading of Roman numerals. One of these will correspond to his own area number—to be found on page 293 and it is *this* portion of the calendar *only* which concerns him.

For instance, the gardener living in northern Illinois finds by consulting page 291 that he is living in Area II.

HOW TO USE THE CALENDAR

He then turns to the calendar for the *month* in which he is interested, and in it the section covering Area II, which includes his part of the country.

Second: The reader selects, from the list of projects of activities suggested for this area, the ones in which he is particularly interested. He may wish to jot them down, along with the accompanying page-reference numbers. This *personal* list or calendar may be made up for a month, or for several, or even for the entire year. It is well to keep it in the tool shed or in some other place where it may readily be referred to.

Don't make your personal list too all-inclusive at the start. One is quite likely to plan many more projects than there will be time, money, or energy enough to accomplish. Three projects really completed yield much more satisfaction than a dozen started but not carried through to completion, and consequently ending in a feeling of frustration.

Third: When you've decided on which projects you'll undertake, the page references included will direct you to the main portion of the book and the how-to information necessary for your project. It is well to look over one's personal calendar, once it has been made up, frequently enough to keep somewhat ahead of the game; in this way it is easy to secure and have on hand seeds, plants, bulbs, materials of various kinds that will be needed for future use. In many garden operations even a few days' delay, while not proving fatal, may mean somewhat less perfect results than might otherwise have been attained.

Many major operations—such as building a rock garden, making a pool, or constructing a new fence—can be planned in definite stages, and then the completion of each step yields its own satisfaction.

With these few words of advice—harvested from decades of experiments, experience, and a reasonable degree of success—we leave the reader to pick and choose the items that will make up *his own* tailored-to-measure calendar—and wish him Happy Hunting!

Alphabetical List of States Showing Areas

Where you live will determine *your* AREA NUMBER for the monthly CALENDAR REMINDERS of garden activities and projects on pages 296 to 396

STATES LISTED ALPHABETICALLY WITH AVERAGE MINIMUM WINTER TEMPERATURES, AVERAGE SPRING PLANTING DATES AND CALENDAR AREAS

Area	State	Average minimum winter temperature	Average spring planting dates
V	Alabama, northern and central	0 to 10	Feb. 1 to 15
VI	southern	20 to 30	Jan. 15
IV	Arizona, high elevations	—20 to —10	Mar. 1 to 15
V	central	—10 to 10	Feb. 15 to Mar. 1
VI	desert	20 to 30	Jan. 15
IV	Arkansas, northern	—10 to 10	Mar. 1 to Apr. 1
V	southern	10 to 20	Feb. 1 to Mar. 1
VI	California, coastal	30 to 40	Jan. 15
VI	southern and central	20 to 30	Jan. 15
V	interior valleys	10 to 20	Feb. 1 to 15
IV	mountainous	—10 to 0	Mar. 1 to 15
I	Colorado, mountainous	—40 to —30	May 1 to 15
II	eastern	—20 to —10	Apr. 15 to May 1
III	Connecticut, coastal	—5 to 5	Apr. 1 to 15
II	central and northern	—20 to —10	Apr. 15 to May 1
IV	Delaware	0 to 10	Mar. 15 to Apr. 1
IV	District of Columbia	0 to 10	Mar. 15 to Apr. 1
VI	Florida	20 to 30	Jan. 15 to Feb. 1
VI	extreme south	30 to 40	Jan. 1 to 15
VI	Georgia, coastal and Southern	20 to 30	Jan. 15 to Feb. 1
V	central	10 to 20	Feb. 1 to 15
V	northern	0 to 10	Feb. 15 to Mar. 1

LIST OF STATES AND AREAS

Area	State	Average minimum winter temperature	Average spring Planting dates
I	Idaho, mountainous	−30 to −20	May 1
II	intermountain	−20 to −10	Apr. 15 to May 1
II	Illinois, northern	−20 to −10	Apr. 15 to May 1
III	southern	−10 to 0	Apr. 1 to 15
II	Indiana, northern	−20 to −10	Apr. 15 to May 1
III	southern	−10 to 0	Apr. 1 to 15
II	Iowa, northern	−30 to −20	Apr. 15 to May 1
III	southern	−20 to −10	Apr. 1 to 15
III	Kansas	−20 to −10	Apr. 1 to 15
IV	southeastern	−10 to 0	Mar. 15 to Apr. 1
IV	Kentucky	−10 to 10	Mar. 1 to Apr. 1
V	Louisiana, northern	10 to 20	Feb. 1
VI	southern	20 to 30	Jan. 15
I	Maine, northern interior	−40 to −30	May 1
II	coastal and southern	−20 to −10	Apr. 15 to May 1
IV	Maryland	− 5 to 10	Mar. 15 to Apr. 1
II	Massachusetts	−20 to −10	Apr. 15 to May 1
III	Cape Cod	− 5 to 5	Apr. 1 to 15
II	Michigan	−20 to −10	Apr. 15 to May 1
I	Minnesota, northern	−40 to −30	May 1 to 15
II	southern	−30 to −20	Apr. 15
V	Mississippi, northern	0 to 10	Feb. 15
V	central	10 to 20	Feb. 1 to 15
VI	southern	20 to 30	Jan. 15
III	Missouri, northern	−20 to −10	Apr. 1 to 15
IV	southern	−10 to 5	Mar. 15 to Apr. 1
I	Montana	−40 to −20	May 1 to 15
II	Nebraska, northern	−30 to −20	Apr. 15
III	southern	−20 to −10	Apr. 1 to 15
I	Nevada, mountains	−30 to −20	May 1
III	western and central	−20 to −10	Apr. 1
IV & V	southwestern	0 to 20	Feb. 15 to Mar. 1
I	New Hampshire, northern	−40 to −30	May 1
II	southern	−20 to −10	Apr. 15
IV	New Jersey	− 5 to 10	Mar. 15 to Apr. 1

SELECTIVE COUNTY-WIDE CALENDAR

Area	State	Average minimum winter temperature	Average spring planting dates
III	New Mexico, northern	—20 to —10	Apr. 1 to 15
IV	central	—10 to 0	Mar. 1 to 15
V	southern	0 to 10	Feb. 15
I	New York, northern	—35 to —20	May 1
II	balance	—20 to —10	Apr. 15 to May 1
III	Long Island	—5 to 5	Apr. 1 to 15
V	North Carolina, coastal	20 to 30	Feb. 1
IV	western	0 to 10	Mar. 1 to 15
V	central	10 to 20	Feb. 15 to Mar. 1
I	North Dakota	—40 to —30	May 1
II	Ohio, northern	—20 to —10	Apr. 15
III	central and southern	—10 to 0	Apr. 1 to 15
III	Oklahoma, western	—20 to 0	Apr. 1 to 15
IV	central and eastern	—10 to 5	Mar. 1 to Apr. 1
V	Oregon, coastal	20 to 30	Feb. 1 to Mar. 1
III, IV	interior	5 to 20	Mar. 1 to Apr. 1
II	intermountain	—50 to —20	Apr. 15
II	Pennsylvania, northern	—20 to —10	Apr. 15
III	southern	—10 to 0	Apr. 1 to 15
II	Rhode Island	—10 to 0	Apr. 15
III	coastal	—5 to 5	Apr. 1 to 15
VI	South Carolina, coastal	20 to 30	Jan. 15
V	interior	10 to 20	Feb. 1 to Mar. 1
IV	western	0 to 10	Mar. 1 to Apr. 1
II	South Dakota	—30 to —20	Apr. 15 to May 1
IV	Tennessee	0 to 10	Mar. 1 to 15
VI	Texas, gulf coast	20 to 30	Jan. 15
V	south central	10 to 20	Feb. 1
V	southwestern	10 to 20	Feb. 1 to Mar. 1
IV	northwestern	—10 to 10	Mar. 1 to Apr. 1
IV	north central	0 to 10	Mar. 1 to Apr. 1
I	Utah, mountainous	—30 to —20	May 1
II	balance	—20 to —10	Apr. 15
I	Vermont, northern	—40 to —30	May 1
II	balance	—30 to —10	Apr. 15 to May 1
IV	Virginia	0 to 20	Mar. 1 to Apr. 1
IV	Washington State, coastal	10 to 30	Mar. 1 to Apr. 1
III	interior	—10 to 10	Apr. 1 to 15
II	mountainous	—20 to —10	Apr. 15 to May 1

LIST OF STATES AND AREAS

III	West Virginia	—10 to 0	Apr. 1 to 15
I	Wisconsin, northern	—40 to —30	May 1 to 15
II	southern	—20 to —10	Apr. 15 to May 1
I	Wyoming, mountainous	—30 to —20	May 1
II	balance	—20 to —10	Apr. 15 to May 1

AREA I

Colorado, mountainous
Idaho, mountainous
Maine, northern
Minnesota, northern
Montana
Nevada, mountainous
New Hampshire, northern
New York, northern
North Dakota
Utah, mountainous
Vermont, northern
Wisconsin, northern
Wyoming, mountainous

AREA II

Colorado, eastern
Connecticut, central
  northern
Idaho, intermountain
Illinois, northern
Indiana, northern
Iowa, northern
Maine, coastal
  southern
Massachusetts
Michigan
Minnesota, southern
Nebraska, northern
Nevada, mountainous
New Hampshire, southern
New York, central
  southern
Ohio, northern
Oregon, intermountain
Pennsylvania, northern
Rhode Island, inland
South Dakota
Utah, lower altitudes
Vermont
Washington, mountainous
Wisconsin, southern
Wyoming, lower altitudes

AREA III

Connecticut, coastal
Illinois, southern
Indiana, southern
Iowa, southern
Kansas (except southeastern)
Massachusetts, Cape Cod
Missouri, northern
Nebraska, southern
Nevada, western
  central
New Mexico, northern
New York, Long Island
Ohio, central
  southern
Oklahoma, western
Oregon, interior
Pennsylvania, southern
Rhode Island, coastal
Washington, intermountain
West Virginia

AREA IV

Arizona, high elevations
Arkansas, northern
California, mountainous
Delaware
District of Columbia
Kansas, southeastern
Kentucky
Maryland
Missouri, southern
Nevada, southern
New Jersey
New Mexico, central
North Carolina, western
Oklahoma, central
  eastern
Oregon, interior
South Carolina, western
Tennessee
Texas, northwestern
  north central
Virginia
Washington, coastal

AREA V

Alabama, northern and central
Arizona, central
Arkansas, southern
California, interior valleys
Georgia, central and northern

Louisiana, northern
Mississippi, central and northern
Nevada, southwestern
New Mexico, southern
North Carolina, coastal and central
Oregon, coastal
South Carolina, interior
Texas, south central and
    southwestern

AREA VI

Alabama, southern
Arizona desert
California, coastal
    southern and central
Florida
Georgia, coastal and southern
Louisiana, southern
Mississippi, southern
South Carolina, coastal
Texas, gulf coast and southeastern

The Calendar

JANUARY

> Every fence, and every tree
> Is as white as white can be.
> JAMES STEPHENS

For Areas I, II, III, IV

INDOORS

Most garden activities this month are indoors. It's a fine time to catch up on the planning you can't get done during the growing season (Chapter 1).

BOOKS: Read a few garden books on subjects of special interest to you.

CATALOGS are coming in every day. Look each one over as it arrives and then file it. Later in the month, seed, nursery stock, and roses should be ordered. If any catalogs you need have not been sent, write for them before the stock is exhausted.

PLANS made to scale are a big help in executing any garden project. If new beds, borders, or other features are to be added to the garden in spring, draw plans *now* before sending in seed and nursery orders. Plan for color combinations, periods of bloom, permanent background plantings as well as for garden design (page 21).

ORDER seeds, nursery stock, roses, tender or half-hardy, summer-flowering bulbs as soon as plans are completed. Don't order more than you have room for; but on the other hand, be sure you order everything you need. Later on, choice varieties may be sold out.

STORED BULBS, *corms, and tubers* should be examined this month. Discard rotted bulbs. Cut away withered or rotted portions of tubers and dust with sulfur. Provide ventilation

THE CALENDAR 297

to prevent further rotting. If tubers are too dry and withering, moisten peatmoss or other storage medium slightly.

Pack gladiolus corms in plastic bags, adding one ounce naphthalene flakes per 100 corms. Store at 35 to 40 degrees, to discourage thrips.

BRING AMARYLLIS BULBS, in their pots, to full light, and increase water. Feed when buds first develop.

REDUCE WATER gradually on Christmas cactus; also on poinsettias when leaves begin to drop. Keep palms on dry side this month.

GARDENIAS can bloom indoors. Give them day temperature of 60 to 70 degrees and don't let it drop below 55 degrees at night. Avoid drafts and see that they get morning sun. Water daily and soak the pot in a bucket of water once a week. Feed once a month.

HOUSEPLANTS get dusty in midwinter. Take them to the kitchen, the laundry, or the bathroom once a week. Wash glossy leaves with soapy water; rinse with clear water. Treat hairy-leaved sorts to a fine misting of the leaves and let dry completely *in the shade*. Except for hairy-leaved specimens, sprinkle or mist leaves freely during this weekly treatment. Use bath, or dish-spray head.

SOW SEEDS of *Vinca rosea* and *Nierembergia* indoors if you want them for the garden next summer. They are very slow-growing. Jerusalem-cherry berries should be dried now and sown in February. Open "cherries" and remove seeds for sowing. You'll have quite a crop for next Christmas! (Pages 65; 279.)

WOOD ASHES from the fireplace make excellent fertilizer to bring up the pH toward neutral if your garden soil is acid. *Store* in tubs or boxes and save for use around lilacs, dianthus, *Daphne cneorum,* and in rose beds.

OUTDOORS

EVERGREENS, both coniferous and broad-leaved, should have snow removed from the branches and from the centers of dense specimens soon after each storm. If it freezes on, permanent damage may result. Boxwood is especially susceptible to this sort of injury because of its dense, globular growth.

FOUNDATION SHRUBS may suffer severely if drip from the eaves or from a downspout turns to ice in a sudden temperature drop. Check eaves, gutters, and downspouts for possible leaks *before* this happens.

PRUNE GRAPES AND FRUIT TREES this month during sunny spells when a few hours outdoors are enjoyable (Chapter 17).

GRAFTING FRUIT TREES is a sport enjoyed by many amateurs. This is the time to cut the scions of trees to be used later for grafts. Mark each variety, make them into bundles, and keep them in a cool place or bury them in peatmoss in a coldframe (Chapter 4).

BAGWORMS have formed cocoons by this time and may sometimes be found on evergreens, especially arborvitae. The brown, pointed cocoons, shaped like Japanese lanterns, should be cut off and burned.

BIRDS need food now. See that they have suet as well as seeds. A bird "pudding" made of suet, seeds, oatmeal, cornmeal, and peanut butter is a real treat. If you have no evergreen cover, set up one or more discarded Christmas trees to give your feathered friends shelter.

PROTECTION FOR TREES AND SHRUBS from rabbits and other rodents should have been completed last month. If it was neglected at that time, see that something is done about it before a heavy snowfall (Appendix, page 448).

JANUARY THAWS often cause heaving of plants in perennial beds. If the ground thaws, walk around the garden and press firmly back into place any plants which have had their roots loosened.

WINDOW BOXES which hold living plants, either evergreens or bulbs, should be checked now and then for moisture. If dry, give a thorough watering when the temperature is above freezing.

TOOLS should have been checked and stored when the garden was "put to bed," but if any need sharpening or repair, January is a good time to do these odd jobs. If the handles of small hand tools like weeders and trowels are painted bright red with an enamel paint, they will be lost less easily, come spring.

COLDFRAMES which contain living plants need attention, even in mid-winter. During very cold spells, additional cover over the glass is a wise precaution. Tarpaulins or heavy plastic, securely tied down, may be used. Or a covering of salt hay or of straw *under* the sash may be substituted. If a warm spell develops, give a little ventilation during the sunny hours, closing the sash again before the thermometer begins to drop sharply toward evening. If there has been a snowfall which remains on the sash, do not disturb it. The frame could not have a cozier winter blanket.

WIND BURN is a serious winter threat in some areas. Place screening, burlap, or heavy plastic on the windward side of broad-leaved evergreens. Wrap trunks of young trees and shrubs where necessary. Spray with Wilt-Pruf (page 151).

MICRO-CLIMATES: A study of midwinter conditions in your garden may reveal several micro-climates (page 86). In severe storms or after heavy snow, note sheltered areas. Doubtfully hardy trees, shrubs, and other plants should be tried out in these locations.

GRAPES may be pruned any time after they go dormant. Before sap begins to flow in February or March, remove a third of old vines and all undergrowth (page 262).

For Area V

BULBS: Check condition of stored, tender bulbs (page 188). In damp fir bark or peatmoss start tubers of tuberous begonias, gloxinias, caladiums (page 188). Pot up calla-lilies. Under glass sow seeds of gloxinias, tuberous begonias, streptocarpus. Day temperature 75°, night 55°.

SOIL PREPARATION: Prepare garden beds as soon as ground can be worked (pages 94-96). Work rich compost or well-rotted manure into beds where established perennials are about to start active growth.

PESTS: Apply dormant sprays to deciduous trees and shrubs (Appendix, page 452). Put out poison bait for mice in mole runs (Appendix, page 448).

TOP-DRESS winter-blooming primroses with all-purpose fertilizer mixed with leafmold.

VEGETABLES: Harvest winter crops as needed. These include endive, Savoy cabbage, Swiss chard, spinach, leeks, Brussels sprouts, kale, salsify, parsnips.

Sow seed of hardy vegetables in frame. Set out perennial vegetable plants (pages 237-239).

PRUNE: Camellia, fuchsia, fig trees, fruit trees, grapes, hydrangeas, roses, wisteria.

Deciduous hedges: beech, hawthorn, laurel, privet, barberry, etc.

Remove dead wood: catalpa, daphne, golden-chain tree, lilacs (including suckers), locust, magnolia, paulownia (Chapter 6).

CUTTINGS: Start fuchsia and camellia cuttings from prunings (page 76).

WATER: In dry weather give deep waterings to evergreens, shrubs, and any plants soon to bloom (pages 89-91).

FRAME: Sow seeds of hardy annuals and vegetables (pages 65-72; 117).

PLANT FLOWERING TREES (pages 148-151): Among the best for the Upper South are dogwood, magnolia, mimosa (*Albizzia julibrissin rosea*), crape-myrtle, fringe tree, and redbud (see Appendix).

For Area VI

PESTS: Apply dormant spray to deciduous trees, roses, and shrubs, if not already attended to. Use general-purpose spray once a week on plants in active growth, especially roses (Appendix, page 451).

WATER: In dry weather, apply deep watering to evergreens, shrubs, and plants soon to bloom (pages 89-91).

FROST: Have light covering of evergreen branches or plastic ready to protect doubtfully hardy plants if frost is predicted. After frost, water tender plants freely in early morning. In frost-free areas, Christmas gift plants do well on the patio or terrace, if brought in on cold nights.

HEDGE PLANTS which may be planted this month are listed on page 422.

BULBS: Do not disturb *Eucharis grandiflora* (Amazon-lily). Top-dress with rich fibrous soil and water well to produce winter bloom. Order new, tender, summer-flowering bulbs.

PLANT AND TRANSPLANT: azaleas, citrus fruit, deciduous trees, evergreens, evergreen shrubs, camellias, figs, fuchsias, flowering trees, fruit trees, magnolias, nut trees, rhododendron (pages 148-151), roses (Chapter 15), perennials, biennials (Chapter 11).

SOW OUTDOORS: ageratum, calendula, California poppy, candytuft, cynoglossum, dianthus, gypsophila, larkspur, lupine, petunia, salvia, snapdragon, verbena, *Vinca rosea* (Chapter 11), hardy vegetables (Chapter 16).

SOW IN FRAMES OR INDOORS: wax begonia, China-aster, cinerarias, fever-few, geranium, heliotrope, lobelia, mesembryanthemum (pages 65; 117).
Tender vegetables: eggplant, peppers, tomatoes (pages 65-71).

SET OUT: onion sets; perennial vegetables; plants of cabbage, cauliflower, broccoli. *Half-hardy bulbs:* anemones, achimenes, bessera, calla, erythronium, freesia, galtonia, gladiolus, hedychium, hymenocallis, ismene, lapeirousia, leucocoryne, milla, montbretia, nerine, spreklia, tritonia, tigridia, watsonia, zephyranthes (page 188). Start sweet potato sprouts (page 239).

FROST-FREE AREAS: Plant tuberous begonias, gloxinia, caladium, amaryllis, gloxinia, etc. (page 188).

FEED: azaleas, camellias, figs, hydrangeas, irises, pansies, primulas, spring-flowering bulbs, violets, other early-blooming plants and shrubs (pages 91; 98).

PRUNE: allamanda, banana (severely if frozen back), camellia, clematis, hibiscus (past freeze), honeysuckle and other rampant vines, lantana (past freeze), mandevilla, pecans, roses, late fall-blooming shrubs (Chapter 6).

FEBRUARY

> With blue and purple hollows,
>   With peaks of dazzling snow,
> Along the far horizon
>   The clouds are marching slow.
>   *The Heavenly Hills of Holland*
>   by HENRY VAN DYKE

For Areas I, II

PRUNE, after each storm, broken and damaged branches of shrubs and trees and remove snow and ice from evergreen branches which may bear them down and cause damage.

THAW: In case of a thaw, examine perennials and other small plants to ascertain if they have "HEAVED" out of the ground. If so, press the roots in firmly, and mulch heavily.

SOWING: Do *not* be tempted to start seeds indoors too early in the far north. Ascertain from seed packets the number of days from sowing to germination. Except for those which germinate very slowly, sow about six weeks before seedlings can be hardened off in a coldframe (page 279).

STUDY your property and note areas which are wind-swept; those which lie deep in snow; are deeply or partially shaded, or in full sun. This knowledge is helpful when planting hardy specimens.

ORDER: Among the SHRUBS which may be ordered now for spring planting are the following hardy sorts: *Cotoneaster apiculata*, a low shrub with arching branches and red berries; *Cotinus coggygria* or Purple Smokebush; *Caryopteris incana* or Blue-beard, which must be treated as a perennial that is cut back in spring; Potentillas, in variety (see also lists in Appendix).

PRUNE: When weather permits, prune fruit trees, grapes, and shrubs which flower in summer or autumn (Chapter 6).

CHECK: Have all needed seeds and nursery stock, including roses, been ordered? If not this should be done at once.

POTS OF BULBS to be forced may still be brought indoors. Those which have finished blooming can be kept in a cool place, watered occasionally, and replanted in the garden when ground can be worked.

HOUSEPLANTS need all the sunshine they can get now. They do not care for cold drafts, but indirect fresh air each day is good for them.

ROOTED CUTTINGS of houseplants which have been transplanted during the winter, may be about to bloom. Feed these before buds show color.

PESTS: Keep an all-purpose houseplant insecticide on hand ready to treat any specimen which develops aphids, white fly, red spider, or other pest (Appendix, page 451).

Syringing the foliage of houseplants each week helps to keep them healthy, discouraging red spider and other troubles aggravated by dry air and dust.

For Areas III, IV

INDOORS

TUBERS: Start dahlia tubers in damp peatmoss. New shoots which have started on these may be rooted like any other cutting. Start tuberous begonia, caladium, and gloxinia tubers by placing, bud side up, in flats of damp peatmoss or fir bark. Tops should remain exposed. Pot up calla-lilies. Set out after last frost.

HOUSEPLANTS: Young flowering plants are about to bloom. Feed, until buds show color. Watch for pests and disease. Do not dry off Christmas cactus too quickly. By treating it as you did during the fall months, you may be rewarded by another burst of bloom.

FORCED HARDY BULBS which have finished bloom should be watered moderately until foliage matures, then placed in a cool dry cellar or frame until ground can be worked, when they can be replanted in the garden. (Discard bulbs of paper whites when bloom is over.) Bring in any remaining pots for forcing.

SEEDS: Sow indoors or under glass seeds of: broccoli, cauliflower, cabbage, *Cobaea scandens,* dwarf dahlias, nierembergia, verbena, stocks, Jerusalem-cherry, lobelia, *Begonia semperflorens, etc.* (page 279).

For Areas III, IV

OUTDOORS

WINTER PRUNING of fruit trees, grapes, and late-flowering shrubs can be done this month if it was not completed in January (Chapter 6).

SPRAY with dormant oil spray when the temperature goes above 45 degrees—but while plants are still dormant—bittersweet, other euonymus, lilac, fruit trees, roses (Appendix, page 451).

COLDFRAMES need management from now on. When temperature rises above 40 degrees, in sun and warm rain, open to give ventilation. Close again before sundown. If soil is dry in frame 6 inches down, give slow, deep watering directly in soil (do not wet plants) on a warm day (Chapter 7).

SHRUBS AND ROSES should have been ordered by now for March planting. If not already done, see to this.

FREEZING AND THAWING may still occur. After each thaw, go

over perennial beds for possible heaving and press roots back into the soil.

FLOWERING SHRUB BRANCHES force easily and quickly if brought indoors in February. Syringe the entire branches every day, and keep the stems in deep water. Hard wood absorbs water better if the ends of the branches are slit or crushed.

SOIL PREPARATION: Prepare garden beds as soon as ground can be worked (pages 94-96).

LAWN: As soon as ground is thawed, fill in bare and low spots on lawn and seed (Chapter 10). Distribute pre-emergence crabgrass killer plus plant food on lawns (Appendix, page 454).

VEGETABLES: As soon as ground can be worked in February or early March, sow peas, and sweet peas, and plant onion sets. Lettuce and radish seeds may be sown in a coldframe (Chapter 7).

PLANTING: Prepare PLANTING HOLES as early as possible for planting trees, roses. Flowering fruit trees, dogwoods, cane and bush fruits should be spring-planted (pages 148; 255).

Has your SEED ORDER arrived? Have seeds been ordered? If not, do it now! The same advice applies to perennial plants for setting out in March.

MULCH GRAPE vines with well-rotted manure if available. If not, fertilize and mulch with rough compost or peatmoss.

For Area V

PLANT: shrubs and trees (page 148), roses (page 223), half-hardy bulbs (page 188), perennial vegetable plants, potatoes, onion sets (Chapter 16), perennial flower plants, including rock garden subjects (pages 179-183; 440).

SOW OUTDOORS: peas and sweet peas, hardy vegetables, early in month (Chapter 16), half-hardy vegetables, half-hardy annuals (page 238).

SET OUT hardy vegetable plants such as cabbage, broccoli, etc. (page 239).

SOW INDOORS or UNDER GLASS: tender annuals, tender vegetables (page 278).

PRUNE: hydrangeas (root-prune if old and not blooming well), late-blooming shrubs, geraniums, fuchsias (Chapter 6), roses, while still dormant (page 226).

FERTILIZE: newly prepared beds (page 92), lawns (page 160), roses (page 225), bulb beds as soon as bloom is over.

SPRAY PROGRAM should be started as soon as roses, shrubs, etc., start new growth. Until then, use dormant sprays where needed (Appendix, page 452).

DIVIDE and transplant mature perennials, if not done previously (page 184).

POT UP tuberous begonias, gloxinias, and caladiums started last month in damp fir bark or peatmoss (page 187).

For Area VI

LAWNS: Prepare seedbeds for new lawns which are to be sown, sprigged, or plugged. Sprigging or plugging can be done this month (Chapter 10).

All established lawns except those of Centipedegrass may be given an application of ammonium sulfate to green them up (Chapter 10).

PLANT: windbreaks and hedges (Appendix); perennials; also divide and replant established clumps (page 184); perennial vegetables; dracaena; palms; gerberias, tritomas, and tender bulbs, such as gloriosa lily, tuberose, canna (page 188); tender water-lilies in boxes to set out in March. In shade houses: begonias, gloxinias, orchids, ferns. Set out tender vegetable plants (page 239).

SOW: tender vegetable seeds (page 238), tender annual seeds (pages 67-71), decorative grasses.

SPRAY: azaleas for petal blight with dithane, camellias for scale with malathion, evergreens and shrubs for aphids with lindane, figs for mealybug with malathion, gladiolus for thrips with miticide, roses once a week with all-purpose spray (Appendix, page 451).

CUTTINGS can be taken now of: allamanda (hard or soft wood), bamboo (2 or 3 joints below ground and the same above), fig, pomegranate (hardwood), passion vine (Chapter 4).

POINSETTIAS are cut back now, leaving 12 inches of stem. When new growth starts, pinch out tips several times to assure branching growth.

PRUNE: fuchsias (Chapter 6).

FERTILIZE: azaleas (acid), camellias (acid), palms, bulbs, after bloom is over (page 98).

AZALEAS may suffer from chlorosis (yellowing). If so, spray with a mixture of 1½ ounces iron sulfate and 1½ ounces hydrated lime to a gallon of water. After bloom, prune plants severely to shape as desired (Chapter 6).

WATER deeply in dry weather (pages 89-91).

FROST may strike early this month. Cover tender subjects, if a freeze is forecast, with burlap, plastic, newspapers, or soil. Uncover as soon as possible. If shrubs freeze back, do *not* prune at once as this may encourage early, soft growth which will again freeze. Crotons, hibiscus, ixoras, etc., may be defoliated by frost but usually the wood is undamaged.

Sprinkle foliage copiously early in morning after frost to prevent damage to tender subjects.

PREPARE NEW BEDS and borders for tender plants to be set out in March (pages 94-96).

MARCH

The wind at the flue, the wind strumming the shutter;
The soft, antiphonal speech of the doubled
   brook, never for a moment quiet;
The rush of the rain against the glass,
   his voice in the eaves-gutter!

EDNA ST. VINCENT MILLAY

For Areas I, II

While the rest of the country starts gardening in earnest this month, spring has not come to most parts of the far north. Some work can be done, however, to save time later, when spring really arrives.

Attend spring flower shows if any are within traveling distance. Take a notebook so that you can use some of the new ideas and grow some of the new varieties shown.

Those who cannot reach any of the shows can read the garden magazines and learn about what's new in plant material and gardening.

Have you a GREENHOUSE or HOTBED? If so, you are now gardening under glass and getting a head start on your neighbors. If not, read Chapters 18 and 7.

PRUNE away damaged tree and shrub branches. Paint over large wounds with tree paint, after scraping away any decay that has set in (page 111).

Prune and trim deciduous trees, late-blooming shrubs (Chapter 6), and grapes, if not already done (Chapter 17). Maples and birches should not be pruned until midsummer, as then the sap is flowing less freely than in the spring.

Do *not* prune spring-flowering shrubs until after bloom

and at no time shear them so as to destroy their natural, graceful forms (Chapter 6).

ROSE BEDS which have been heavily protected should be gradually uncovered as early as possible. When snow is gone and lawns begin to green up, remove heavy mulches and gradually uncover climbers which have been laid down and buried in soil. Do not unhill until April (Chapter 15).

PLANTING: If nursery stock or roses are delivered before it is time to plant, unwrap plants, place them in a trench, and keep roots covered with moist loam or damp peatmoss until the job can be done (page 150).

As soon as frost is out of ground, prepare planting holes for evergreens, shrubs, roses (pages 148-151).

Evergreens should be planted in spring *before* new growth appears.

PESTS: Dormant oil sprays may still be applied this month (see Appendix, page 452).

FRAMES: Open coldframe or hotbed to air, sun, and rain when temperature is above freezing. Close again before evening and night temperatures drop too low (page 117).

SOW INDOORS or UNDER GLASS seeds of broccoli, cauliflower, cabbage, petunia, verbena, dwarf dahlia (page 279).

For Areas III, IV

Attend SPRING FLOWER SHOWS and make notes for use on the home place.

PRUNE away winter-damaged limbs of trees and branches of shrubs (Chapter 6). Remove dead wood and weak stems from shrubs. Do not prune spring-blooming shrubs. Never shear these in a way that will destroy their natural grace (Chapter 6).

SOIL PREPARATION: As soon as ground can be worked, prepare beds, borders, and vegetable area (pages 94-96). Prepare planting holes for the stock that is to be planted soon (pages 148-151).

Prepare soil in frames or seedbeds for sowing (pages 68-71).

LAWNS: Prepare areas to be spring-planted; treat with pre-emergence weed killer. Clean up and fertilize established lawns, repair bare spots in lawn (Chapter 10).

PLANT as soon as holes can be prepared: beech, birch, dogwood, hawthorns, lilacs, magnolias; evergreens (before new growth starts) (page 148); fruits, bush fruits, grapes, strawberries (Chapter 17); roses (page 223).

ROSES: Remove mulch as soon as snow is gone. Unhill and work hilling into beds. Add fertilizer. Give dormant spray if plants are still dormant. Start summer spray program as soon as growth starts. Plant new roses. Prune (Chapter 15).

HEEL into trench any nursery stock, roses, or trees delivered before they can be planted. Unwrap, heel in, and water if necessary. *Keep* moist (page 148).

MULCH: Gradually remove all winter mulches.

FEED: bulb beds, fruits, perennial beds, rock gardens, shrubs and trees, roses, perennial vegetable rows (page 91).

SOW OUTDOORS: peas, sweet peas, hardy vegetables such as beets, carrots, spinach, Swiss chard, radishes, lettuce (Chapter 16), hardy annuals.

IN FRAME: half-hardy annuals (page 117).

DIVIDE AND TRANSPLANT early-flowering perennial flowers (page 184), perennial vegetables.

COLDFRAMES need much attention now. Leave open on sunny and rainy days, if above freezing. Cover only when frost threatens, or in drying winds (Chapter 7).

DORMANT SPRAYS can be applied only before plants come into growth. If scale is still present on euonymus, lilac, etc., use a combination of DDT and malathion every ten days *in late May or June* (Appendix, page 451).

When cultivating and fertilizing perennial beds where LILIES and other late-starting plants are present, be careful not to injure first shoots as they emerge or while they are still just below the soil level.

Where CRAPE-MYRTLE is root-hardy but is killed back above ground, cut back stems to 6 inches after removing mulch. Fertilize.

SUMMER TUBERS: Tuberous begonias, caladiums, and gloxinias can be started now in trays of moist peatmoss or in pots, if not already attended to in February (page 188).

For Area V

LAWNS: Feed, reseed and repair bare spots, apply crabgrass or other weed controls, begin mowing as soon as needed (Chapter 10). Use Bonus selective weed killer for dichondra lawns (Appendix, page 454).

PRUNE: albizzia, camellia after bloom, fuchsia (cuttings may be made from prunings), roses, geraniums (Chapter 6).

FEED: agapanthus (established), azaleas after bloom, camellia after bloom (page 98), bulb plantings, early-blooming perennials, trees, shrubs.

DIVIDE and transplant late-blooming perennials (page 184).

WIND SCALD: In the Southwest, guard against wind scald (page 128); provide ample water.

PREPARE all planting areas (pages 94-96); fertilize and have ready for setting out.

SOW half-hardy annual and vegetable seeds (pages 175; 238); tender annual and vegetable seeds as soon as soil warms up.

AZALEAS: Select new varieties during the blooming season when you can see them in flower.

SOW INDOORS: In cooler areas, seeds of tender annuals and perennials (page 278).

SET OUT: plants of broccoli, cabbage, cauliflower (page 239), first gladiolus corms (page 188), perennials (page 181).

PLANT: deciduous trees, shrubs (page 148), fruits (Chapter 17), roses (page 223).

SPRAY: holly and other specimens affected by scale, *before* March 15. Begin regular summer spray program as plants start into active growth (Appendix, page 451).

For Area VI

LAWNS: Mow winter grass very close. Feed established areas and apply weed killers. Sprig or plug new lawn areas, or sow seed. Repair bare spots and reseed. Treat Dichondra lawns with Bonus selective weed killer. Then apply fertilizer (Chapter 10).

SOW: seeds of tender annuals (pages 67; 175); tender vegetables (page 238); shrubs like *Cassia alata* and erythrinas.

PLANT: avocado, agapanthus, bamboo, caladiums in pots, crape jasmine, citrus fruits (pages 148-151), ground covers, subtropicals in warm areas, summer-flowering bulbs, corms, and tubers (page 188).

PRUNE: azaleas after bloom; camellias after bloom—take cuttings, fuchsias—take cuttings, geraniums—take cuttings (Chapter 4), shrubs after bloom (Chapter 6).

FEED: all established plantings; use cottonseed meal or other acid fertilizer where soil is alkaline, or for acid-loving plants such as azaleas, camellias, citrus fruits, evergreens, gardenias, hydrangeas (page 98); bulb beds, after bloom, summer-flowering bulbs.

SET OUT: water-lily boxes prepared last month. Leave ⅓ open water; early-flowering annual plants (page 184); hardy vegetable plants; tender vegetable plants in warmest sections (page 239); strawberries (page 268).

CUTTINGS: Start chrysanthemum cuttings for fall bloom (pages 73; 77).

Select new AZALEA varieties during blooming season.

SPRAY: Start regular spring and summer spray program: azaleas and gladiolus plants for thrip; roses weekly (Appendix, page 451).

WATER: In dry areas water regularly and deeply, especially plants about to bloom. Sprinkle foliage frequently. Protect recently planted areas from drying winds (pages 78-81).

APRIL

> Across the plains of April,
> Fresh regiments of rain
> With slanting silver bayonets
> March to the front again;
> And emerald green their banners fly
> Against the dark, disheveled sky.
>
> FREDERICK FRYE ROCKWELL

For Area I

In the extremely cold portions of the north and at high altitudes, winter has not loosened her grip.

On first warmer days, do not make the mistake of uncovering plants until sure that there will be no more nights of hard freeze.

As soon as weather moderates *consistently,* all operations listed for April for Area II may be undertaken in Area I.

For Area II

At last the winter should be on the run and many garden jobs can be done as the weather moderates.

UNWRAP TREE TRUNKS and branches. REMOVE MULCHES gradually from beds and shrubs.

As soon as the ground can be worked, PREPARE NEW BEDS and borders for planting (page 94); new lawn areas (page 156); planting holes for nursery stock, roses (pages 148; 223).

SELECTIVE COUNTRY-WIDE CALENDAR

LAWNS can be treated with needed soil amendments (lime or sulfur) as soon as snow melts. Apply pre-emergence weed killer-fertilizer one week later. Repair bare spots. Remove snow mold. Prepare new lawn areas as soon as ground can be worked (Chapter 10).

PLANT: beech, birch, dogwoods, evergreens (until new growth appears), fruit trees, bush fruits, grapes, hawthorns, lilacs, magnolias, shrubs, roses, perennials, strawberries.

ROSES: When planting roses, hill temporarily to 6 inches until re-established. If completely dormant, apply dormant spray (page 451). Established rose beds may now be unhilled. Work hilling material into the beds. Prune roses. Start summer spray program as soon as new leaves appear (Chapter 15).

SOW INDOORS OR UNDER GLASS: seeds of annuals which germinate slowly (page 278) and tomatoes, peppers, and eggplant, late in month.

VEGETABLES: As soon as soil is prepared and enriched (page 236) sow hardy vegetable seeds (page 238). Plant onion sets, rhubarb, asparagus, horseradish.

DIVIDE and transplant perennials. Take rooted cuttings from chrysanthemum: crowns are set out in rows (pages 72-73).

FEED: bulb beds, flower beds and borders of perennials, flowering trees and shrubs (page 98), lawns (pages 98; 161), rock gardens (also add compost around roots), roses (page 225).

PESTS: Treat flower beds and lawn areas with chlordane for insects which live in soil. *Do not* use on vegetable garden (page 451).

FRAMES need careful attention now. Remove heavy mulch around plants in frames. Open sash unless mercury goes below freezing. Water if dry (page 117).

WATER: Where springs are dry, WATER as needed (pages 89-91).

CUT BACK to ground root-hardy, top-tender SHRUBS like buddleias, hydrangeas, caryopteris, etc.

BULBS: Start tuberous begonia tubers and caladiums in damp

peatmoss indoors. Pot up canna roots and keep indoors until May.

For Area III

As soon as it seems safe, remove all mulches; weed bulb beds and perennial borders. Do not injure emerging bulb shoots, especially lilies.

PERENNIALS: Dig all perennials that are to be divided. Cut back tops of buddleias, caryopteris, hydrangeas. Before replanting perennials, loosen soil in beds, add humus, fertilizer, compost (or well-rotted manure). Work in thoroughly. Replant divided perennials. Chrysanthemum cuttings with roots are taken from outsides of crowns and planted in rows in the garden or in peat pots in a frame, to grow on.

FERTILIZE before bloom: bulb beds, ericaceous plants, with acid fertilizer, flowering shrubs, flowering trees, early-blooming perennials, rock garden perennials, with wood ashes and bonemeal (pages 91-98).

LAWNS: If lawns were not attended to in March, see to them now (Chapter 17).

SET OUT in their beds plants of pansies, violas, English daisies, primulas, and other very early-blooming perennials supplied from your own frames or from growers (page 184).

SUMMER BULBS: As soon as danger of frost is over, plant the first gladiolus corms; follow with ismenes and other half-hardy summer-flowering bulbs, corms, tubers (pages 185-187).

START INDOORS in very early April: tender annuals; tomatoes; peppers; and eggplant later in month (page 278).

IN COLDFRAME about middle of month: half-hardy annual seeds; perennial seeds and tender annuals late in month (page 117).

PREPARE A CUTTING BED in the vegetable garden. Sow in rows now: hardy annual seeds, plants of perennials, half-hardy bulbs. When soil and air warm up: tender annual seeds, dahlia tubers, etc.

SOW now in the open garden, after ground has been thoroughly prepared: beets, carrots, Swiss chard, parsnips, spinach, turnips, and other cool-weather vegetables (page 238). Late in month try some bush beans, covering seedlings with soil on cold nights.

SET OUT plants of broccoli, cabbage, cauliflower, lettuce, and anything else not affected by slight frost (page 239). Harden young plants for a week in coldframe before setting out.

PLANT STRAWBERRIES if not already done. Place straw around established plants, after weeding and fertilizing the bed (pages 267-270).

PEST CONTROL: Use chlordane on lawns and flower beds (*not* on vegetable garden at this time) for ants, earwigs, and larvae living in soil.

USE SLUG and SNAIL BAIT once every two weeks, at night (page 451).

SPRAY: Begin regular fruit spray program following closely instructions of your local county agent, or State Experiment Station (page 456).

ROSES: Before growth starts take down hilling and work into beds. Last dormant spray is given at this time. If growth has started, omit dormant spray and begin regular summer spray program. Apply fertilizer, working in lightly (Chapter 15).

FEED: Before new growth starts feed azaleas, camellias, rhododendrons, *Pieris japonica*, hollies, *Leucothoe catesbei*, etc. (page 98).

PLACE NETS or strings for sweet peas, brush for garden peas, poles for beans to be planted in early May.

BULBS: Continue planting GLADIOLUS in succession, every two weeks from first planting, for six weeks. Begin spraying for thrips when plants are 6 to 8 inches tall (Appendix, page 451).

For Areas IV, V

LAWNS: Repair, fertilize and topdress with compost, aerate; on alkaline soil apply ammonium sulfate to kill weeds and feed grass; on acid soil, apply lime; plant plugs of Bermudagrass in new lawn areas; mow winter grass very close (Chapter 10).

FEED: all plants soon to bloom; azaleas and camellias *after* bloom; iris with fertilizer high in phosphorus and potash (page 98).

ROSES: Prune, feed, start regular summer spray program (Chapter 15).

SET OUT: early-blooming annuals and bedding plants, after hardening off for a week in a frame (page 184); strawberries (page 269); broccoli, cabbage, cauliflower, lettuce (page 239); tomatoes, peppers, eggplants as soon as ground warms up; American-grown lilies; gladiolus corms and other half-hardy summer-flowering bulbs (page 188); hedges and windbreaks (page 148).

SOW SEEDS: Half-hardy annuals, half-hardy vegetables, tender annuals and vegetables as soon as ground is warm (pages 67-71).

PRUNE: shrubs after bloom, hedges, crape-myrtle, santolina, rosemary, teucrium, nierembergia (Chapter 6).

BULBS: Continue succession plantings of gladiolus corms every two weeks from first planting, for six weeks. Begin spraying for thrips when plants are 6 to 8 inches tall (Appendix, page 451).

Sow *dwarf* dahlia seeds in coldframe (page 117).

Mark clumps of daffodils so crowded they have ceased to bloom freely. Dig these next July (page 188).

Encourage foliage of spring-flowering bulbs to remain green as long as possible. Water, fertilize. Do not cut until foliage turns yellow (page 187). Set out annual plants to conceal maturing foliage.

As soon as soil warms up, plant tuberous begonias and other tender summer-flowering bulbs and corms. Caladiums should not be set out until temperature remains above 40° around the clock, as they are damaged at lower readings (page 188).

For Area VI

PLANT: tuberous begonias; caladiums when night temperature is above 40°; cannas, dahlia tubers, divide and replant; gladiolus (second or third planting); gloxinias, tuberoses (page 188); water-lilies.

SOW SEEDS of tender annuals (pages 67; 175); cool-weather vegetables (page 238).

SET OUT young annual plants, replacing old exhausted ones; perennials (page 184); crape jasmine; bamboo; chrysanthemums, rooted cuttings from old crowns.

LAWNS: Sprig or plug new lawn areas, fertilize established lawn areas, mow regularly (Chapter 10).

FEED: After bloom, spring-flowering bulb beds; azaleas, camellias, avocado, citrus fruits, grapes with superphosphate and potash, early-flowering perennials (page 98).

TAKE CUTTINGS of abutilon, geranium, fuchsia, vitex (pages 76-77). AIR-LAYER jasmine, *Magnolia soulangeana*, viburnum (page 74).

PLANT tropicals in southern or eastern exposure but where early morning sun does not strike them (in shade of building or tree); palms just before new growth starts.

DUST OR SPRAY regularly for pests and diseases (Appendix, pages 451-454). Watch out for mildew. Use Mildex. For black spot on roses, use phaltan. For thrips on gladiolus, use dieldrin. Clean up all beds. Burn trash.

Begin summer mulching of all beds, borders, shrubs, trees.

THE CALENDAR

Use 2 to 3 inches of pine needles, coarse, rotted sawdust, peatmoss, shredded fir bark, chopped sugar cane, etc. (pages 88-89).

PICK DAILY: Pansies, violas, and other early-blooming flowers.

PRUNE any plants which were injured by freezes during winter: spring-flowering shrubs after bloom, azaleas, hedges (Chapter 6).

WATER: Give deep waterings in dry spells (pages 89-91).

BULBS: Mark clumps of spring-flowering bulbs too crowded to bloom (dig and divide in July) (page 188).

MAY

> Fragrance and beauty come in with the green!
> The ragged bushes put on sweet attire!
> JAMES STEPHENS

For Area I

As soon as ground can be worked, add soil amendments, humus, manure, fertilizer, chlordane (except in vegetable garden where it should be applied in fall after crops are out), work over well, and prepare for planting and sowing (Chapter 2).

DIVIDE AND TRANSPLANT perennials. Set out rooted cuttings of chrysanthemums taken from outside of old crowns (pages 72-73).

SOW: As soon as ground can be prepared, sow sweet peas, peas. Plant onion sets and perennial vegetable plants (Chapter 16).

SOW INDOORS or in frame half-hardy annual seeds: tomato, eggplant, and pepper seeds (page 278); outdoors: hardy vegetable seeds (page 238).

HARDEN OFF in frame for 10 days or two weeks cool-weather vegetable and flower plants started indoors. Then set out in garden, protecting transplants from prevailing, dry winds. Keep well watered. Shade from hot sun for a week or until re-established (page 239).

LAWN: Clean up winter damage. Remove snow mold. Loosen bare spots, add compost, reseed. Fertilize and use weed killers (Chapter 10).

PLANT trees (pages 148-151; also see planting list for April, Area II).

ROSES: Uncover; unhill; prune; spray; plant new bushes (Chapter 15).

FLOWERS: After mulch is removed from beds and border, feed and water.

In WEEDING and fertilizing beds, be careful not to injure young shoots of lilies and other late-starting plants.

FRUITS: Follow spray program closely (Appendix, page 456).

SPRAY: If plants are still dormant apply dormant spray for scale to apples, crabapples, euonymus, lilacs, mountain-ash, viburnum (page 451).

FRAMES need attention this month: open for warm rain and sun; close only if temperature drops near freezing (page 117).

For Area II

SOW half-hardy annuals like marigolds, zinnias, etc., in frame (page 117) or seedbed; tender annuals late in month, cool-weather vegetable seeds outdoors (page 238).

SET OUT plants of cabbage, broccoli, cauliflower (page 239); pansies and other early-flowering, hardy plants (page 184). (Harden in frame from 10 days to 2 weeks before setting out if plants have been raised indoors or under glass.)

HARDEN OFF tomato plants in frames after May 15, ready for setting out late in month (page 239).

SET OUT peppers and eggplants when soil warms up and weather has really settled.

BULBS: If dry, WATER DAFFODILS after bloom. Keep foliage growing. Remove dead flowers. Mark clumps which are overcrowded for dividing in July (page 187).

WHEN CLEANING, CULTIVATING, AND FERTILIZING beds and borders, do not injure the young shoots of plants like lilies, which start late.

SPRAY program for fruit trees and roses should be followed (page 456).

THE CALENDAR 329

IN WINDY AREAS, do not set houseplants outdoors without wind protection; or wait until windy period is over. Young transplants should also be protected on side of prevailing winds.

LAWN: Sow new lawns as soon as areas are ready; *the earlier the better*. Fertilize established lawns, begin mowing (Chapter 10).

PLANT gladiolus corms. Make succession plantings every two weeks, for six weeks. Other half-hardy bulbs can go in now. Tuberous begonias are set out when weather has settled and soil is frost-free; caladiums not until night temperature is above 40° (page 188).

PINCH BACK young annuals to make bushy plants; also perennials like chrysanthemums, hardy asters.

FERTILIZE all beds and borders of plants about to bloom; also spring-flowering shrubs and trees. Keep well watered in dry areas (pages 89-91).

MULCH: Begin placing summer mulch around trees and shrubs, and on beds and borders as time and opportunity offer (pages 87-89).

HOTKAPS of plastic or paper give a head start with tender vegetables. May be used over vine crops, tomatoes, eggplant, peppers (Chapter 8).

For Areas III, IV

PLANT: summer-flowering bulbs if not already attended to. Set out tuberous begonias late in month; caladiums in June (page 188).

BULBS: Keep foliage growing after bloom. Remove flower heads. Mark overcrowded clumps for transplanting in July (page 187).

THIN beets, carrots, lettuce, radishes, spinach, etc.; half-hardy and hardy annual seedlings (page 240).

SOW: After May 15 seeds of beans, corn, okra, squash, cucumber, cantaloupe—all tender vegetables; tender annuals like portulaca, torenia (page 175).

SET OUT plants of tomato, eggplant, pepper, sweet potato (page 239).

In seedbed or frame in part shade sow seeds of perennials, biennials (pages 67-68).

STRAWBERRIES: Put straw around strawberry plants.

SPRAY fruit trees according to schedule (page 456); roses regularly.

FEED: Has everything had its spring feeding? If not, do it now (pages 91; 98).

WATER if dry, then mulch, trees, shrubs, beds. Acid-lovers should have acid mulch; others any available material (pages 87-89).

PINCH BACK all too leggy young annuals and perennials.

TWIST or PLAIT BULB foliage and set out bedding plants in bulb beds.

PRUNE: All spring-flowering shrubs after bloom is over. Don't spoil their natural grace of growth (Chapter 6).

HOUSEPLANTS should be kept indoors in windy areas until wind has abated; or set out where they will have complete protection from prevailing winds. Sink to rims in well-prepared bed, with filtered sun.

STAKE tall-growing, early perennials to prevent breakage (page 177).

LAWNS: Sod new lawn areas with Zoysia or Bermuda. Plugs or sprigs of these grasses are available now (Chapter 10).

For Area V

FEED: perennials and biennials, now in strong growth, with a low-nitrogen fertilizer; roses after bloom; spring-flowering, broad-leaved evergreens, after bloom; all perennials and shrubs, after bloom; tulips, after bloom (pages 91-98).

SOW seeds of very tender annuals; perennials, biennials (pages 67-71), vine crops, corn, okra, in seedbeds or frames; second sowings of cool-weather vegetables for fall harvest (page 238); annual seeds in bulb beds (do not cut bulb foliage until mature).

SET OUT eggplant and peppers (page 239); bedding plants; summer-flowering bulbs, including tuberous begonias (page 188); water-lilies in their boxes when water temperature reaches 70°.

ROSES: Remove dead flowers; cut back blooming sprays of large-flowered climbers, removing two or three buds, after bloom; remove old canes of ramblers, after bloom; fertilize after bloom; keep well watered; spray regularly; summer mulch. Pot-grown plants can still be set out. Or keep in containers on patio (floribundas) (Chapter 15).

CLEAN UP and compost spent annual plants. Replace with young plants of summer bloomers.

SPRAY camellias after bloom; holly and lilac for leaf miner; roses weekly; elm, hackberry, honey locust, fruits for cankerworm (page 451).

CHRYSANTHEMUMS: Feed every 3 or 4 weeks; pinch back 3 times, last pinching in early July; water deeply; mulch for summer; give all-purpose spray as needed.

LAWNS: Seed or sod new areas, previously prepared; feed those already established; apply weed control; water deeply in dry spells (Chapter 10).

PINCH BACK late-flowering perennials to create bushy plants (page 179).

REMOVE DEAD FLOWERS from delphinium, foxglove, and other early-blooming perennials; also from spring-flowering bulbs. Prune all shrubs after bloom is over (page 102).

HOUSEPLANTS: Plunge pots outdoors in shady, enriched bed, after repotting if necessary. Feature large specimens on patio.

STAKE tall-growing plants, tubers, and corms (page 177).

For Area VI

ROSES: Give plants a chance to rest a little after their first heavy bloom. Remove dead flowers. Feed lightly. Prune back very tall canes. Water as needed and do not let up on spraying. Summer mulch. Prune back old canes of ramblers to ground, after bloom (Chapter 15).

SET OUT plants of tomatoes, eggplant, and peppers, if not already done; young plants for later bloom in bulb beds (keep bulb foliage growing); all bedding plants (page 184); dahlias and other tender, summer-flowering bulbs not already in (page 188).

SPRAY schedule should be rigidly adhered to. Keep ahead of pests and diseases (Appendix, page 451).

FEED chrysanthemums every 3 or 4 weeks; established lawns (Chapter 10); citrus fruit, with sulfate of ammonia; plants about to bloom (pages 91-98).

CITRUS FRUITS: Plant now; feed established trees—add iron sulfate; spray for scale, aphids (Appendix, page 451).

CLEAN UP all beds containing plants exhausted after bloom. Replace with young plants of later bloomers, or sow seed of hot-weather annuals.

BULBS: Make succession plantings of gladiolus corms every two weeks for six weeks (page 188). See list of summer-flowering bulbs for southern gardens (page 426).

WATERING should not be neglected in dry areas (pages 89-91).

DIG and STORE tulips and hyacinths when foliage matures (page 188).

VEGETABLES: Keep rows thinned as young plants develop. Give side-dressing to half-grown plants. Keep after weeds. Keep watered and well mulched (Chapter 16).

SUMMER MULCH beds, borders, trees, and shrubs to retain moisture, keep down weeds (pages 87-89).

JUNE

A fragrant rose;
A tall calm lily from the waterside;
A half-blown poppy hanging at the side
Its head of dream,
Dreaming among the corn.
           JAMES STEPHENS

For Area I

SOW half-hardy annual seeds in frame, or where they are to grow; late in month, tender annual and vegetable seeds, or earlier in a frame (pages 67-71).

HARDEN OFF plants started indoors or under glass by placing in frame for ten days to two weeks (page 239).

SET OUT annual, young perennial, and all but most tender vegetable plants, after hardening off; tomato plants after all danger of frost is past (page 184); peppers and eggplant somewhat later when soil warms up; summer-flowering bulbs like gladiolus, ismene; tuberous begonia, gloxinia, caladium, canna when soil warms up (page 188).

SHADE newly set out plants for a few days with berry boxes or shingles on the windward side.

IN CULTIVATING beds and borders be careful not to damage plants which are late appearing above ground.

FEED and WATER, then SUMMER MULCH all beds and garden areas.

STRAWBERRIES: Arrange straw mulch under plants in strawberry beds.

PINCH BACK late-blooming perennials like chrysanthemums, hardy asters, to make them bushy. Then feed, water, and mulch.

THE CALENDAR

SPRING-FLOWERING BULBS: Keep foliage growing after bloom by giving plant food and water; remove dead blossoms; mark clumps which are overcrowded and need digging and dividing in July (page 187).

THIN seedling vegetables and annuals (page 71).

ROSES: Remove dead blooms; water, summer mulch (Chapter 15).

LAWN: Feed, water as needed, and mow once a week (Chapter 10).

FLOWER BEDS: After weeding beds and borders, add compost, fertilizer. Water well and then apply summer mulch (Chapter 5). Faded blooms should be removed from early-blooming perennials.

PRUNE spring-flowering shrubs after bloom (Chapter 6).

DIVIDE lily-of-valley, primroses, etc. after flowering (pages 181; 184).

PESTS: Watch seedling nasturtiums for black aphids. Spray with malathion of Black Leaf 40 (Appendix, page 451). Regular summer spray program should now be in full swing (Chapter 5).

CUT BACK and feed very early-blooming PERENNIALS like myosotis, pansies, violas, and others.

BEDDING PLANTS may be set out in bulb beds but *do not cut* bulb foliage (page 187).

In high altitudes of late frosts, young plants can be protected with Hotkaps until weather warms up (page 128).

For Areas II, III

LAWN: Feed, water, and mow once a week. Keep up crabgrass and other weed-control measures (Chapter 10 and Appendix, page 454).

PLANT caladiums, tuberoses, cannas, and other very tender bulbs, corms and tubers, if not done (page 188).

SET OUT very tender annual and vegetable plants, if not done previously (pages 184; 239).

SHADE and protect newly set out annuals for a few days with berry boxes or shingles on windy side (page 128). Keep watered.

STAKE tall-growing perennials that have not yet bloomed (page 177).

CUT BACK early-blooming perennials: remove dead blossoms from pansies, violas, and other early, low-growing biennials and perennials.

SOW a second lot of candytuft, nigella, cornflowers, and other annuals which bloom only a short time, to keep up succession of bloom (page 175).

PESTS: Watch nasturtium seedlings closely for black aphids. Spray with malathion or Black Leaf 40 (Appendix, page 451).

PINCH BACK tall-growing annuals, chrysanthemums, hardy asters, dahlias, and others as needed, to produce sturdy, bushy plants (page 178).

DIG and divide primroses, lily-of-the-valley. Wait until July or August for iris and June-blooming perennials (pages 72-73; 184).

SPRAY: Continue regular summer spray program.

ROSES: Feed just before June bloom; keep dead blossoms cut, just above *outfacing* bud; spray weekly; water deeply when needed without wetting foliage; after bloom remove old canes of ramblers; cut dead blooms from large-flowered climbers, removing 2 or 3 eyes (Chapter 5).

BULBS: Dig tulips when foliage matures, or leave in ground another year if still blooming well; keep daffodil and other bulb foliage growing vigorously; water and feed if necessary (page 187); lilies, at their height in July, should be fed and kept moist this month; mulch to keep soil cool around roots. Set out bedding plants in bulb beds, but do *not* remove healthy bulb foliage; simply lay it aside or tie it together.

SUMMER MULCH may now be applied to everything after beds have been weeded, plants fed, and watered (pages 87-89).

TROPICAL WATER-LILIES can be placed in pools when water reaches 70 degrees. Plan for one third open water, full sun.

FEED, after bloom: delphinium, lupine, Oriental poppies, aquilegia, peonies, iris (pages 91-98).

TOMATOES: Begin tying up plants to supports and pinching out new growths (page 244).

For Areas IV, V

BULBS: Remove matured yellow foliage of tulips, or dig and store bulbs for replanting in autumn. Keep foliage of other spring-flowering bulbs growing by giving deep waterings (page 187).

FEED perennials which have finished bloom, first removing dead flower stalks or stems. Water if dry; then summer mulch (pages 88-91; 98).

VEGETABLES: Begin tying to supports and continue pinching out new growths of tomatoes (page 244); side-dress half-grown plants like cabbage, broccoli; thin out corn, beans, planted late in May (page 240); cut every other lettuce head, giving more room to those remaining; give second thinning to carrots, beets, turnips, and other hardy and cool-weather vegetables. Beet and turnip thinnings make delicious greens. Make second sowing for a late crop of carrots, beets, etc. Sow Chinese-cabbage, celery, Brussels sprouts (Chapter 16).

SET OUT all very tender plants like dwarf dahlias, caladiums, etc., if not done already (page 188).

PLANT tropical water-lilies in pool when water reaches 70 degrees. Leave one third open water.

LAWN: Mow weekly, feed, water, treat for weeds (Chapter 10).

PINCH BACK tall-growing annuals and late-blooming perennials to make bushy plants.

DIVIDE May-blooming plants such as primroses, iris, lily-of-the-valley.

SPRAY: Watch nasturtiums for black aphids. Spray with malathion. One treatment will make a 100 per cent kill (Appendix, page 451). Continue regular SPRAY program.

ROSES: Water every 7 to 10 days; apply 2- to 3-inch summer mulch; prune back lightly after June bloom; spray weekly; fertilize lightly after heavy bloom; remove all old canes to ground from ramblers; large-flowered climbers are pruned like Hybrid Teas (Chapter 15).

FEED and WATER azaleas, camellias, chrysanthemums (pages 89-91; 98).

SUMMER MULCH should be applied to all parts of the garden to conserve moisture, discourage weeds; continue deep watering in dry sections (pages 87-89).

STAKE tall-growing plants which have not yet bloomed (page 177).

FRUITS: Keep fruit trees, small fruits, and strawberries well watered while fruit is developing (Chapter 17).

SOW: For constant bloom, make monthly sowings this month and next of short-term bloomers like candytuft, nigella, and cornflower; sow seeds of torenia to take place of pansies in late garden; sow perennial and biennial seeds in frame (page 175).

PRUNE all spring-flowering shrubs which have finished blooming (Chapter 6).

AZALEAS, RHODODENDRONS: Prune and remove dead flowers (page 104); water frequently; stir and add to mulch; feed every 6 weeks with acid food (pages 90-98); make tip cuttings and layers (Chapter 6).

SET OUT young chrysanthemum plants. Feed. Water. Spray bimonthly.

FEED and water fuchsias and hydrangeas—the latter with acid fertilizer (page 98).

TUBEROUS BEGONIAS may be purchased in pots now and set out in shaded bed or patio. Mist with fine water spray on hot afternoons.

For Area VI

AZALEAS and RHODODENDRONS: Start cuttings (page 79); prune, also removing all dead blossoms (page 104); stir and add to mulch; feed with acid plant food every 6 weeks. Give iron; water frequently.

FEED and WATER established shrubs, agapanthus, bamboo, summer-flowering bulbs, citrus fruits (acid food), chrysanthemums, fuchsias, camellias (acid food), ixoras, gardenias, hydrangeas (acid food), tibouchina, palm trees, violets, ground covers (pages 90-98).

LAWNS: Mow 1½ to 2 inches high; Bermudagrass to ½ inch; apply weed controls; Bonus controls weeds in dichondra lawns; feed monthly; water weekly, twice a week when temperature is over 90 degrees; sow dichondra seed (Chapter 10).

PLANT crotons, dracaenas, large palm trees.

PRUNE bauhinia, oleander, and other tropical shrubs after bloom (use rubber gloves when handling oleander to prevent skin poisoning); keep geraniums groomed (Chapter 6).

PINCH BACK chrysanthemums, dahlias; new growths of tomatoes (pages 178; 244).

FRUITS: Keep watered. Prop up fruit-laden branches to prevent breakage.

TREES: Newly or recently planted trees and shrubs should be kept well watered and shaded to prevent sunburn (page 150).

STAKE UP gladiolus, dahlias, other tall-growing plants that have not bloomed (page 178).

DRAINAGE: If soil is poorly drained, improve by tiling or open ditches (pages 33-37).

PESTS: Regular spray program is most important; check figs

for red spider, thrips, thread blight; spray roses weekly; Malathion on passion vine for caterpillars, Chlordane for ants (Appendix, page 451).

DIVIDE and replant bearded iris (page 184); leucocoryne bulbs (replant in pots).

Remove dead flower stalks from early-blooming perennials, annuals.

MULCH to protect roots from heat with well-rooted manure, compost, or straw (pages 87-89).

SOW perennial, biennial, hot-weather annual and vegetable seeds (Chapters 11 & 16).

JULY

> I turned my head and saw the wind
> Not far from where I stood,
> Dragging the corn by her golden hair
> Into a dark and lonely wood.
> *The Villain* by WILLIAM HENRY DAVIES

For Areas I, II, III, IV

WATER deeply in drought, and regularly in areas where dry summers are the rule (pages 89-91).

MULCHING: After light cultivation of the soil, an application of fertilizer, and a deep watering, the application of a mulch is good preparation for summer heat. It conserves moisture, keeps down weeds, and maintains coolness around plant roots (pages 87-89).

LAWNS: Fertilize established lawns with high-nitrogen formula; water thoroughly as needed; mow high in hot weather; apply weed controls; spray for pests and diseases (Chapter 10).

SPRING-FLOWERING BULBS may be dug, dried off, and stored for fall planting *after* foliage turns brown; tulips may remain in ground or be dug each year and replanted in October or November; overcrowded clumps of daffodils can be dug, divided, and replanted now, or stored until September (page 187); remove dead flower stalks from all early-blooming perennials, and from lilies which have bloomed, *after* stalks die.

IRIS foliage should mature after bloom. Bearded iris can be dug, divided, and replanted, *six weeks* after bloom ceases. Cut away any rotted or pest-ridden parts, dust cuts with disinfectant, cut rhizomes into small clumps, and replant near

THE CALENDAR

surface. Before resetting, work over beds, adding peatmoss and superphosphate.

DIG AND DIVIDE rock garden perennials such as: arabis, *Alyssum saxatile,* heuchera, iberis, *Phlox nivalis, Phlox subulata.* Small sections, set in a row of well-prepared soil and kept watered until they root, will increase stock easily.

Do not remove foliage from peonies but keep it growing like bulb foliage. Feed peonies after bloom (page 187).

FEED: aquilegia, chrysanthemums, day-lilies, delphinium, iris, lupine, hardy asters, late-flowering annuals, roses, including climbers (lightly after heaviest bloom), peonies, potted amaryllis bulbs (pages 91-98).

REMOVE SUCKERS from roses, flowering crabs, plums, peaches, flowering almond, and any grafted plant where sucker comes from *below* graft; also from lilacs.

CHRYSANTHEMUMS: Pinch back every two weeks to July 15; feed with liquid manure.

ROSES: Remove all dead flowers, cutting above an eye or bud; ramblers *only:* cut back old canes to ground after bloom; feed lightly this month to give a little rest after heavy June bloom; keep well watered, mulched, sprayed weekly (Chapter 15).

PRUNE: wisteria runners, and other hardy perennial vines to keep growth under control; yews and sheared coniferous evergreen hedges; broadleaf evergreen hedges like box and privet; deciduous hedges. Shape up shrubs like forsythia, shrub roses, but do not destroy natural grace (Chapter 6).

CUTTINGS can now be taken and rooted of coleus, fuchsia, geraniums, lantana, heliotrope, and other tender plants for winter bloom indoors. Box, yew, euonymus, pachysandra, perennials, and deciduous shrubs are ready to be slipped for cuttings (Chapter 4).

SOW SEED of hardy perennials in partly shaded frame: delphinium as soon as seed is ripe; annuals like calendula, candytuft, sweet alyssum, to keep up succession of bloom (page 175); vegetables like beets, endive, Chinese-cabbage, lettuce, radish, spinach, turnips, for fall crop; beans and corn for a late crop (page 238).

For Areas III, IV

SET OUT late cabbage, cauliflower, and celery plants; keep well watered (page 239).

STRAWBERRIES: Keep weeded, feed with 5–10–5 formula, 2 to 3 lbs. per 100 square ft.; water and keep mulched. As soon as young plants have formed at tips or runners, pot in rich soil in peat pots and sink near parent plants without cutting runners. In August or September these can be separated from old plants, and set out in a new row (pages 267-270).

HERBS: Harvest lavender flowers before they fade; also prime leaves of culinary and fragrant herbs. Dry on trays in airy shed or attic; store in airtight containers. Pick everlastings when in early full bloom, tie in bunches, hang upside down in shed to dry (pages 210-211). Pick flowers and sprays while in perfect condition, to dry for winter bouquets in Flora-gel, or borax and cornmeal.

BULBS: Plant last gladiolus bulbs in July—by July 15 in the north; keep after thrips (page 63).

PERENNIALS: Order day-lilies, Oriental poppies, iris, madonna lilies, colchicums, fall-blooming crocus, sternbergia, and such minor bulbs as winter-aconite. All of these should be planted as soon as received.

TUBEROUS BEGONIAS, CALADIUMS: Mist spray thoroughly during hot, dry afternoons (page 91); use all-purpose rose spray for mildew, leaf spot (Appendix, page 453).

SPRAY OR DUST REGULARLY and keep eyes open for midsummer pests and diseases: beetles, aphids, bag worms, berry moths, borers, ear worms in corn, clover mite (lawns), grasshoppers, mealy bugs, mites, thrips, leaf blights, mildew, lawn diseases, nematodes (Appendix, pages 451-453).

WATER IS NEEDED ESPECIALLY BY azaleas, rhododendrons,

coniferous evergreens, magnolias, dogwood, flowering and other fruits (pages 89-91).

For Areas V, VI

CUT BACK exhausted annuals (replacing with young plants if necessary); remove old flower stalks of perennials.

SHEAR hedges such as box, coniferous evergreens, privet, barberry (Chapter 6).

If SPRING-FLOWERING BULBS that need division and replanting have not already been attended to, do it now; foliage has matured.

DIG AND DIVIDE bearded iris, Oriental poppies, primulas (if not done), and others; allow six weeks after end of blooming period (page 184).

CHLOROSIS (yellowing of leaves) may appear in lawns or on plants in summer. It is caused by excess alkalinity. Apply an iron chelate such as Sequestrene to soil. Also apply to foliage as a spray.

LAWN: In drought, when grass turns blue-green and wilts, sift compost over surface and work down gently around roots; if turf turns yellow, see CHLOROSIS above. Feed, on cool, cloudy days; water weekly, twice a week if temperature is above 90°; mow high in hot weather. Plug or sprig new lawn areas with St. Augustine, Centipede or Bermudagrass (this last may also be seeded) (Chapter 10).

GROUND COVERS: Shear off ground covers which are setting seeds (Chapter 10).

VEGETABLES: Cut back artichokes after bearing, to produce a crop next spring.

SOW last of warm-weather vegetables (page 238) in flats or partly shaded frame; broccoli, cabbage, cauliflower; amaryllis; perennials; winter and spring-flowering annuals (page 175).

PLANT pot-grown trees, shrubs; annuals from nurseries (page

184); *Lycoris radiata;* broad-leaved evergreens; fruits (page 255). Keep all well watered.

FEED fast-growing annuals; late-blooming perennials; chrysanthemums, with liquid manure; clivias; ixoras; hibiscus (pages 91-98). Withhold fertilizer for two months from roses to give rest; from doubtfully hardy evergreen shrubs in areas where early frosts may injure tender foliage.

BULBS: Raise amaryllis bulbs which have sunk too deep in ground.

DRAINAGE: In areas of summer rain, check drainage and install tiles or ditches if necessary; use raised beds (pages 33-37).

WATER consistently and deeply in dry areas, with special attention to all trees and shrubs, broad-leaved evergreens, fruits, and plants about to bloom (pages 89-91).

SPRAY: Keep up consistent SPRAY program. This is the peak month for pests and diseases in many areas.

PRUNE hydrangeas after bloom, poinsettias, rampant perennial vines (Chapter 6).

PINCH BACK dahlias, hardy asters, chrysanthemums, up to July 15.

SOFTWOOD CUTTINGS may now be taken of camellias (root under glass), Japanese yew, pomegranate, poinsettia (page 76).

MULCHING and GROUND COVERS protect plants from hot wind and sun (pages 88; 168).

AUGUST

> Sometimes too hot the eye of heaven shines.
> SHAKESPEARE

For Areas I, II, III, IV

In the coldest regions, annuals from seed are at their best this month. Keep dead blooms cut off to prevent seeding. Remove weeds, give copious water, fertilize lightly between bursts of bloom, and mulch to conserve moisture and protect from heat.

Where short growing season and low winter temperatures keep roses and other plants from attaining tall, heavy growth, cut flowers with short stems to conserve stem growth and foliage.

WATER, and plenty of it, is needed this month in most sections of the country. Give deep, slow waterings and measure depth to which it permeates. It should reach to 6 or 8 inches (pages 89-91).

SUMMER MULCHES help to hold moisture, protect plants from heat by keeping root-runs cool, and help to keep down weeds (pages 87-89).

LAWN areas for fall seeding should be prepared early this month (pages 154-158); seeding can be undertaken late in August or in early September; fertilize and water established lawns; apply weed killers and spray for diseases, pests (Appendix, page 451); mow high in hot weather.

In areas subject to very early frosts, withhold plant food and water after August 15 from roses, azaleas, rhododendrons, and other woody plants, soft growth of which may be in-

THE CALENDAR

jured by early frost. Reduce water on broad-leaved evergreens in the above class.

FEED chrysanthemums, hardy asters, dahlias, tomatoes, lawns, strawberry beds for the last time (pages 91-98).

STAKE tall-growing plants before heavy blooms bend them over (page 177).

SPRAY programs should be followed closely and a sharp lookout kept for new pests. August is the time when many troubles reach their peak.

Mildew may attack delphinium, hardy asters, chrysanthemums, lilacs, phlox, roses, zinnias (Appendix, page 453); *lawn diseases* may appear (Appendix, page 449); for *leap hoppers, peach tree borers, spider mites, euonymus scale, Japanese and other beetles, aphids, mealy bug* (Appendix, page 451).

BULBS: Order spring-flowering bulbs; include unusual species: alliums, chionodoxas, crocus, fritillarias, scillas, winter-aconite. Minor bulbs should be planted on delivery, especially fall colchicums and *Sternbergia lutea*, and winter-aconite. Order lily bulbs. Plant madonna lilies at once; others as soon after delivery as possible.

BULB BEDS can be prepared between the time of ordering and delivery of the bulbs.

Crocus, freesia, paper-white narcissus; calla-lily, amaryllis, and other winter-flowering bulbs can now be planted in pots for winter bloom indoors (page 120).

SOW SEEDS of perennials and biennials: aquilegia, catanache, coreopsis, delphinium, gloriosa daisy, Shasta daisy, Canterbury bells, centauria, foxglove, hollyhock (page 178).

STRAWBERRY runners can now be detached from parent plants. Dig up potted runner plants and set out in a row (page 269).

DIG AND DIVIDE, if crowded, or set out new plants or bulbs of: crown-imperial, day-lilies, foxglove, bearded iris, madonna lilies, mertensia, Oriental poppy, peony, Shasta daisy (pages 72; 184).

IRIS: In Areas III and IV, where they are hardy, set out new Japanese and other tender iris plants.

CANE FRUIT: If not done previously, prune back cane fruits after bearing (page 265).

BLUEBERRIES are shallow rooted. Be sure they are well mulched and watered (pages 87-91).

ORDER: Where fall planting is safe, order azaleas and other shrubs; also perennials and roses.

VEGETABLES: Sow lettuce seed in frame for fall crop (page 238). Where autumns are long and mild, set out fall vegetable plants (page 239). When asparagus tops are faded, remove from bed. Mulch with well-rotted manure. As vegetable crops are harvested, clean up the areas, place undiseased or pest-free trash on compost heap, cultivate soil and sow winter cover crop.

FALL COLOR: Exhausted annuals can now be replaced with chrysanthemums—transplant even in bud; or with fall-blooming annuals.

For Areas V, VI

FEED: long-season annuals, between bursts of bloom; dahlias; and disbud for show blooms azaleas, camellias, and fuchsias; chrysanthemums with liquid plant food; roses; strawberry beds for last time; fall- and winter-flowering shrubs; tomato plants.

STAKE as needed all tall-growing plants still in bloom or about to flower (page 177).

WATER: In dry areas keep watering and keep plants, beds, and borders mulched to conserve moisture, keep roots cool, and control weeds (pages 87-91).

PLANT Easter lily bulbs—varieties Croft or Creole—as soon as delivered; also madonna lilies, Louisiana and Japanese iris, fall- and winter-flowering bulbs.

LAWNS: Last call to sow Bermudagrass now; fertilize and water established lawns, apply weed killer and spray for disease and pests (Chapter 10).

REFRIGERATE cool-weather perennial seeds like delphinium, pansy, and viola before sowing (far South).

CUT BACK or remove rampant perennials in borders that threaten to crowd out more desirable species. Continue to cut back rampant vines that encroach on trees, shrubs, or other plants.

SET OUT plants of cool-weather annuals, perennials, and vegetables (page 184); pot-grown shrubs, roses, broad-leaved evergreens (pages 148-151).

PLANT calla-lily, clivia, ranunculus.

DIVIDE and TRANSPLANT day-lilies, clivia, Oriental poppies, peonies, Shasta daisy (pages 73; 184).

SOW: calendula, myosotis, stock, viola, wallflower. Transplant in six weeks for December bloom (page 175); beets, beans, collards, carrots, Chinese-cabbage, radishes, for fall crop (page 238).

ROSES: Order roses for October–November planting; take cuttings and start under glass jars; feed and water; spray weekly; remove dead blooms and keep beds clean (Chapter 15).

WATER consistently in all dry areas or dry spells (pages 89-91). Azaleas, camellias, and fuchsias need constant moisture.

SPRAYS and DUSTS should be applied at regular intervals. This is the peak time for pests and diseases; watch chrysanthemums and dahlias for aphids, red spider; dahlias for stem borers (slit stems and remove borers); watch figs for rust; pyracantha for lace-wing bug; watch for mildew on annuals, perennials, lilacs (Appendix, page 453).

SEPTEMBER

> To bronze Jove changed
> Earth's golden time.
> *Odes* by HORACE

For Areas I, II, III, IV

Though there are great variations in temperatures in the above planting areas, frost may strike even the mildest of them before the end of September. Operations suggested for this month can be executed as dictated by local weather conditions.

LAWNS: Seed new areas if not already done; the earlier the better; fertilize and repair established lawns (page 160); have soil tested and add amendments if necessary; mow high—to 2½ inches; water in dry areas (Chapter 10).

COMPOST is worth its weight in gold! Build a new heap now (page 41).

DIVIDE and REPLANT early-blooming perennials (page 184).

BULBS: Plant spring-flowering bulbs; tulips go in last; minor bulbs and lilies on delivery; lift bulbs, corms, and tubers of summer-flowering tender subjects before or just after first frost; dry off and store (page 188).

HARVEST onion and root crops and store; store winter squash at 50 to 60 degrees (Chapter 16).

CLEAN UP beds from which dead or matured plants have been removed. Cultivate and SOW COVER CROPS (page 41).

WATER chrysanthemums, hardy asters, and other fall bloomers; newly set evergreens; recently planted shrubs and trees (pages 89-91).

FEED chrysanthemums, asters before they show color; use a *low*-nitrogen food to stimulate blooms, not foliage (page 98).

GATHER PODS of wildflowers and garden subjects; dry and store for winter bouquets.

EVERGREENS can be transplanted from now until ground freezes (pages 148-151).

FRAMES: If you have no coldframe, build one now (Chapter 7).

SOW completely hardy annual seeds where they are to grow: calliopsis, California-poppy, cornflower, larkspur, Shirley poppy (pages 67-71).

STOP FERTILIZING roses and shrubs: this will encourage dormancy.

SOIL PREPARATION: Where fall planting of roses is successful, prepare beds; order plants (Chapter 15).

CUTTINGS: Start cuttings of tender, flowering houseplants (page 76).

For Areas I, II, III, IV

INDOORS

Loosen pots of houseplants in their beds; in three days to a week, remove to a sheltered spot; cut back rank growth; repot where necessary, then bring indoors before first frost, which may injure tender specimens.

Place in north or west windows, ferns, ivies, tolmieas, philodendrons, tradescantias, and large-leaved begonias; place flowering plants in south or east windows; African-violets do best in east or west exposures.

Feed Christmas cactus every two weeks. Syringe frequently. Water moderately.

Watch for aphids and other pests. Treat at once. Weekly syringing of leaves discourages pests.

Houseplants which do not throw out new growth should be watered moderately, and plant food withheld until new growth starts.

If portions of houseplants die back after bringing indoors, prune back to live wood.

For Area V

LAWNS: Seed new areas; repair poor spots in established lawns, then top dress with compost and fertilize; keep up treatments for crabgrass; spray for snow mold if necessary (Chapter 10).

DIG, DIVIDE, and REPLANT peonies and other early-blooming perennials such as day-lilies, iris, Oriental poppies (pages 72; 184).

SET OUT young perennial plants in permanent locations (page 184).

MULCH young perennials after planting with light, nonmatting material (pages 87-89).

CHRYSANTHEMUMS and HARDY ASTERS should be fed every two weeks until buds show color; and should be kept well watered.

SOW SEEDS of hardy annuals; early-blooming perennials like primroses (pages 65-71); hardy and half-hardy vegetables such as lettuce, leek, mustard, spinach, Swiss chard, turnip (page 238).

BULBS: Plant spring-flowering bulbs (page 185); half-hardy bulbs; Candidum lilies.

PRUNE roses lightly. Feed for last time. Continue spray program (Chapter 15).

FERTILIZER should be *withheld* after the middle of month from deciduous trees, shrubs, and roses to prevent soft new growth which may be injured by frost. Withold water also.

BULBS: Prepare lily beds for November planting. Feed amaryllis and other established bulb plantings with one teaspoon muriate of potash to ½ gallon of water, to harden for cold weather.

FEED camellias and winter-blooming shrubs that have not bloomed. Remove dead flowers from those which have (page 98).

CUTTINGS: Take camellia cuttings and root in frame (page 78).

TREES AND SHRUBS: Prepare planting holes for later planting (pages 148-151).

SET OUT winter-blooming flower plants (page 184).

CUT BACK exhausted annuals severely, to encourage new growth.

SPRAY: Keep up regular spray program on all plants in growth (Appendix, page 451).

For Area VI

LAWNS: Feed; water; mow high. Overplant Bermuda or other summer grass lawns with annual ryegrass and keep constantly moist until germination (Chapter 10).

FEED: citrus fruits for last time (early in month); avocados, camellias, with acid fertilizer (page 98); chrysanthemums; established bulb beds; sweet peas, wallflowers, and other winter bloomers (page 91).

WATER: In dry areas, keep beds, borders, trees, shrubs, and lawns well watered.

SOW SEEDS of hardy and half-hardy annuals; perennials (page 175).

THE CALENDAR

SET OUT plants of winter-blooming flowers. Keep moist until established (page 184).

DIVIDE and REPLANT spring-flowering perennials: iris, peony, Oriental poppy, primula, etc. (pages 73; 184).

SPRAY PROGRAM should be continued.

PLANTING HOLES may now be dug for trees and shrubs to be moved later (Chapter 9).

WITHHOLD fertilizer and heavy watering from hibiscus, citrus fruits, figs, tibouchina, etc., in areas where soft new growth may be killed by frost.

MULCH tender surface roots before cool weather (pages 87-89).

VEGETABLES: Sow seeds of cool-weather vegetables (page 238). Set out plants of hardy perennial vegetables now or later in fall (Chapter 16).

STAKE and TIE chrysanthemums, hardy asters, climbing roses, vines.

ANNUALS: Cut back exhausted plants, feed and water.

ROSES: Prune lightly to force November bloom; feed for the last time; water; spray (Chapter 15).

SOIL PREPARATION: Prepare beds for pansies and other winter bloomers to be set out later (pages 94-96).

CAMELLIAS: Remove dead blooms to prevent petal blight; water if needed; take cuttings and root in frame (page 78).

OCTOBER

> Golden leaves in an amber pool,
>   And rocks all warm in the sun;
> Why should we fret that summer is gone—
>   When autumn has just begun?
>
> ESTHER C. GRAYSON

For Area I

PLANT spring-flowering bulbs; lilies as soon as delivered; winter rye on garden areas after they are cleaned of all trash, weeded, and cultivated (page 185).

PRUNE back tall growths of climbing roses which may whip in winter winds (page 226); cane fruits which have finished bearing (page 266).

ROSES: Hill up to 12 inches around all bush roses, with compost or top soil; have winter mulch ready to apply to rose beds over hilling just before or just after first hard freeze; prepare to lay down and cover with soil climbing and tree roses before ground freezes (Chapter 15).

GRAPES: Young vines should be laid down and covered like climbing roses, above.

GARDEN CLEAN-UP should include removal and *burning* of all trash in which pests or diseases may winter over.

VEGETABLES: Harvest before hard frost; dry off and store; follow directions (page 241).

TOOLS and POWER EQUIPMENT: Clean, check, and store after garden work is completed (Chapter 8).

For Areas II, III, IV

BULBS: Tulips can be planted as soon as the daffodils and other spring-flowering bulbs are in (page 185). Plant all lily bulbs as soon as delivered. Divide and replant lily-of-the-valley clumps (page 73). Mulch lily-of-the-valley beds with well-rotted, strawy manure, if available; otherwise with rough compost reinforced with dried manure. Pot up daffodils, tulips, muscari, hyacinths, etc., for forcing (page 120). Tender bulbs should be dug just before or just after first frost; dry off and then store (page 188).

ROSES: Have topsoil or compost dumped near rose beds ready to hill them up before hard freeze (page 230).

CHRYSANTHEMUMS: Observe and make notes on varieties which bloom well in your locality before hard freeze. Discard those which flower so late that they suffer severe frost damage before they make a show. Heel into coldframe varieties which are doubtfully hardy. Later mulch these with nonmatting mulch.

WINTER PROTECTION: Have nonmatting mulch ready to mulch beds and borders just before hard freeze (pages 87-89).

EVERGREENS and choice shrubs may be protected by placing stakes around each specimen and nailing to these a screen of burlap, canvas, or heavy plastic. Inside this screen pack dry hardwood leaves, pine needles, or locally available mulch. In milder sections, chicken wire may be used to hold the mulch in place.

GARDEN CLEAN-UP: As plant material matures or is touched by frost, clean up beds and borders, as well as vegetable garden, burning trash which may carry over pests or disease. Loosen up soil and plant winter rye as cover crop (page 41).

PESTS: Apply chlordane to soil infested by ants, earwigs, maggots, sowbugs (Appendix, page 451).

LAWNS: If grass is heavy, give last mowing. In areas where snow mold is a problem, treat with lawn fungicide to kill surviving spores (page 453). Seed new lawns; renovate old ones (Chapter 10).

WATER deeply before hard freeze all newly planted or transplanted trees and shrubs (pages 89-91).

VEGETABLES: Root crops are dug now and stored in coolest frost-free place available (page 241). Place in frame celery, lettuce, Chinese-cabbage, heel in; cover on cold nights; use as needed (Chapter 7).

WINTER SQUASH and sweet potatoes should be stored in temperature 50 to 60 degrees.

SOIL PREPARATION: Prepare planting holes for nursery stock which may not be delivered until after ground freezes. Cover prepared ground with straw, leaves, or burlap, held down by boards to keep from freezing. In areas where fall planting is possible, prepare new rose beds ready for planting roses when delivered (page 221). Peonies and phlox may also be planted or divided and replanted now. Mulch beds after planting (pages 87-89).

CUT BACK long vines and rose canes which may whip in winter wind (page 226); *old* raspberry canes to the ground; and prune off a third of young canes (page 266).

HOUSEPLANTS: Bring houseplants indoors, if this has not already been attended to. Prune back rank growth and repot if needed.

Do not feed houseplants until they have recovered from shock of new environment. Watch for aphids and other pests at this time. Syringe foliage at least once a week. Keep moist but not soggy.

Feed Christmas cactus every two weeks. Water moderately, but syringe frequently.

November is the rest period for fuchsia, clivia, and crown-of-thorns. Reduce water. Do not feed until plants show signs of new growth.

While garden is in full color with berries and autumn foliage, make notes on areas which need more colorful autumn shrubs. Order these for late winter or early spring planting. If marked stakes are placed at points where new shrubbery is to be planted, this will hasten the job when it is time to dig holes and set shrubs.

FRUITS: Harvest and store tree fruits as they ripen.

For Area V

PLANT spring-flowering bulbs; half-hardy bulbs; lilies (page 185); camellias; lilacs and other shrubs and trees as soon as they become dormant; roses, fuchsias, heathers; azaleas as soon as new flower buds form (page 148). (Magnolias, dogwoods and hollies should be *spring-planted*.) Columbine, Canterbury bells, wallflower, calendula, snapdragon; ground covers such as ajuga, liriope, *Hedera helix*, and *Vinca minor* (pages 168-170).

DIVIDE and TRANSPLANT: Peonies, iris, phlox, Oriental poppies (pages 72; 184).

PREPARE beds for pansies and other winter-blooming flowers (page 94); vegetable garden for sowing (page 236); planting holes for trees and shrubs to be planted later (pages 148-151).

SET OUT plants of cabbage, cauliflower, broccoli (page 239).

SOW late in month: carrot, beet, onion, spinach, Swiss chard, lettuce, broccoli, kale (page 238); hardy annuals (page 67); in frame: perennials and biennials (page 67); lawns with domestic ryegrass for winter color (page 164).

SPRAY broad-leaved evergreens for tea scale (Appendix, page 451).

LAWNS: Sprig new lawns with Bermudagrass. Plug St. Augustine, centipede, and Zoysia turf areas. Feed established Bermuda, carpet, St. Augustine, and Zoysia turf (Chapter 10).

REPLANT hardy water-lilies late in month.

BANK around tender shrubs and trees with soil before hard frost.

WATER deeply in dry climates so shrubs and trees will not go into cold weather with dry roots. Chrysanthemums last longer if kept well watered (pages 89-91).

HOUSEPLANTS: Bring in before hard frost; cut back and repot if necessary; watch for pests; do not feed until plants have recovered from shock of move; take cuttings of geranium, heliotrope, lantana, fuchsia (page 76).

For Area VI

PLANT and TRANSPLANT early-blooming perennials (page 184); azaleas when flower buds have set; camellias, fuchsias, heathers, lilies, bulbs. Tulip bulbs which have been in refrigerator for a few weeks may now be planted.

PLANT or TRANSPLANT tropical subjects no later than October.

FEED established bulb beds; roses; established lawns (pages 91-98).

WITHHOLD fertilizers from shrubs and tender plants which may sustain frost injury to soft growth. If dormant, or partially so, there is less danger of damage. This rule applies to citrus fruit.

SET OUT winter-blooming plants; hardy vegetables (pages 184; 239).

SOW perennial seeds in seedbed; cool-weather vegetables in garden (pages 67; 238).

LAWNS: Sprig new lawns with Bermudagrass; plug in St. Augustine, centipede, or Zoysia (page 159); feed established turf, continue mowing (Chapter 10).

WATER: See that there is ample moisture around roots of shrubs, trees, and plants to prevent cold damage (pages 89-91); after a frost, spray leaves of affected plants and protect from strong sun.

PRUNING is to be avoided in autumn, as heavy growth helps

to prevent frost damage; also because pruning may encourage soft growth, which is susceptible to injury.

PROTECTION: Keep ready at hand burlap, slats, or black plastic, to protect tender specimens if frost is forecast. Remove covering as soon as danger is over. (Smaller plants may be wrapped in newspaper.)

NOVEMBER

The Wind

The wind stood up, and gave a shout;
He whistled on his fingers and
Kicked the withered leaves about,
And thumped the branches with his hand,
And said he'll kill, and kill, and kill;
And so he will! And so he will!

JAMES STEPHENS

For Area I

MULCHES: Spread well-rotted, strawy manure or compost over surface of perennial flower and vegetable beds just before or just after first hard freeze. Mulch plants in coldframes with dry hardwood leaves, pine needles, or other locally available mulching material that does not mat down. Mulch recently set or doubtfully hardy shrubs with a foot or more of nonmatting mulch (pages 87-89). Have extra insulation available to place over coldframe sash when weather becomes severe. One-inch thick Fiberglas bats covered with plastic are excellent for this purpose.

ERECT WINDBREAKS around doubtfully hardy shrubs, and those in exposed positions. Place protection on windward side to prevent sun scald. Wrap trunks of young fruit trees in heavy aluminum foil or hardware cloth to guard them from rabbits. Erect snow fence on windward side of exposed garden areas where there is no natural protection.

TREES: Place guy wires on newly set trees. Check these and metal labels to be sure they will not cut into the bark in wind or snow (page 151).

LARGE TREES may be moved by digging around them, permitting root ball to freeze, then transplanting when opportunity offers (pages 148-151).

BRING IN SOIL, sand, and peatmoss for seed sowing later. Store, damp, in plastic bags or cartons.

ROSES: Mulch hilled rose beds with nonmatting material held with evergreen boughs before they are covered by heavy snow (page 230).

BULBS: Cover newly planted bulb beds with evergreen boughs.

PERENNIALS: Pack in a pit or 3-foot-deep frame covered with sash: anemones, chrysanthemums, Canterbury bells, delphiniums, foxgloves. Heel the plants in close together.

TOOLS: When all outdoor work is completed, collect, clean, sharpen, and paint handles. Store in reasonably dry place (Chapter 8).

LAWNS: Treat for possible snow mold (Appendix, page 453).

For Areas II, III, IV

BULBS: Finish planting all spring-flowering bulbs and lilies (page 185). Where temperatures go very low in winter, cover newly planted bulb beds with evergreen boughs.

MULCH perennial and strawberry beds with strawy manure and compost, not covering crowns of plants. Where temperatures go very low, cover mulch with evergreen boughs. Use evergreen boughs *alone* to cover iberis, heuchera, madonna lily, and other plants with evergreen foliage.

ROSES: Cut rose bushes and climbers back to prevent damage from whipping. Hill up rose bushes with compost or topsoil, 6 to 12 inches, depending on severity of winter in your area. Where necessary, lay down and cover with soil climbing and/or tree roses, and young grapevines. Where winters are less severe, protect with evergreen boughs, straw or corn stalks (Chapter 15).

LAWNS: Treat lawns now for possible snow mold (Appendix, page 453).

CLEAN UP flower beds and vegetable garden after hard frost. Burn any trash which may carry over pests or disease.

SOW cleared areas to a cover crop of winter rye (page 42).

WATER evergreens deeply before hard freeze (pages 89-91).

FRAME: Dig plants of doubtfully hardy chrysanthemums and other perennials and heel in close together in a deep frame. Mulch plants with nonmatting mulch (page 88).

VEGETABLES: Bank celery in vegetable garden for blanching. Bring in roots of witloof chicory and plant in deep boxes of soil, peatmoss, and sand in cellar, for winter salads. Complete harvest of winter vegetables (page 241).

PESTS: Put out metaldehyde bait for slugs and snails; dust soil with chlordane for sowbugs and earwigs (Appendix, page 451).

DRAINAGE: Watch for poor drainage during fall rains. Few plants can survive constantly wet feet; chrysanthemums are especially susceptible. For correcting such conditions, see pages 33; 37.

BRING IN soil, sand, peatmoss and store—preferably in plastic bags—for use later in seed sowing or repotting (pages 279-282).

WATER PIPES in the garden and all outdoor faucets should be checked to be sure they are turned off and drained before hard freeze.

For Area V

PLANT spring-flowering bulbs (page 185); lilies; perennials (page 179); roses (page 223); evergreens, shrubs, berried shrubs, trees (pages 148-151).

SOW seed of hardy annuals, including sweet peas (page 71); cover crops on beds—if they are to remain unused through the winter (page 42)—after clean-up, weeding, and cultivation.

CLEAN-UP of all beds and garden areas should be undertaken as soon as plants are bloomed out or killed by frost; *burn* any trash which may carry over winter disease or pests; place clean plant material in compost heap.

VEGETABLES: Harvest root vegetables (page 241); leave winter-hardy crops such as kale, leeks, parsnips in garden and harvest as needed; sow in frame or seedbed, lettuce, radishes; thin seedlings sown in October (pages 66-71).

STRAWBERRIES: Reset runners or new pot plants (page 269).

WATER where falls and winters are dry; give regular, deep waterings (pages 89-91).

LAWN: If overseeded with domestic ryegrass, keep moist until seed germinates.

BULBS: Dig summer-flowering bulbs, corms, and tubers not hardy in your locality; dry off and store (page 188); plant hardy spring-flowering types up to hard freeze (page 185); water established bulb beds if weather is dry.

SPRAY or dust as needed to control pests, diseases.

CUT BACK to the ground when bloom is over, chrysanthemums, hardy asters, and peonies.

CUTTINGS can now be taken of tender, shrubby plants (page 77).

TREES: Fertilize hardy, deciduous shade trees, 6 pounds plant food for each 100 square feet of spread; water fall-planted specimens; brace or stake recently planted trees and shrubs before winter (page 150).

MULCH doubtfully hardy garden subjects, half-hardy bulbs, or prepare mulch ready for use when needed (pages 87-89).

For Area VI

PLANT refrigerated tulips, lily bulbs, bulbs listed in January calendar; evergreens, trees, shrubs, berried shrubs (pages 148-151); plants of winter-blooming annuals, biennials, perennials, including violets (page 184).

DIG, dry off, and store corms, tubers, and bulbs not hardy outdoors in your locality (page 188).

PRUNING, shaping, and repair of trees and shrubs can be begun this month (Chapter 6).

LAWNS: Cut winter grass weekly; feed established turf each month; water as needed (Chapter 10).

FEED established bulb beds, winter-blooming shrubs, shade trees (pages 91-98).

VEGETABLES: Sow seed of cool-weather sorts; thin seedlings previously sown (page 238).

COMPOST HEAP: Build a new one now (page 41).

MULCH with nonmatting material tender subjects such as amaryllis, datura, gerberia, hibiscus, plumbago; azaleas, rhododendrons, and camellias with *acid* mulch of hardwood leaves, pine needles, or acid peatmoss.

TREES: Brace and stake recently set specimens before winter (page 150).

FROST DAMAGE may be prevented in many cases by covering tender plants temporarily when frost threatens. Have ready for use burlap bags, slatting, or heavy plastic. Remove as soon as possible. Sprinkling foliage copiously the morning after a frost may prevent injury. If frost damage occurs, cut back root-hardy, tender-topped plants as soon as extent of injury is ascertained. Banana, canna, and dahlias are examples.

DECEMBER

> Winter! Winter! Do not fear!
> You shall wear an icy crown
> At the falling of the year
> When the leaves are tumbling down.
> JAMES STEPHENS

For Area I

INDOOR ACTIVITIES: See December calendar for Areas II, III, IV.

PRUNE and shape evergreens before Christmas; use prunings for holiday decorations; remove dead or injured branches of trees and shrubs when weather is pleasant (Chapter 6).

CHRISTMAS TREES may be collected after the holiday and used for extra protection on beds and borders and for climbing or tree roses (page 230).

Attend programs of garden clubs, special plant societies, horticultural societies.

SNOW: After storms, remove at once from branches of trees and shrubs that might be broken by the snow's extra weight. Check that all garden areas and plants are adequately protected from coming storms.

For Areas I, II, III, IV

Water Christmas cactus every other day; syringe weekly; feed with liquid fertilizer every 10 days until buds show color.

BULBS: Start French-Roman hyacinths, Dutch hyacinths, paper-whites for bloom later.

Plant amaryllis bulbs in 6-inch pots; set in cool, dark place; water once a week; bring to light in eight weeks.

Bring in first spring-flowering bulbs to be forced (page 120).

Go over gladiolus corms; pack in plastic bags with naphthalene flakes.

Are other tender bulbs cleaned and stored (page 188)?

Let begonia and crassula plants dry out between waterings; this is their rest period.

Move holiday gift plants to cool room or sunporch each night; they will last longer if not kept at too high a temperature.

Have tools been cleaned, sharpened, and stored? (Chapter 8).

For Areas II, III, IV

OUTDOORS

CUTTINGS: Take hardwood cuttings of deciduous shrubs after several hard frosts. Mark each variety, wrap in bundles, and bury in moist sand and peatmoss mixture (half and half) at a temperature between 40 and 50 degrees; do not let dry out; in spring, start in frame. Cuttings of coniferous evergreens may also be taken now (page 77).

WATER: Check outdoor water pipes and faucets before hard freeze; install one or two frostproof faucets on outer house wall for convenience in emergency winter and early spring watering.

FRAMES: Mulch plants in coldframes with nonmatting material; have extra insulation ready for placing over sash in severe weather; try one-inch thick Fiberglas bats covered with plastic; spread well-rotted strawy manure or compost over surface of perennial vegetable and flower beds just before or just after the first hard freeze (page 241).

ROSES: Cut back canes on climbing roses which may whip and break in wind (page 226). In severe climates, lay down climbing and/or tree roses and cover with soil (page 230). Elsewhere, protect with evergreen boughs, straw, or corn shocks.

MULCH azaleas, shrubs, and broad-leaved evergreens with 6 inches to a foot of pine needles, hardwood dry leaves, salt hay, or other material that will not mat down when wet. Where winters are very severe, place extra mulch of nonmatting material and/or evergreen boughs over perennials and hilled rose beds (pages 87-89).

PROTECTION: Erect windbreaks around doubtfully hardy shrubs. Wrap trunks of young fruit trees in heavy aluminum foil, hardware cloth, or Tree-wrap to guard from rabbits; make it high enough for protection *when there is heavy snow on the ground* (page 448). Prevent winter traffic across lawns by erecting barriers across short cuts likely to be used by tradesmen, children, or animals. Place tree guards on windward sides of trunks of young deciduous trees to prevent sunscald.

TREES: Place guy wires on newly set trees (page 151). Larger trees may be moved by digging, permitting root ball to freeze; then transplant. Prune holly, yew, etc., before ground freezes hard, and save for Christmas decorations (Chapter 6).

Purchase or collect discarded Christmas trees after the holiday; use boughs to cover and hold mulches on top of coldframe sash, over Dutch Iris plantings. Lash several small trees in upright position around standard roses, climbers, and half-hardy shrubs to protect against wind and sun. Check labels and guy wires on shrubs and trees. Do not let these cut into bark.

TOOLS: When all outdoor activities are completed, check, clean, sharpen, and store tools; collect, check, clean, sharpen, and paint handles of hand tools; check, clean, and store power equipment (Chapter 8).

For Area V

PLANT fruit trees (page 255); deciduous shrubs and trees; broad-leaved and coniferous evergreens; heathers, avocados, pecans (pages 148-151); perennial vegetables and onion sets (page 239); plants of pansies, violas, snapdragons, dianthus, etc. (page 193); roses (page 223).

LAWN: Apply rock phosphate where lawn moss grows in winter. Agricultural lime also discourages growth of moss. Water regularly in dry areas; mow as needed (Chapter 10).

FEED winter-blooming plants like primroses, pansies, camellias; violets and pecans should be fertilized with a formula high in potash (pages 91-98). Withhold plant food from fuchsias, roses, and other plants in which dormancy should be encouraged at this time.

MULCH beds not in use with compost and strawy manure; cover perennial borders as above. Azaleas, camellias, and other acid-lovers should be mulched with an acid material as peatmoss or pine needles; have protective material ready in case a freeze threatens (pages 87-89).

SOW seeds of hardy annuals, including sweet peas; cool-weather vegetables (page 238).

PRUNE grapes as soon as dormant; remove one third to one half old wood and thin out undergrowth; roses as they become dormant (page 226); shrubs and heathers as they finish blooming.

VEGETABLES: Let parsnips, salsify, leeks, Brussels sprouts, kale, Swiss chard remain in garden; harvest as needed.

PESTS: Put out bait for slugs and snails; chlordane soil where nothing edible is to be planted before spring; use dormant sprays only while plants treated are actually dormant; before using, prune away all damaged or diseased wood (page 104).

SHIFT to sheltered positions plant boxes and tubs containing living plant material or bulbs or set in deep frame.

LAVENDER, lantana, day-lilies, dianthus, gaillardia, marguerites, and sedums grow well in soil for CITRUS FRUITS.

FROST INJURY may frequently be prevented by sprinkling foliage copiously with water in *early* morning after freeze; then cover to shade from sun; if damage occurs, cut back only after extent of injury is evident; some portions of plants may recover.

For Area VI

FROST: To save plants touched by frost, water with sprinkler or hose early in the morning; keep coverings handy for tender subjects in case frost threatens.

SET OUT plants of winter bloomers like calendula, cineraria, dianthus, pansies, stock, primroses, snapdragons, violas (page 184); perennial vegetables and onion sets (page 239).

BULBS: Dig and store tuberous begonias and other tender bulbs, corms, and tubers which cannot survive winter outdoors; plant spring-flowering bulbs, if not done already pages 185-187); plant half-hardy bulbs; see list, page 426.

SOW SEED of half-hardy annuals (pages 67-71); early vegetables (page 238).

PLANT trees, shrubs, broadleafed evergreens, evergreens; see lists (pages 420-424); for plants compatible with citrus fruits, see list in Area V.

FEED each month: lawns, camellias, roses, other winter-blooming flowers (pages 91-98).

Do not feed plants that have finished bloom and are resting.

PRUNE shrubs and heathers, as soon as they finish blooming; grapes, as soon as they go dormant; evergreens—use the prunings for holiday decorations; trees. If surgery is required, see Chapter 6.

WATER: In dry weather, give regular deep waterings to trees, shrubs, plants in active growth, especially those about to bloom; to lawns and bulb beds (page 89-91).

PREPARE rose beds for January planting (page 221).

SPRAYS: Use summer strength oil spray on plants not fully dormant; put out bait for snails and slugs; keep after pests and diseases (pages 451-454).

Notes on Country-wide Gardening Problems

THE WEST COAST

WASHINGTON
OREGON
CALIFORNIA

Gardening on the West Coast cannot be covered by any one set of rules because of the many micro-climates. Although some are within a few miles of each other, each has its own special conditions and limiting factors of temperature and humidity.

In the *Sunset Western Garden Book*, thirteen separate zones are specified in the coastal states alone, between the Canadian border and Southern California; and some of these are again subdivided several times for greater accuracy.

It is understandable, then, that our calendar for the West Coast must be modified to fit local conditions, especially in coordinating gardening operations with spring and fall frost dates. The selection of suitable plant material for each zone or section is also of supreme importance.

The Pacific Northwest in the *Puget Sound* area provides an average of 250 growing days near the water and about 160 a few miles inland. Winter temperatures only occasionally drop below zero, and most planting is done on the assumption that material will seldom have to weather below-zero periods.

This is a section where many borderline plants thrive, provided they do not require high summer temperatures, and if they enjoy plenty of moisture. Broadleaved evergreens of all sorts flourish in this mild but cool area, while perennials and hardy bulbs are at their best.

The northern two thirds of the Oregon coastland, in the long valley between Vancouver and Portland on the north and Rosenberg on the south, receives 80 to 120 inches of rain annually, most of it during the winter, with only 10 to 12 inches falling in the summer. Growing seasons average more than 200 days, with many nearer 300. It is small wonder that this part of the Northwest is a horticulturist's paradise: summers are cool and winter temperatures along the coast average from 20 to 30 degrees F.; 10 to 20 degrees is the average just inland from the coast, with mean temperatures in the 40s.

Winter rains taper off gradually, usually ending in May, so that spring and early summer flowers, strawberries, and hardy vegetables have ideal conditions for development.

The commercial production of spring-flowering bulbs is concentrated in this area and the best lilies in the United States are bred and grown here. Portland (known as the Rose City) commonly produces rose blooms the size of coffee cups and tea saucers! Primulas, dianthus, delphinium, and other species which thrive in a cool, moist climate are unexcelled here. These include azaleas, rhododendrons, and some of the less hardy broadleaved evergreens.

The dry summer period does not last long so that artificial watering is necessary for only a comparatively short period of time.

In fact, gardening poses few problems for the homeowner in the Pacific Northwest, unless his grounds are poorly drained. In this case, artificial drainage may be necessary (pages 33-37). Alkaline and saline soils are found in some sections of eastern Washington and this condition must be corrected (Chapter 2, page 47).

Where high rainfall constantly replenishes the humus content of the prevalent gray-brown soils characteristic of cool, humid regions, the home gardener should adhere to a consistent fertilizer program by applying home-produced compost or by adding soil amendments or complete plant foods (Chapter 2).

The intermountain areas of western Washington, Oregon, and California are covered in the Mountain and Intermountain section to be found on page 387.

In the *Siskiyous* around Medford and Grant's Pass, Oregon, and in the foothills of northern California between Redding and Bakersfield, the sharply defined climate ranges from winter lows of zero to six above, yet average 30 to 35 degrees. Crops mature quickly as the summer temperatures rise to 85 or even 90 degrees, yet the growing season lasts only about 182 days.

Because of cold winters, deciduous trees and shrubs, lilacs, flowering fruits, peonies, and hardy vegetables thrive in this area.

The *Central Valley* of California, just west of the section described above, ranges from Red Bluff on the north to Bakersfield on the south. Here the growing season averages 270 days, with some areas warm enough for the growing of citrus fruits and ornamentals like crape-myrtle, gardenias, nandinas, and oleanders. Tuberous begonias, fuchsias, and other plants which prefer cool summers can be successfully grown under shading.

Summer highs during June, July, August, and early September reach 90 to 100 degrees; but the cool, pleasant springs, lasting from February to the end of May, are ideal for gardening.

The Northern Coast of California and the San Francisco Bay runs from Eureka on the north to Carmel on the south —a narrow strip of ocean-tempered land where the growing season averages 350 days per year in and around San Francisco Bay and over 300 days in Monterey. Although the growing season is long in the foggy Bay section, summer highs average 65–68 degrees. Only plants which thrive in cool, moist air can be grown successfully here. Some, like subtropicals, are not actually injured by cold temperatures, but need more sun and many more warm days in order to flourish. Here rhododendrons, azaleas, fuchsias, ferns, geraniums, and begonias are thoroughly at home.

A few miles south, in Santa Cruz, summer temperatures average 74 to 76, with more sunshine. Here it often drops to 39 degrees in winter, as it does at the north end of the strip around Crescent City, where summer temperatures are not as high.

Gardeners along this coastal strip must select plant material by trial and error. One can experiment with all sorts of borderline plants. An area like Berkeley, where fog is less prevalent than around San Francisco, offers an opportunity to grow such tender plants as hibiscus, which cannot survive in the center of the fog belt.

Along the *Southern Coast of California* from Santa Barbara to San Diego, lies a subtropical strip where summer temperatures average in the 70s, with winter averages well up in the 40s. In this ideal climate, pleasant at all times of the year, an average of 335 growing days makes horticulture an exciting hobby. Frosts may occur, of course, sometimes years apart, sometimes several years in a row, so the tenderest of plants grown should be placed against buildings or near massed plantings that offer shelter.

The desert areas of Southeastern California are covered after the section on the Southwest on page 383.

THE SOUTHWEST

SOUTHEASTERN CALIFORNIA
ARIZONA
NEW MEXICO
NEVADA
WESTERN AND CENTRAL TEXAS

Throughout the vast areas of the Southwest, there are major problems for the home gardener which are not encountered in most other areas.

Elevation is an all-important factor here where high mountains, plateaus, and low valleys are encountered.

Maximum temperatures drop about one degree for every 225 feet of elevation. At high altitudes therefore, the number of growing days per year rapidly decreases until the period between last spring and first autumn frosts reaches less than 100 days at higher elevations. This naturally limits the kind of plant material which may be successfully grown. (See page 387 for a discussion of *Mountain and Intermountain* conditions, and the Appendix for lists of plants suitable for these regions. At the other extreme, *Desert Gardening* is discussed later on in this chapter.)

Given a similar elevation, each hundred miles of distance north or south makes a difference of from one to two weeks in season changes, and therefore, in plant development. This is true everywhere in the country. (We ourselves have moved three times during the past thirty-five years, each time approximately one hundred miles farther north. We have found that the planting dates in our present home in Massachusetts are about three weeks later than in Philadelphia—and we are on Cape Cod, where the average temperatures are much milder than in the rest of the state.)

In the Southwest, where winter and summer temperatures, soils, wind, and rainfall vary so greatly, native plant life and the horticultural possibilities are equally varied.

Beginning near the Gulf, where subtropical plants are at home, each hundred miles northward marks a change in the natural vegetation, caused not only by cooler temperatures but by soil characteristics, winds, and moisture—or the lack of it.

It is impossible in a limited space to give specific gardening advice to those living in any given part of the area, but the following general directives, taken in conjunction with the rest of this chapter, should be helpful:

1. Ascertain the type of soil on which your home is built by consulting your local county agent or nearest Agricultural Experiment Station. (See Soils of the Southwest, below.)

2. Arrange for as generous a supply of *water* as you can afford.

3. Observe native *plants* of the area and cultivated plants successfully grown in the vicinity, and choose your plant material accordingly. (See lists in the Appendix.)

4. If drying winds present a problem in winter, summer, or both, make the planting of windbreaks a first consideration. The protection of newly or recently set trees, shrubs, and other plants is most important to success under these conditions.

5. Where winters are extremely cold, adequate winter protection for plant material should be applied.

6. For desert conditions, see page 383.

SOILS OF THE SOUTHWEST

WESTERN NEW MEXICO
EASTERN ARIZONA

Gardeners have to work with soils composed largely of alkaline adobe sands at both high and low elevations.

EASTERN NEW MEXICO
WESTERN TEXAS
WESTERN OKLAHOMA

All have highly alkaline adobe soil—that combination of alluvial clay, silt, and sand which must be handled as clay soil (see Chapter 2). By adding humus, sand, and other needed amendments, its potential richness can be activated. Sufficient *water,* deep tilling, and an adequate drainage system are essential.

CENTRAL TEXAS

Soil is composed of black limestone on calcareous bases, reaction being alkaline to neutral to acid as the Mississippi River is approached.

COUNTRY-WIDE GARDENING PROBLEMS

These calcareous soils are extremely rich and easily managed. They are characterized by the deep cracks which develop in dry weather. Instead of forming hard clods like typical clay soil, however, they crumble easily and can be worked without difficulty. Only humus is needed to maintain their high productivity.

CENTRAL OKLAHOMA

Soil is similar in character, but less rich, being deficient in phosphorus, which must be added to make it productive. Hot summer winds and severe winter temperatures add to the problems of successful gardening in this section.

SOUTHWESTERN ARIZONA
SOUTHEASTERN CALIFORNIA

Include extensive desert regions, where special problems exist. Only where irrigation has been introduced is it possible for man to live and for plant life to flourish. Most of the soil is highly alkaline. *Salinity* may also be a problem, especially in soils irrigated by the Colorado River, which is loaded with soluble salts that sometimes build up in the surface soils to a point where many plants will not grow. In agricultural land, this is leached away by forming temporary ponds on the affected areas (see page 50).

On irrigated land, the fertility is often extremely high, especially where the Colorado River deposits its rich silts. Soils vary from heavy clay through sandy loam to pure sand. Nitrogen and phosphate are the two nutrients most needed in the growing of commercial vegetable crops, together with animal manure and other humus. Green manuring, achieved by planting a cover crop to be dug under 60 days before planting, helps keep up the humus content (see Chapter 2). If a cover crop is planted and dug under before a new home is built, or before a lawn is seeded, humus in the soil is assured for the first year at least.

DESERT LIVING

In reclaimed desert regions, where irrigation has brought fertility to vast sections formerly producing only cacti and sagebrush, temperatures reach 125 degrees in midsummer and 100 as early as March and as late as October. Frost is unusual in the short, mild winters, and the mercury occasionally climbs as high as 85 degrees.

Water. Humidity is extremely low, rainfall averaging only 2 to 3 inches per year. Because of these conditions, irrigation and wells have been introduced to make the land productive. Tremendous quantities of water are needed to produce healthy plant life, so the first need of the would-be gardener is to see that an ample supply is available.

Soil. After the soil has been analyzed and resulting recommendations carried out, it is time to consider what to grow and how to grow it.

Plantings. Once established on a home site, shade trees, shrubs, and lawns reduce wind and temper dry heat beating on roof and ground, while lawns, vines, and foliage plants cool and moisten the surrounding air by convection and evaporation. Ground surfaces ranging in temperature from 150 to 130 degrees may be cooled an average of 36 degrees when tempered by shade. Vines grown on house walls, pergolas, and verandas help to reduce the intense heat in locations where no shade is thrown by trees or shrubs.

A lawn actually reduces glare and heat radiation and so is a "must" for desert homes. Bermudagrass, lippia, or St. Augustinegrass are the three species most often used, while annual ryegrass is seeded into Bermudagrass turf for winter color.

Trees, shrubs, and flowers which will survive and even flourish in reclaimed desert areas are found listed in the Appendix. Windbreaks for protection against blowing sand and trees to provide shade are of utmost importance.

Service areas may be screened with bougainvillea, passion-vine, climbing roses, and trumpet-vine, all husky climbers which rapidly cover a fence or lattice.

For color in the borders, tender, summer-flowering bulbs like dahlias, gladiolus, montbretias, and tigridias are showy and heat-resistant. Among the annuals, heat-loving species include marigolds, nasturtiums, and zinnias.

Completion of a home landscape may take years of planning and planting, but when the work is done it will have greatly enhanced the beauty as well as increased the value of the property.

Important in desert areas is the tolerance of plants to alkali and saline conditions.

ALKALI TOLERANCE OF PLANTS

High	Moderate	Not tolerant

COVER CROPS, GRASSES, AND CEREAL GRAINS

High	Moderate	Not tolerant
Bromegrass	Alfalfa	Bluegrass
Millet	Barley	Giant wild rye
Orchardgrass	Field peas	
Rye	Oats	
Timothy	Ryegrass	
Tussockgrass	Sweet clover	
Western wheat	Wheat	

FRUITS AND SHRUBS

High	Moderate	Not tolerant
Date palm	Desert saltbush	Creosotebush
Greasewood	Grapes	Mesquite
Salt sage		Sagebrush
White sage		
		Apples
		Figs
		Oranges
		Pears

VEGETABLES

High	Moderate	Not tolerant
	Sugar beets	Corn
		Potatoes

TOLERANCE OF PLANTS TO SALINITY

High	Moderate	Not tolerant

VEGETABLES

High	Moderate	Not tolerant
Asparagus	Broccoli	Beans, snap
Beets (garden)	Cabbage	Celery
Kale	Cantaloupe	Radish
Spinach	Carrots	
	Cucumber	
	Lettuce	
	Peas	
	Peppers	
	Squash	
	Sweet corn	
	Tomato	

FRUITS

High	Moderate	Not tolerant
Fig	Date	Apple
Grape		Apricot
Olive		Grapefruit

Pomegranate   Lemon
                                     Orange
                                     Peach
                                     Pear
                                     Plum

COVER CROPS AND GRASSES

Alfalfa	Bermudagrass	Clover,
Clover, Sweet	Saltgrass	Ladino
Dallisgrass		White
Fescue, Tall		
Vetch		

ALKALINE-TOLERANT TREES AND SHRUBS

North

TREES

Chinese Elm
Junipers
Piñon Pine
Spruce, Colorado Blue

SHRUBS

Buckthorn
Buffaloberry
Chokecherry
Lilacs
Mugo Pine
Roses, Austrian Briar
Russian Olive
Silverberry
Tamarix

South

Greasewood   Salt Sage
Date Palms   White Sage

SENSITIVE TO ALKALINE SOILS

North

Birches   Privets
Firs   Roses, Rugosa
Maples   Sandcherry
Lodgepole Pine   Spireas
Poplar, Bolleana
    Silver
Willows

South

Apples	Creosotebush
Figs	Mesquite
Oranges	Sagebrush
Pears	

MOUNTAIN AND INTERMOUNTAIN

WESTERN MONTANA
IDAHO
WYOMING
WESTERN AND CENTRAL COLORADO
UTAH
NEVADA (MOUNTAINOUS)
ARIZONA (MOUNTAINOUS)
NEW MEXICO (MOUNTAINOUS)

In the mountainous parts of the West most soils are lithosols—that is, they are made up of rock fragments of varied texture. Other sections are arid, most of these being alkaline and sometimes saline (pages 49-50).

Some intermountain soils like those near Salt Lake City, Utah, and Boise, Idaho, are rich in nutrients and therefore productive.

Growing conditions in high elevations vary so greatly that it is difficult to give any very specific directions to beginning gardeners. They must consult experienced neighbors and the nearest Agricultural Experiment Station. Home gardening can be attempted only if equipment for artificial watering is available during the growing season. A regular program of soil management must also be followed to maintain humus, fertilizer, and needed soil amendments at the necessary levels.

In the coldest portions of the area there are less than 100 growing days per year, temperatures dropping one degree for every 25 feet of elevation. Because of late frosts in spring, early frosts in autumn, and severe sub-zero temperatures during the winter, only very hardy trees, shrubs, and perennials can be grown. Native material is inexpensive and easy to grow if correct transplanting practices are observed (Chapter 9).

Where heavy snow covers the ground throughout the winter, a greater variety of plants can be grown than where bare ground accompanies sub-zero weather. Lists of trees and shrubs for mountain plantings will be found in the Appendix.

With a coldframe or hotbed (Chapter 7), annuals of all sorts, biennials and perennials to be treated as annuals, can be grown on for summer color. A greenhouse or conservatory attached to the home (Chapter 18) makes it possible to garden all year round instead of only during the meager number of frost-free days to be expected in many parts of this region.

In fertile *intermountain* areas, winter temperatures in mild seasons may not go below 10 degrees above, and the average number of growing days is 170 to 180. Under such conditions, successful gardening is not difficult if plenty of water is available and if good soil management is practiced (Chapter 2).

THE GREAT NORTHERN PLAINS

MINNESOTA
NORTH DAKOTA
SOUTH DAKOTA
EASTERN MONTANA
EASTERN WYOMING
NORTHERN AND CENTRAL NEBRASKA
NORTHERN IOWA

Here on the Great Plains, the climate is characterized by low winter temperatures which vary from −20 to −40 degrees. In most of the area, summer highs reach 90 degrees and rainfall is between 15 and 20 inches, 2 to 9 inches of which falls during the growing season for home gardeners.

Minnesota is favored by a higher rainfall: 25 to 30 inches annually, with 10 to 13 inches falling in summer. Here, as in the most easterly portions of the Dakotas, lies the rich "black soil" originally covered by prairie grass; year after year over the centuries this prairie grass died back and replenished the soil until it made deep, dark topsoil. Typical prairie soils are found in the southeastern portion of the state.

Soils in the west and south of the Northern Plains are mostly brown or chestnut grassland types, with some deposits of shallow, arid soils. Although most of this land is moderately rich in nutrients, home gardening is limited by the supply of available water and by the severity of the winters. With plenty of water, however, the gardener can achieve success by providing humus, needed soil amendments, fertilizers, and appropriate plant material.

The growing season varies from 150 to 120 frost-free days; fall frost occurs in September, and the last spring frosts in May in the colder regions. Only very hardy species can survive the cold and wind, but much work has been done by

COUNTRY-WIDE GARDENING PROBLEMS

local State Experiment Stations in selecting and developing iron-hardy varieties of many ornamental plants, including roses and chrysanthemums (see Appendix).

Massive winter protection of many ornamentals is essential, as is wrapping or other cover to prevent sunscald and wind burn. (For windbreak material, see Appendix.)

CENTRAL PLAINS

EASTERN COLORADO
KANSAS
SOUTHERN NEBRASKA

Most of the fertile land of the Central Plains is watered by an annual rainfall of approximately 25 inches per year, though a few sections receive as little as 15 inches. Six to 9 inches falls in the growing season, when it can be helpful in the home garden.

From 140 (in the west) to 210 (in the east) frost-free days are enjoyed, but despite the comparatively long growing season, and the basic richness of the soils, which were originally covered by grasses, home gardening is difficult and in many portions impossible without plenty of supplementary water.

Given the means to irrigate as needed, it is comparatively easy to add fertilizers and humus according to local soil requirements, which can be ascertained by having samples analyzed by the county agent or nearest Agricultural Experiment Station.

An additional hazard to cultivated plants is the drying wind which sweeps across this country from the foothills of the Rocky Mountains, making it necessary for the gardener to take precautions against wind burn and winter sunscald.

HEARTLAND PRAIRIE

CENTRAL ILLINOIS
CENTRAL AND SOUTHERN IOWA
SOUTHEASTERN KANSAS
NORTHERN MISSOURI

The richest of the prairie soils of the United States lie in eastern Kansas, Iowa, and southern Minnesota, with one section east of the Mississippi in southern Wisconsin and northern Illinois. Reddish prairie soils, not quite so rich, adjoin this area on the south as do the rich "black soils" to the north.

Here in the "corn belt" lies the only soil in the country which can boast 15 to 20 inches of humus, developed by the prairie grasses over the centuries and retained in the upper soil layers because the rainfall is not excessive—30 inches annually, 10 to 13 inches falling during the growing season.

We well remember a friend who spent her childhood in northern Illinois telling us of the wonderful vegetable gardens her father raised each year, never adding a pound of fertilizer or an ounce of humus. Such practices, however, exhaust even the richest of soils in time. This is certainly true of the comparatively small areas occupied by home gardens. It is worth-while to ask the local county agent for advice on the management of land in your vicinity.

NORTH CENTRAL, NORTHEAST, EAST CENTRAL, AND MID-ATLANTIC STATES

WISCONSIN	NEW YORK	PENNSYLVANIA
MICHIGAN	VERMONT	NEW JERSEY
NORTHERN ILLINOIS	NEW HAMPSHIRE	DELAWARE
INDIANA	MAINE	MARYLAND
OHIO	MASSACHUSETTS	WEST VIRGINIA
KENTUCKY	RHODE ISLAND	VIRGINIA
	CONNECTICUT	

Strange as it may seem to group these diverse states under one heading, the fact remains that they vary chiefly in the severity of their winter climates. The soils of the entire northeast quarter of the United States are derived from the primeval forests which covered them.

Northern Wisconsin and Michigan soils are the rich, acid forest soils also found in northern New York, Vermont, New Hampshire, and Maine. They are richer and more acid than the soils of southern Michigan, Indiana, Ohio, Kentucky, West Virginia, western Pennsylvania, and much of New York State and the Mid-Atlantic States. Soils in these areas also derive from the original forests, but much of the humus and nutrients have leached away.

Growing conditions in northern Michigan or central Maine, where winter lows may drop to −40 degrees, are the most rugged, especially as late spring and early fall frosts may reduce the growing season to little more than 120 days per year. In Maryland and Virginia, on the other hand, one can expect from 210 to 250 frost-free days and winter lows of from zero to plus 20 degrees. For directives on when garden operations should be performed, see the calendar.

Except for this disparity, however, gardening is quite similar from Michigan to Maine, and from New York to Virginia.

The entire section receives between 30 and 40 inches of rain annually, most of it nearer 40 than 30, while one section of central New York State receives an average of 50 inches. From 10 to 13 inches of this rain falls during the growing season. In short, no portion of the northeast quarter of the country suffers from prolonged dry seasons.

Soil Management. As practically all these soils are acid (alkaline soils of the West are invariably in areas of low rainfall), the addition of lime is essential (page 47). Fertilizers and humus must be applied periodically to soils in which the humus and nutrients have leached away, or been reduced by poor management in the past (Chapter 2).

Plants of a similar nature can be grown throughout the entire area, the only limitation being that of hardiness. Although Philadelphia is usually considered the northern limit for many half-hardy plants, many of these grow farther north, especially near the seashore where the cold is less severe and the climate more humid. On our home grounds on Cape Cod, for instance, we winter outdoors *Camellia sasanqua,* franklinia (*Gordonia alatamaha*), cherry-laurel (*Prunus laurocerasus*), and Virginia Boxwood. Even figs have survived for five years but we are keeping our fingers crossed.

In our north central area, where winters are extreme, only the hardiest of decorative evergreens and deciduous shrubs are safe without protection, yet a tremendous backlog of material is available. With adequate winter protection, somewhat less hardy species are successfully grown.

SOUTH CENTRAL

EASTERN OKLAHOMA
EASTERN TEXAS
SOUTHERN MISSOURI
ARKANSAS
NORTHERN LOUISIANA

Clay soils predominate in the South Central portion of the country. They are alkaline or neutral in the west and become more acid as they approach the Mississippi River. Approximately 30 per cent of Eastern Oklahoma, however, has very acid soils to which lime must be added if plants that thrive only in neutral soils are to be successfully grown (see Chapter 2).

Here the annual rainfall averages from 40 to 50 inches, of which only 10 to 13 inches fall during the summer. The growing season here has from 200 to 230 frost-free days, so that watering during the dry season and proper management of the local soils are the chief problems.

In western portions, high, drying winds make successful gardening difficult. Precautions should be taken against wind burn and sunscald.

Plants which thrive in western Louisiana are also at home in the adjoining eastern part of Texas, where soils are similar.

UPPER SOUTH

SOUTHERN KENTUCKY
TENNESSEE
NORTHERN MISSISSIPPI
NORTHERN ALABAMA
NORTHWESTERN GEORGIA

Red and yellow soils typical of warm, temperate regions prevail throughout the entire southeastern quarter of the United States. This area ranges from eastern Texas and Oklahoma (see South Central section) to North Carolina and Georgia, and from Tennessee to northern Florida, with the exception of the half-bog soils along the coast, and the alluvial deposits along the Mississippi River.

In the western portions this soil is alkaline, but gradually becomes neutral, and then acid as it nears the Mississippi, where rainfall increases.

On the eastern side of the Mississippi soils are predominantly acid, and rather low in nutrients and in humus because of the high annual rainfall of 50 inches which leaches both humus and nutrients down to a deep level.

Soil management includes the constant replacement of humus plus plentiful feedings of fertilizer. The long growing season of 200 to 250 frost-free days and the abundant rainfall make it easy to grow and turn under cover crops to keep up the humus supply. This area is ideal for the culture of a great variety of food and ornamental plants, including the acid-loving azaleas and rhododendrons which are the glory of the South.

Those who live near the southern boundary of the Upper South should read the section on the Lower South and Gulf Coast, while those residing near the northern limits will find additional information in the sections on the North Central and Mid-Atlantic States.

LOWER SOUTH AND GULF COAST

ATLANTIC COAST:
  FROM NORTH CAROLINA
  TO FLORIDA
GULF COAST OF FLORIDA
ALABAMA
MISSISSIPPI
LOUISIANA
TEXAS

Along the Coastal Plain from Charleston to Southern Florida, and along the west coast of Florida and the Gulf Coast of Florida, Alabama, Mississippi, Louisiana, and southeastern Texas, lie chiefly half-bog or waterlogged soils containing much humus, though some of it is far below the surface. Soil from the higher elevations inland is constantly being washed down by the rivers and deposited on the Coastal Plain, so that these half-bog soils are very fertile *if well drained*.

Under these conditions, open ditches running with the grades toward water courses are usually dug—especially in spots where roots of large trees would invade pipes. If the ditches are partially filled with large stones their efficiency is increased.

Tile drainage (page 35) is perfectly adequate for open lawn areas and flower beds and borders where no shrub or tree roots may clog the tile pipes.

Inland from the Coastal Plain, the soils of the Lower South are largely sandy loams with some areas of clay or clay subsoils. These soils are commonly low in nutrients and humus. Successful gardening in these areas depends upon soil management: the constant replenishment of nutrients and humus which leach away through the porous soil.

Peaty soils found in and near the Everglades, and in other portions of the Lower South, usually lack potash and phosphorus, and even nitrogen is sometimes present only in nonsoluble forms. The addition of copper sulfate at the rate of 30 to 50 pounds per acre has been found effective in improving the fertility of peat soils in Florida.

Along the Mississippi River in southern Louisiana and Mississippi, much of the soil is alluvial. This is rich in plant nutrients and high in organic matter, though in some areas it is necessary to add humus regularly by growing cover crops to be turned under. For other soil improvement methods, see Chapter 2.

Conditions along the immediate coastline, in seashore areas, are discussed on the following pages.

Although with few exceptions soils of the Lower South and Gulf Coast are acid in reaction, it is not usually necessary to add lime since many of the ornamentals and vegetables grown are acid-lovers, or at least tolerant of low pH reactions. Acidity may even have to be increased in growing azaleas and rhododendrons. This is accomplished by applying acid muck or leafmold from nearby marshes or by using one of the acidifiers described in Chapter 2.

Throughout this section of the country *air circulation* is an important consideration, because of the rapidity and luxuriance of plant growth. The objective should be to plant and maintain plantings in such a way that they permit air to circulate freely in both winter and summer and yet provide some protection from cold winter winds.

High shade is another essential feature of gardening here —shade which gives protection from too hot sun in summer and also shields shrubs, trees, and perennials that are winter bloomers.

ATLANTIC SEASHORE

There are special difficulties in establishing and maintaining gardens on the immediate seashore, either in the north or in the south.

Sand or sandy, unfertile soil, high, driving winds, and salt spray are the chief problems to be met and overcome. Each year, however, more Americans are establishing summer homes and even year-round residences in such locations. For such pioneers, a few basic principles for seashore gardening may be of considerable help in achieving success.

Wind protection is the first problem to be solved, preferably by the architect or the landscape architect. If professional help is not available, a solution must be found by the owner himself. Especially if it is to be a one-story design, a new home can be planned so that it provides considerable protection. Walls and fences extending far enough and high enough beyond the house walls to protect the foundation plantings and gardens often solve the problem. Very tough, wind-resistant native material may be used instead, or as a supplementary windbreak. The more extensive such a mixed planting may be, the better.

One objection to the wall or fence is the fact that the wind barrier obstructs the ocean view. At a recent flower show in Boston, a class for ocean-front gardens offered several practical plans. The one that we liked best was a solid fence-barrier on the ocean side with heavy gates which opened inward and fastened back against the inside of the fence. This arrangement permitted an unbroken view of the water from the garden and its lounging terrace, yet was capable of being closed and securely fastened (with iron posts fitting into metal sleeves sunk in the ground) in high winds in summer, fall, and winter. Such fences or walls also act as barriers against drifting sand, which is apt to inundate unprotected ocean-front garden areas.

Wind barriers of wind- and salt-resistant native shrubs should be a combined planting of such species as red-cedar (*Juniperus communis*), beach plum, bayberry, and scrub oak, interplanted with dwarf huckleberry and *Rosa rugosa*. Ground covers for such a planting include bearberry (*Arctostaphylos uva-ursi*), a beautiful evergreen ground cover with pink flowers and red berries, which grows all along the Atlantic in favorable areas; beach wormwood (*Artemesia stelleriana*); and the beach pea (*Lathyrus maritima*). A length of snow fence securely erected within the plant barrier helps to hold back drifting sand.

On open, shifting dunes or sand, beach grass should be plugged in (see Chapter 10). Once established, its roots will hold the slopes. Bearberry and beach wormwood, mentioned above, may also be used. Farther south, sand myrtle, with its boxlike evergreen foliage and starry pink and white flowers in May and June, may be substituted for bearberry. It is native from New Jersey to Florida.

Soil improvement is, perhaps, too polite a term for building garden soil on the ocean front. We live more than two miles back from the Atlantic, yet we have had to fill every bed, border, and planting hole with soil transported from our compost heap (Chapter 2) and from topsoil brought in for the purpose. The only exception is a locust grove where natural grass flourishes in the shallow soil. On the other hand, there are advantages to seaside gardening. One has a limitless supply of sand which can be used for everything from propagating cuttings to mixing concrete for building. And of course there is the mild climate induced by the salt water and the welcome moisture it transmits to the air.

Near the ocean front, it is advisable to remove the native sand and to build beds, borders, and lawn areas (if any) from scratch, with good loam in which plenty of humus and fertilizer are incorporated. Drainage in the sand is almost too good, so that nutrients leach away rapidly and have to be replaced frequently. When applying plant foods the rule to follow is "little and often," so that none are wasted.

Paved terraces edged by plant and flower borders are often more practical than a lawn. If a turf area is attempted, Seaside Bent in the north makes a fine lawn and is salt-resistant. Perennial ryegrass gives a coarse but adequate green cover. In the South, Bermudagrass, St. Augustinegrass, or *Zoysia matrella* resist salt spray.

All the commonly grown annuals, especially those which enjoy hot sun and sandy soil, do well at the seashore. The owner of a summer house should use them for color rather than perennials, which need winter care. Popular annuals include portulaca, petunias, ageratum, marigold, calliopsis, larkspur, sweet alyssum, and zinnia.

For shrubs, trees, and other plants especially suitable for seashore planting, north and south, see Appendix, pages 433-435.

PART FOUR

APPENDIX

HARDY TREES AND SHRUBS

TREES, SHRUBS, AND OTHER PLANTS FOR VERY COLD CLIMATES

TREES, SHRUBS, AND OTHER PLANTS FOR THE SOUTH AND FOR RECLAIMED DESERT LANDS

TREES, SHRUBS, AND OTHER PLANTS FOR THE ATLANTIC SEASHORE

GARDEN FLOWERS: ANNUALS, BIENNIALS, PERENNIALS; BULBOUS PLANTS; PLANTS FOR ROCK, WALL, WATER, AND BOG GARDENS; FRAGRANT PLANTS AND HERBS

GARDEN TROUBLES: PESTS, DISEASES, WEEDS, AND THEIR CONTROLS

BOTANICAL GARDENS AND ARBORETUMS

PARKS AND DISPLAY GARDENS

AGRICULTURAL COLLEGES AND AGRICULTURE EXPERIMENT STATIONS

SPECIAL PLANT SOCIETIES

OTHER NATIONAL ORGANIZATIONS

BOOKS FOR FURTHER REFERENCE

BIBLIOGRAPHY

> I would make a list against the evil days
> Of lovely things . . .
>
> RICHARD LA GALLIENNE

Hardy Trees and Shrubs

(See also Chapter 9.)

TALL, HARDY CONIFEROUS EVERGREENS

BOTANICAL NAME	COMMON NAME	HEIGHT (IN FEET)
Abies	Fir	
concolor	White	120'
homolepis	Nikko	120'
nordmanniana	Nordmann	60'
veitchi	Veitch	60'
others		
Chamaecyparis	False-cypress	
obtusa	Hinoki	100'
pisifera	Sawara	50–100'
Cryptomeria	Cryptomeria	
japonica	Japanese	125'
Juniperus	Juniper or Red-cedar	
chinensis	Chinese	60'
communis	Common	35'
virginiana	Eastern	100'
Picea	Spruce	
abies	Norway	150'
engelmanni	Engelmann	100–150'
glauca densata	Black Hills	40'
pungens	Colorado Blue	50'
kosteriana	Koster Blue	40'
Pinus	Pine	
bungeana	Lace-bark	70'
densiflora	Japanese Red	100'
nepalensis	Himalayan	75–100'
nigra	Austrian	50'
strobus	Eastern White	100'

APPENDIX

Pseudotsuga		
taxifolia	Douglas-fir	100–300'
taxifolia glauca	Rocky Mountain	100'
Taxus	Yew	
baccata	English Yew and varieties	60'
cuspidata	Japanese Yew and varieties	20–50'
Thuja	Arborvitae	
occidentalis	American	60'
orientalis	Oriental	60'
plicata	Giant	180'
Tsuga	Hemlock	
canadensis	Canadian	90'
caroliniana	Carolina	75'
heterophylla	Western	200'

LOW-GROWING, HARDY CONIFEROUS EVERGREENS

BOTANICAL NAME	COMMON NAME	HEIGHT	REMARKS
Chamaecyparis	False-cypress	6–15'	
obtusa, dwarf forms	Dwarf Hinoki		slow-growing; dense, shrub-like; after years of growth attain size of very large shrubs
compacta			
gracilis			
nana			
Pisifera, dwarf forms	Dwarf Sawara		same as above, but less dense in growth; form pyramidal
filifera	Thread Sawara		
aurea	Golden Thread Sawara		
Juniperus, dwarf and spreading forms	Juniper		
chinensis varieties	Pfitzer	6'	spreading; slow-growing to large shrub
	Sargent	1½'	prostrate
communis depressa	Oldfield Common	4'	spreading
conferta	Shore	1'	procumbent, spreading
excelsa stricta	Spiny Greek	2'	spreading
horizontalis varieties		1'	prostrate
	Bar Harbor	1'	blue foliage
alpina	Alpine	2–3'	blue-gray foliage
douglasi	Waukegan	1'	blue summer, purple winter foliage; trailing
plumosa	Andorra	1½'	spreading, crested
sabina varieties	Savin	3'	spreading
squamata meyeri	Meyer	4'	prostrate stems; ascending shoots
virginiana globosa	Globe	10'	dense, rounded, slow-growing
kosteri	Koster	5'	spreading
others.			

HARDY TREES AND SHRUBS

Pinus mugo mughus	Mugo Pine	2–8'	globular
Taxus, dwarf forms	Dwarf Yews		
baccata, dwarf forms	Dwarf English	4–10'	
canadensis	Ground-hemlock	2–4'	straggling
cuspidata and dwarf varieties	Dwarf Japanese	1–8'	
media varieties	Chadwick; Hatfield; Hicks'; Stoveken	8'	hybrids of vigorous habit and fine form
others.			
Thuja	Arborvitae		
occidentalis, dwarf forms	American	2–6'	globular or dense shrubs
orientalis, dwarf forms	Oriental	4–6'	pyramidal or globular
Tsuga, low-growing forms	Hemlock		
canadensis compacta	Dwarf Canada	6–8'	conical
globosa	Globe	6–8'	globular
nana		5'	spreading
pendula	Sargent's	6'	tall
	Weeping	10'	broad

HARDY DECIDUOUS TREES

BOTANICAL NAME	COMMON NAME	HEIGHT
Acer, in variety	Maple	various
negundo	Boxelder	70'
Aesculus	Horse-chestnut, Buckeye	
carnea	Red	40'
hippocastanum	Common	100'
Ailanthus altissima	Tree-of-Heaven	60'
Betula, in variety	Birch	50–100'
Carpinus, in variety	Hornbeam	50–70'
Carya	Hickory	120'
laciniosa	Shellbark	120'
ovata	Shagbark	120'
Castanea	Chestnut	
mollissima	Chinese	60'
pumila	Chinquapin	45'
Catalpa bignonioides	Common Catalpa	60'
Celtis occidentalis	Hackberry	120'
Fagus	Beech	60'
grandiflora	American	
sylvatica and varieties	European	
Fraxinus, in variety	Ash	70–150'
Ginkgo biloba	Maidenhair Tree	120'
Gleditsia triacanthos and varieties	Honey Locust	140'
Gymnocladus dioica	Kentucky Coffee Tree	100'
Juglans	Walnut	60–150'
cinerea	Butternut	100'
major	Western Walnut	60'
nigra	Black Walnut	40–150'

Larix	Larch	60'
decidua	European	60'
laricina	American, Tamarack, or Hackamatack	60'
leptolepis	Japanese	60'
Liquidambar styraciflua	Sweet Gum	140'
Liriodendron tulipifera	Tulip Tree	200'
Maclura pomifera	Osage-orange	60'
Morus, in variety	Mulberries	80'
Paulownia tomentosa	Empress Tree	40'
Platanus, in variety	Plane Tree, Sycamore, or Buttonwood	100–150'
Populus, in variety	Poplars	45–90'
Prunus serotina	Wild Black Cherry	90'
Quercus, in variety	Oaks	various to 100'
Robinia pseudoacacia and varieties	Black Locust	80'
Salix, in variety	Willows	20–75'
Sassafras albidum	Sassafras	60'
Tilia	Linden, Lime, or Basswood	120'
americana	American	
europaea	European	
Ulmus	Elm	
americana	American	120'
chinensis	Chinese	40'

HARDY BROADLEAVED EVERGREENS

BOTANICAL NAME	COMMON NAME	BLOOM—FRUIT	HEIGHT
*Abelia grandiflora	Glossy Abelia	pink bloom	5'
Azaleas, hardy varieties	Snow; Torch; Kurume	various	5–10'
Berberis, hardy varieties	Barberry		
Julianae	Wintergreen	yellow bloom, blue berries	5'
mentorensis	Mentor	yellow bloom, red berries	4–6'
ilicifolia	Holly	yellow bloom, blue berries	10'
triacanthophora	Threespine	pale yellow bloom, blue berries	4'
verruculosa	Warty	yellow bloom, black berries	4'
Buxus	Boxwood		
	Littleleaf		4'
	Common		20'
	Dwarf		4'
Camellia sasanqua varieties Selected japonica varieties	Camellia	various	4–8'
*Cotoneaster	Rock-spray	red fruit	3–10'

HARDY TREES AND SHRUBS

dammeri	Bearberry	red fruit	6'
francheti	Franchet	red fruit	8–10'
horizontalis	Rock-spray	red fruit	low
microphylla	Small-leaved	red fruit	3'
salicifolia floccosa	Willow-leaved	red fruit	15'
Cytisus	Broom	various	2–10'
Daphne cneorum	Rose Daphne	pink	1'
Erica, in variety	Heaths	various	1–10'
Euonymus	Euonymus		
fortunei		pinkish fruit	1' trailing
carrierei			1' trailing
colorata		red fruit	2'
kewensis		red fruit	2'
minima		red fruit	3'
radicans		red fruit	3–4'
vegeta		orange fruit	4–5'
other	Corliss Emerald Hybrids	various	2–5'
Ilex	Holly	various	5–15'
crenata	Japanese	black berries	5–10'
convexa	Box-leaved	black berries	6–8'
glabra	Inkberry	black berries	5–8'
opaca	American	red berries	30–50'
pernyi	Perny	red berries	30'
rotunda	Japanese variety	red berries	15'

BOTANICAL NAME	COMMON NAME	BLOOM—FRUIT	HEIGHT
other varieties and hybrids			
Kalmia latifolia	Mountain-laurel	pink bloom	5–10'
Ledum groenlandicum	Labrador-tea	white bloom	6'
Leucothoë	Leucothoe		
catesbaei	Drooping	cream bloom	6'
keiskei	Japanese	cream bloom	3½'
*Ligustrums	Privets	white bloom	6–12'
*Lonicera pileata	Privet Honeysuckle	white bloom	4'
*Mahonia aquifolium	Oregon Holly-grape	yellow bloom	3–6'
others			
Pieris	Andromeda	white bloom	6–20'
floribunda	Mountain	white bloom	6'
japonica	Japanese	white bloom	5–10'
*Pyracantha coccinea	Firethorn	white bloom, orange berries	5–10'
Rhododendrons, in variety	Rhododendrons	various	4–20'
Viburnum rhytidophyllum	Leatherleaf	white bloom, red berries	10'

* Foliage persistent, not reliably evergreen, North.

HARDY, DECIDUOUS, FLOWERING, AND ORNAMENTAL TREES AND TREE-LIKE SHRUBS, WITH THEIR SEASONS OF BLOOM

BOTANICAL NAME	COMMON NAME	COLOR OF BLOOM	TIME OF BLOOM	FOLIAGE OR FRUIT	HEIGHT
Acer	Maple				
japonicum	Full-moon	purple	May	red foliage	30'
palmatum atropurpureum	Japanese	purple	May	red foliage	30'
multifidum		purple	May	red foliage	25'
ornatum		purple	May	red foliage	25'
rubellum		purple	all summer	red foliage	25'
Aesculus parviflora	Bottlebrush Buckeye	white	July–Aug.	spiny fruit	12'
Amelanchier canadensis	Shadbush	white	May	dark blue fruit	6–15'
Aralia chinensis	Angelica Tree	whitish	August	dark blue fruit	15–20'
Cercis canadensis	Redbud	rose-red, before leaves	spring	berry-like fruit	15–30'
alba		white	spring		15–20'
Chionanthus virginicus	White Fringe Tree	greenish-white	May		15'
Cornus	Dogwood				
florida	Flowering	white, pink	spring	dark blue fruit	15–20'
kousa	Chinese	white	spring	red autumn foliage	15–20'
Crataegus	Hawthorn			red fruit	12–15'
arnoldiana	Arnold	white	May	red fruit	20–30'
mollis	American	white	May	scarlet fruit	20–30'
monogyna	English	pink, red, white	May	red fruit	15–20'
oxycantha	English	pink, red, white	May	red fruit	12–20'
phaenopyrum	Washington Thorn	white with pink anthers	June	red fruit	25–35'
submollis	American Thorn	white	May	orange-red fruit	20–30'
Davidia involucrata	Dove Tree	white	late May		10–30'
Eleagnus angustifolia	Russian-olive	yellowish	June	silvery foliage, yellowish fruit	15'

BOTANICAL NAME	COMMON NAME	COLOR OF BLOOM	TIME OF BLOOM	FOLIAGE OR FRUIT	HEIGHT
Franklinia alatamaha	Gordonia	white or pinkish	Aug.–Sept.	red autumn foliage	15'
Halesia carolina monticola	Silver-bell	white white	spring spring		12–20' 20–25'
Hamamelis japonica mollis virginiana	Witch-hazel Japanese Chinese American	yellow reddish yellow	Dec.–Jan. Jan.–Mar. Oct.–Nov.		20' 12–20' 12–20'
Hibiscus syriacus	Rose-of-Sharon	various	Aug.–Sept.		10'
Koelreuteria paniculata	Goldenrain Tree	yellow	July–Aug.		15–20'
Laburnum watereri	Goldenchain Tree	yellow	June		15'
Magnolia denudata liliflora nigra sieboldi soulangeana stellata virginiana glauca	Magnolia Lily Siebold's Saucer Star Sweet Bay	white, fragrant purple-red white, fragrant white and rose white or pink white	spring spring June–July May April May–Aug.	brown fruit brown fruit crimson fruit brownish fruit red fruit red fruit	20' 15' 15' 20' 25' 20'
Malus, in variety	Flowering Crabs Bechtel Dolga Hopa Sargent Tea	pink rose-red pink white rose-red white	May May May May May June	red fruit red fruit red fruit red fruit scarlet foliage red fruit and foliage	30' 20' 10x10' 10' 20' 60'
Oxydendron	Sourwood	white	July–Aug.		12–15'
Photinia villosa	Oriental Photinia	white			
Prunus, in variety *cerasifera*	Flowering Cherries Cherry Plum	white, rose-purple	May	purple fruit	15'

BOTANICAL NAME	COMMON NAME	COLOR OF BLOOM	TIME OF BLOOM	FOLIAGE OR FRUIT	HEIGHT
sargenti	Sargent's	clear pink	May	purple fruit	40′
seiboldi	Seibold's	pale pink	May	black fruit	20′
serrulata	Japanese	white, pink	May	black fruit	20′
yedoensis	Yedo	pale pink	May	black fruit	25′
Sorbus, in variety	Mountain-ash	white	fall	orange-red berries	20′
Stewartia ovata	Stewartia	white	June-Aug.	yellow autumn foliage	20′
Styrax japonica	Storax	whitish	late June		15′
Viburnum	Viburnum				
lentago	Nannyberry	cream	May-June	blue fruit, plum autumn foliage	12′
opulus	Cranberry-bush	cream	June	scarlet fruit, red autumn foliage	10′
prunifolium	Black-haw	cream	May	blue fruit, plum autumn foliage	15′
setigerum		cream	June	red-orange fruit	12x12′
trilobum	American Cranberry-bush	cream	June	scarlet fruit, red autumn foliage	10′

HARDY DECIDUOUS SHRUBS

BOTANICAL NAME	COMMON NAME	COLOR OF BLOOM	TIME OF BLOOM	FOLIAGE OR FRUIT	HEIGHT
Aesculus parviflora	Bottlebrush Buckeye	white	spring		12'
Amelanchier stolonifera	Dwarf Juneberry	white	spring	red fruit	4'
Berberis, in variety	Barberries	yellow	spring	red fruit	4-6'
Buddleia alternifolia	Butterfly Bush	blue, pink, white	summer		10'
Callicarpa japonica	Beautyberry	pink, white	spring	lavender fruit	5'
Calycanthus floridus	Sweet-shrub	brown	spring	yellow autumn foliage	10'
Caragana microphylla	Pea-shrub	yellow	spring		10'
Caryopteris incana	Blue-spiraea	lavender-blue	late summer		4-8'
Chaenomeles japonica (Cydonia maulei)	Flowering Quince Dwarf Japanese Flowering	red	spring	yellow fruit	3'
lagenaria (Cydonia japonica)	Japanese Flowering	various	spring	green-yellow fruit	10'
Clethra alnifolia	Pepperbush Sweet Pepper	white	late summer		10'
rosea	Pink Sweet Pepper	pink	late summer		10'
Colutea arborescens	Bladder Senna	yellow	spring	bladder-like pods	15'
Cornus, in variety	Dogwood Shrubs	white, cream	spring	red or white fruit	4-10'
Corylopsis glabrescens	Winterhazel	yellow	winter		20'
Cotinus coggyria	Smoke Tree	purple	summer		15'
Cotoneaster, in variety	Rock-spray	white	spring	red fruit	3-12'
Crataegus, in variety	Hawthorns	white, pink, red	spring	red fruit	20'
Daphne mezereum	Daphne	lavender	April	scarlet fruit	4'
Deutzia, in variety	Deutzia	white, pinkish, purplish	early summer		6'

BOTANICAL NAME	COMMON NAME	COLOR OF BLOOM	TIME OF BLOOM	FOLIAGE OR FRUIT	HEIGHT
Elsholtzia stauntoni	Elsholtzia	lilac-purple	autumn		5'
Enkianthus perrulatus	Enkianthus	white	spring	red foliage	6'
Euonymus, in variety	Spindle-tree	whitish	spring	red-orange fruit	15'
Exochorda giraldi wilsoni	Pearl-bush	white	spring		15'
Forsythia, in variety	Forsythia	yellow	spring		12'
Hamamelis vernalis	Witch-hazel Spring	yellow	winter (Jan.–Mar.)		6'
virginiana		yellow	autumn		15'
Hibiscus syriacus	Althea; Rose-of-Sharon	various	late summer		12'
Hydrangea, in variety	Hydrangea	white, blue, pink	summer		3–10'
Hypericum, in variety	St. John's-Wort	yellow	summer		4–5'
Ilex, deciduous in variety	Holly Shrubs	whitish	spring	red, blue, or white fruit	12'
Itea virginica	Sweet Spire	white	early spring		10'
Jasminum nudiflorum	Winter Jasmine	yellow	spring		15'
Kerria japonica	Kerria	yellow	spring		8'
pleniflora	Double	yellow, double	spring		8'
Kolkwitzia amabilis	Beautybush	pink	spring		8'
Ligustrum, in variety	Privet	white, cream	early summer	black fruit	15'
Lindera benzoin	Spicebush	yellow	early spring	yellow autumn foliage	10'
Lonicera, in variety	Honeysuckle	cream, yellow, red	summer	red, blue, or black fruit	12'
Lycium chinense	Matrimony-vine	purple	spring	scarlet fruit	12'
Magnolia shrubs in variety	Magnolia	white, cream, pink, red, purple	spring; summer	red or brownish fruit	to 20'
Paeonia suffruticosa, in variety	Tree Peony	various	spring		6'
Philadelphus, in variety	Mock-orange	white	spring		12'

BOTANICAL NAME	COMMON NAME	COLOR OF BLOOM	TIME OF BLOOM	FOLIAGE OR FRUIT	HEIGHT
Photinia villosa	Photinia	white	spring	red fruit	15'
Potentilla fruticosa	Cinquefoil	yellow, cream	summer		4'
Prunus glandulosa, double	Flowering-almond Plum	pink, white	spring	purple fruit	3–5'
maritima	Beach Plum	cream, blush, pink, white	spring	purple fruit	to 12'
triloba	Flowering-almond	cream, blush, pink, white	spring	red fruit	to 10'
Rhamnus cathartica	Buckthorn Common	yellowish	spring	black fruit	6–14'
frangula	Alder	greenish	spring	red fruit	12'
Rhododendron, deciduous	Azaleas, in variety	various	spring		2–12'
Rhodotypos scandens	Jetbead	white	spring	black fruit	6'
Rhus aromatica	Sumac Fragrant	yellowish	spring	red fruit	12'
copallina	Shining	white	summer	red fruit	to 20'
typhina laciniata	Staghorn	greenish	summer	red fruit	to 20'
Ribes aureum	Golden Currant	yellow, fragrant	spring	dark purple fruit	6–8'
Robinia hispida	Rose-acacia	pink	late spring	hairy pods	7'
Rosa, shrub types in variety	Rose	various	early summer	red fruit	10'
Sambucus, in variety	Elder	white, cream	summer		15'
Sorbaria sorbifolia	False-spirea	white	spring, summer	blue, red fruit	6'
Spiraea, in variety	Spirea	white, pink	spring		8'
Stephanandra incisa	Stephanandra	white	spring		7'
Symphoricarpos, in variety albus	Snowberry	white, pink	spring	white fruit	7'
orbiculatus	Coral-berry, Indian-currant	white	early summer	red fruit	7'

BOTANICAL NAME	COMMON NAME	COLOR OF BLOOM	TIME OF BLOOM	FOLIAGE OR FRUIT	HEIGHT
Syringa, in variety	Lilac	white, pink, lavender, purple	spring		10–20'
Tamarix	Tamarisk				
odessana		pink	summer		6'
parviflora		pink	spring		15'
pentandra		pink	late summer		15'
Viburnum, in variety	Viburnum	white, blush	spring	red, blue fruit, red or plum autumn foliage	20'
Vitex Agnus-castus	Chaste-tree	lavender, white	late summer		10'
Weigela, in variety	Weigela	pink, red	spring		10'

Trees, Shrubs, and Other Plants for Very Cold Climates

HARDY EVERGREEN GROUND COVERS

BOTANICAL NAME	COMMON NAME	BLOOM	HEIGHT	REMARKS
Arctostaphylos uva ursi	Bearberry, Hog-cranberry	white bloom, red berries	trails	seashore
Asarum europaeum	Wild Ginger	brown	5"	moist shade
Calluna, species and varieties	Heathers	white to red	4"–2'	acid, sandy soil; sun
Cotoneaster, creeping species	Rock-spray	red berries	flat	
Daphne cneorum	Rose Daphne	pink	1'	
Epigaea repens	Trailing Arbutus	pink	creeping	acid, sandy soil
Erica, species and varieties	Heaths	white to red	2"–1'	acid, sandy soil; sun
Euonymus fortunei, and varieties	Winter Creeper	white	to 1'	
Galax aphylla	Galax	white	6"	moist shade
Gaultheria procumbens	Wintergreen, Checkerberry, or Teaberry	pink, red berries	4"	moist shade
Iberis sempervivens	Evergreen Candytuft	white	1'	sun
Juniperus, procumbent species	Junipers		1'	procumbent shrubs
Leiophyllum buxifolium	Sand-myrtle	white, pink	2'	seashore
Liriope spicata	Lily-turf	blue	8–10"	
Mitchella repens	Partridgeberry	pink, red berries	6–10"	moist shade
Pachistima canbyi	Pachistima	reddish	1'	
Pachysandra terminalis	Japanese-spurge	white	6"	shade
Teucrium chamaedrys	Germander	rose-purple	1'	sun
Vinca minor	Periwinkle	blue or white	6"	shade

DECIDUOUS TREES FOR THE ROCKY MOUNTAINS

BOTANICAL NAME	COMMON NAME	HEIGHT
NATIVE:		
Acer negundo	Boxelder	40'
Celtis occidentalis	Hackberry	60'
Populus	Poplar	
angustifolia	Narrowleaf	60'
deltoides	Cottonwood	100'
tacamahaca	Balsam	40'
tremuloides	Quaking Aspen	50'
Salix mygdaloides	Peach-leaf Willow	80'
INTRODUCED:		
Fraxinus pennsylvanica lanceolata	Green Ash	60'
Gleditsia triacanthos	Honey Locust	60'
Populus	Poplar	
candicans	Balm of Gilead	90'
grandidentata	Largetooth Aspen	40'
Salix	Willow	
alba	White	40–60'
daphnoides	Russian	40'
Ulmus	Elm	
americana	American	80'
parvifolia	Chinese	40'
pumila	Siberian	35'

SHRUBS FOR THE ROCKY MOUNTAINS

BOTANICAL NAME	COMMON NAME	FLOWER	TIME OF BLOOM	FRUIT	HEIGHT
Amelanchier alnifolia	Serviceberry	white	spring	black	7'
Aronia arbutifolia	Chokeberry	blush	spring	red	5–10'
Caragana arborescens	Siberian Pea-shrub	yellow	spring		6–10'
Eleagnus commutata	Silverberry	white	late spring	silvery	12'
Prunus americana	Wild Plum	white	spring	red	15'
Rhamnus cathartica	Buckthorn	yellow-green	spring	black	10–14'
Rhus	Sumac				
aromatica	Fragrant	yellowish	summer	red	6'
typhina	Staghorn	greenish	summer	red	15'
Shepherdia argentea	Buffaloberry	yellowish	spring	red or yellow	6'
Tamarix odessana	Tamarisk	pink	summer		6–14'

TREES, SHRUBS, OTHER PLANTS FOR VERY COLD CLIMATES 413

TREES FOR THE GREAT PLAINS FOR IRRIGATED LAND

BOTANICAL NAME	COMMON NAME	HEIGHT
*Acer negundo	Boxelder	50'
*Celtis douglasi	Hackberry	20'
*Eleagnus angustifolia	Russian-olive	15–25'
*Fraxinus pennsylvanica lanceolata	Green Ash	50–60'
*Gleditsia triacanthos	Honey Locust	50'
Juglans nigra	Black Walnut	40–60'
Juniperus	Juniper or Red-cedar	
*virginiana	Eastern Red-cedar	25–35'
*scopulorum	Rocky Mountain Red-cedar	20–30'
Picea pungens	Blue Spruce	30–40'
Pinus ponderosa	Ponderosa Pine	40–60'
Populus	Poplar	
alba	White	60–80'
deltoides	Cottonwood	80–100'
Prunus armeniaca siberica	Russian Apricot	20'
Salix	Willow	
amygdaloides	Peach-leaf	30'
lucida	Shiny	18'
Tilia americana	American Linden	40–60'
Ulmus	Elm	
americana	American	80'
parvifolia	Chinese	40'

* Indicates species that can be planted in unirrigated soil.

WINDBREAKS FOR THE GREAT PLAINS

BOTANICAL NAME	COMMON NAME	HEIGHT
TALL:		
Populus deltoides	Cottonwood	80–100'
Ulmus americana	American Elm	80'
MEDIUM:		
Acer negundo	Boxelder	50'
Fraxinus pennsylvanica lanceolata	Green Ash	50–60'
Ulmus parvifolia	Chinese Elm	40'
EVERGREEN:		
Juniperus	Juniper or Red-cedar	
scopulorum	Rocky Mountain	20–30'
virginiana	Eastern	25–35'
Picea pungens	Blue Spruce	30–40'
Pinus	Pine	
ponderosa	Ponderosa	40–60'
sylvestris	Scotch	40–50'
SHRUBS:		
Aronia arbutifolia	Chokeberry	5–10'
Caragana arborescens	Siberian Pea-shrub	6–10'
Prunus pumila	Sandcherry	3–5'

WINDBREAKS FOR THE CENTRAL PLAINS

BOTANICAL NAME	COMMON NAME	HEIGHT	REMARKS
EVERGREEN:			
Juniperus communis	Common Red-cedar	35'	tolerates thin, dry soils
Picea	Spruce		
excelsa	Norway	50–60'	prefers moist, well-drained, fertile soils
glauca	White	50–60'	similar to Norway Spruce but more drought-resistant
densata	Black Hills	50–60'	drought-resistant
Pinus	Pine		
resinosa	Red	60'	prefers sun; well-drained, sandy soils
strobus	White	70–80'	requires well-drained soils
Pseudotsuga texifolia	Douglas-fir	50–60'	prefers well-drained, porus soils; tolerates other soils
Thuja occidentalis	American Arborvitae	30–60'	prefers swampy, moist or thin, moist soils
DECIDUOUS:			
Eleagnus angustifolia	Russian-olive	15–25'	grows well in thin, sandy, poor soils
Populus deltoides	Cottonwood	80–100'	brittle; grows rapidly; prefers lowlands
Morus rubra	Mulberry	60'	grows well in sandy soil
Quercus palustris	Pin Oak	50–80'	prefers lowlands
Salix aurea	Golden Willow	25–40'	prefers moisture but tolerates dry soils
Ulmus	Elm		
chinensis	Chinese	35–45'	quick-growing; drought-resistant
americana	American	70–80'	subject to Dutch elm disease

HEDGE PLANTS FOR VERY COLD CLIMATES

BOTANICAL NAME	COMMON NAME	UNTRIMMED HEIGHT
Acer negundo	Boxelder	50–70'
Aronia arbutifolia	Chokeberry	10–20'

TREES, SHRUBS, OTHER PLANTS FOR VERY COLD CLIMATES

Berberis thunbergi	Japanese Barberry	4–8'
Celtis occidentalis	Hackberry	25–50'
Cornus alba	Tatarian Dogwood	6–10'
Caragana	Pea-tree	
arborescens	Siberian	10–25'
microphylla	Russian Pea-shrub	6–10'
Eleagnus angustifolia	Russian-olive	10–25'
Physocarpus	Ninebark	
bracteatus	Colorado	6–8'
monogynus	Dwarf	1½–3'
Pinus mugo mughus	Mugo Pine	3–6'
Rhamnus cathartica	Common Buckthorn	10–25'
Ribes alpinum	Mountain Currant	3–8'
Syringa	Lilac	
josikaea	Hungarian	5–10'
persica	Persian	5–10'
vulgaris	Common	5–10'
Thuja occidentalis	American Arborvitae	25–60'
Ulmus pumila	Dwarf Asiatic Elm	25–50'
Viburnum lentago	Nannyberry	10–25'

SHRUB ROSES FOR VERY COLD CLIMATES

NAME	BLOOM	TIME OF BLOOM	HEIGHT
Agnes	golden-yellow double, fragrant	May–June	4–5'
Amelie Fravereaux	bright red double	*remontant	4–5'
Belle Poitevine	large, pink double	*remontant	3½'
Betty Bland	double pink, *very hardy*	June	6'
F. J. Grootendorst	small, bright red	*remontant	3'
Hansa	reddish double, fragrant	*remontant	4–6'
Harison's Yellow	small yellow double	June	4–6'
Rosa rubrifolia	single, small pink; maroon foliage	June	4–6'
Sir Thomas Lipton	white, fragrant	*remontant	2–3'
Yellow Persian	small yellow double	June	5'

* Profuse bloom in June, repeating with fewer flowers throughout the season.

HARDY VINES FOR COLD CLIMATES

BOTANICAL NAME	COMMON NAME	COLOR OF BLOOM	HEIGHT	REMARKS
Akebia quinata	Five-leaved Akebia	purplish	15-20'	evergreen or persistent; prune severely; use as screen, climbs by twining
Ampelopsis brevipedunculata	Porcelain-berry	greenish; blue berries	10-20'	deciduous; prune severely; use as screen, wall cover; climbs by twining tendrils
Aristolochia durior	Dutchman's Pipe	yellowish	20-30'	deciduous, thin; cut back lightly; use as screen shade; climbs by twining stems
Campsis radicans	Trumpet Creeper	orange	20-30'	deciduous; thin out; blooms on new wood; use on dead trees, pergolas; climbs by aerial roots
Celastrus scandens	Bittersweet	orange fruit	10-20'	deciduous; prune frequently; spray for scale; use on rocks, banks, walls, climbs by twining stems
Clematis flammula	Clematis	rose	15'	deciduous; prune in fall; use on fence, trellis; climbs by twisting petioles
jackmani	Jackman	purple	12-15'	deciduous; prune in fall; use on fence, trellis; climbs by twisting petioles
paniculata	Sweet	white	30'	deciduous; prune in fall; use on fence, trellis; climbs by twisting petioles
texensis	Scarlet	red	6-10'	deciduous; prune in fall; use on fence, trellis; climbs by twisting petioles
virginiana	Virginia	white	18'	deciduous; prune in fall; use on fence, trellis, wall, or bank; climbs by twisting petioles
others				

BOTANICAL NAME	COMMON NAME	COLOR OF BLOOM	HEIGHT	REMARKS
Forsythia suspensa	Forsythia	yellow	8–10'	deciduous; train and tie; use on banks, walls
Hedera helix and varieties	English Ivy	white	50–90'	evergreen; cut back; use on walls, banks, shady areas on ground; climbs by rootlets on stems
Hydrangea petiolaris	Hydrangea	white	30–50'	deciduous; train when young; use on house walls; climbs by holdfasts on stems
Lonicera	Honeysuckles	white, yellow, red	40–80'	deciduous or evergreen; prune severely; use on banks, lattices; climbs by twining stems
Lycium halimifolium	Matrimony vine	lilac berries	5–9'	deciduous; thin; use on banks, lattices; climbs by trailing stems
Parthenocissus quinquefolia	Virginia Creeper	greenish	30–50'	deciduous, blue berries, red foliage; prune severely; use on trees and walls; climbs by rootlets with holdfasts along stems
Polygonum auberti	Fleece-vine or Silver-lace-vine	white, lacy	15–30'	deciduous, prune severely; use on trellis, walls; climbs by twisting stems
Rosa	Rose	various	4–30'	deciduous; prune after bloom; fragrant; use on trellis, fence, walls, banks; climbs by arching canes
Wisteria sinensis	Wisteria	violet, white	25–30'	deciduous; train when young; prune severely when rampant; use on pergolas, walls; climbs by twining stems

HARDY HEDGE ROSES FOR THE GREAT PLAINS

NAME	BLOOM	TIME OF BLOOM	HEIGHT
Rosa			
multiflora	small white; fragrant	June	6'
primula	small pale yellow; fragrant foliage	June	6'
rugosa and hybrids	large singles in many colors; very fragrant	June; some varieties *remontant	6'
spinossisima altaica and hybrids	various	June	6'
Therese Bugnet	pink single	*remontant	6'

* Profuse bloom in June, repeating with fewer flowers throughout season.

HARDY CHRYSANTHEMUMS FOR VERY COLD CLIMATES

HARDIEST

NAME	COLOR	TYPE	RELATIVE SEASON OF BLOOM
Aglow	orange-bronze	tall double	early-mid
Arikara	bronze	semidouble	early
Chippewa	purple	double	late-mid
Dakota	yellow-bronze	double	very early
Delight	yellow	tall double	early
Hidatsa	red	small double	late-mid
Violet	lavender	double	mid
Waku	white	large double	late

LESS HARDY

Apache	red-bronze	large double	early
Crowning Glory	wheat-bronze	tall large double	mid
Dr. Longley	lavender	double	early
Early Gold	yellow	small double	early-mid
George Luxton	bronze	double	early
Murmurs	lavender	double	early-mid
Nanook	cream	small double	early-mid
Reverence	pale yellow	large double	very early
Rouge Cushion	red	semidouble	mid
Wanda	raspberry	double	early

BEARDED IRIS FOR VERY COLD CLIMATES

White: Gudrun, Lady Boscawen, Matterhorn
Cream: Desert Song, Sunny Ruffles
Yellow: Cloth of Gold, Ola Kala, Soveg
Pink: Pink Cameo, Coralie, Twilight Sky

Light Blue:	Azure Skies, Great Lakes
Medium Blue:	Blue Frills, Blue Rhythm, Chivalry
Deep Blue:	Danube Wave
Purple:	Sable, Vatican Purple
Lavender or Violet:	Mulberry Rose, Violet Symphony
Red:	Ranger, Solid Mahogany
Bicolor:	Wabash
Plicata:	Blue Shimmer, Kansas Bouquet
Variegata:	City of Lincoln, Mexico

Trees, Shrubs, and Other Plants for the South and for Reclaimed Desert Lands

EVERGREEN TREES FOR THE SOUTH AND SOUTH CENTRAL

BOTANICAL NAME	COMMON NAME	BLOOM	FRUIT	HEIGHT
Arbutus unedo	Strawberry-tree	blush		30'
*Cedrus	Cedar			
atlantica	Atlas		cones	120'
deodora	Deodor		cones	150'
Cinnamomum camphora	Camphor Tree	yellow		40'
Cryptomeria japonica, and varieties	Cryptomeria	yellow	cones	125'
Cyrilla racemiflora	Southern Leatherwood	white		30'
*Ilex	Holly			
aquifolium	English	whitish	red berries	40'
cornuta		whitish	red berries	20'
c. burfordi	Burford	whitish	red berries	20'
crenata	Japanese	whitish	black berries	20'
opaca	American	whitish	red berries	50'
Juniperus virginiana, and varieties	Eastern Juniper or Red-cedar		blue berries	to 100'
*Magnolia	Magnolia			
glauca	Sweet Bay	cream	red fruit	to 60'
grandiflora	Bull Bay	white	red fruit	to 100'
Myrica cerifera	Wax Myrtle		whitish fruit	35'
Osmanthus fragrans	Sweet-olive	whitish		30'
Photinia serrulata		white	fruit	
Picea, in variety	Spruces		cones	40–100'
Pinus, in variety	Pines			
Quercus virginiana	Oak, Live		acorns	to 60'
Symplocos tinctoria	Sweetleaf	yellowish	orange berries	30'
Taxus, in variety	Yews		red fruit	various
Thuja	Arborvitaes		cones	60'

* South Central only.

ORNAMENTAL DECIDUOUS TREES FOR LOWER SOUTH AND CALIFORNIA

BOTANICAL NAME	COMMON NAME	COLOR FEATURE	HEIGHT
Acer palmatum	Japanese Maple	red foliage	25'
Aesculus	Horse-chestnut		
californica	California Buckeye	white, pink blossom	40'

SOUTH AND RECLAIMED DESERT LANDS

carnea	Red Horse-chestnut	rose blossom	40'
Albizzia julibrissin	Silk Tree	pink blossom	40'
Catalpa bignonioides	Common Catalpa	white and lavender blossom	20–50'
Cercis	Redbud		
canadensis	Eastern	magenta blossom	25–35'
chinensis	Chinese	rose-purple blossom	25–50'
occidentalis	Western	magenta blossom	15'
siliquastrum	European	magenta blossom	25–40'
Crataegus, in variety	Hawthorn	white, pink, red blossom	to 25'
Delonix regia	Royal Poinciana	orange-scarlet blossom	40'
Firmiana simplex	Chinese Parasol Tree	green fruit	15–50'
Koelreuteria	Chinese Flame	yellow fruit; flame blossom	20–40'
formosana	Tree		
paniculata	Goldenrain Tree	yellow blossom	20–30'
Lagerstroemia	Crape-myrtle		
indica	Common	various colors	20'
speciosa	Queen	purple blossom	60'
Magnolia, deciduous forms in variety	Magnolia	various colors	20–80'
Malus, flowering, in variety	Flowering Crabapples	various colors	15–25'
Melia azedarach	Chinaberry	purplish blossom	40'
Paulownia tomentosa	Empress Tree	lavender blossom	30'
Prunus, in variety	Ornamental fruits	various colors	15–20'
Zizyphus jujuba	Chinese Jujube	brown fruit	15'

FLOWERING EVERGREEN SHRUBS FOR THE SOUTH

BOTANICAL NAME	COMMON NAME	HEIGHT	BLOOM	FRUIT
Abelia grandiflora	Arbutus-shrub	6'	pink	
Aucuba japonica variegata	Gold Dust Tree	15'	purple	red
Buxus	Boxwood	various		
Camellias	Camellia	various	various	
Daphne odor	Daphne	3–4'	lavender	
Feijoa sellowiana		15'	pink	
Gardenia jasminoides	Gardenia	8–9'	white	
Ilex, in variety	Hollies	various	cream	red
Jasminum, in variety	Jasmines	6'	yellow or white	
Leucothoë catesbaei	Drooping Leucothoe	6'	cream	
Ligustrums	Privets	various	cream	black
Loropetalum chinense		8–9'	white	
Mahonia	Mahonia			
bealei	Chinese	12'	yellow	blue
aquifolium	Holly	6'	yellow	blue
pinnata		12'	yellow	blue
Michelia fuscata	Banana shrub	7–8'	cream, red edge	

Nandina domestica		8–9'	white	red
Neriums	Oleander	to 20'	various	
Osmanthus fortunei	Sweet-olive	6'	white	
Pieris	Andromeda			
floribunda	Mountain	6'	white	
japonica	Japanese	10'	white	
Pittosporums		10–15'	white, yellow, purple	
Pyracanthas	Firethorns	to 10'	cream	orange
Raphiolepis indica	India Hawthorn	5'	pink	
Rhododendrons	Rhododendrons	to 15'	various	
Skimmia japonica	Skimmia	5'	white	red
Viburnum tinus	Laurestinus	8–9'	blush	black
Zenobia pulverulenta	Zenobia	6'	white	

HEDGE PLANTS FOR THE SOUTH

BOTANICAL NAME	FOLIAGE	BLOOM
Abelia grandiflora	evergreen	pink
Acacia, Star	evergreen	yellow
Berberis (Barberry), in variety	evergreen	
Buxus (Box) in variety	evergreen	
Camellias, in variety	evergreen	various
Ceanothus thyrsiflorus	evergreen	blue
Cotoneaster lucida	evergreen	
Euonymus japonicus, and varieties	evergreen	pink fruit
Hibiscus rosa-chinensis	deciduous	various
Ilex	evergreen	red fruit
aquifolium		
cornuta		
crenata		
Lantana camara	deciduous	orange and yellow
Ligustrums (Privets)	evergreen	white
Myrtis communis (True myrtle)	evergreen	white
Mahonias	evergreen	yellow
Neriums (Oleanders)	evergreen	white to rose
Osmanthus	evergreen	white
fragrans		
ilicifolius, and varieties		
Pittosporums	evergreen	
Plumbago capensis	deciduous	blue
Punica franatum (Pomegranate), and varieties	deciduous	orange-red red fruit
Rhamnus crocea ilicifolia Red berry buckthorn	evergreen	red fruit
Tamarix	heath-like	pink
aphylla		
odessana		
parviflora		
pentandra		

DECIDUOUS FLOWERING SHRUBS FOR THE LOWER SOUTH

BOTANICAL NAME	COMMON NAME	FLOWERS	FRUIT
Aronia arbutifolia	Chokeberry	pink	
Asimina	Pawpaw	yellowish	
Azaleas		various	
Calliandra guildingi		greenish white, red stamens	
Callicarpa americana		blue	blue
Caryopteris incana		lavender-blue	
Deutzia, in variety		white	
Euphorbia pulcherrima	Poinsettia	white, pink, red	
Hibiscus, in variety		various	
Hydrangea, in variety		various	
*Lagerstroemia indica	Crape-myrtle	various	
*Lonicera, in variety	Honeysuckle	various	red
*Philadelphus, in variety	Mock-orange	white	
Photinia		white	
*Plumeria rubra	Frangipani	various	
*Prunus glandulosa	Flowering Almond	pink	
Punica granatum	Pomegranate	orange-red	red
*Spiraea, in variety	Spirea	white	
Thryallis glauca		yellow	
Tibouchina semidecandra	Glory Bush	purple	red
Viburnum, in variety		white	blue
Weigela		white, pink, red	

* Fragrant

BROADLEAVED EVERGREEN TREES FOR THE SOUTH

BOTANICAL NAME	COMMON NAME	FLOWERS	FRUIT	HEIGHT
*Acacias		yellow		various
Cinnamomums	Camphor Trees	yellow		to 40'
*Citrus fruits	Oranges, lemons, grapefruit	white	edible	to 40'
Eucalyptus, in variety	Gum Tree	various		tall
Ficus, in variety	Rubber-plant			various to 80'
Gordonia	Gordonia			
alatamaha	Franklinia	cream		10'
lasianthus	Loblolly Bay	white, large		60'
Grevillea robusta	Silk-oak	orange		150'
Ilex	Holly			
aquifolium	English	white	red	40'
cassine	Dahoon	white	red	25'
opaca	American	white	red	50'
Jacaranda acutifolia	Jacaranda	blue		50'
Magnolia	Magnolia			
*grandiflora	Bull Bay	cream	red	100'
*virginiana	Sweet Bay	cream	red	60'
**Palms, in variety	Palms			various
Persea americana	Avocado	white	edible	
Photinia serrulata	Chinese Photinia	white	red	40'
Quercus virginiana	Live Oak		acorns	60'

* Fragrant
** See list for Reclaimed Desert Lands for botanical names.

VINES FOR THE LOWER SOUTH AND SOUTHERN CALIFORNIA

BOTANICAL NAME	COMMON NAME	BLOOM	HEIGHT	REMARKS
Allamanda cathartica	Common Allamanda	yellow	20'	
Antigonon leptopus	Coral-vine	rose-pink	40'	prefers poor soil
Bauhinia variegata	Mountain-ebony	lavender to purple	30'	very tender
Bignonia capreolata	Trumpet-vine	yellow-red	50'	evergreen
Bougainvilleas, in variety		various	to 10'	showy
Boussingaultia baselloides	Madeira-vine	white	20–30'	fragrant
Clerodendron thomsoniae	Glory-bower	red and white	10–15'	evergreen
Clematis, in variety		various	10–20'	
Clitoria ternatea	Butterfly-pea	blue, yellow throat		very tender perennial; slender twiner
Clytostoma callistegioides	Trumpet Flower	lavender	10'	evergreen
Cocculus trilobus	Snail-seed	lavender	15'	evergreen; slender twiner
Doxantha unguis-cati	Rat's-claw	yellow	10'	tall
Ficus pumila	Creeping Fig		8'	wall cover
Gelsemium sempervirens	Carolina-jessamine	yellow		fragrant evergreen
Ipomoea tuberosa		yellow, showy; seed pods	15'	very tender perennial
Jasminum	Jasmine			
humile		yellow	15'	fragrant
officinale	Poet's Jasmine	white	30'	fragrant
pubiscens		white	30'	fragrant
Kadsura japonica		yellow; red fruit	6–8'	evergreen
Pandorea jasminoides	Bower-plant	white	20–30'	fragrant
Passiflora	Passion-flower		15–30'	rampant growth
alba (subpelata)		white; yellow fruit		
caerulea		white, lavender, chartreuse; yellow fruit		
coccinea		red; yellow fruit		

incarnata	Maypop	white, purple, pink; yellow edible fruit		
Plumbago capensis	Leadwort	azure blue	8'	
Senecio confusus	Mexican flame-vine	orange red	20'	rampant
Schisandra sphenanthera		green and orange	10–20'	
Smilax lanceolata	Southern smilax	red fruit	20'	slender, evergreen
Thunbergia grandiflora	Clock-vine	blue or white	30–50'	
Trachelospermum jasminiodes	Confederate-jasmine Star-jasmine	white	10'	fragrant, evergreen

BULBOUS PLANTS FOR THE SOUTH INCLUDING BULBS, CORMS, TUBERS, TUBEROSE ROOTS, AND RHIZOMES

NAME	HEIGHT	COLOR	TIME OF BLOOM	CARE	TYPE
*Acidanthera	18"	white	S.	dig and store	C
Alpinia nutans speciosum	8'	white, pink tips	S. A.	outdoors	T
Alstroemerias	2–3'	white, pink, red	Sp. S.	outdoors	B
*Amarcrinum howardi	2–3'	pink	S.	outdoors	B
Amaryllis belladonna striata	3'	deep pink, white salmon pink	S. W.	outdoors outdoors	B B
Amaryllis—see Hippeastrum					
Anemone, St. Brigid	18"	various	W. Sp.	outdoors	C
*Brunsvigia rosea	2–3'	rose	S.	outdoors (Upper South only)	B
Caladiums	1–3'	various	S.	dig and store	T
Cannas	2–5'	foliage	S.	outdoors	
Clivia miniata	2–4'	various	Sp.	Lower South outdoors	
		orange		in pots	
*Crinums	2–4'	white-red	Sp. S.	Lower South	B
Dahlias	2–5'	various	S.	outdoors dig and store	T
Eucharis grandiflora	1–2'	white	W.	outdoors Lower South	B

NAME	HEIGHT	COLOR	TIME OF BLOOM	CARE	TYPE
Eucomis punctatum	2–3'	chartreuse-yellow	Sp. S.	outdoors	B
*Freesia	18"	various	W.	outdoors (Upper South only)	C
Gladiolus	1–3'	various	Sp. S. W.	outdoors	C
Gloriosa Lily	climbs to 8'	red and yellow	S.	outdoors	T
Habranthus	1'	pale pink	Sp. S.	outdoors	B
Haemanthus	2–3'	red, white	S.	outdoors in pots (protect from freezes)	B
Hedychium coronarium	3–5'	white, orange, yellow	S. A.	outdoors	Rhiz.
*Hymenocallis (Ismene)	2–3'	white, yellow	Sp. S.	outdoors	B
Iris	1–2'	various	Sp. S. W.	outdoors	B
Bulbous					
Dutch					
English					
Spanish					
Ixias	1–1½'	various	Sp.	outdoors Upper South	B
Lycoris					
alba	3'	white	A.	outdoors	B
aurea	3'	yellow	A.	outdoors	B
incarnata	2'	pale flesh	A.	outdoors	B
radiata	2'	salmon	A.	outdoors	B
sprengeri	2'	lavender	A.	outdoors	B
squamigera	3'	lavender-pink	S.	hardy	B

NAME	HEIGHT	COLOR	TIME OF BLOOM	CARE	TYPE
Montbretia	2–3'	various	S.	outdoors	C
Nerines	18"	pink, white	A.	outdoors	B
Oxalis	1'	various	S.	outdoors	B
*Polianthes (Tuberose)	18"	white	S.	outdoors	T
Sparaxis	1'	various	S.	outdoors Lower South	B
Strelitzia	4–20'	blue-orange	W.	outdoors	Rhiz.
Tigridia	18"	various	S.	outdoors	C
Tritelia uniflora	8'	blue, white throat	S.	outdoors	B
Zantedeschias (Calla-lilies)	1–4'	white, pink, yellow	Sp. S.	outdoors	T

* Fragrant
Sp.—Spring
S—Summer
A—Autumn
W—Winter

BROADLEAVED EVERGREENS FOR CALIFORNIA

BOTANICAL NAME	COMMON NAME	BLOOM, FRUIT	HEIGHT	REMARKS
Acacia	Acacia or Wattle		10–20'	showy, Australian flowering trees; fragrant
baileyana		yellow bloom	10–20'	
decurrens dealbata	Silver	yellow bloom	50'	
decurrens mollis	Black	yellow bloom	50'	
longifolia	Sydney Golden	yellow bloom	20'	
melanoxylon	Blackwood	cream bloom	50'	
Arbutus menziesi	Madrone	cream bloom	50–100'	
Arctostaphylos	Manzanita	white bloom; red fruit	2–40'	
Cinnamomum camphora	Camphor Tree	yellow	40'	
Ceanothus thyrsiflorus	Ceanothus or Blue-blossom	blue bloom	8'	
Eucalyptus	Gum Tree		30–300'	
corynocalyx	Sugar	yellowish bloom	120'	tender, drought-resistant
ficifolia	Red-flowering	crimson to white bloom	30'	tender
globus	Blue	yellowish bloom	300'	coastal
maculata	Lemon-scented	white bloom	150'	tender
citriodora	Red-box	white bloom	150'	
rostrata	Red	yellowish bloom	200'	frost and drought-resistant
sideroxylon	Red Ironbark	pink bloom	60'	tender
viminalis	Manna	yellowish bloom	300'	frost-resistant
Eugenia paniculata myrtifolia	Bottle-bush cherry	white bloom	25'	continuous bloom
Fremontia californica	Flannel bush	golden bloom	10'	drought-resistant
Grevillea robusta	Silk-oak	orange bloom	150'	for coastal areas
Melaleuca leucadendron others	Cajeput tree	white, pink, red blooms	25'	
Maytenus boaria	Mayten tree	greenish bloom	25'	coastal to Berkeley
Olea europaea	Olive	white (also olives)	25'	fragrant
Pittosporum undulatum	Orange Pittosporum	white bloom	40'	fragrant

APPENDIX

Persea americana	Avocado	edible fruit	60'	south
Quercus	Oak		60'	Los Angeles area
ilex	Holm			
suber	Cork		60'	south
Schinus molle	California Pepper Tree	yellowish bloom; yellowish, red fruit	20'	south
Umbellularia californica	California-laurel	yellowish-green bloom; purplish fruit	80'	south

CONIFEROUS TREES FOR CALIFORNIA

BOTANICAL NAME	COMMON NAME	LOCATION	HEIGHT
Abies	Fir		60–200'
concolor	White	north	150–200'
grandis	Giant	north coastal	150–200'
magnifica	Red	north central	60–150'
nordmanniana	Nordmonn	Sacramento	60–150'
pinsapo	Spanish	San Francisco	60–100'
venusta	Bristlecone	Monterey	60–100'
Araucaria	Araucaria		
bidwilli	Bunya Bunya	south	150'
excelsa	Norfolk Island-pine	south	200'
imbricata	Monkey Puzzle	south	100'
Cedrus	Cedar		
atlantica	Mt. Atlas	entire coast	120'
deodora	Deodor	entire coast	150'
libani	Lebanon	entire coast (also in mts. to 4000')	150'
Chamaecyparis	False-cypress		
lawsoniana	Lawson	north coastal	200'
obtusa	Hinoki		120'
pisifera	Sawara		100'
Cryptomeria japonica elegans	Plume sawara	general	50–125'
Cupressus	Cypress		
arizonica	Arizona	dry land	40–70'
goveniana pygmaea	Pygmy	dry land	6'
sempervirens	Italian	general	80'
macrocarpa	Monterey	Monterey	40–70'
Libocedrus decurrens	Incense-cedar	general	100'
Picea	Spruce		
abies	Norway	general	70–80'
orientalis	Oriental	general	
pungens	Colorado Blue	general	50–80'
Pinus	Pine		40–100'
canariensis	Canary Island	coastal	80'
coulteri	Coulter	coastal	80'
halepensis	Aleppo	hot, dry	60'
pinea	Italian stone	Sacramento	80'

torreyana	Torrey	San Diego	40'
radiata	Monterey	Monterey and general	100–140'
mugo	Mugo or Swiss Mountain	general	6–40'

SHADE AND ORNAMENTAL TREES FOR RECLAIMED DESERT AREAS

BOTANICAL NAME	COMMON NAME	HEIGHT	BLOOM
DECIDUOUS:			
Brachychiton populneum	Australian Bottle-tree	60'	yellow, red
Cercidium floridum	Paloverde, Blue	25'	yellow
Chilopsis linearis	Willow, Desert	20'	lavender, white
Cydonias, (Chaenomeles)	Quinces	20'	various; edible fruit
Dalea spinosa	Smoke Tree or Thorn	25'	violet
Fraxinus velutina	Arizona Ash	50'	
Ficus carica	Fig	25–30'	
Jacaranda acutifolia	Jacaranda	50'	blue
Melia azedarah	Chinaberry	50'	purplish; fruit showy
Morus	Mulberry	60'	whitish; edible fruit
Parkinsonia aculeata	Jerusalem Thorn	30'	golden
Populus fremonti	Cottonwood	80'	
Prosopis juliflora	Mesquite	20'	yellow
Punica granatum	Pomegranate	20'	orange-red; edible fruit
Robinia pseudoacacia	Black Locust	80'	white
Tamarix aphylla	Athel Tree	30'	pink
Ulmus pumila	Siberian Elm	40'	
Zizyphus jujuba	Jujubes	40'	whitish, edible fruit
EVERGREEN:			
Acacia melanoxylon	Acacia		yellow
Casuarina stricta	Beefwood		
Citrus	Citrus fruits		white
Cupressus	Cypress	6–8'	
arizonica	Arizona	40–70'	
sempervirens	Italian	80'	
Eriobotryal japonica	Loquats	20'	white
Eucalyptus	Gum Tree		
rudis	Desert	100'	yellowish
tereticornis	Gray	150'	yellowish
ficifolia	Red Flowering	30'	red
rostrata	Red	200'	red
sideroxylon	Red Ironbark	40'	pink
Juniperus chinensis pfitzeriana	Juniper, Pfitzer	10–15'	
Olea europaea	Olive	25'	yellow
PALM:	Palm		
Arecastrum australe (Cocos plumosa)	Plume	30'	

APPENDIX

Phoenix
  canariensis — Canary Island — 60'
  dactylifera — Date — 100'
  Trachycarpus fortunei — Windmill — 10–40'
Washingtonia
  filifera — Fan — 80'
  robusta — Fan — 100'
Pinus halapensis — Aleppo Pine — 60'
Thuja orientalis — Oriental Arborvitae — 60'
Ulmus parviflora — Chinese Elm — 40'

SHRUBS FOR RECLAIMED DESERT LANDS

BOTANICAL NAME	COMMON NAME	HEIGHT	FOLIAGE	BLOOM
Acacia farnesiana	Sweet Acacia; Popinac	10'	evergreen	yellow fruit
Carissa grandiflora	Natal Plum	18'	evergreen	white; scarlet fruit
Cassia artemisioides	Wormwood Senna	8'	deciduous	yellow
Euonymus japonicus	Japanese Euonymus	15'	evergreen	pink fruit
Lagerstroemia indica	Crape-myrtle	20'	deciduous	white, pink, rose
Ligustrum ovalifolium	California Privet	15'	deciduous	white
Malvaviscus arboreus	Turkscap	4'	deciduous	red
Myrtus communis	Myrtle	10'	evergreen	white
Nandina domestica		8'	evergreen	white; red fruit
Nerium oleander	Oleander	20'	evergreen	various
Plumbago capensis		8'	deciduous	blue, white
Pittosporum tobira	Japanese Pittisporum	10'	evergreen	white bloom
Pyracantha	Firethorn	20'	evergreen	white; orange-red fruit
Spiraea vanhouttei	Spirea	6'	deciduous	white
Tamarix tetranda	Tamarisk	12'	persistent	pink
Thevetia puruviana	Yellow Oleander	30'	evergreen	yellow

Trees, Shrubs, and Other Plants for the Atlantic Seashore

NATIVE TREES AND SHRUBS FOR SEASHORE

BOTANICAL NAME	COMMON NAME	HABITAT
Amelanchier canadensis	Shadbush, Serviceberry	pond edges and woodlands
Baccharis halimifolia	Groundsel bush	salt flats and swamps
Cornus amomum racemosa	Dogwood shrubs	sandy woodlands
Crataegus	Hawthorns	sandy woodlands, hedgerows
Ilex	Holly	Upper South
cassine	Dahoon	pond edges
glabra	Inkberry	swamps, moist spots
verticillata	Winterberry	Virginia and South
vomitoria	Yaupon	open fields, woods
Juniperus communis virginiana	Red-cedar	
Myrica cerifera	Bayberry	poor, sandy, dry
Nyssa sylvatica	Tupelo, Pepperidge, Black Gum	pond edges
Pinus rigida	Pitch Pine	sandy woodlands
Prunus		
laurocerasus	Cherry-laurel	Upper South
maritima	Beach Plum	poor, sandy, dry
virginiana	Chokecherry	sandy woodlands
Rhus copallina	Shiny Sumac	waste places, roadsides
Robinia		
pseudoacacia	Black Locust	sandy woodlands and open spaces and swamps
hispida	Rose-acacia	
Sassifras albidum	Sassifras	sandy woodlands

CULTIVATED TREES AND SHRUBS FOR THE SEASHORE

THE NORTH

BOTANICAL NAME	COMMON NAME
Berberis	Barberries, hardy varieties
Buxus microphylla koreana	Box, Korean
Cytissus and *Genista* species	Brooms, in variety

APPENDIX

Eleagnus angustifolia — Russian-olive
Gleditsia species — Honey locusts
Hippophae rhamnoides — Sea-buckthorn
Ilex crenata convexa — Box-leaf Holly
Juniperus, spreading types — Junipers, in variety
Ligustrum — Privets, hardy varieties
Pinus — Pine
  densiflora — Japanese
  nigra — Austrian
  resinosa — Red
  sylvestris — Scotch
Pyracantha c. lalandi — Firethorn
Rosa — Rose
  rugosa
  wichuraiana
Tamarix — Tamarisk
  parviflora
  pentandra
Yucca

THE SOUTH

BOTANICAL NAME	COMMON NAME
Agave, in variety	
Araucarias	Australian pines
Cacti	Cacti
Carissa grandiflora	Natal-plum
Coccolobia uvifera	Sea-grape
Palms	
Phoenix	
canariensis	
sylvestris	Wild date palm
Washingtonia	California fan palm
robusta	
Pittosporum tobira	Australian Laurel
Raphiolepis umbellata	Yeddo-hawthorn
Rosa	Roses
rugosa	
wichuraiana	
Succulents, in variety	
Yuccas, in variety	

GROUND COVERS FOR SEASHORE

BOTANICAL NAME	COMMON NAME	HABITAT	COLOR FEATURE
Arctostaphyllos uva-ursi	Bearberry		evergreen, pink flowers
Artemesia stelleriana		in sea sand	
Callunas, in variety	Heather		
Celastrus scandens	Bittersweet		red berries
Ericas, in variety	Heath		
Euonymus, creeping			evergreen
Hedera helix, varieties	English Ivy	shade	
Leiophyllum buxifolium	Sand-myrtle	New Jersey and South	

Loniceras, vines and bush forms	Honeysuckle	
Opuntia vulgaris	Prickly-pear cactus	rampant, full sun
Vinca minor	Myrtle, Periwinkle	shade

Garden Flowers

ANNUALS, BIENNIALS, PERENNIALS
BULBOUS PLANTS
PLANTS FOR ROCK, WALL, WATER, AND BOG GARDENS
FRAGRANT PLANTS AND HERBS

HARDY ANNUALS

Adonis
Argemone
California-poppy
Candytuft
Centaurea cyanus
Clarkia

Collinsia
Coreopsis
Dianthus

Evening-primrose
Four O'clock
Gaillardia
Glaucium
Honesty
Larkspur

Limnanthes
Love-in-a-mist
Mexican fire plant

Pansy
Polygonum
Poppies
Rudbeckia
Snapdragon
Snow-on-the-mountain
Sweet Alyssum
Sweet Pea

HALF-HARDY ANNUALS

Arctotis
Balsam
Calendula
Celosia
Centaurea americana
Cleome
Cypress vine
Datura
Dimorphotheca
Dusty Miller
Flax

Gilia
Godetia
Gypsophila
Hunnemannia
Hyacinth bean
Lavatera
Linaria
Lobelia
Lupine
Lychnis
Marigolds

Nasturtium
Nemesia
Nicotiana
Petunia
Phlox drummondi
Portulaca
Scabiosa
Statice
Sunflowers
Tahoka-daisy
Thunbergia
Zinnia

TENDER ANNUALS

Ageratum
Anagallis
Begonia
Bells-of-Ireland
Blue Lace-flower
Browallia
Castor-bean
China-aster
Chrysanthemum
Cobaea scandens
Dahlia (bedding)

Everlastings
Gourds
Heliotrope
Immortelles
Mesembryanthemum
Mignonette
Monkey Flower
Moonflower
Morning-glory
Nemophila
Phacelia

Salpiglossis
Salvia
Sanvitalia
Scarlet Runner bean
Schizanthus
Star of Texas
Stocks
Tassel Flower
Tithonia
Torenia
Verbena

GARDEN FLOWERS

LIST OF ANNUALS

FOR SUN	FOR PART SHADE	SHORT SEASON
Ageratum L	Amaranthus T	Baby's Breath M
Antirrhinum M/T	Anchusa M	Calliopsis M
Balsam M	Balsam M	Candytuft L
Bells-of-Ireland M	Calendula M	Cape-marigold M
Browallia M	Celosia T/M/L	*Centaurea cyanus* M
Calendula M	China-aster M	(Bachelor's Button)
Castor-bean T	Centaurea M	*Cobaea scandens* V
Celosia T/M/L	Clarkia M	(north)
Cleome T/M	Cleome T/M	Hunnemannia M
Cosmos T	Cosmos T	Mignonette M/L
Dahlia, bedding M	Cynoglossum M	Moonflower (north) V
Datura T	Godetia M	Nigella M
Dianthus, annual L	Larkspur T/M	Pansy (north) L
Gaillardia, annual M	Lobelia M/L	*Phlox drummondi* L
Larkspur T	*Mathiola bi-*	Poppies, annual M
Lobelia M/T	*cornis* M	Swan River-daisy L
Marigold T/M/L	*Matricaria chamo-*	Sweet Alyssum L
Mesembryanthemum L	*milla* M	Sweet Pea (north) V
Morning-glory V	Mimulus M	Thunbergia (north) V
Nasturtium V	Nemesa M	Sunflower T
Petunia M/L	Nicotiana M	
Portulaca L	Petunia M/L	
Rudbeckia M	Snapdragon T/M	
Salvia splendens M	Sweet Alyssum L	
Scabiosa M	Torenia L	
Snapdragon T/M	Virginia-stock L	
Tithonia T	Verbena L	
Vinca major M		
Zinnia T/M/L		

KEY: T—tall M—medium L—low V—vine

ANNUAL VINES

NAME	HEIGHT	BLOOM	TIME	CLIMBS BY
Cardiospermum halicacabum (Balloon vine)	6–10'	white	summer	tendrils
Cobaea scandens (Cup-and-saucer vine)	10–40'	lavender-blue or white	summer	tendrils
Dolichos labab (Hyacinth bean)	15–25'	purple or white	summer	twining stems
Eccremocarpus scaber (Chilean Glory Vine)	6–12'	orange-red, showy	summer	tendrils on leaf tips

APPENDIX

Ipomoea bona-nox (Moonflower)	10–30'	white or pink	late summer	twining stems with holdfasts
Morning-glory	10–20'	various	summer	holdfasts
Gourds in variety	10–20'	golden	summer	vines and tendrils
Lathyrus odoratus (Sweet Pea)	6–7'	various, fragrant	all season	tendrils
Phaseolus coccineus Scarlet Runner bean	10–20'	red	summer	stems
Quomoclit pennata (Cypress vine)	1–20'	scarlet	summer	stems
Thunbergia alata Clock vine Black-eyed Susan	5–9'	white or orange-buff	summer	twining
Tropaeolum majus (Nasturtium)	3–15'	various	all season	clambering stems
Peregrinum (Canary-bird vine)	10'	yellow	summer	clambering stems

BIENNIALS

Take two years to complete growth. Planted this summer, they bloom next year, then die.

> *Althea rosea* (Hollyhocks)
> *Bellis perennis* (English daisies)
> *Campanula calycanthema* (Canterbury bells) medium
> *Chieranthus allioni* (Siberian wallflowers) cheiri (English wallflowers)
> *Dianthus barbatus* (Sweet William)
> Digitalis (Foxgloves)
> Myosotis (Forget-me-nots)
> *Papaver nudicaule* (Iceland poppies)
> Pansies
> *Verbascum phoeniceum* (Verbascum)

PERENNIALS

FULL SUN

Achilleas (Yarrow) T/M/L
Althaea (Hollyhock) T
Alyssum saxatile L
Achusas T/M
Anthemis M
Arabis L
Asclepias tuberosa (Butterfly-weed) M
Aster, hardy, in variety T/M/L
Aubretias L
Bellis perennis (English Daisy)
Catanache M
Centaureas T/M
Cerastiums M/L

Chrysanthemums T/M/L
Chrysanthemum maximum (Shasta Daisy) M
Coreopsis M
Delphinium T
Dianthus L
Echinops (Globe Thistle) M
Gaillardia M
Geraniums (Cranesbill) M/L
Geum M
Heleniums T
Helichrysum (Everlasting) M/L
Helianthus (Sunflower) T/M
Heliopsis T/M

GARDEN FLOWERS

Hemerocallis (Day-lily) M/L
Heuchera (Coral Bells) M
Hibiscus (Mallows) T/M
Iberis sempervirens L
Kniphofia (Red Hot Poker) M
Lavender
Liatrris (Gayfeather) M
Limoniums (Statice) M/L
Linums (Flax) M
Lupines T/M
Lychnis M/L
Nepeta mussini M
Oenotheras
  (Evening primrose) M

Peony, herbaceous T/M
  Tree T
Penstemons T/M/L
Phlox nivalis L
  paniculata T/M
  subulata L
Physostegia T
Platycodon M
Plumbago L
Polemoniums L
Rudbeckia M
Salvias M
Thermopsis T
Veronicas M/L
Yucca T

PART SHADE

Aconitum (Monkshood) T/M
Ajuga (Bugle Weed) L
Aquilegia M
Astilbe M
Brunnera *(Anchusa myosotiflora)* M
Campanulas M/L
Cimifugas T
Corydalis lutea M
Dicentras M/L
Dictamnus (Gas Plant) M
Digitalis (Foxglove) T/M
Dodecatheons (Shooting Star) M/L
Doronicum T/M
Epimedium M
Eupatorium M
Filipendula (Meadow Sweet) T/M
Helleborus niger
  (Christmas-rose) L
  orientalis
  (Lenten-rose) L

Hemerocallis (Day-lily) T/M
Hostas M/L
Lamiums L
Lobelia, M/L
Lythrums T
Mertensia virginica M
Monardas M
Myosotis L
Phlox divaricata M
Primulas in variety M/L
Pulmonarias L
Thalictrums
  (Meadowrue) T/M
Vinca minor
Violas

KEY: T—tall M—medium L—low

BULBOUS PLANTS

HARDY AND HALF HARDY

Acidanthera hh
Alliums
Anemones, tuberous hh
Brodiaeas hh
Calochortus
Chionodoxas
Claytonia (shade)
Colchicums
Cooperias hh
Convallaria (Lily-of-the-valley)
Crocuses
Cyclamen, hardy species

Erythroniums (moist shade)
Eranthis
Fritillarias
Galanthus
Galtonia hh
Gladiolus hh
Hyacinths
Iris, bulbous hh
Ismene hh
Ixias hh
Leucojum (moist shade)
Lilies, in variety

440 APPENDIX

Lycoris squamigera
Montbretias hh
Muscari
Narcissus in variety
Orchids (hardy terrestrial)
Ornithogalum
Oxalis hh
Puschkinias
Ranunculus, hardy varieties

Scillas
Sparaxis hh
Sternbergia
Tigridias hh
Tritonias hh
Tulips
Watsonias hh
Zantedeschia (Calla) hh
Zephyranthes hh

hh–half hardy

FOR ROCK AND WALL GARDEN

PLANTS FOR THE SUNNY ROCK GARDEN

Achillea
Alliums
Alyssums
Anagallis
Anchusa
Anthemis
Arabis
Arenaria
Armeria
Aubretia

Brachycome
Bulbocodium

Cacti
Calluna
Calochortus
Campanulas
Centranthus
Cerastium
Cistus
Colchicum
Crocus
Cytisus

Daffodils
Dicentra
Dianthus

Echeveria

Edelweiss
Erigeron
Erysimum
Eschscholzia
Euphorbias

Genista
Gentians
Geraniums (dwarf)
Geum
Gypsophila

Helianthemum
Heuchera
Hyacinthus *azureus*
Hypericum

Incarvillea
Iris, dwarf
Ixias
Ixiolirion

Lewisia
Linum
Lobelias
Lychnis

Mesembryanthemum
Muscari
Nepeta

Nierembergia

Oenothera

Papaver alpinum and *nudicale*
Penstemons (dwarf)
Portulaca
Puschkinia

Roses, baby

Santolina
Saxifraga
Scilla
Sedum
Sempervivum
Silene
Statice
Sternbergia

Teucrium
Thalicteum
Thymes
Tulips, species

Valerians
Veronicas

Wahlenbergia
Wallflowers

ROCK PLANTS FOR PARTIAL SHADE

Adonis
Anemones
Aquilegias
Auriculas

Campanulas
Chionodoxa

Cotyledon
Crocus
Cyclamen
Cypripedium

Daffodils
Daphnes

Dicentra

Epimedium
Eranthis
Ericas
Erythroniums

GARDEN FLOWERS

Ferns
Fritillaria
Funkias

Galanthus
Gaultheria
Gentians

Iris, dwarf

Leucojum
Linaria

Mertensia
Mimulus
Mitraria

Orchids
Ornithogalum
Oxalis

Platycodon
Primulas
Pulmonaria

Ranunculus

Sanguinaria
Saxifraga
Sedums
Shortia

Thalictrum
Tiarella cordifolia
Troillius

Violas
Vinca minor

ROCK PLANTS FOR SUMMER BLOOM

*Achillea argentea
  tomentosa*
Alyssum montanum
Anchusa myosotidiflora
Arenaria
Armeria
Aubretia
Asters, dwarf

Campanulas, in variety
Cerastium tomentosum
Ceratostigma plumbaginoides
Cherianthus
Cytissus

Dianthus

Erodium
Euphorbia myrsinites

Gaultheria procumbens
Genista pilosa
Gentians, in variety
Geraniums, in variety
Geums
Globularia
Gypsophila repens

Helianthemum

Linums
Lychnis

Nepeta mussini

Oenotheras

Portulaca

Santolina
Sedums

Teucrium

Veronicas
Violas

PLANTS FOR THE SUNNY WALL

Acaenas
Achillea tomentosa
*Alyssum alpestre
  montanum
  saxatile*
Arabis
Arenaria
Asperula
Aubretia

Campanulas, in variety
Cerastium tomentosum
Cheiranthus

Dianthus
Draba

Erigeron

Gypsophila repens

Helianthemum
Hypericum

Iberis sempervirens

Lewisia rediviva
Linaria alpina
Linum alpinum
Lychnis alpinum

Nepeta mussini

Oenotheras
Origanum

*Phlox nivalis
  subulata*

Portulaca
Primulas

Santolina incana
Saponarias
Saxifragas
Sedums
Sempervivums
Silene alpestris

Thymus, in variety
Teucrium

Verbenas
Veronicas

Wahlenbergia

PLANTS FOR MOIST WALL OR ROCK GARDEN

Aquilegias
Arenaria
Asarums (Wild Ginger)
Cornus canadensis
Eranthis
Erythroniums
Ferns
Galax
Geum reptans
Hepaticas
Heucheras
Mitchella repens
Mertensia
Myosotis
Mitraria
Oxalis
Primulas
Pyrolas
Sanguinaria
Saxifraga
Vinca minor
Violas
Violets

PLANTS FOR THE BOG GARDEN

Acorus (Sweet Flag)
Anagallis (Pimpernel)
Astilbe
Cyprepediums
Darlingtonia californica
  (California pitcher-plant)
Ferns, in variety
Hibiscus (Mallows)
Hostas
Houstonia caerulea (Bluets)
Iris aurea
  kaemferi
  monnieri
  monspur
  pseudacorus
Lilium *martagon*
  superbum
Lobelia *cardinalis*
  (Cardinal flower)
  syphilitica
  (Blue Cardinal flower)
Lythrums
Mitella diphylla
Mimulus, in variety
  (Monkey-flower)
Monardas
Myosotis
Orchises
Podophyllums (May-apple)
Polyogonatum multiflorum
  (Solomon's Seal)
Primulas, in variety
Ranunculus
Sarracenia drummondi
  flava
  purpurea
  (Pitcher-plants)
Spiraea aruncus (Aruncus)
  palmata (Filipendula)
Thalictrums
  (Meadowrue)
Trilliums
Trollius
Vinca minor (Myrtle)
Violas

PLANTS FOR WATER GARDENS

MARGINAL

Calla palustris (Water-arum)
Caltha palustris (Marsh-marigold)
Dracocephalums (Dragonhead)
Lobelia cardinalis
Menthas (Mint)
Menyanthes trifoliata
Mertensia virginica
Myosotis palustris semperflorens
Ranunculus aquatilis
Veronica beccabunga (Brooklime)

IN WATER

Nymphaeas (Water-lilies)
  in variety
Orontium aquaticum
  (Golden-club)
Pontederia cordata
  (Pickerel-weed)
Sagittarias, in variety
  (Arrowhead)

GARDEN FLOWERS

FRAGRANT PLANTS

SHRUBS AND VINES

Azalea arborescens
  canescens
  nudiflora
  poukhanensis
  rosea
  viscosa
Benzoin
Calycanthus
Clematis heracleaefolia
  paniculata
  recta
  virginiana

Clethra alnifolia
Crataegus
Cystisus
Daphne mezereum
  odora
Deutzias
Eleagunus multiflora
Forsythia
Jasmines
Leucothoë catesbaei
Lilacs
Magnolias

Philadelphus
Pieris floribunda
  Japonica
Pyrus angustifolia
  (Flowering Crabs)
Roses
Viburnums
Vitex (Chaste Tree)
Vitis (grape)
Wisteria

PERENNIALS

Achilleas
Alyssum maritimum
  saxatile
Angelica (herb)
Anthemis
Aquilegia
Artemisias
Asperula (herb)
Buddleia
Centaureas
Cheiranthus
Chrysanthemum

Cimifuga
Dianthus
Dill (herb)
Dictamnus
Iberis
Hemerocallis (Day-lily)
Lavender (herb)
Loniceras
Lupines
Melissa (Lemon Balm, herb)
Monardas
Nepeta mussini (herb)

Nymphaeas
  (Water lilies)
Oenotheras
Peonies
Phlox
Primulas
Santolina (herb)
Sweet Cicely
Thymes (herb)
Teucrium (herb)
Violas
Yarrow

ANNUALS

Borage (herb)
Centaureas
Datura metel
  stramonium
Dianthus, annual
Geraniums
Heliotrope

Mignonette
Mirabilis (Four o'clock)
Moonflowers
Nicotiana
Nasturtiums
Pansy
Petunias

Scabiosa
Stocks
Summer Savory (herb)
Sweet marjoram (herb)
Sweet Pea
Sweet basil (herb)
Verbena

TENDER SHRUBS

Heliotrope
Lemon-verbena
Pelargoniums, Scented (Geraniums)
Rosemary
Sweet-olive (Osmanthus fragrans)

CULINARY HERBS

FOR SALADS

Anise A
Balm, Lemon P
Burnet P
Caraway A
Cardoon P
Chervil A
Chicory (Witloof) A
Houseleek P
Jerusalem artichoke P
Nasturtium A
Rampion P
Sorrel P

FOR FLAVORING

Angelica B/P
Basil, Sweet A
Bay, Sweet S
Borage A
Burnet P
Caraway A
Coriander A
Chives P
Dill A
Lovage P
Marjoram, Sweet A
   Pot P
Mints P
Parsley B
Pelargoniums (Geraniums) TS
Rosemary, scented TS
Sage, Garden P
   Pineapple TS
Savory, Summer A
   Winter P
Tarragon P
Thymes, in variety P

KEY: A–annual B–biennial P–perennial S–shrub TS–tender shrub

FRAGRANT BULBS

Acidanthera bicolor T
Amaryllis belladonna T
Childanthus fragrans T
Convallaria (Lily-of-the-valley)
Crocus
Cyclamen indicum
Eucharis T
Freesia T
Fritillaria imperialis
Galtonia candicans T
Hyacinths
Hymenocallis (Ismene)
Iris reticulata

Lilies
Muscari
Narcissus jonquilla and hybrids
   odorus
   Paperwhite T
   poetaz
   poeticus
   Soleil d'Or T
   tazetta and hybrids
Pancratium maritimum T
Tuberose
Tulip, Single Early varieties

KEY: T–tender

Garden Troubles

PESTS, DISEASES, WEEDS, AND THEIR CONTROLS

GARDEN PESTS AND THEIR CONTROLS

(See Chapter 5.)

PEST	CONTROL
Ants	Chlordane—5% dust
Aphids, various	Malathion or nicotine sulfate; trithion for citrus fruits
BEETLES	
Asiatic	Hand pick; DDT, cryolite, or methoxychlor
Asparagus	Rotenone, 5% dust in cutting season; DDT, 5% dust after season
Bean, Mexican	Rotenone after beans form; DDT before beans form; or malathion to within 3 days of harvest; or methoxychlor to within 7 days of harvest
Blister	As for Mexican Bean Beetle
Cucumber, Striped	Methoxychlor from germination until fruit forms; also hand pick
Elm bark	DDT 1 qt. 25% emulsion to 5 gal. water in mid-May; repeat at half strength in early July
Flea	Rotenone on leaf vegetables; DDT on ornamentals
Japanese	Chlordane, 5% dust for grubs; DDT on ornamentals; DOOM or JAPONEX (milky white disease) as directed; Traps, baited; hand pick
June	Chlordane for grubs; DDT for beetles
Potato, Colorado	
White fringed	Chlordane or DDT in soil for grubs
BORERS	
Corn	Slit stalks and remove; burn all affected stalks in autumn; DDT, 10% dust 3 times, 5 days apart; or DDT, 25% emulsified, 1 tbs. per gal. water. Spray until wet when silks appear, 3 times as above; spray is most effective
Crabapple—see Peach Borer	
Dogwood—see Peach Borer	

Iris	DDT and malathion mixed, 25% spray; used as directed in May and June
Lilac	As for Iris Borer, but in June and July
Peach	As for Iris Borer, but in July or August
Stalk	Slit up from entry; remove borer; bind wound and water plant
Squash	Open stem, remove borer; then mound up moist soil over wound and nearest joint to encourage root growth; also use ¾% rotenone dust

BUGS

Chinch gray-brown patches in lawn; small reddish bugs and larger black ones marked with white visible on grass blades	Chlordane spray June and early August
Harlequin	Toxaphene; rotenone or sabadilla powder for edible plants
Lace, various	Lindane; 25% wettable powder used as directed; 2 treatments
Squash	Hand pick; remove all rubbish in fall and burn. Fertilize well; 20% sabadilla dust kills nymphs; adults hard to control

Stink
  Ornamentals
  Edible parts of food plants
	10 to 20% sabadilla dust

Tarnish Plant	As for Stink Bugs, above
Crickets, Mole	Chlordane 5% dust before planting, as directed

FRUIT PESTS AND DISEASES

(See fruit tree spray formula and schedule, pages 455-456.)

Small fruits and cane fruit	Dibrom used as directed
Grasshoppers	Chlordane or malathion
Grubs in soil, Asiatic, Japanese, and June beetles	Chlordane or dieldrin
Leaf hoppers (transmit aster yellows virus)	Malathion or methoxychlor
Leaf miners, Hawthorn, Holly, etc.	When flies are present spray with 25% lindane in 25 gals. water; repeat 10 days later
Leaf tier, Hydrangea	Arsenate of lead
Loopers, various	Arsenate of lead
Maggots, Root	5% chlordane in soil before planting, as directed
Onion	Treat seed with heptachlor

GARDEN TROUBLES

Mealybug	Dormant oil spray
	Plants in growth with malthion or all-purpose spray every 2 weeks
Millipedes	DDT, 5% dust or spray
Mites, various	Aramite, dimite, karathane, kelthane, malathion, sulfur or trithion
Moths, Berry, Codling, etc.	DDT
Nematodes	DD mixture (POISON) or Vapam
PINE PESTS	
Needle Miner	
Needle Scale	
Sawfly	DDT and malathion mixture, June 1 and June 15
Shoot Moth, European	
Pitch Twig Moth	
SCALES	
Cottony maple and vine	Dormant oil spray when temperature is *above* 60 degrees, but when plants are *dormant*
Euonymus	
Oyster shell	
apples	
crabs	DDT and malathion mixture when plants are in bloom
lilac	
magnolias	
mountain-ash	
Viburnum	
Pine	
Spruce	
St. Jose	
Slugs	Metaldehyde bait
Snails	Metaldehyde bait
Termites	Chlordane in soil
Thrips, gladiolus, onions, etc.	Dieldrin or malathion; dust every 10 days; see limitations on food plants under insecticides
WEEVILS, ROOT	Lindane
Taxus	Chlordane or lindane
Vine, Black	DDT
Whitefly	Dormant oil spray
	In growth, malathion or all-purpose spray every two weeks
WORMS	
Army	Cutworm bait
Bag	Arsenate of lead or malathion in July; spray on; hand pick bugs when they appear
Cabbage	Rotenone dust or spray
Canker	Arsenate of lead or malathion
In spring on apple, elm, hackberry, honey locust, plum	
In fall on ash, box-elder, sugar maple	
Cut	10% toxaphene when *preparing* soil for planting; use collars around plants set out if damage occurs
Ear (corn)	¼ tsp. mineral oil dropped at base of silk on each ear as silk begins to shrivel; methoxychlor or DDT if ornamentals are attacked

448　APPENDIX

Eel	See nematodes
Wire	Chlordane in soil before planting
Web, Sod	Dieldrin or chlordane (moths appear in May)
Wood Ticks	Dieldrin, or chlordane

ANIMAL PESTS

Dogs	Chaperone and other repellents
Gophers	Poison bait in gopher-bait dispenser (See Colo. Agr. Exp. Sta. Pamphlet 1-S)
Moles	Chlordane areas where grubs are present. Use mole bait or cyanogas in runs
Deer	Repellent Z.I.P.; bone tar oil or electrical devices
Rabbits	Rabbit Repellent No-Nibl and others; traps; wrap trunks of young trees in heavy foil or hardware cloth to prevent winter damage. Soak soft cord or felt stripping in Conservo or other creosote mixture and place around beds that must be protected; creosote will kill grass or ornamental plants, however
RODENTS—rats, field mice Orchard, meadow, and pine mice, and rats	Warfarin and other rodenticides Zinc phosphide rodenticide, poison. Get from State Agr. Exp. Sta. and use as directed
Squirrels	Traps
Shrews (in coldframes)	Bait mousetraps with peanut butter
Skunks	Chlordane soil to kill grubs, which skunks eat

DISEASES

Black Spot	All-purpose rose sprays; phaltan
BLIGHTS	
Botrytis on tulips	Maneb, zineb, or ziram
Flower blight on azalea, camellia	As above
Fireblight	Agri-mycin at early and full bloom
Helminthosporium ("melting-out")	Captan
Leaf blights	Bordeaux mixture, captan, or zineb
Chlorosis Yellowing of leaves between veins; stunting; bud drop, caused by excess alkalinity	Feed with iron sulfate or chelate such as Sequestrene, applying to soil and foliage once a month or as often as needed to maintain healthy plants
GLADIOLUS	
Blight, Rot, and Scab	Soak corms in solution of Semesan
LAWN DISEASES	Lawn fungicides under trade names are effective, used as directed. Be

GARDEN TROUBLES

	sure the one purchased applies to the specific trouble
Brown patch Circular brown spots with grayish or black edges; in hot, humid weather	Fungicide containing captan, Calo-chlor, or other calomel-corrosive-sublimate material; or captan
Copper spot Three- to 6-inch spots, irregular margins, running together; copper colored. In warm, humid weather	A cadmium fungicide such as Cadminate or Caddy
Dollar spot Small brown, then bluish, dollar-size spots, merging. Warm days and cool nights in late spring and early fall	As for Copper spot
Fairy ring Bright green rings, brown on inner edge of circle	Calo-chlor or PMAS
Melting-out (Helminthosporium)	Captan
Mildew, powdery	Actidione as directed or karathane ¼ oz. to 2 gal. water; or Mildex
Pythiums Grass dies out in spots or streaks; blackish, greasy, cottony fungus on blades. In warm, humid weather on poorly drained ground	Improve drainage; stop watering and mowing until controlled; captan or zineb applied at five-day intervals
Rust Yellow to orange pustules on grass blades in warm weather	Zineb, 2–4 oz. to 2 gal. water; or dust with sulfur
Snow mold Spring die-out in areas where snow is deep and long-lasting	Spray fall or/and in midwinter thaw when ground is bare with 3 oz. Calo-chlor to 2 gal. water or one of commercial lawn fungicides as directed. Give 2 fall treatments in areas where problem is serious
Leaf curl on fruits	Dormant oil spray, winter; lime-sulfur dormant spray, spring
Leaf gall (azaleas)	Bordeaux mixture, maneb, zineb
Leaf scorch (horse-chestnuts)	Ziram or zineb
Leaf spots (attack many species)	Bordeaux mixture, ferbam, phaltan, maneb, or ziram; all-purpose sprays containing fungicides
Mildew Downy Powdery	 Copper fungicide See under lawn diseases Sulfur dust
Mosaic, see virus diseases	
Rhizoctonia diseases cause damping-off in seedlings	Soil fumigants and soil drenches (see page 454)
ROTS Blossom end (tomato)	Avoid nitrogenous fertilizer, including stable manure; use plenty of superphosphate; water *evenly*

APPENDIX

Iris	Remove affected parts; soak unaffected rhizomes in inorganic or organic mercury
RUSTS	Bordeaux mixture, ferbam, phaltan, sulfur spray, or zineb
Scab, Potato	Do not use lime, wood ashes, or fresh stable manure if soil is already infected; preferably plant in new ground; grow scab-resistant varieties
TOMATO DISEASES	Apply maneb or zineb just before rain and every five days, beginning six weeks after setting out
VIRUS DISEASES	Disinfect tools, etc.
Mosaic, Bulb spread by aphids	
Yellows, Aster spread by leaf hoppers	Spray or dust with malathion to destroy insetcs that spread virus

WEEDS AND THEIR CONTROLS

Bermudagrass	Methyl bromide
Bindweed	Bonus; MCPA
Beggars ticks	2-4-D
Buckthorn	2-4-D
Burdock	2-4-D
Chickweeds, common and mouse-ear	2-4-5-T or silvex; DMA or SMDC for seedlings
Cocklebur	2-4-D
Crabgrass	Pre-emergence seed killers; post-emergence: chlordane and arsenicals; Zytron
Dandelion	Bonus; MCPA; silvex
Dock, Curly Field	2-4-D
Ground-ivy	Silvex
Goosegrass	As for crabgrass
Knotweed	2-4-D
Heal-all	2-4-D
Henbit	Silvex
Johnsongrass	Methyl bromide
Nightshade, Black	Mow close and keep cut and cultivated
Nutgrass	Mow; hand weed
Oxalis, wild	2-4-D
Pigweed	SMDC pre-emergence
Pokeweed	Pull seedlings; dig out roots of mature plants
Plantains	2-4-D; Bonus
Poison-ivy and -oak	2-4-5-T or silvex
Purslane	2-4-D
Quackgrass	Pull by hand or cover with black plastic for a month
Ragweeds	2-4-D
Sheep laurel	2-4-D
Smartweed	Mow close and cultivate
Spurge, Leafy	Mow close and cultivate
Spotted	Silvex

GARDEN TROUBLES

Squirrel-tail grass	Mow close and cultivate
Thistle, Canada	2–4–D
Russian	Mow close and keep cultivated
Tick trefoil	2–4–D
Vetch	2–4–D
Violets	Silvex
Yarrow	Mow close and cultivate

INSECTICIDES AND PESTICIDES

NAME	USE
ALL-PURPOSE SPRAYS available under trade names marketed by many large companies	Combined insecticides and fungicides for: fruits, small perennials; fruit trees, roses; lawns, vegetables; ornamentals
Aramite for ornamentals or vegetables up to fifteen days before harvest; fruits up to twenty-one days before harvest	Mites, various; 15% wettable powder emulsions, and dusts
Arsenate of lead for ornamentals only	Chewing insects—largely replaced by modern chemicals
Chlordane Long residual effects; can be absorbed through skin. Apply to food gardens *in fall* after harvest	Soil inhabiting grubs and insects; 5% and 10% dusts; 40 and 50% wettable powder
Cryolite (Do not use with Bordeaux mixture or lime, DDT, parathion, or nicotine.) If applied to food plants or fruit, must be thoroughly washed off before being eaten	Chewing insects; 2½ oz. cryolite to 1 gal. water. Detrimental to birds and desirable insects
DD Mixture (POISON) Delay planting one to two weeks after soil treatment	Nematodes; soil fumigant
DDT Do not apply to large vegetables within seven days of harvest; to berries after fruit forms; to celery after stalk is half formed or bunching starts; to leaf vegetables after seedling stage	Chewing insects; borers; millipedes; scales; thrips; 5 or 10% dust; 25 or 50% wettable powder
Diazinon valuable for citrus fruits, fig and olive trees	Aphids, flies; use as directed
Dibrom on bush and cane fruits; vegetables. Do not apply within four days of harvest	Aphids, caterpillars, leaf hoppers, mites; dust, low percentage; emulsion

Dieldrin (POISON) Work into soil like chlordane; for ornamentals	Soil inhabiting insects including termites; thrips; use as directed
Dimite ornamentals only	Mites; use as directed
Heptachlor ornamentals only	Grasshoppers, grubs, white grubs, wireworms; soil insecticide; dusts and sprays available; use as directed
Karathane (POISON) ornamentals only	Mites; see also under fungicides; use as directed
Kelthane ornamentals and some vegetables and fruits, that can be washed	Mites; low percentage dust; 18½% wettable powder; use as directed
Lime-sulfur ornamentals only	Dormant spray in spring on ornamentals, for scales; lower concentrations used during growing season for aphids, mites, and as a fungicide; see table of fungicides
Lindane ornamentals; food crops, except roots, when plants are very young	Aphids; soil insecticide; usually combined with other materials in mixed formulations; use as directed
Malathion ornamentals; vegetables to within seven days of harvest, except leaf vegetables, within fourteen days; okra only before pods develop	General insecticide effective against sucking and chewing insects; 5% dust, 25% wettable powder
Metaldehyde	Slugs and snails; usually present in commercial baits; sold under trade names
Methoxychlor on ornamentals; fruit and vegetables: do not use within a week of harvest; leaf vegetables within two weeks	Chewing insects, including beetle larvae; dusts; sprays and in mixed formulas, according to directions
Milky white disease sold as Doom, Japonex, etc.	Japanese beetles; placed in soil to infect succeeding generations of beetles, thus reducing infestation over a long period
Nicotine sulfate sold as Black Leaf 40; ornamentals; leaf vegetables to within seven days of harvest; others within three days	Aphids; lice; malathion has largely replaced this old aphicide in the home garden
OIL (Volck) SPRAYS, DORMANT sold under trade names by all big companies	Scales; mealy bug; white fly; summer strength for use when plants are in growth, 0.24 to 2%
Pyrethrum not harmful, as sold	General insecticide from ground flower heads; not toxic; often used with chemical insecticides
Rotenone not harmful; safest material for use on all food plants	An insecticide derived from ground derris and cube roots; dusts and sprays

GARDEN TROUBLES

Sabadilla not harmful	Chewing insects; dust or powder from ground seeds
Sevin for ornamentals; fruits and vegetables as directed on package	Chewing insects; 5 and 10% dusts; 50% wettable powder
Sulfur	Mites; also as fungicide, which see; dusts and sprays
Toxaphene ornamentals; leaf vegetables as seedlings only; others to within seven days of harvest	Chewing insects; as wettable powders and in mixed formulas
Trithion ornamentals, nuts, fruits, including citrus; vegetables	Mites and aphids; 5% dust; 25% wettable powder; in liquid concentrates; use as directed
Vapam (soil fumigant) two-week interval between treatment of soil and planting date	Nematodes; see also under fungicides and herbicides; apply when temperature is above 60 degrees
Wilt-Pruf (trade name) anti-transpirant	For sunburn, sunscald, salt spray and wind injury when transplanting woody subjects; also for winter protection against dehydration and sunscald; use as directed

FUNGICIDES

Available as dusts or sprays

NAME	USE
Actidione	Mildew
Agri-mycin	Fireblight, other blights, rots and bacterial wilts
Bordeaux mixture	Anthracnose, blights, downy mildew, leaf spots, etc.
Captan ornamentals	For diseases on plants and as a soil drench
Chloropicrin (POISON)	Larvacide; soil fumigant which kills weed seeds, fungi, and insects; use as directed
Copper compounds, various sold under many trade names	Use as directed
Ferbam	Rusts, scab, and as a soil drench to prevent damping-off diseases
Formaldehyde (POISON)	Soil fumigant; 1 tb. in 5 tbs. water sprinkled over a 20x14x3 flat of soil; let stand *covered* for 24 hours; then sow seed and *water well*
Karathane	Mildew; see also under insecticides
Lime-sulfur	Fungicide; see also under insecticides
Maneb (Dithane M-22; Manzate); use on food plants according to directions	Anthracnose; blights; leaf spots; 6 and 8% dusts and sprays
Nabam (Dithane D-14; Liquid Nabam Fungicide, etc.) ornamentals and as directed on food plants	Liquid; often used with zineb, which see; soil drench

APPENDIX

Panodrench (trade name)	Soil drench for rhizoctonia; damping-off diseases
Phaltan ornamentals, especially roses	Blackspot, leaf spots, powdery mildew, etc.; 5 to 75% dusts
Soil Fumigants see under chloropicrin, formaldehyde	For damping-off diseases
Seed Treatment Chemicals available under many trade names	For seed protection before sowing
Semesan (trade name) stunts some plants such as pansy, petunia, snapdragon when used as drench	As a seed protectant and as a drench on living plants for rhizoctonia diseases
Sulfur	Mildew, etc.; dust; see also under insecticides
Thiram (Arasan)	Fungicide; soil drench; seed treatment chemical; use as directed
Vapam	Soil fumigant; fungicide; see also under insecticides
Zineb (Dithane Z-78)	Blights; fungus leaf spots; rusts; also for russet mites on citrus; use as directed
Ziram available under several trade names; ornamentals only except as directed; almonds; pecans	Blights; leaf spots; anthracnose; brown rot, etc.

HERBICIDES

Weed killers are available under many trade names, often sold by lawn-seed companies. Selection can be made to suit special needs.

Amiden	Brush killer; makes soil sterile for two years
Ammate	Brush and poison-ivy; sterilizes soil for two months
Ammonium sulfate	For weeds in lawns set mower low and "scalp" weeds, then apply 4 lbs. per 100 sq. ft.; poisons weeds and feeds permanent grass
Bonus (trade name)	For broad-leaved weeds in summer growth; dandelion, buckthorn, plantains, etc.; also fertilizes soil; use on dichondra lawns
Calcium cyanamid available under trade names; allow 60 days from treatment to seeding	A high lime and nitrogen fertilizer and weed seed killer for acid soils and compost heaps; kills soil bacteria and every living seed
Chlordane available under trade names; apply in late winter or very early spring	Crabgrass seedlings and other weed seedlings; arrests all growth for three weeks; 5, 10, 20, and 25% granules; 40% wettable powder; see also under insecticides

GARDEN TROUBLES

Chloropicrin	Weed seed killer; see under fungicides
Dacthal allow 60 days from treatment to planting; use in early spring	Crabgrass and broad-leaved weeds when germinating
Dalapon	Brush killer; sterilizes soil for two months
DMA	For seedling crabgrass, common chickweed, other grasses; do not use on carpet, centipede or St. Augustine grasses; use as directed
Dybar	Brush killer; sterilizes soil for two years
MCPA	Dandelion, bindweed, ground-ivy, purslane, speedwell
Methyl bromide	For unwanted Bermuda- or Johnsongrass, annual weeds and grasses; use as directed
Pre-emergence weed killers available under many trade names	For seeds of crabgrass, goosegrass, etc.; use as directed
Randox	Brush killer; sterilizes soil for two years
Silvex see 2-4-5-T	
SMDC allow 5 days to seeding; 21 days for food crop areas	Germinating chickweed, pigweed, ragweed, Bermuda and Johnson grasses
2-4-D	Destroys a large variety of weed seedlings and most broad-leaved weeds in growth, including many hard-to-eradicate species; use as directed
2-4-5-T (Silvex)	Chickweed, common and mouse-ear Henbit; poison-ivy and poison-oak; spotted spurge; when combined with Dalapon, kills everything and arrests growth for three weeks; grasses for six weeks
Vapam allow two weeks from treatment to planting	Liquid herbicides; use as directed; see also under fungicides

SPRAY AND SPRAY SCHEDULE FOR THE HOME ORCHARD

All-purpose Spray

Captan, 50% wettable powder 1½ cups to 10 gal. water
Methoxychlor, 50% wettable powder 1½ cups to 10 gal. water
Malathion, 25% wettable powder 1½ cups to 10 gal. water
  The above mixture may also be used on ornamentals.

PARKS AND DISPLAY GARDENS

COLORADO	Roosevelt Park rose garden	Longmont
	Pan-American Seeds, Inc. trial grounds, petunias	Paonia
	Washington Park (Martha Washington Gardens)	Denver
	Mineral Palace Park rose garden	Pueblo
CONNECTICUT	Bristol Nurseries chrysanthemums, perennials	Bristol
	Elizabeth Park rose garden	Hartford
DELAWARE	Josephine Gardens roses, iris	Brandywine Park, Wilmington
	Winterthur Museum and Gardens azaleas, spring flowers	Henry Francis du Pont estate (near Wilmington)
DISTRICT OF COLUMBIA	West Potomac Park Tidal Basin flowering cherries	Washington
	Dumbarton Oaks	Washington
	East Potomac Park flowering cherries	Washington
	The Bishop's Garden, Washington Cathedral	Washington
FLORIDA	Bok Tower	Lake Wales
	Simpson Park tropicals, subtropicals	Miami
	St. Petersburg Park tropicals	St. Petersburg
	Edwin A. Menninger trees	Stuart
	Killearn Gardens azaleas, gardenias	Tallahassee
	Florida Cypress Gardens	Winter Haven
	Corkscrew Swamp Sanctuary	Immokalee
GEORGIA	Hurt Park magnolias, shrubs, flowers	Atlanta
	Piedmont Park rare trees	Atlanta
	H. G. Hastings Co. Flower Acres test garden	Lovejoy
	Dunaway Gardens roses, rock garden, old-fashioned garden	Newman

Spray Schedule for Fruit Trees

TIME	APPLE	PEAR QUINCE	PEACH PLUM APRICOT	CHERRY
Dormant Before buds show green tips in spring	X		X	
Prebloom When blossom buds show color but before they open	X	X	soil under trees only	
Petal-fall When most petals have fallen from apple	X	X	X	X
First Cover 7 to 10 days after petal-fall	X	X	X	X
Second Cover 7 to 10 days after first cover	X	X	X	X
Third Cover 7 to 10 days after second cover	X			
Fourth Cover 7 to 10 days after third cover	X		X	X
Fifth Cover 10 to 12 days after fourth cover	X	X	X	X
For late apples, pears, and peaches every 10 days	X	X	X	

Eight to 10 sprays are minimal to achieve success.
(Information taken from Iowa State University Pamphlet 175.)

Botanical Gardens and Arboretums

State	Name	Address
ALASKA	Experiment Station	Palmer
	Experiment Station	College
ARIZONA	Desert Botanical Garden of Arizona	Papago Park (near Phoenix)
	Boyce Thompson Southwestern Arboretum	Superior

BOTANICAL GARDENS AND ARBORETUMS 457

CALIFORNIA	Los Angeles State and County Arboretum	301 N. Baldwin Ave., Arcadia
	Regional Parks Botanic Garden	Tilden Regional Park, Berkeley
	University of California Botanical Garden	Strawberry Canyon, Berkeley
	Rancho Santa Ana Botanical Garden	1500 N. College Ave., Claremont
	University of California Arboretum	College of Agriculture, Davis (near Sacramento)
	Descanso Gardens	1418 Descanso Drive, La Canada
	Botanical Garden, University of California	405 Hilgard Ave., Los Angeles
	Joseph McInnes Memorial Botanical Gardens, Mills College	Seminary Ave. and MacArthur Blvd., Oakland
	Joseph R. Knowland State Arboretum and Park	96th Ave. at Mountain Blvd., Oakland
	Eddy Arboretum	Institute of Forest Genetics, Placerville
	Strybing Arboretum and Botanic Garden	Golden Gate Park, San Francisco
	Huntington Botanical Gardens	1151 Oxford Rd., San Marino
	Santa Barbara Botanic Garden	1212 Mission Canyon Rd., Santa Barbara
	Saratoga Horticultural Foundation	Verde Vista Lane, Saratoga
	Villa Montalvo Arboretum	Saratoga
COLORADO	The Glenmore Arboretum	Buffalo Creek
	Denver Botanical Gardens	909 York St., Denver
CONNECTICUT	Marsh Botanical Garden	Yale University, New Haven
	Connecticut Arboretum	Conn. College, New London
DELAWARE	Henry Francis du Pont Winterthur Arboretum	Wilmington
DISTRICT OF COLUMBIA	Kenilworth Aquatic Gardens	Douglas St., N.E., Washington
	United States National Arboretum	Montana Ave. and Bladensburg Rd., N.E., Washington
FLORIDA	Gifford Arboretum	University of Miami, Coral Gables
	Flamingo Groves Tropical Botanic Garden	3501 S. Federal Highway, Fort Lauderdale
	Thomas A. Edison Winter Home and Botanical Gardens	2341 McGregor Blvd., Fort Myers

	Wilmot Memorial Garden	University of Florida, Gainesville
	Fairchild Tropical Garden	10901 Old Cutler Rd., Coconut Grove, Miami
	McKee Jungle Gardens	Vero Beach
	Highlands Hammock State Park	Sebring
GEORGIA	Founders' Memorial Garden and Living Arboretum	Athens
	Ida Cason Callaway Gardens	Pine Mountain (85 miles south of Atlanta)
HAWAII	Foster Park Botanical Garden	45 North School Street, Honolulu
	Harold L. Lyon Arboretum	University of Hawaii, Honolulu
	Harold L. Lyon Botanical Garden	Koko Head, Oahu
	Wahiawa Botanical Garden	1396 California Ave., Wahiawa, Oahu
IDAHO	The Charles Houston Shattuck Arboretum	College of Forestry, University of Idaho, Moscow
ILLINOIS	Garfield Park Conservatory	300 N. Central Park Avenue, Chicago
	Lincoln Park Conservatory	2400 N. Stockton Drive, Chicago
	The Morton Arboretum	Lisle
INDIANA	James Irving Holcomb Botanical Gardens	Butler University, Indianapolis
	Christy Woods Botanical Garden	Ball State Teachers College, Muncie
IOWA	College Gardens	Iowa State Teachers College, Cedar Falls
	Lilac Arboretum, Ewing Park	McKinley Avenue and Indianola Rd., Des Moines
KANSAS	Indian Hill Arboretum	3617 West South Ave., Topeka
LOUISIANA	Jungle Gardens	Avery Island
	Gardens of the Louisiana Polytechnic Institute	Ruston
MAINE	Botanical Plantations of the University of Maine	Orono
MASSACHUSETTS	The Arnold Arboretum of Harvard University	Jamaica Plain (near Boston)
	Botanic Garden of Smith College	Northampton
	Alexandra Botanical Garden and Hunnewell Arboretum	Wellesley College Wellesley
	Walter Hunnewell Arboretum	845 Washington St., Wellesley

BOTANICAL GARDENS AND ARBORETUMS

MICHIGAN	The Nichols Arboretum of the University of Michigan	Ann Arbor
	Anna Scripps Whitcomb Conservatory	Belle Isle, Detroit
	Beal-Garfield Botanic Garden	Michigan State University, East Lansing
	Slayton Arboretum of Hillsdale College	Hillsdale
MINNESOTA	University of Minnesota Landscape Arboretum	St. Paul (near Excelsior)
	Botanical Garden of the University of Minnesota	Minneapolis
	Hormel Foundation Arboretum	Austin
MISSOURI	Missouri Botanical Garden	2315 Tower Grove Ave., St. Louis
NEBRASKA	Arbor Lodge State Park Arboretum	Nebraska City
NEW HAMPSHIRE	Lilac Arboretum	University of New Hampshire, Durham
NEW JERSEY	Hanover Park Arboretum	Mt. Pleasant Ave., East Hanover
	New Jersey Agricultural Experiment Station Arboretum	Rutgers University, New Brunswick
NEW YORK	Cornell Plantations	Cornell University, Ithaca
	Thomas C. Desmond Arboretum	Newburgh
	Brooklyn Botanic Garden	1000 Washington Ave., Brooklyn
	The New York Botanical Gardens	Bronx Park, New York City
	Bayard Cutting Arboretum	Oakdale, Long Island, N.Y.
	Buffalo Botanic Garden	South Park Ave. and McKinley Drive, Buffalo
	Planting Fields Arboretum	Oyster Bay, L.I.
	Highland and Durand—Eastman Park Arboretum	5 Castle Park, Rochester
NORTH CAROLINA	The Coker Arboretum	University of North Carolina, Chapel Hill
	Sarah P. Duke Memorial Garden	Duke University, Durham
OHIO	Eden Park Conservatory	950 Eden Park Drive, Cincinnati
	The Dawes Arboretum	Newark
	Kingwood Center	Mansfield
	The Secrest Arboretum	Ohio Agricultural Experiment Station, Wooster

APPENDIX

OREGON	The Peavy Arboretum	Oregon State College, Corvallis
	Hoyt Arboretum	4000 S.W. Fairview Blvd., Portland
PENNSYLVANIA	Taylor Memorial Arboretum	10 Ridley Drive, Garden City, Chester
	Botanical Garden of the Reading Public Museum and Art Gallery	500 Museum Road, Reading
	Longwood Gardens	Kennett Square
	The John J. Tyler Arboretum	Lima, Delaware County
	Masonic Homes Arboretum	Elizabethtown
	Botanical Garden of the University of Pennsylvania	38th and Spruce St., Philadelphia
	Ellis School Arboretum	Newtown Square
	The Morris Arboretum of the University of Pennsylvania	9414 Meadowbrook Ave., Philadelphia
	Elan Memorial Park	116 E. Front St., Berwick, Lime Ridge
	Phipps Conservatory	Schenley Park, Pittsburgh
	Mont Alto State Forest Arboretum	Mont Alto
	Bowman's Hill Wild Flower Preserve	Washington Crossing State Park, Washington Crossing
	Westtown School Arboretum	Westtown
	Arthur Hoyt Scott Horticultural Foundation	Swarthmore College, Swarthmore
	Arboretum of the Barnes Foundation	300 Latch's Lane, Merion
SOUTH CAROLINA	Brookgreen Gardens	near Georgetown
TENNESSEE	Southwestern Arboretum	Southwestern College, Memphis
	The W. C. Paul Arboretum	Audubon Park, Memphis
	The Tennessee Botanical Gardens and Fine Arts Center	Cheekwood Mansion, Nashville
TEXAS	Texas A. & M. Arboretum and Trial Grounds	Texas A. & M. College, College Station
	Fort Worth Botanic Garden	3220 Botanic Garden Drive, Fort Worth
UTAH	Botanical Garden	Brigham Young Univ., Provo

PARKS AND DISPLAY GARDENS

State	Name	Address
VIRGINIA	Virginia Polytechnic Institute Arboretum	Blacksburg
	Orland E. White Arboretum	Blandy Experimental Farm, University of Virginia, Boyce (60 miles west of Washington)
	Norfolk Botanic Garden	Granby & 35th St., Norfolk
WASHINGTON	University of Washington Arboretum	Lake Washington Blvd., Seattle
	Finch Arboretum	W. 3404 Woodland Blvd., Spokane
	Wind River Arboretum	Carson
WEST VIRGINIA	West Virginia University Arboretum	Morgantown
WISCONSIN	Alfred L. Boerner Botanical Garden	Whitnall Park, Hales Corners (near Milwaukee)
	University of Wisconsin Arboretum	Madison
	Paine Art Center and Arboretum	Oshkosh
WYOMING	Cheyenne Horticultural Field Station	Cheyenne

Parks and Display Gardens

State	Name	Address
ALABAMA	Bellingrath Gardens	Mobile
ARIZONA	Pioneer Park Rose Garden	Mesa
	Memorial Rose Garden	Prescott
	Tucson Rose Garden	Tucson
ARKANSAS	AA Gladiolus Trial Garden	Jonesboro
	Territorial Capitol Gardens	Little Rock
CALIFORNIA	Patrick's Point State Park azaleas, lilies	north of Eureka, Coast Highway
	Oakhurst Gardens bulbs, tropicals, subtropicals	345 W. Colorado, Arcadia
	Municipal Rose Garden	Berkeley
	Vetterle & Reinelt Nursery delphiniums, primroses, tuberous begonias	Capitola
	Bodger Seeds, Ltd. trial grounds	1600 S. Tyler Ave., El Monte

APPENDIX

Roeding Park roses, trees, shrubs	Fresno
Domoto Nursery camellias, bonsai trees, gerberias, tree peonies, magnolias	Western Rd., Hayward
Howard Rose Co.	Hemet
Denholm Seed Co. trial grounds	Lompac
Exposition Park Rose Garden	Figueroa St., Los Angeles
Gardens of Sunset Magazine	Willow and Middlefield Rds., Menlo Park
Melrose Iris Gardens	Rt. 6, Modesto
Armstrong Nurseries roses	Ontario
Jackson & Perkins Co. roses	Pleasanton
White Park roses, trees	3900 Eighth St., Riverside
Capitol Park camellias	Sacramento
McKinley Park Municipal Rose Garden	Sacramento
Ferry-Morse Seed Co. trial grounds	Salinas
Balboa Park rose garden, dahlias	San Diego
California Camellia Gardens	13531 Fenton Ave., San Fernando
Golden Gate Park	San Francisco
San Jose Municipal Rose Garden	Naglee Ave., San Jose
Palomar College cacti, succulents	San Marcos
Alameda Park	Santa Barbara
Mission Park rose garden	Santa Barbara
Memorial Rose Garden	700 E. Canon Perdido St., Santa Barbara
Redwood Highway (U.S. Rt. 101)	northern Calif.
William McDonald Seed Co. trial grounds	Santa Maria
Sequoia and Kings Canyon National Parks	Three Rivers
Victory Park rose garden	Stockton
Public Rose Garden	Visalia

APPENDIX

	Todd's Dahlia Farm	Suches
	Fulwood Park	Tifton Park
	azaleas	
	Camellia Trail	Valdosta
HAWAII	Hawaii National Park	Kilauea-Mauna Loa Sect., Island of Hawaii
	Liliuokalani Park Japanese Garden	Hilo
IDAHO	Julia Davis Park rose garden	Boise
	Memorial Rose Garden	Lewiston
	Lakeview Park rose garden	Nampa
	Ross Park Rotary Rose Garden	Pocatello
ILLINOIS	Humboldt Park roses, lilies	Chicago
	Jackson Park flowering trees, spring flowers, chrysanthemums	Chicago
	Marquette Park roses, azaleas, tropicals	Chicago
	Hill-Dundee Nursery evergreens	Dundee
	Eldorado Memorial Park flowering trees, bulbs, roses	Eldorado
	Merrick Park roses	Evanston
	Shakespeare Garden	Northwestern Univ. campus Evanston
	Cook Memorial Library roses	Libertyville
	Lilacia Park lilacs	Lombard
	Dr. Ernest H. Wilson Memorial Garden	Peoria
	Lincoln Memorial Garden flowering trees, wild flowers	Springfield
	George K. Ball trial grounds, chrysanthemums	West Chicago
	Catigny Farm; Vaughan's Seeds trial grounds	Wheaton
	David F. Hall	809 Central Ave., Wilmette

PARKS AND DISPLAY GARDENS

INDIANA	Foster Park iris, peonies, lilacs, tulips	Fort Wayne
	Jaenicke Gardens flowering trees, azaleas, bulbs	Fort Wayne
	Lakeside Rose Gardens	Fort Wayne
	Lawton Park chrysanthemums	Fort Wayne
	Kundred Gladiolus Farms	Goshen
	Earl R. Roberts iris	Rt. 4, Indianapolis
	International Friendship Gardens demonstration garden, Persian roses	Michigan City
	E. G. Hill Memorial Rose Garden	Richmond
	Leeper Park: garden of fragrance for the blind	U.S. Highway 31, South Bend
IOWA	Iowa State College test gardens	Ames
	Vander Veer Park roses	Davenport
	Grandview Park peonies	Dubuque
	Interstate Nurseries trial grounds	Hamburg
	Edmondson Park peonies	Oskaloosa
	Byrnes Park rose demonstration garden	Waterloo
KANSAS	University of Kansas campus lilacs, flowering crabs	Lawrence
	Reinisch Gardens rose demonstration	Topeka
KENTUCKY	Shawnee Park perennials—old-fashioned garden	Louisville
LOUISIANA	Laurel Farms test garden	Forbing
	Southeastern Louisiana College camellia garden	Hammond
	Audubon Memorial State Park Louisiana iris	Oakley, St. Francisville
	City Park Rose Garden	New Orleans
	Cross Lake Gardens	Shreveport
	Hodges Gardens roses, camellias	Many

MAINE	Asticou Gardens	Northeast Harbor
	Bok Memorial Garden alpines	Camden
	Municipal Rose Garden	Portland
MARYLAND	Sherwood Gardens azaleas, bulbs	Stratford and Underwood Rds., Baltimore
	Dr. and Mrs. William A. Briggs' daffodil trial garden	Lutherville
	Mr. and Mrs. Jesse Hakes' daffodil trial garden	Sylvanville
MASSACHUSETTS	Harlan P. Kelsey Nurseries	East Boxford
	Bay State Nurseries	North Abington
	Worcester County Horticultural Society Orchard old apple varieties	North Grafton
	Springfield Park gardens	Pittsfield
	Mount Holyoke College greenhouses	South Hadley
	Bee Warburton iris test garden	Rt. 1, Westboro
	Berkshire Garden Center herbs	Stockbridge
	University of Massachusetts trial grounds	Waltham
	Weston Nurseries	Weston
MICHIGAN	Johnson Memorial Gardens	Detroit
	Centennial Park spring and autumn flowers	Holland
	Cooley Gardens rose demonstration	Lansing
	Grand Mere Nurseries chrysanthemum test garden	Rt. 4, Niles
	Emlong Nurseries chrysanthemum test garden, demonstration garden	Stevensville
	R. M. Kellogg Co. chrysanthemum test garden	Three Rivers
	Cranbrook Institute of Science formal gardens	Bloomfield Hills
MINNESOTA	Brand Peony Farm peonies, lilacs	Faribault
	Lyndale Park rose garden	Minneapolis
	Northrup-King & Co. trial grounds	Minneapolis
	University of Minnesota chrysanthemum trial grounds	St. Paul

PARKS AND DISPLAY GARDENS

MISSISSIPPI	Beauvoir on the Beach roses, azaleas, camellias, woodland	Biloxi
	Mississippi State College rose garden	Long Beach
	Mississippi State College camellia test garden	Poplarville
MISSOURI	Capaha Park rose display garden	Cape Girardeau
	University of Missouri chrysanthemum trial grounds	Columbia
	Municipal Rose Garden	Kansas City
	Forest Park Municipal Rose Garden	St. Louis
MONTANA	City Park System	Great Falls
	Roselawn Park roses	Libby
	Sunset Park municipal rose garden	Missoula
	Memorial Rose Garden	Polson
NEBRASKA	Antelope Park municipal rose garden	Lincoln
	Joslyn Art Museum conservatory	Omaha
	Omaha Hemerocallis Display Gardens	Omaha
NEVADA	Squires Park Rose Garden	Las Vegas
	Washoe Medical Center municipal rose garden	Reno
NEW HAMPSHIRE	Thomas Bailey Aldrich Memorial old-fashioned garden	Portsmouth
NEW JERSEY	Nomahegan Park flowering cherries	Cranford
	Warinanco Park	Elizabeth
	Mattano Park Rose Garden	Elizabeth
	Cedar Brook Park varied plantings through season	Plainfield
	Julius Roehrs Co. indoor plants	Rutherford
NEW MEXICO	Baptist Assembly Gardens iris, roses, delphiniums, tuberous begonias	Glorieta
	Municipal Rose Gardens	Roswell
NEW YORK	Landscape Association, Inc. display gardens	Brookville, L.I.
	Lilac Land	Brookville, L.I.
	Louis Smirnow peonies	Brookville, L.I.
	Humboldt Park rose garden	Buffalo

APPENDIX

Kelly Bros. Nurseries — Dansville
  trees,
  fruits,
  shrubs,
  chrysanthemums
Maloney Bros. Nursery — Dansville
Beacon Hill Rock Garden Nursery — Dobbs Ferry
Stillwell-Perine House — Dongan Hills, Staten Island
  colonial gardens
Hammond House — Grasslands Parkway, Eastview
  eighteenth century gardens
James I. George and Son — Fairport
  clematis
Long Island Agricultural and Technical Institute — Farmingdale, L.I.
  trial grounds,
  dahlias
Rose Garden — Great Neck
  trees,
  summer flowers
The L. H. Bailey Hortorium — Cornell Univ., Ithaca
Old Westbury Gardens — Westbury, L.I.
Jackson & Perkins Co. — Newark
  roses,
  perennials,
  display garden
The Cloisters: garden of the Middle Ages — Fort Tryon Park, Riverside Drive, New York City
Van Cortlandt House — Van Cortlandt Park, The Bronx, New York City
  formal Dutch garden
Vassar College Campus — Poughkeepsie
  flowering trees,
  shrubs
Maplewood Park — Rochester
  roses,
  flowering trees
Chase Bros. — 2405 East Ave., Rochester
  demonstration herb garden
Joseph Harris Seed Co. — Moreton Farms, Rochester
  trial grounds
Congress Park: Italian garden — Saratoga Springs
Yaddo Estate — Saratoga Springs
  rose garden,
  rock garden,
  trees
Skyland Nursery — Sloatsburg
  formerly private estate,
  great variety of material,
  large acreage,
  scenic

PARKS AND DISPLAY GARDENS

	Thornden Park roses, bulbs, herbs, annuals, perennials	Syracuse
	Sterling Forest Gardens great variety of plant material, large acreage	Tuxedo Park
NORTH CAROLINA	Rhododendron Park	West Asheville
	Biltmore Estate extensive plantings	Asheville
	Sunnyside Rose Garden	Charlotte
	Sarah P. Duke Memorial Garden	Duke University, Durham
	Airlie Gardens	Wilmington
	C. C. O'Brien iris trial grounds	1212 Bellevue, Greensboro
	Clarendon Gardens and Nursery	Pinehurst
	North Carolina State College trial grounds	Raleigh
	Manteo Gardens hemerocallis	Roanoke Rapids
	Municipal Iris Gardens	Runnymede Rd., Winston-Salem
	Tanglewood Park roses, azaleas, shrubs, wild flowers	Winston-Salem
OHIO	Goodyear Memorial Rose Garden	East Akron
	Cahoon Park Memorial Rose Garden	Bay Village
	Ault Park summer flowers, dahlias	Cincinnati
	Fleischman Gardens bulbs, flowers	Cincinnati
	Lytle Park tulips, annuals	Cincinnati
	Cleveland Cultural Gardens international	Rockefeller Park, Cleveland
	Fine Arts Garden flowering trees, bulbs, formal garden, sculpture	East Blvd. at Euclid Ave., Cleveland
	Wade Park herb garden	Cleveland

APPENDIX

	Municipal Rose Garden	Cleveland
	Waterfront Gardens (Donald Gray Gardens) formal	Cleveland
	Euclid Park Rose Garden	Cleveland
	Park of Roses	4015 N. High St., Columbus
	Ohio State University Rose Garden	Columbus
	Bohlken Park Rose Garden	Forest City
	Kingwood Center roses	Mansfield
	Gerard K. Klyn, Inc. rose test garden	Mentor
	Bosley Gardens roses	Mentor
	Wayside Gardens nursery with many rare species and varieties, bulbs, perennials, shrubs, trees	Mentor
	Library Rose Garden	Rocky River
	Spring Hill Nurseries trial grounds, chrysanthemums	Tipp City
OKLAHOMA	Ardmore Rose Garden	Whittington Park, Ardmore
	Johnstone Municipal Park Rose Garden	Bartlesville
	Will Rogers Park rose garden, bulbs, hibiscus, annuals, wild plants	Oklahoma City
	Woodward Park Municipal Rose Garden	Tulsa
OREGON	Mirror Pond Park rose gardens	Bend
	Walter Marx Gardens lilies, iris, hemerocallis	Boring
	Clark's Primroses	Clackamas
	Oregon State College Experimental Gardens clematis, chrysanthemums, azaleas, hemerocallis, holly	Corvallis
	Hendricks Park rhododendrons	Eugene
	Oregon Bulb Farms lilies	Gresham
	Ambrose Brownell hollies	Milwaukie

PARKS AND DISPLAY GARDENS

	Rhododendron Garden	Crystal Springs Island, Portland
	Washington Park roses	Portland
	Duniway Park lilacs	S.W. Sixth and Sheridan Way, Portland
	Lewis and Clark College memorial rose garden	420 S.W. Third Ave., Portland
	Gill Bros. Seed Co. trial grounds	Portland
	Bush Park Municipal Rose Garden	Salem
PENNSYLVANIA	Independence Hall Garden	Philadelphia
	Gross Memorial Rose Garden	Allentown
	Burpee's Fordhook Farms trial grounds	Doylestown
	Rose Garden demonstration	Hershey
	Breeze Hill Gardens trial grounds	Harrisburg
	Riesenhauser Park rose arboretum	McKeesport
	Mellon Park rose garden	Pittsburgh
	City Park rose garden	Reading
	The Conard-Pyle Co. roses, demonstration garden	West Grove
	Farr Nursery Co. hemerocallis	Weiser Park, Womelsdorf
	Farquhar Park municipal rose garden	York
RHODE ISLAND	Roger Williams Park large acreage, varied plantings	Providence
SOUTH CAROLINA	Cypress Gardens azaleas	Strawberry (north of Charleston)
	Magnolia Gardens azaleas, camellias	Johns Island (west of Charleston)
	Middleton Gardens camellias, live oaks	Ashley River Rd., Charleston
	Clemson College camellias, test garden	Clemson
	Municipal Rose Garden	Florence
	Edisto Gardens camellias, azaleas, shrubs, trees, roses, hemerocallis	Orangeburg

APPENDIX

	Memorial Park azaleas	Sumter
	Edmunds Memorial Rose Garden	Sumter
	Swan Lake Gardens iris, camellias	Sumter
	Dundale Gardens hemerocallis, camellias	Columbia Highway, Sumter
	Fortunes Spring Park roses	Winnsboro
SOUTH DAKOTA	South Dakota State College test garden for woody plants	Brookings
TENNESSEE	Warner Park Rose Garden	Chattanooga
	Happy Cabin Dahlia Garden	Signal Mt., Chattanooga
	Great Smoky Mountains National Park native trees, shrubs, flowers	Gatlinburg
	Blount Mansion (spring display)	Hill and State sts., Knoxville
	Eastern State Hospital municipal rose garden	Knoxville
	Overton Park holly, azaleas	Memphis
	Ketchum Memorial Iris Garden	Audubon Park, Memphis
TEXAS	Memorial Park rose garden	Amarillo
	W. J. Rogers test garden	Beaumont
	Spuria Iris Test Garden	2503 Wertheimer Dr., Houston
	Texas Camellia test garden	Orange
	Tyler Municipal Rose Garden	Tyler
	Arp Nursery Co. roses	Tyler
	Lindsey Lane azaleas	Tyler
UTAH	Statehouse Museum rose garden	Filmore
	Municipal Memorial Rose Garden	Nephi
	City and County Park formal	Ogden
	Rose Garden: State Industrial School	Ogden
	Wallace Iris Gardens	Orem
	Sowiette Park memorial rose garden	Provo

PARKS AND DISPLAY GARDENS

	Tell's Iris Gardens	691 E. 8th St. N., Provo
	Municipal Rose Garden	Salt Lake City
VIRGINIA	Wakefield: Washington's birthplace colonial gardens	Westmoreland County
	Mount Vernon: Washington's home colonial gardens	Mount Vernon
	Memorial Rose Garden	Arlington
	Little England Daffodil Farm	Gloucester
	Lafayette Park	Norfolk
	Norfolk Municipal Gardens azaleas, camellias, woodland	Norfolk
	Colonial Williamsburg colonial gardens	Williamsburg
WASHINGTON STATE	San Benn Park roses	Aberdeen
	Cornwall Park roses	Bellingham
	Chehalis Rose Garden	Chehalis
	Lewis & Clark Park woodland	south of Chehalis
	Woodland Park Rose Gardens	Seattle
	Maneto Park varied plantings	Spokane
	Western State Hospital primroses	Stielacoom
	Point Defiance Park roses, rhododendrons, dahlias	Tacoma
	Ohme Gardens trees, alpines	Wenatchee
WEST VIRGINIA	Rose Garden, Y.M.C.A.	Charleston
	Ritter Park Rose Gardens	Huntington
	Oglebay Park gardens, peonies	Wheeling
WISCONSIN	Riverside Park flowers on the levee	La Crosse
	University of Wisconsin gardens	Madison
WYOMING	Storm Gardens	Chugwater

Agricultural Colleges
Agricultural Experiment Stations

(From U. S. D. A. Agriculture Handbook No. 116. Workers in Subjects Pertaining to Agriculture in Land-Grant Colleges and Experiment Stations, May 1962.)

State	Name	City
ALABAMA	School of Agriculture, Auburn University	Auburn
	Agricultural Experiment Station	Auburn
	Alabama Agricultural and Mechanical College	Normal
ALASKA	Department of Agriculture, University of Alaska	College
	Agricultural Experiment Station	Palmer
ARIZONA	College of Agriculture, University of Arizona	Tucson
	Agricultural Experiment Station	Tucson
ARKANSAS	College of Agriculture, University of Arkansas	Fayetteville
	Agricultural Experiment Station	Fayetteville
CALIFORNIA	College of Agriculture, University of California	Berkeley
	Agricultural Experiment Station	Berkeley
	Agricultural Experiment Station	Davis
	Agricultural Experiment Station	Los Angeles
	Agricultural Experiment Station	Riverside
COLORADO	College of Agriculture, Colorado State University	Fort Collins
	Agricultural Experiment Station	Fort Collins
CONNECTICUT	College of Agriculture, University of Connecticut	Storrs
	Storrs Agricultural Experiment Station	Storrs
	The Connecticut Agricultural Experiment Station	New Haven
DELAWARE	School of Agriculture, University of Delaware	Newark
	Agricultural Experiment Station	Newark
	Delaware State College	Dover

AGRICULTURAL COLLEGES AND EXPERIMENT STATIONS 475

FLORIDA	College of Agriculture, University of Florida	Gainesville
	Agricultural Experiment Station	Gainesville
	School of Agriculture, Florida Agricultural and Mechanical University	Tallahassee
GEORGIA	College of Agriculture, University of Georgia	Athens
	Georgia Coastal Plain Experiment Station	Tifton
	Georgia Agricultural Experiment Station	Griffon
	The Fort Valley State College	Fort Valley
HAWAII	College of Tropical Agriculture, University of Hawaii	Honolulu
	Agricultural Experiment Station	Honolulu
IDAHO	College of Agriculture, University of Idaho	Moscow
	Agricultural Experiment Station	Moscow
ILLINOIS	College of Agriculture, University of Illinois	Urbana
	Agricultural Experiment Station	Urbana
INDIANA	School of Agriculture, Purdue University	Lafayette
	Agricultural Experiment Station	Lafayette
IOWA	College of Agriculture, Iowa State University of Science and Technology	Ames
	Agricultural Experiment Station	Ames
KANSAS	Kansas State University of Agriculture and Applied Science	Manhattan
	Agricultural Experiment Station	Manhattan
KENTUCKY	College of Agriculture, University of Kentucky	Lexington
	Agricultural Experiment Station	Lexington
	Kentucky State College	Frankfort
LOUISIANA	Louisiana State University and Agricultural and Mechanical College, University Station	Baton Rouge
	Agricultural Experiment Station, University Station	Baton Rouge
	Southern University and Agricultural and Mechanical College	Baton Rouge
	Southern Branch Post Office	
MAINE	College of Agriculture, University of Maine	Orono
	Agricultural Experiment Station, University of Maine	Orono

APPENDIX

MARYLAND	College of Agriculture, University of Maryland	College Park
	Agricultural Experiment Station	College Park
	Maryland State College, University of Maryland	Princess Anne
MASSACHUSETTS	College of Agriculture, University of Massachusetts	Amherst
	Agricultural Experiment Station	Amherst
MICHIGAN	Michigan State University of Agriculture and Applied Science	East Lansing
	Agricultural Experiment Station	East Lansing
MINNESOTA	Institute of Agriculture, University of Minnesota, St. Paul Campus	St. Paul
	Agricultural Experiment Station, St. Paul Campus	St. Paul
MISSISSIPPI	School of Agriculture and Forestry, Mississippi State University of Applied Arts and Sciences	State College
	Agricultural Experiment Station	State College
	School of Agriculture, Alcorn Agricultural and Mechanical College	Lorman
MISSOURI	College of Agriculture, University of Missouri	Columbia
	Agricultural Experiment Station	Columbia
	Lincoln University	Jefferson City
MONTANA	Montana State College	Bozeman
	Agricultural Experiment Station	Bozeman
NEBRASKA	College of Agriculture, University of Nebraska	Lincoln
	Agricultural Experiment Station	Lincoln
NEVADA	Max C. Fleischmann College of Agriculture, University of Nevada	Reno
	Agricultural Experiment Station	Reno
NEW HAMPSHIRE	College of Agriculture, University of New Hampshire	Durham
	Agricultural Experiment Station	Durham
NEW JERSEY	State College of Agriculture and Mechanic Arts, State University	New Brunswick
	Agricultural Experiment Station of Rutgers	New Brunswick
NEW MEXICO	College of Agriculture, New Mexico State University	University Park
	Agricultural Experiment Station	University Park

AGRICULTURAL COLLEGES AND EXPERIMENT STATIONS 477

NEW YORK	New York State College of Agriculture, Cornell University	Ithaca
	Agricultural Experiment Station	Ithaca
	New York State Agricultural Experiment Station	Geneva
NORTH CAROLINA	North Carolina State College of Agriculture and Engineering, University of North Carolina	Raleigh
	Agricultural Experiment Station	Raleigh
	The Agricultural and Technical College of North Carolina	Greensboro
NORTH DAKOTA	College of Agriculture, North Dakota State University of Agriculture and Applied Science	Fargo
	State University Station Agricultural Experiment Station	Fargo
OHIO	College of Agriculture, Ohio State University	Columbus
	Ohio Agricultural Experiment Station	Wooster
OKLAHOMA	Oklahoma State University of Agriculture and Applied Science	Stillwater
	Agricultural Experiment Station	Stillwater
	Langston University	Langston
OREGON	School of Agriculture, Oregon State University	Corvallis
	Agricultural Experiment Station	Corvallis
PENNSYLVANIA	College of Agriculture, Pennsylvania State University	University Park
	Agricultural Experiment Station	University Park
PUERTO RICO	College of Agriculture, University of Puerto Rico	Rio Piedras
	Agricultural Experiment Station	Rio Piedras
RHODE ISLAND	College of Agriculture, University of Rhode Island	Kingston
	Agricultural Experiment Station	Kingston
SOUTH CAROLINA	Clemson Agricultural College of South Carolina, School of Agriculture	Clemson
	Agricultural Experiment Station	Clemson
	South Carolina State College	Orangeburg

APPENDIX

SOUTH DAKOTA	South Dakota State College of Agriculture and Mechanic Arts	College Station
	Agricultural Experiment Station	College Station
TENNESSEE	College of Agriculture, University of Tennessee	Knoxville
	Agricultural Experiment Station	Knoxville
	Martin Branch, University of Tennessee	Martin
	Tennessee Agricultural and Industrial State University	Nashville
TEXAS	Agricultural and Mechanical College of Texas	College Station
	Prairie View A. and M. College	Prairie View
	Agricultural Experiment Station	College Station
UTAH	Utah State University of Agriculture and Applied Science	Logan
	Agricultural Experiment Station	Logan
VERMONT	College of Agriculture, University of Vermont	Burlington
	Agricultural Experiment Station	Burlington
VIRGINIA	School of Agriculture, Virginia Polytechnic Institute	Blacksburg
	Agricultural Experiment Station	Blacksburg
	Virginia Truck Experiment Station	Norfolk
WASHINGTON	College of Agriculture, Washington State University, Institute of Agricultural Sciences	Pullman
	Agricultural Experiment Station	Pullman
WEST VIRGINIA	College of Agriculture, West Virginia University	Morgantown
	Agricultural Experiment Station	Morgantown
WISCONSIN	College of Agriculture, University of Wisconsin	Madison
	Agricultural Experiment Station	Madison
WYOMING	College of Agriculture, University of Wyoming	Laramie
	Agricultural Experiment Station	Laramie

Special Plant Societies

African Violet Society of America, Inc.	Mrs. J. Addison MacLean 49 Saunders Rd. Norwood, Ma. 02062
American Begonia Society	Mrs. Virginia Barnett 1213 S. Mullender Ave. W. Covina, Calif. 91790
American Camellia Society	Mr. Joseph H. Pyron Box 212 Fort Valley, Ga. 31330
American Daffodil Society	Mrs. Robert F. Johnson 2537 W. 89th St. Leawood, Kansas 66206
American Dahlia Society, Inc.	Mr. Edward B. Lloyd 10 Crestmont Rd. Montclair, N.J.
American Fuchsia Society	California Academy of Science Golden Gate Park San Francisco, Calif.
American Gesneria Society	Mrs. Thomas Neel 6504 Dresden Indianapolis, Ind. 46227
American Gloxinia Society, Inc.	Miss Diantha Buel Eastford, Conn. 06242
American Hemerocallis Society	Mrs. Lewis B. Wheeler Box 28786 Memphis, Tenn. 38128
American Hibiscus Society	Mrs. C. H. Calais Goldenrod Orlando, Fla.
American Iris Society	Mr. Clifford W. Benson Missouri Botanical Garden 2237 Tower Grove Blvd. St. Louis, Mo. 63110
American Orchid Society, Inc.	Mr. Gordon W. Dillon Botanical Museum of Harvard University Cambridge 38, Mass.
American Penstemon Society	Mrs. Merle Emerson P. O. Box 64 Somersworth, N.Y. 03878
American Peony Society	Mr. C. Dan Pennell 107½ W. Main St. Van Wert, Ohio 45891
American Plant Life Society (includes American Amaryllis Society)	Dr. Thomas Whitaker Box 150 La Jolla, Calif.
American Poinsettia Society	Mrs. R. E. Gaunt Box 94 Mission, Texas 78572
American Primrose Society	Mrs. Alice Hills Baylor Johnson, Vt. 05656

APPENDIX

American Rhododendron Society	Mrs. Wm. Curtis Rt. 2, Box 105 Sherwood, Ore. 97140
American Rock Garden Society	Mr. Richard W. Redfield Box 26, Closter, N.J. 07624
American Rose Society	Mr. O. Keister Evans, Jr. 4048 Roselea Place Columbus, Ohio 43214
Bromeliad Society, Inc.	Miss Victoria Padilla 647 S. Saltair Ave. Los Angeles 49, Calif.
Cactus and Succulent Society of America, Inc.	Mr. Charles Blass Box 167 Reseda, Calif. 91335
Gourd Society of America, Inc.	Mrs. Raymond Wheeler Elmwood, Mass.
Herb Society of America	Mrs. Edmund K. Dawes 300 Massachusetts Ave. Boston 15, Mass.
Holly Society of America	Mr. Bluett C. Green P. O. Box 8445 Baltimore, Md. 21234
International Geranium Society	Mrs. Vernon Ireland 1413 Bluff Drive Santa Barbara, Calif.
National Chrysanthemum Society, Inc.	Mrs. George S. Briggs 8504 Laverne Dr. Adelphi, Md. 20783
National Tulip Society	Mr. Felix R. Tyroler 55 West 42nd St. New York 36, N.Y.
North American Gladiolus Federation	H. E. Frederick 234 South St. South Elgin, Ill. 60177
North American Lily Society	Mr. Fred M. Abbey N. Ferrisburg, Vermont 05473
Palm Society	Mrs. Lucita H. Wait 7229 S.W. 54th Ave. Miami 43, Fla.
Saintpaulia International	Mrs. J. M. Beetem 1247 Eastern Parkway Louisville, Ky. 40204

Other National Organizations

American Horticultural Society	1600 Bladenburg Rd., N.E. Washington 2, D.C.
Garden Club of America	598 Madison Ave. New York 22, N.Y.
Men's Garden Clubs of America	Mr. George A. Spader 50 Eaton St. Morrisville, N.Y.
National Council of State Garden Clubs, Inc.	Mrs. Earl H. Hath 4401 Magnolia Ave. St. Louis 10, Mo.
Woman's National Farm and Garden Association	Mrs. W. Donald Miller R.D. #2, Box 194 Havre de Grace, Md.

Books For Further Reference

LANDSCAPING AND PLANNING

The Art of Home Landscaping. Garrett Eckbo. McGraw-Hill, 1956.
Budget Landscaping. Carlton B. Lees. Holt, 1960.
Ladies' Home Journal Book of Landscaping and Outdoor Living. Richard Pratt. Lippincott, 1963.
Landscape for Living. Garrett Eckbo. McGraw-Hill, 1950.
Landscaping Your Own Home. Alice L. Dustan. Macmillan, 1955.
Color and Design for Every Garden. H. Stuart Ortloff and Henry B. Raymore. Barrows, 1951.
Garden Design Illustrated. John A. and Caroll Grant. Univ. of Washington Press, 1954.
Imaginative Small Gardens. Nancy Grasby. Hearthside Press, Inc., 1963.

GENERAL GARDENING

American Home Garden Book. Editors and staff, American Home. M. Evans, Co., 1963.
America's Garden Book. Louise and James Bush-Brown. Scribners, rev. 1958.
Better Homes & Gardens Garden Book. Meredith Press, 1954.
10,000 Garden Questions. F. F. Rockwell (ed.). Doubleday, 1959.
Taylor's Encyclopedia of Gardening. Norman Taylor. Houghton Mifflin, 1961.
How to Landscape Your Own Home. J. I. Rodale and staff. Rodale Books, Inc., 1963.

REGIONAL GARDENING

Gardening in the Lower South. Harold H. Hume. Macmillan, 1954.
Gardening in the South and West. Mrs. Gross R. and M. A. Scruggs (eds.). Doubleday, 1947.
How to Have Good Gardens in the Sunshine States. George W. Kelly. Littleton, Colo. 1957.
Modern Tropical Garden. Loraine E. Kuck and Richard C. Tongg. Tongg Publishing Co., Honolulu, 1955.
The Southern Gardener. Mary B. Stewart. Crager, 1961.
Sunset Western Garden Book. Editors of Sunset Magazine. Lane, 1961.
Your Florida Garden. J. V. Watkins and H. S. Wolfe. Univ. of Florida, 1961.

SPECIAL GARDENS

FRUITS:
Encyclopedia of Fruits, Berries and Nuts. Albert E. Wilkinson. Blakiston, 1945.
Small Fruits for Your Home Garden. J. Harold Clarke. Doubleday, 1958.

BOOKS FOR FURTHER REFERENCE

GREENHOUSE:
Greenhouse Gardening as a Hobby. James Underwood Crockett. Doubleday, 1961.
The New Greenhouse Gardening for Everyone. Ernest Chabot. Barrows, 1955.
How to Grow Rare Greenhouse Plants. Ernest Chabot. Barrows, 1952.

LAWNS:
The Complete Book of Lawns. F. F. Rockwell and Esther C. Grayson. Doubleday, 1956.
The Lawn Book. Robert W. Schery. Macmillan, 1961.

INDOORS:
Garden in Your House. Ernesta D. Ballard. Harper, 1958.
All About House Plants. Montague Free. Doubleday, 1946.
The World Book of House Plants. Elvin McDonald. World, 1963.

CONTAINERS:
Gardening in Containers. Editors of *Sunset Magazine.* Lane, 1959.
Outdoor Gardening in Pots and Boxes. George Taloumis. Van Nostrand, 1962.
Window-box Gardening. Henry Teuscher. Macmillan, 1956.

ROCK AND WALL:
Rock Garden Plants. Doretta Klaber. Holt, 1959.

VEGETABLES:
Burrage on Vegetables. Albert C. Burrage. Van Nostrand, 1954.

WATER:
Garden Pools, Water Lilies, and Goldfish. G. L. Thomas, Jr. Van Nostrand, 1958.
Water Gardens. Frances Perry. Penguin, 1962.

SPECIAL PLANTS AND PLANT GROUPS

AFRICAN VIOLETS:
African Violets, Gloxinias and Their Relatives. Harold E. Moore, Jr. Macmillan, 1957.
All about African Violets. Montague Free. Doubleday, 1951.

ANNUALS:
The Complete Book of Annuals. F. F. Rockwell and Esther C. Grayson. Doubleday, 1955.
How to Grow and Use Annuals. Sunset Editorial Staff. Lane, 1962.

BULBS:
The Complete Book of Bulbs. F. F. Rockwell and Esther C. Grayson. Doubleday, 1953.
How to Grow and Use Bulbs. Sunset Editorial Staff. Lane, 1963.
Hardy Garden Bulbs. Gertrude S. Wister. Dutton, 1964.

CACTI AND SUCCULENTS:
The Book of Cacti and other Succulents. Claude Chidamian. Doubleday, 1958.
Desert Plants—Cacti and Succulents. Oliver and Margaret Leese. Transatlantic. 1959.

CAMELLIAS:

Camellia Culture. E. C. Tourje (ed.). Macmillan, 1959.
Camellias in America. Harold H. Hume. McFarland, 1955.
You Can Grow Camellias. Mary Noble and Blanche Graham. Harper, 1962.
The Camellia Book. John Threlkeld. Van Nostrand, 1962.

CHRYSANTHEMUMS:

The Complete Book of Chrysanthemums. Cornelius Ackerson. Doubleday, 1957.

GERANIUMS:

Geraniums for Home and Garden. Helen K. Krauss. Macmillan, 1955.
Geraniums (Pelargoniums) for Windows and Gardens. Helen Van Pelt Wilson. Barrows, 1957.

GROUND COVERS:

Ground Covers. Daniel J. Foley. Chilton Co., 1961.
Ground Cover Plants. Donald Wyman. Macmillan, 1956.

HERBS:

Gardening for Good Eating. Helen M. Fox. Macmillan, 1943.
Magic Gardens. Rosetta E. Clarkson. Macmillan, 1939.
Herbs: Their Culture and Uses. Rosetta E. Clarkson. Macmillan, 1942.

IRIS:

Iris for Every Garden. Sydney B. Mitchell. Barrows, 1960.
Garden Irises. L. F. Randolph. American Iris Society, 1959.

LILACS:

Lilacs for America. John C. Wister (ed.). Swarthmore College, 1953.

LILIES:

The Complete Book of Lilies. F. F. Rockwell and Esther C. Grayson with Jan de Graaf. Doubleday, 1961.

ORCHIDS:

Orchids: Their Botany and Culture. Alex D. Hawkes. Harper, 1961.
Home Orchid Growing. Rebecca T. Northen. Van Nostrand, 1962.

PERENNIALS:

New Perennials Preferred. Helen Van Pelt Wilson. Barrows, 1961.
Contemporary Perennials. Roderick W. Cumming and R. E. Lee. Macmillan, 1960.
The Picture Book of Perennials. Arno and Irene Nehrling. Hearthside Press, 1964.
The Rockwells' Complete Book of Roses. F. F. Rockwell and Esther C. Grayson. Doubleday, 1958.
Anyone Can Grow Roses. Cynthia Westcott. Van Nostrand, 1960.
Climbing Roses. Helen Van Pelt Wilson. Barrows, 1955.

VINES:

Landscaping with Vines. Frances Howard. Macmillan, 1959.
All about Vines and Hanging Plants. Bernice Brilmayer. Doubleday, 1962.

TREES AND SHRUBS

Book of Broadleaf Trees. Frank H. Lamb. Norton, 1939.

BOOKS FOR FURTHER REFERENCE

The Book of Shrubs. Alfred C. Hottes. Dodd, Mead, revised, 1959.
Climbing Plants and Wall Shrubs. Douglas Bartram. Gifford, London, 1959.
The Concise Encyclopedia of Favorite Flowering Shrubs. Majorie J. Dietz. Doubleday, 1963.
Crab Apples for America. Donald Wyman. American Association of Botanical Gardens and Arboretums, 1955.
The Evergreens. James H. Beale. Doubleday, 1960.
Evergreens for Every State. Katharine M-P. Cloud. Chilton Co., 1960.
Flowering Trees. Robert B. Clark. Van Nostrand, 1963.
The Friendly Evergreens. L. L. Kumlien. Rinehart, 1954.
Handbook of Hollies. Harry William Dengler (ed.). American Horticultural Society, 1957.
Hollies. H. Harold Hume. Macmillan, 1953.
The Home Owner's Tree Book. John S. Martin. Doubleday, 1962.
Maples Cultivated in the United States and Canada. Brian O. Mulligan. American Association of Botanical Gardens & Arboretums, 1958.
Modern Shrubs. E. H. M. Cox and P. A. Cox. Nelson, 1960.
Shrubs and Trees for the Home Landscape. James Bush-Brown. Chilton, 1963.
Shrubs and Trees for the Small Place. P. J. Van Melle. Doubleday, revised, 1955.
Shrubs and Vines for American Gardens. Donald Wyman. Macmillan, 1949.
Tree Care. John M. Haller. Macmillan, 1957.
Tree Maintenance. P. P. Pirone. Oxford, 1959.
Trees for American Gardens. Donald Wyman. Macmillan, 1951.

SOILS AND THEIR MANAGEMENT

A Book about Soils. H. Stuart Ortloff and Henry B. Raymore. Barrows, 1962.
Your Garden Soil. R. Milton Carleton. Van Nostrand, 1961.

TECHNIQUES

Create New Flowers and Plants. John James. Doubleday, 1964.
Growing for Showing. Rudy J. Favretti. Doubleday, 1961.
How to Control Plant Diseases. Malcolm Shurtleff. Iowa State University Press, 1962.
How to Increase Plants. A. C. Hottes. Dodd, Mead, 1956.
Plant Breeding for Everyone. John Y. Beaty. Branford, 1954.
Plant Propagation and Garden Practice. R. C. M. Wright. Criterion, 1956.
Plant Propagation in Pictures. Montague Free. Doubleday, 1957.
Plant Pruning in Pictures. Montague Free. Doubleday, 1961.
Propagating House Plants. Arno and Irene Nehrling. Hearthside, 1962.
Pruning Guide for Trees, Shrubs, and Vines. Tom Stevenson. Robert B. Luce, Inc., 1964.
Pruning Made Easy. Edwin F. Steffek. Holt, 1958.
Simple, Practical Hybridizing for Beginners. D. G. Thomas. St. Martin's Press, 1962.

ARRANGEMENT

Contemporary Flower Arrangement. Rae L. Goldson. Hearthside, revised, 1962.
New Horizons in Flower Arrangement. Myra J. Brooks and others. Barrows, 1961.
Period Flower Arrangement. Margaret Fairbanks Marcus. Barrows, 1952.
The Rockwell's New Complete Book of Flower Arrangement. F. F. Rockwell and Esther C. Grayson. Doubleday, 1960.

Bibliography

America's Garden Book by Louise and James Bush-Brown. Scribners. New York. 1958.
Basic Horticulture by Victor R. Gardner. Macmillan. New York. 1951.
The How and Why of Better Gardening by Laurence Manning. Van Nostrand. New York. 1951.
Entoma. E. H. Fisher, editor. Entomological Society of America. 14th Edition. 1961–62.
Flower Grower, The Home Garden Magazine. New York. 1960–63.
Flower and Garden Magazine. Kansas City, Mo. 1962–63.
Gardener's Directory. J. W. Stephenson, compiler. Doubleday. New York. 1962.
Gardening in the Lower South by H. Harold Hume. Macmillan. New York. 1954.
Gardening in the South and West. Mrs. Gross R. Scruggs, editor. Doubleday. New York. 1947.
Gardening for Fun in California by Jean-Marie Consigny. George Palmer Putnam, Inc. Hollywood, Calif. 1940.
Ground Covers for Easier Gardening by Daniel J. Foley. Chilton Co. Philadelphia. 1961.
Hortus Second Compiled by L. H. Bailey and Ethel Zoe Bailey. Macmillan. New York. 1947.
Modern Gardening by P. P. Pirone. Simon and Schuster. New York. 1952.
Plant Disease Handbook by Cynthia Westcott. Van Nostrand. New York. 1960.
Plant Propagation by R. C. M. Wright. Criterion Books. New York. 1956.
Plant Propagation in Pictures by Montague Free. Doubleday. New York. 1957.
Plant Pruning in Pictures by Montague Free. Doubleday. New York. 1961.
Secret of the Green Thumb by Henry and Rebecca Northen. Ronald Press Co. New York. 1954.
Shrubs and Trees for the Small Place by P. J. Van Melle. Revised by Montague Free. Doubleday. New York. 1955.
Soil Science (Fundamentals of) by C. E. Millar and L. M. Turk. John Wiley & Sons, Inc. New York. 1961.
Standard Cyclopedia of Horticulture, 3 vol. Liberty Hyde Bailey, editor. Macmillan. New York. 1927.
Sunset Magazine. Palo Alto, Calif. 1962–63.
Sunset Western Garden Book, Staff of Sunset Magazine, and Sunset Books, 1961. Editors. Lane Publishing Co. Menlo Park, Calif.
10,000 Garden Questions. F. F. Rockwell, editor. Doubleday. New York. 1959.
The Friendly Evergreens by L. L. Kumlien. D. Hill Nursery Co. Dundee, Ill. 1946.
The Garden Encyclopedia. E. L. D. Seymour, editor. Wise & Co. New York. 1941.
The Gardener's Bug Book by Cynthia Westcott. Doubleday. New York. 1956.

The W. C. System for Producing Healthy, Container-Grown Plants. Kenneth F. Baker, editor. University of California. 1957.

What's New in Gardening by P. P. Pirone. Hanover House. Garden City, N.Y. 1956.

Brochures, bulletins, and leaflets of the agricultural colleges of all state universities, and of the U. S. Department of Agriculture, Washington, D.C.

INDEX

Acid-loving plants, 45, 196
Acid soils, 33, improvement, 47–48; plants for, 96
Adobe soil, 38, 49
African violets, propagation, 77
Agricultural colleges, 474–78
Agricultural Experiment Stations, 46, 49, 50, 474–78
Air, 59, 61, 62
Air layering, 74, *ill.* 74, *ill.*
Airwrap, 74
Ajuga, 185
Akebia, 146
Alabama: agricultural colleges and experiment station, 474; area, 290; gardens and parks, 461; problems, 393
Alaska, 456; agricultural college and experiment station, 474; gardens, 456
Alkaline-saline soils, improving, 50–51
Alkaline soils, 33, 39; improving, 49–50
Alkali tolerance: plants, 385; trees, 386; shrubs, 386
Altitude, 86
Amaryllis, 57, 186, 297; propagation, 75
American Horticultural Society, 481
Ampelopsis, 146
Amur River Privet, 145
Anatomy, plant, *ill.* 53
Angel's-trumpet (*Datura*), 175
Animal pests, 448
Animals—plants, difference, 52, 54
Annuals, 174–78; books on, 483; buying, 176; end-of-season care, 178; fertilizer, 93, 98, 174, 177; fragrant, 191, 443; half-hardy, 436; hardy, 436; life cycle, *ill.* 55; list, 437; mulching, 177; pinching back, 178; for pool, 207; pruning, 104; quick growers, 175; soil preparation, 95, 176; sowing and planting, 176; for streams, 207; supports, 177–78, *ill.* 178; tender, 436; thinning out, 176–77, *ill.* 177; vegetables, 251; vines, 175, 437–38; water gardens, 207

Apple trees: culture, 257–58; orchards, spraying, 256; pruning, *ill.* 259
Apricot trees, 261
Aquatic plants, 209
Arabis, 183
Arboretums, list, 456–61
Arbors, 129, 147, *ill.* 130; climber roses, 219; grapes, 261–62; rambler roses, 223–24
Arborvitaes, 141
Arches, 147
Areas, states, 290–93
Area I: calendar: January, 296–99, February, 304–05, March, 312–13, April, 319, May, 327, June, 334–35, July, 342–43, August, 348–50, September, 353–54, October, 359, November, 366–67, December, 372–73; grass, 162; lawnmaking, 152–53; spring planting date, 288; states in, 293
Area II: calendar: January, 296–99, February, 304–05, March, 312–13, April, 319–20, May, 328–29, June, 335–36, July, 342–43, August, 348–50, September, 353–54, October, 360–61, November, 367–68, December, 373–74; grass, 162; lawnmaking, 152–53; spring planting date, 288;

states in, 293; trees, 139, 140, 141
Area III: calendar: January, 296–99, February, 305–07, March, 313–14, April, 321–22, May, 329–30, June, 335–36, July, 342–44, August, 348–50, September, 353–55, October, 360–61, November, 367–68, December, 373–74; grass, 162; lawnmaking, 152–53; spring planting date, 288; states in, 293; trees, 139, 140, 141
Area IV: calendar: January, 296–99, February, 305–07, March, 313–14, April, 323, May, 329–30, June, 337–38, July, 342–44, August, 348–50, September 353–55, October, 360–61, November, 367–68, December, 373–74; lawnmaking, 152–53; spring planting date, 288; states in, 293; trees, 139, 140, 141
Area V: calendar: January, 299–300, February, 307–08, March, 315–16, April, 323, May, 330–31, June, 337–38, July, 345–46, August, 350–51, September, 355–56, October, 362–63, November, 368–69, December, 375–76; lawnmaking, 152–53; spring planting date, 288; states in, 293–94
Area VI: calendar: January, 301–02, February, 308–10, March, 316–17, April, 324–25, May, 332, June, 339–40, July, 345–46, August, 350–51, September, 356–57, October, 363–64, November, 370, December, 376–77; lawnmaking, 152–53; spring planting date, 288; states in, 294
Arid soils, fertility and fertilizers, 51
Arizona: agricultural college and experiment station, 474; area, 290; gardens and parks, 456, 461; problems, 381–83, 387; soil, 382, 383
Arkansas: agricultural college and experiment station, 474; area, 290, gardens and parks, 461; problems, 391
Arrangement, flower, books on, 486
Asexual propagation, 72–76; *See* Propagation
Asparagus, 248–49; beetle, 249; in flower border, 235
Atlantic seashore, gardening problems, 394–96
Autumn: flowers, 216; rose feeding, 226; shrubs, list, 143
Azaleas, 215; acid-loving, 45; bank garden, 200–01; chlorosis, 309; fertilizer, 98; layering, 73; propagation, 77; soil for, 48, 96

Bagasse, 230
Bagworms, 298
Balloon-vine (*Cardiospermum halicacabum*), 146
"B and B" (balled and burlapped) stock, 148
Bank gardens, 200–01; advantages, 192; natural settings for, 203; trailer roses, 219
Banks: sods, 158–59; turf for, 155
Barberry, 145; for hedges, 145; pruning, 106
Bark grafting, 81
Beans, 245–46, *ill.* 247, *ill.*
Bearberry (*Arctostaphylos uva-ursi*), 168
Beech trees, 141
Beetles, 445
Begonias, 188; propagation, 77; seed sowing, 70; tuberous, propagation, 76
Bents grasses, 162–63
Bermudagrass, 162, 166; mowing, 339
Berries, picking, 267
Berry boxes, 184

INDEX

Biennials, 179, 438; defined, 438; life cycle, 179, *ill.* 55
Birch trees, 141
Birds: blueberries, 263; feeding, 298; water in patio, 213, 214
Blights, 448
Blossom-set, 243
Blueberries, 263–64; acid soil, 254; location, 254; mulched and watered, 87–91, 350
Bluegrasses, 163
Bog garden, 208; design, 205; plants 205, 442
Borders, planting, 23. *See* Flower beds and borders
Borers, 252, 445–46
Boron, 51, 97
Botanical gardens, list, 456–61
Bougainvillea, 147
Bovung, 42, 157, 244
Box protectors, 128. *See* Protecting plants
Boxwood, 298; pruning, 107
Bracing, 149, 151, *ill.* 149. *See* Supports
Budding, 80–81, *ill.* 83; time for, 81. *See* Grafting and budding
Buffalograss, 168
Bugle-weed (*Ajuga reptans*), 168
Bugs, 446
Bulbils, 76
Bulblets, 76
Bulbous plants, 439–40; propagation, 75; for South, 426–28
Bulbs, 185–87; books on, 483; culture, 186–87; dividing, 73; early, 26; fall planting, 57; fertilizer, 187; flowering, skipping a year, 121; foliage, care of, 187–88; "forcing," 120–21; fragrant, 191, 444; hardy, replanting, 187; life cycle, *ill.* 57; overwintering, 188; pans, 120; planting trowel, Slim Jim, 187; soil, 186–87; for South, 426–28; springflowering 215; spring planting, 187–89; tender, 57
"Burning," 93
Bush fruits, 263–65
Bush roses, planting holes, 223

Calendar: how to use, 287–89; lawn schedule, 170–71
Calendulas, seed sowing, 67
California: agricultural college and experiment stations, 474; area, 290; broadleaved evergreens, 429–30; coniferous trees, 430–31; gardens and parks, 457, 461–62; ornamental deciduous trees, 420–21; privets, 145; problems, 378–82; soil, 383; vines, 424–25
Callas, 188
Cambium layer (bark), 80–81
Camellias: propagation, 77; soil, 48, 96
Camomile (*Cotula squalida*), 169
Canada Bluegrass, 163
Cane fruits, 265–67, 350
Carpetgrass, 166
Carson, Rachel, 100
Castor-oil bean (*Ricinus*), 175
Catalogs, 296
Centipedegrass, 166
Central Plains, gardening problems, 389
Cherry trees, 141
Chestnut soils, 39
Chinese junipers, pruning, 107
Chionodoxa, 186
Chlorosis, 345, 448
Chrysanthemums, 80–84, 185, 215; books on, 484; for very cold climates, 418; dividing, 73; pruning, 105; special bed, 27
Clay or plastic pots, in coldframe, 118
Clay soils, 30, 37, 183; acidifying, 48
Clematis vines, 147
Climbing roses, 145, 147, 219;

on greenhouse, 272; planting holes, 223; pruning, 227–28; supports, 129, 223–24, *ill.* 225
Clover, 36, 41, 93, 156, 164–65; White Dutch, 164–65
Coal, 37
Coldframes and hotbeds, 87, 112 ff, 299; attention to, 113; building frame, 115–17; bulbs for indoors, 120–21; cleaning, 119; drainage, 114; frames, kind, 113; hotbed, 119–20; lettuce, 242–43; location, 114; management, 117–19; melons, 249; patio garden, 215; placement, 173; removable divider, 114; roses, 224; sash, 113; shading, 119; soil for frames, 117; spacing in, 118; temperature, 278; tomatoes, 244; vegetable plants, 238; ventilation, 306
Colleges, agricultural, 474–78
Color: evergreens, 140; in flower beds and borders, 180; shrubs, 142
Colorado: agricultural college and experiment station, 474; area, 290; gardens and parks, 457, 463; problems, 387–88, 389
Columbia River Basin, 50
Composition planter trays, 69
Composition pots, 282
Compost, 93; for lawn, 156–58; storing, 274
Compost heap, 41–44, 93, *ill.* 43; placement, 173; weeds and, 240
Composts for the Home Grounds, 43
Connecticut: agricultural college and experiment stations, 474; area, 290; gardens and parks, 457, 463; problems, 390–91
Conservatory, 271
Conservo, 115

Control of conditions, in seed sowing, 66–67
Copper beech trees, 139
Coral bells (*Heuchera*), in wall garden, 201
Cormous plants, propagation, 75, 76
Corms, for the South, 426–28
Corn. *See* Sweet corn
"Corn belt," 390
Cosmos, 177, 178
Cotoneaster horizontalis, 145
Cottonseed meal, 49
County agricultural agent, 86, 139, 157, 248, 254, 276
Cover crops, 51; alkali tolerance, 385, salinity tolerance, 386
Cowpeas, 93
Crab trees, flowering, 141
Creeping Bents, 163
Creeping fig (*Ficus pumila*), 146
Crested wheatgrass, 168
Crimson Pygmy barberry, 145
Crocking, 282; *ill.* 281
Crocuses, 186; "forcing," 120
"Crowns," 73
Cucumber beetle, 252
Cultivars, 72
Cultivation, 89; necessity of, 126; rock garden 199–200; tools for, 126; tree fruits, 257–63; vegetables, 240–42; of vines, 147–48
Cup-and-saucer vine (*Cobaea scandens*), 146, 175, 177
Currants, 264
Cutting garden, 172–73, *ill.* 173; -patio garden, 212
Cuttings, 76–77; hardwood, 79; keeping, 77; leaf, 76–77; root, 76; rooting media, 77–78; softwood stem, 77; stem, 76
Cyclamen, 276

Daffodils, 186, 189, 215; dividing, 73; foliage, 187; "forcing," 120; life cycle, 57;

INDEX

propagation, 75; replanting, 187

Dahlias, 178, 188; propagation, 76; pruning, 105; special bed, 27

Daisy, 185; English, 179; Shasta, 187

Damp-off diseases, 69

Day-lilies, 183, 185

Dead wood, removal of, 104

Deciduous flowering shrubs, list, 143

Deciduous trees, 140; list, 141

Delaware: agricultural colleges and experiment station, 474; area, 290; gardens and parks, 457, 463; problems, 390–91

Delphinium, pruning, 105

Desert living, 383–84

Desert soils, 39. See Adobe

Dichondra carolinensis, 169

Dieffenbachia, air layering, 74

Disbudding, 105

Diseased plants, pruning, 105

Diseases, 63, 86, 97, 448–49; black spot, 222, 448; of currants and gooseberries, 264–65; damping-off, 69; fruit trees, 257; lawn, 448–49; mildew, 222; rhizoctonia, 69, 283; rose petals, decayed, 230; tomato, 245, 450; virus, 450

Disinfectants, seedlings 70

Display gardens, 461–73

District of Columbia: area, 290; gardens and parks, 457, 463

Division, of plants, 184–85

Dogwood trees, 141

Domestic or Italian ryegrass, 164

Double digging, 34, *ill.* 36

Drainage, 34–35, *ill.* 37; alkaline-saline soils, 50; coldframes, 114; lawn, 156; pools in winter, 209; rock garden, 193; rose garden, 221, 222; for seed sowing, 67; tile, installing, *ill.* 37; vegetable garden, 234

Driconure, 42, 157, 244

Drought, mulching, 63

Dryness, 63

Dry well, *ill.* 155

Dusting: application, 100; equipment, 130–31, *ill.* 131; roses, 230

Dwarf fruit trees, 257–58, *ill.* 260

Dwarf junipers, pruning, 108

Edging roses, 220

Elm, 141; growth rate, 138

Emerald Zoysia, 167

England: gardens, 94; John Innes mixtures, 68; Malling, 257; topiary work, 106

English daisies (*Bellis perennis*), 179

English ivy (*Hedera helix*), 146, 169

Entertainment, planning area for, 24

Erosionet, 159

Espaliered fruits, 106, *ill.* 107; apricots, 261; nectarines, 261; trees, 212

Espaliered plants, pruning, 147–48

Europe: topiary work, 106; window boxes, 215

Evaporation: mulching and, 88; *Wilt-Pruf* spray, 128

Evergreens: bank garden, 200; bracing, 149, 150–51; color, 140; -deciduous trees, difference, 140; patio garden, 211; planting, 314; pruning, 107; rock garden, 193, 194; for screens and hedges, list, 143–44; snow, 297; trees, list, 141

Experimental gardening, 62n

"Eye," in pruning, 111

Feeding of plants, 92–93; in coldframe, 118

Fences, 24, 129

Fertilizers, 32, 92; annuals, 93, 98, 175, 177; application 93, 98; liquid form, 131; for arid soils, 51; bulbs, 187; "complete," 32, 45, 92; formulas, and recommended uses, 98; greenhouse seedlings, 280, 281; inorganic, 92–93; lawn, 98, 157, 160–61; liquid, 54, 131; nitrogenous, 92; nutrients contents, 98; organic, 92–93; -base, 98, 184; percentage in "complete," 92; in planting hole, 148; reaction, 98; roses, 98, 221, 225; and seed distributor, 134, 157; shrubs, 93, 98; storing, 272; strawberries, 268; trees, 98; type to use, 95–96; for vegetables, 93, 98, 239

Fescues, 164

Fieldstone, 197

Fig tree, 263

Fireblight, 257

Fir trees, 141

Fish, in pools, 209

Flats, 68, 69, 176, 239; setting out plants from, 184

Florida: agricultural colleges and experiment station, 475; area, 290; gardens and parks, 457–58, 463; problems, 393

Flower beds and borders, 26, 172–91; annuals, 175–78; backgrounds, 173, 174; biennials, 179; borders: edging roses, 220; bulbs, 185–87; tender, 188; daffodils, 188–89; evening fragrance, 191; fragrant gardens, 191; herbs, 190; lettuce in, 243; long flowering season, 174; number, 174; perennials, 179; *ill.* placement, 172, of flowers, 180; planning, 174, border, 180–83; "plunging border," *ill.* 212; preparation, 183–85; setting out plants, 184; soil preparation, 174, 183, depth of, 95; tulips, 188–89; vegetables in border, 235

Flower pots, 68

Flowers: cool-house subjects, 276; over-crowded, 254. *See* Annuals, Biennials, Flower Beds and borders, Perennials *and* Plants

Foliage, roses, 222

Foliar feeding, 54

Food (plant), 61, 91–93

"Forcing" bulbs, 120–21

Forget-me-not (*Myosotis*), 179

Forsythia: *suspensa,* 145; dividing, 73; layering, 73; pruning, 107

Foundation planting, 25; lists of plants, 400, 402–03; shrubs, 298

Fountains, in patio, 213

Fragrant gardens, 191

Fragrant plants, 443–44

Frames: for seed sowing, 67; soil for, 67. *See* Coldframes and hotbeds

Freezing, vegetables, 242, 248

Fruit gardens: books, 482; pests and diseases, 446–48; planning, 27. *See* Fruits *and* Fruit trees

Fruits, 253; alkali tolerance, 385; blackberries, 265, 267; blueberries, 263–64; bush, 263–65; cane, 265–67; culture, 253; currants, 264; dewberries, 265; frozen, 253; gooseberries, 264; grapes, 261–62, *ill.* 262; location, 254; loganberries, 265; nitrogen deficiency, 97; over-crowded, 254; pests, and diseases, 446–47; planting, 255; raspberries, 265–66, *ill.* 266; salinity tolerance, 385–86; soil, 254; space, 254; strawberries, 267–70, *ill.* 268, 269;

tree, 254. (*See* Tree fruits *and* Fruit trees); why cultivate?, 253

Fruit trees: apple, 257–58; bloom, 256; diseases, 257; espaliering, 212; fig, 262; grafting, 298; harvesting, 257; mulching, 256; peach, 260, 261, *ill.* 261; pear, 258; pests, 257; plum, 258, 260; protecting, 256; pruning, 104, 258, *ill.* 259; "scaffold," 258; spraying, 256, 456, and schedule, 456; storing, 257; "whips," 261

Fungicides, 100–01, 453–54; precautions, 101

Garden Club of America, 481
"Garden consultant," 20
Garden house, 24
Gardenia, 215, 297; air layering, 74
Gardening: books, 462; defined, 85; greenhouse, 278 (*See* Greenhouse); "mobile," 215; organic, 96; problems, 378–96; under glass (*See* Coldframes *and* Greenhouse)
Garden roses, 219. *See* Roses *and* Rose garden
Gardens: bank, 200, 203; bog, 208; botanical, list, 456–61; clean-up, 359, 360; cutting, 173, *ill.* 173; display, 461–73; fragrant, 191; herb, 190; marsh, 208; patio, 210; pests, and control, 445–46; plan, *ill.* 21; planning area for, 23; rock, 192–200, 203; rose, 218–31; special, planning, 22; temperature for sowing, 278; vegetable, 232–51; wall, 201–03; water, 204, 205, 208–09
Gas-plant (*Dictamnus*), 179
Gates, 129
Georgia: agricultural colleges and experiment stations, 475; area, 290; gardens and parks, 458, 463–64; problems, 392
Geraniums: propagation, 77
Germination. *See* Seed germination
Gladiolus, 188; cormlets (propagation), 76; storing, 297; diseases, 448–49; thrip, 64, 324
Gooseberries, 264
Grading, lawn preparation, 154–55
Grafting, 80–84; and budding, 80–84; time for, 81; fruit trees, 298
Gramagrasses, 168
Grandiflora rose, *ill.* 219
Granite, 197
Grapes, 261–62, *ill.* 262; vines, mulch, 307; pruning, 299, *ill.* 263
Grass: area affinity, 162; cool climate, 162; seed 157, 162; warm-climate, 162
Grasses: alkali tolerance, 385; for cool climates, 162–65; cool-weather schedule, 170; dry land, 168; ground cover substitutes. 168–70; hot climate, 166–67; mixtures, 165; "nurse," 162; salinity tolerance, 386; types, 154; warm-weather schedule, 170–71
Grass seed, 157, 162
Great Northern Plains, gardening problems, 388–89
Greenhouse, 112; books on, 483; construction, 271; -conservatory difference, 271; crocking, 282; cutting bed, 283, dual-purpose, 272; equipment, 276–77; even-span or lean-to, 272, *ill.* 273; function determines design, 272; "growing" or construction, 271; for "growing" or "enjoyment," 271; heating, 274–76; home, 271–84; melons, 249;

"misting" system, 78; operations, 278–79; patio garden, 212, 215; potting and repotting, 281–82; prefabs, 271; propagation box, 278; propagation by cuttings, 283; seed sowing, 279–84; shade, 276; spraying, 283; starting seedlings, 278–79; *ill.* vegetable plants, 238, 239; ventilation, 276; water, 277; work space, 272–77

Green manures, 41, 93, 96, 156, 179; for acidity, 47; crops, 36, 41

Ground covers, 168–70, 179; books on, 484; for very cold climates, 411; Erosionet, 159; hardy evergreen, list, 411; for seashore, 434–35

Gulf Coast, gardening problems, 393–94

Gumbo soils, 38, 39, 49

Gypsum, 49

Hardwood cuttings, 79
Hardy border, 26
Hardy bulbs, "forcing," in coldframe, 120
Hardy shrubs, list, 399–410
Hardy trees, list, 399–410
Hawaii: agricultural college and experiment station, 475; gardens and parks, 458, 464
Hawthorn trees, 141
Heat, 63; greenhouse, 272, 274–76; water and, 87
Heaving, of plants, 298, 304
Hedge plants: for very cold climate, 414–15; for the South, 422. *See also* Hedges
Hedge roses, 220; for very cold climate, 418
Hedges, 23; asparagus, 248; cost, 145; hardy shrubs and evergreens, list, 143–44; hedge roses, 220; instead of fences, 129; pruning, 106; shrubs for, 145; yew, *ill.*

"Heeling in" nursery stock, *ill.* 255
Hemlock trees, 141
Herb garden, 344; plan for, *ill.* 190; vegetables in, 235; walling in, 201
Herbicides, 100–01, 454–55; fertilizer and seed distributor, 134
Herbs, 190; books on, 484; fragrant, 444
Heuchera, 183
Hicks' Yew, 144
Hilling: corn, 246, 248, *ill.* 247; roses, 230; strawberries, 269–70
Holes, planting, 148–50; preparation, 95
Hollies, soil for, 48
Home greenhouse, 271–84
Honeysuckle, 146
Hormodin, 74, 78
Horse-chestnut trees, 141
Hoses: "fog" nozzle, 69, 71, 91, 275, 280; mist spray, 91, 151, 158, 184, 238; perforated, 91, 158; for rose garden, 222; shut-off, 277
Hotbed, 112, 119; temperature, 278–79; vegetables in, 239. *See* Coldframes and hotbeds
Hotkaps, 91, 128, 184, 249, 329
Houseplants, 297, 305
Humus, 37, 51, 88, 93, 174; defined, 31; "friable" soil, 31; fruits, 254; lawn, 156–57; maintenance, 33; organic materials, 30–31; rose garden, 221. *See* Compost heap
Hyacinths, 186; "forcing," 120
Hybrid tea roses, *ill.*
Hydrangea, climbing (*H. petiolaris*), 106, 147

Idaho: agricultural college and experiment station, 475; area, 291; gardens and parks, 458, 464; problems, 387–88

INDEX

Illinois: agricultural college and experiment station, 475; area, 291; gardens and parks, 458, 464; problems, 389–91

Indiana: agricultural college and experiment station, 475; area, 291; gardens and parks, 458, 465; problems, 390–91

Injured plants, pruning, 105
Inoculants, seedlings, 70
Inorganic fertilizers, 92–93
Insecticides, 100–01, 451–53; precautions, 101

Insects, 86; currants, 264; gooseberries, 264

Iowa: agricultural college and experiment station, 475; area, 291; gardens and parks, 458, 465; problems, 388–90

Iris, 185; bearded, 342, for very cold climates, 418–19; books on, 484; dividing, 73

Irish junipers, pruning, 107
Iron sulfate, 49
Irrigation, vegetable garden, 91
Ismenes, 188; propagation, 75

Japanese-spurge. *See* Pachysandra
John Innes mixtures, 68
Juniper trees, 141

Kalmias, soil, 96

Kansas: agricultural college and experiment station, 475; arboretum, 458; area, 291; gardens and parks, 465; problems, 389–90

Kentucky: agricultural colleges and experiment station, 475; area, 291; gardens and parks, 465; problems, 390–92

Kentucky Bluegrass, 163
Knot gardens, *ill.*
Korean Lawngrass (*Zoysia japonica*), 167

Laburnum trees, 141
Landscape architect, 20

Landscaping: books on, 482; expensive features, 148; flower beds and borders, 172; trees, shrubs, vines: planting first, 137; value of, 137

Larch trees, 140, 141
Larkspur, 177, 178

Lawn, 152–70; books on, 483; "chocolate icing" layer, 153; clippings, 161; cover crop, 156; defined, 76; diseases, 349, 448–49; drainage, 156; equipment, 132–34; example, 153; feeding, 161; fertilizer, 98, 157, 161; grading, 154, 155; grass, kinds, 162–68, 170–71; grasses, types, 154; ground cover as grass substitutes, 168–70; humus for, 156; laying out areas, 155; lime for, 161; maintenance, 160–61; mowing, 161; nitrogen for, 92; planning area for, 23; plugging, 159; preliminary preparations, 154–56; primary work, 152; purpose, 153; renovation, 160; "scalping," 156; seeding, 157–58; sodding, 158, 159; soil, 156; depth of preparation, 95; sprigging, 159; status symbol, 132; stripping, 159; summer, 152; surface soil–the "chocolate icing" layer, 156–58; type, 153; winter, 152. *See* Grasses

Layering, 73
Leaching, 39, 50
Leaf cuttings, 76–77
"Leaf scorch," 97
Legume Aid, 70
Lemmons Alkaligrass, 168
Lettuce, 233, 242–43
Life cycle, of plants, 55–57
Light, 61, 61n, 62; seedlings, 71

Lilacs: mildew, 63; pruning, 105
Lilies, 186, *ill.* 182; germina-

tion, 67; life cycle, 57; pool, 205; propagation, 76, *ill.* 75; "scaling," *ill.* 75; special bed, 26–27
Lime: for lawns, 161; -loving plants, 196; sulfur, 49–50
Limestone, 196; raw ground for acidity, 47–48
Linden trees, 141
Lippia canescens, 169
Liriope muscari, 169
Loam, 30
Locomotion, planning, 22
Locust trees, 141
Long-range plan, 20
Louisiana: agricultural colleges and experiment station, 475; area, 291; gardens and parks, 458, 465; problems, 391–93
Lupines, 187; pruning, 105
Lythrum, 199

Magnolia *stellata, ill.* 197
Magnolia trees, 87, 141
Maine: agricultural college and experiment station, 475; area, 291; gardens and parks, 458; 466; problems, 390–91
Malling, 257
Manillagrass (*Zoysia matrella*), 167
Manures, 36, 93; commercial, 42; cow, for rose garden, 221; green, 36, 41, 47, 93, 96, 156, 179; for improving soil, 41; substitutes, 41
Maple trees, 87, 141; roots, 211
Marigolds, 175, 177; seed sowing, 67–68
Marsh garden, 208
Maryland: agricultural colleges and experiment station, 476; area, 291; gardens and parks, 466; problems, 390–91
Massachusetts: agricultural college and experiment station, 476; area, 291; gardens and parks, 466; problems, 390–91
Master plan, 22
Meadowgrass, 164
Melon lice, 252
Melons, 249
Men's Garden Clubs of America, 481
Merion Bluegrass, 153, 158, 162, 163
Mertensia, 167
Michigan: agricultural college and experiment station, 476; area, 291; gardens and parks, 459, 466; problems, 390–91
Micro-climates, 139; areas, 62; forming, 86–87
Mildew, 257, 349
Milorganite, 157, 239, 241
Miniature roses, 220
Minnesota: agricultural college and experiment station, 476; arboretum, 459; area, 291; gardens and parks, 466; problems, 388–89
Mississippi: agricultural colleges and experiment station 476; area, 291; gardens and parks, 467; problems, 392–93
Missouri: agricultural colleges and experiment station, 476; area, 291; botanical garden, 459; gardens and parks, 467; problems, 389–90
Mist spraying, 238; trees, transplants, 150
"Mobile" gardening, 215
Model, of water garden, 205
Moisture, 87–91; conservation of, 87 ff; evaporation rate, 91; mulching, 88–89; requirements, measuring, 90; seedlings, 70. *See* Water
Montana: agricultural college and experiment station, 476; area, 291; gardens and parks, 467; problems, 387–89

INDEX 501

Moonflower (*Ipomaea bonanox*), 146, 147, 175
Morning-glory, 175, 177
Mountain area problems, 387–88
Mountain-ash trees, 141
Muck soils, 38
Mugo pine, 144; pruning, 107
Mulberry, propagation, 79
Mulch: annuals, 176; application, 89; consistency, 88; defined, 88; grass clippings, 161; rose garden, 223; for roses, 229; summer, 88–89, 348
Mulching: annuals, 177; defined, 88; drought and, 63; fruit trees, 256; materials, 36; moisture, 87–88; rock garden, 200; roses, 229; transplants, 150; vegetable garden, 241; winter storage of vegetables, 241–42
Myosotis, 187

Nasturtiums, 175; black aphids, 336
National Council of State Garden Clubs, Inc., 481
Natural conditions, and special gardens, 26
Nature, pruning, 102, 105
Nebraska: agricultural college and experiment station, 476; arboretum, 459; area, 291; gardens and parks, 467; problems, 388–9
Nectarine trees, 261
Neutral (or alkaline) soil, 33; plants for, 96
Nevada: agricultural college and experiment station, 476; area, 291; gardens and parks, 467; problems, 387–8
New Hampshire: agricultural college and experiment station, 476; arboretum, 459; area, 291; gardens and parks, 467; problems, 390–1

New Jersey: agricultural college and experiment station, 476; arboretum, 459; area, 291; gardens and parks, 467; problems, 390–1
New Mexico: agricultural college and experiment station, 476; area, 292; gardens and parks, 467; problems, 381–82, 387; soil, 381–82
New York: agricultural college and experiment stations, 477; area, 292; gardens and parks, 459, 467–69; problems, 390–1
Nitricin, 70
Nitrogen, 44, 61, 92; deficiency, symptoms of, 97; lawn fertilizer, 161
Nod-O-Gen, 70
North Carolina: agricultural colleges and experiment station, 477; arboretum, 459; area, 292; gardens and parks, 469
North Dakota: agricultural college and experiment station, 477; area, 292; problems, 388–9
Nozzles, 277; for coldframes, 118, 277; "fog," 69, 70, 277, 280; mist spray, 151, 158, 184, 238; "pressure breaker," 277; sprinkler, 277; three hose
Nursery, home, 138
Nursery stock: care of, 150; "heeling in," *ill.* 255
Nutrient deficiency, symptoms of, 97

Oak trees, 141
Oats, 36
Ohio: agricultural college and experiment station, 477; arboretum, 459; area, 292; gardens and parks, 469–70; problems, 390–1
Oklahoma: agricultural colleges and experiment station, 477;

area, 292; gardens and parks, 470; problems, 391–92; soil, 382–83

Old age, 64

Open ditches, 35–37

Orchard, spraying, 455–56

Oregon: agricultural college and experiment station, 477; arboretum, 460; area, 292; gardens and parks, 470–71; problems, 378–80

Organic fertilizers, 92–93

Organic gardening, 96–97

Organic materials: plus factor, 33; in soil building, 31

Organic soils, 40

Oriental poppies, 185, 187; dividing, 73; propagation, 76

Oscillating rain machine, 91

Oscillating sprayers, 158, 238

Outdoor living: planning area for, 22–23

Oxydendron trees, 141

Pachysandra terminalis, 169

Panodrench, 279, 283

Pansies, 179

Parks, 461–73

Passion-flower, 147

Passion vine, 146

Patio: planning, 214–15; planting border, *ill.* 214; view, importance of, 214–15; walling in, 201. See Patio garden

Patio garden: coldframe, 215; defined, 210–11; greenhouse, 215; plants for, 212–13; "plunging border," *ill.* 212; trees, 211; vines, 211; water features, 213–15

Paulownia trees, 141

Peach trees, 260, 261; harvesting, 261; pruning, *ill.* 261

Pear trees, 258

Peatmoss, 37, 38, 41, 174, 255; pulverized, 78

Peat pots, 281–82; in coldframe, 118

Peat soils, 37–38

Pennsylvania: agricultural college and experiment station, 477; arboretum, 460; area, 292; gardens and parks, 460, 471; problems, 390–1

Peonies, 179, 185

Perennial ryegrass, 164

Perennials, 179–80, 187, 438–39; books on, 484; border, *ill.* 179; color distribution, 180; obtaining plants, 181, 183; spacing, 183; characteristics, 180; crowding 62; dividing, 184–85, *ill.* 181; fertilizer, 93, 98; fragrant, 191, 443; growing from seed, 181; life cycle, *ill.* 56; for pool, 207; pruning, 105; replanting, 184; "run out," *ill.* 181; soil preparation, depth of, 95; for stream, 207; vegetables, 250–51; for water garden, 207

Periwinkle (*Vinca minor*), 170

Perlite, 78

Pesticides, 451–53

Pests, 63, 99; animal, 448; asparagus beetle, 249; of fruit trees, 256, 257; garden, and control, 445–46; vegetable, 252

Petunias, seed sowing, 70

Philodendron, air layering, 74

Phlox, 187; dividing, 73; mildew on, 63

Phosphorus, 44, 61, 92; deficiency, symptoms of, 97

Pillar roses, supports, 224

Pine trees, 141

Pitch pine, 138

Planning, 19–28; books on, 482; carefulness in, 28; important areas, 22–25; long-range, 20; master plan, 22; to scale, 296; special gardens, 26–28

Planting: "B and B" (balled and burlapped) stock, 150; fruits,

INDEX

255–56; holes, size, 148; potting shed, 274; preparation for, 94–96; shrubs, 148–51; soil preparation, 95–96; spring, dates, 290–93; trees, 148–51; vines, 148–51

Planting holes, 148, *ill.* 149; roses, 223

Plants: acid-loving, 196; adaptability of, 54; air, 59; alkali tolerance, 385; anatomy, 52–58, *ill.* 53; animals, difference, 52, 54; aquatic, 209; asexual reproduction, 58–59; methods, *ill.* 60; bog, 205; bog garden, 208; elements necessary, 32, 59–62; enemies, 86; environment, 85; food, 61; fragrant, 443–44; growth of, 59–62; deterrents to, 62–64; keeping vigorous and healthy, 85–101; leaves, 58; life cycle, *ill.* 55; light, 61; 61n; lime-loving, 196; marsh garden, 208; miniature pool, 213–14; parts, 52–54; patio garden, 211–12, 213; pot, 176, 244, 269–70; for pool, 207; reproduction 58; asexual, 58–59; requirements, 85; rock garden, 193, 194–95, 199; roots, 54, 57; salinity tolerance, 385–86; seeds, 59; special and groups, books on, 483–84; stems, 57, 58; for streams, 207; submarine culture, 62 n; surplus, 184; temperature, 62; training, objectives of, 105–08, 184; trunks, 57, 58; wall garden, 201; water, 61; for water garden, 207, 208; window boxes, 215, 216

Plant societies, 479–80
Plant stake, 178
Play, planning area for, 22–25
Pliofilm, 211
Plugging, 159
Plum trees, 258, 260

Pole beans, *ill.* 247
Pools, 204; annuals, 207; construction, 206, 207; design, 205; lily, 205; location, 205; looking-glass in rose garden, *ill.* 238; miniature, plants for, 213–14; mirror, 213; in patio, 213; perennials, 207; plants, 207; small, *ill.* 206; -stream combination, 205; swimming, 204 n; type, 205; -water garden difference, 208; water supply, 207–08; winter care, 209; woodland, 205

Poplar trees, 87
Post-and-chain support, 129, 224, *ill.* 225
Post-and-rail fence, 129
Potash, 45, 61; for roses, 225
Potassium, 45, 92
Potatoes, propagation, 76
Pot plants; 176; "crocking" for, *ill.* 281; strawberries, 267–69, 270; tomatoes, 244
Potting, greenhouse, 281–2
Potting bench, 274, *ill.* 275
Potting shed, 24, 274, *ill.* 275; uses, 274
Power tools, 123
Prairie: gardening problems, 389–90; soils, 39–40
Primroses, 276
Privet(s), 142–44; California, 144; for hedges, 142–44; pruning, 106
Problems, gardening, 378–96; Atlantic Seashore, 394–96; Central Plains, 389; desert living, 383–86; East Central states, 390–91; Great Northern Plains, 388–89; Gulf Coast, 393–94; heartland prairie, 389–90; intermountain, 387–88; lower South, 393–94; mid-Atlantic states, 390–91; mountain, 387–88; North Central states, 390–91; Northeast, 390–91; South

INDEX

Central states, 391–92; Southwest, 381–83; upper South, 392; West Coast, 378–81
Propagation: asexual: air layering, 74; cuttings, 76–84; dividing, 73; layering, 73; natural division, rooting media, 77–79; budding, 80, 81; by cuttings, in greenhouse, 283; dividing, 73; time for, 73; grafting, 80–84; methods (*See* Propagation methods)
Propagation box, 78–79, 278, *ill.* 79
Propagation methods: asexual, 72–76; cuttings, 76–77; grafting and budding, 80–84; growing from seed, 65–71; kinds, 65; rooting media, 77–79; seedlings, starting, 71–72; sowing, 67–70
Protecting plants, 184; mechanically, 128; melons, 249; patio plants, 211; rock garden, 193, 194
Pruning: anticipation, 111; equipment, 108–9; espaliered plants, 148; to forestall injury, 105; fruit trees, 256, 258, *ill.* 259; light, 111, *ill.* 124; lupines, 105; objectives, 104–5, rock garden, 199; roses, 104–5, 223, 226–29; shrubs, 104–5, 107–8, 148, 150; techniques, 109–11; tools, 108–9, 110; trees, 104, 148, 150; vines and other climbers, 145, 147, 148, 150; wounds, 111. *See* Training
Puerto Rico: agricultural college and experiment station, 477
Purple beech trees, 139
Puschkinias, 186
Pyracantha c. lalandi, 145
Pyrethrum, 97

Quality, of seeds, 66

Rambler roses: pruning, 229; supports, 224
Raspberries, 265–66
Recipes: GrayRock French dressing, 243; green corn fritters, 248
Reclaimed desert areas: ornamental trees, 431–32; shade trees, 431–32; shrubs, 432
Red fescue, 164
Redtop, 163
Regional gardening, books, 482
Renewing old plants, pruning, 104
Replanting, 184–85
Repotting: greenhouse, 281–82; potting shed, 272, 274; seedlings, 72
Reproduction, 58; asexual, 58–9
Rest, planning area for, 22–25
Retaining wall, 201, *ill.* 202
Rhizoctonia, 69, 283
Rhizomes, 185; for the South, 426–28
Rhode Island: agricultural college and experiment station, 477; area, 292; gardens and parks, 471; problems, 390–91
Rhododendrons: acid-loving, 45; fertilizers, 98; soil for, 48, 96
Rhubarb, in flower border, 235
Rind grafting, 81
Rock garden, 20, 192–200, *ill.* advantages, 192; annuals, 175; books on, 483; building, 195–99, *ill.* 197, 198; culture, 199; construction, 195–96; drainage, 193; location, 193, 194; mulching, 200; natural setting, 193, 203, *ill.* 195; plan, 27, 195, *ill.* 196; plants, 194, 440–42; selecting, 199; rocks, 196; soil, 195; steps, *ill.* 198; three dimensional, 196; top, 199; trailer roses, 219; watering, 200; winter care, 200

INDEX

Rocky Mountains: deciduous trees, 412; shrubs, 412
Rodents, 448
Root cuttings, 76
Root division, 73
Rooting media, 77–79
Rooting, stem or leaf cuttings, 59
Rootone, 70, 73, 74, 78
Roots, 54
Rose garden, 218–31; drainage, 34, 221, 222; mulch, 223; plan, 219; planting, 223–26; preparing, 221–23; pruning, 226–29; semiformal, moderate-sized, *ill.* site, 221; soil, 221; preparation, 221; self-watering system, *ill.* 222; spring care, 229–31; type, 219–20; walling in, 201; watering system, 221–22, *ill.* 222
Roses: bank garden, 200–01; black spot, 304; bush, 223; cancer, 105; climbing, 145, 147, 219, 223, 224, 227; on greenhouse, 272; planting holes, 223; pruning, 227–28; support for, 129, 223, *ill.* 225; cutting, 230; dividing, 73; edging, 220; feeding, 225; fertilizer, 98, 221, 225; floribundas 219; garden, 219; grandiflora, 219 *ill.* hedge, 220; for very cold climate, 418; hilling up, 230–31; hybrid teas, 219; "knob" or "graft," 223; "knuckle," 224; miniature, 220; mulching, 229; pillar, supports for, 224; planting, 223–26; planting holes, 223; popularity, 218; potash for, 225; propagation, 77; pruning, 104, 223, 226–29, *ill.* 228; rambler, 224, 228, 230; shrub, 218, 220, 223; for very cold climates, 415; layering, 73; single, *ill.* 241; soil preparation, depth of, 95; special bed, 26; spraying, 63, 229, 230; spring care, 225, 229–31; suckers, removing, *ill.* 227; supports, 223–24, *ill.* 225; trailers, 219; variety, 218; winter protection, 230–31. *See* Rose garden
Rotenone, 97
Rototilling, 95
Rots, 449–50
Rough Bluegrass, 164
Rubber-plant, air layering, 74
Rudbeckia, 183
Rusts, 450
Rye, 36, 41
Ryegrass, 36, 41, 156, 164

Saddle grafting, 81
St. Augustinegrass, 166–67
Saline soils, improving, 50
Salinity tolerance, of plants, 385–86
Sandstone, porous, 197
Sandy soils, 30, 37
Sash: for coldframes, 113; slatted, 119
Sassafras trees, 141
Scale, in rock garden, 199
Scion, 80
Screening: for patio garden, 210–11; planning area, 22–23; pole beans, 245–46; temporary, 91
Screens: hardy shrubs and evergreens, list, 143–44; shrubs for, 142–45
Seabrook Farms, 106
Seashore: cultivated trees and shrubs, 433–34; ground covers, 434–35; native trees and shrubs, 433
Seaweed, 241
Sedge peat, 37–38
Seed germination: light, 71; temperature, 70
Seedlings: sowing (*See* Sowing

seedlings); starting, 70–71; in greenhouse, 278–79; plants, *ill.* thinning out, 71; transplanting, 71

Seeds, 58–59; control of conditions, 66–67; grass, 157–58; growing from, 65 ff; protectant, 69–70; quality, 66; sowing, 183–84; timing, 66; watering, 91

Seed sowing: art of, 70; disinfectants, 70; greenhouse, 279–84; inoculants, 70; labels, 70; temperature, 278–79; watering devices, 69

Setting out. *See* Transplanting

Shade: coldframe, 119; creating, 87; estimating cast, 25; greenhouse, 276–77; measure for, *ill.* 25; planning area for, 24–25; trees, 25, 211

Spergon, 70

Sphagnum, 255, 280

Sphagnum moss, 37, 74; milled, 78. *See* Peatmoss

Sphagnum peat, 157

Sphagnum rooting, 59

Spirea: dividing, 73; pruning, 107

"Sport," 59

Spraying: all-purpose fruit tree spray formula and schedule, 456; equipment, 130–32; fruit trees, 256; in greenhouse, 279, 283; mist, of tree transplants, 151; orchard schedule, 455–56; roses, 230; tank sprayers, 131; "trombone" sprayer, 132

Sprays, 100, 314; for coldframe, 119; equipment, 130–32; for roses, 229. *See* Spraying

Spreading Japanese yew, pruning, 108

Sprigging, 159

Spring: -flowering annuals, 215; -flowering bulbs, 215; -flowering perennials, 215; planting dates, 288, 290–93; rock garden flowers, 199; rose care, 229–31; shrubs, list, 143

Spruce trees, 141

Staking, roses, 230

Stay-dry, 241

Stem cuttings, 76

Stems and trunks, 57, 58

Steps, rock garden, *ill.* 198

Sternbergia lutea, 186

Stokesia, 187

Strawberries, 185, 267–70, 344, *ill.* 269; *ill.* hill system, 269, 270; picking, 267; plants, *ill.* 268; reproduction, 58; rooting runners, *ill.* 269; varieties, 267

Stream(s), 204; annuals, 207; construction, 206; design, 205; perennials, 207; plants 207; -pool combination 205–6; water supply, 207–8

Stripping, 159

Submarine plant culture, 62 n.

Subsoil, 33–36; composition, 33–34; depth, 34; "hard pan," 34; in planting hole, *ill.* 149; porous, 36; preparation of, 94–95

Suckers, 104, 107; raspberries, 266; rose, removing, *ill.* 227

Summer: bulbs, 321; -flowering annuals, 207; -flowering perennials, 207; lawn, 152; mulch, 88–89, 348; shrubs, list, 143

Sunflower, 175, 177

Sunshine, limited, providing, 113–14

Supports: annuals, 177–78, *ill.* 178; climbing roses, 129, 223, *ill.* 225; dwarf fruit trees, 258; for gooseberries, 264–65; grapes, 262; plants, 129; post-and-chain, 224, *ill.* 225; raspberries, 265; for tomatoes, 244; for vines, 145, 146–47, 177; when to put in, 224

Sweet corn, 97, 233, 241, 246–48, *ill.* 247
Sweet gum trees, 141
Sweet peas, 177; special bed, 27
Sweet William (*Dianthus barbatus*), 179
Swimming pool, 204 n
Switzerland, miniature roses, 220
Syringing, 305

Tall fescue, 164
Temperature, 62, 86–87; coldframe, 117; greenhouse, 274–76; hotbed, 278; seedlings, 70; in greenhouse, 278; winter, average minimum, 290–93
Tennessee: agricultural colleges and experiment station, 478; area, 292; gardens and parks, 460, 472; problems, 392
Terrace. *ill.*
Texas: agricultural colleges and experiment station, 478; area, 292; gardens and parks, 460, 472; problems, 381–82, 391–92, 393–94; soil, 382
"Thatch," 241
"Thinning out," 238; seedlings, 71; vegetables 240; when to do, 184
Thymus serpyllum, 169
Tigridias, 188
Tile, for drainage, 34, 221; installing, *ill.* 37
Timing, in seed sowing, 66
Tomatoes, 233, 243–45; diseases, 450; Trellis for, *ill.* 244
Tools and equipment, 122 ff; acquisition, "go slow," 122; budding knife, 111, *ill.* 124; buying, 122; care of, 134; for cultivating, 126; dibble, 126; dusting and spraying equipment, 130; edgers, 134; fertilizer and seed distributor, 134; field hoe, 126; greenhouse, 277; hand, 122–28; hand mower, 132; hand pruning shears, 108; hand weeders, 127; hoe, 126; holemaker, 126; knives, 127; lawn equipment, 132–34; lopping shears, 108, 109, 228; mechanical protectors, 128; "onion" hoe, 126, 238; plant supports, 129; pole pruning shears, 108; power, 123; power mower, 132, 134, 156; pruning, 108–09, *ill.* 110; pruning knife, 108; pruning saw, 109; rakes, 127; roller, 134; scuffle or push-hoe, 89, 126; sharpening stone, 109, 128; Slim Jim bulb-planting trowel, 187; spading fork, 123; spades, 123; spike-tamper, *ill.* 133; *tamper-aerator,* 134; for transplanting, 123–26; trowels, 123; turf edger, *ill.* 133; types, 122; water-ballast roller, *ill.* 133; for weeding, 240
Tool shed, 289; planning, 24
Topiary work, 106
Topsoils, 33; "chocolate icing" layer, 154; shallow, 34
Trace elements, 61; "complete" fertilizers, 92
Trailers, for window boxes, 216
Trailing roses, 219
Training plants, *ill.* objectives, 102, 105–08
Transplanting: greenhouse seedlings, 280–81; mulching, 150; organic fertilizers, 93; potting shed, 274; seedlings, 71, 72; time for, 185; tools for, 123–26; shrubs, 138–39; trees, 138–39; watering, 91
Tree fruits, 254; apples, 254; "bearing age," 255; culture, 257–63; planting, 255; pruning, 256; space, 254. *See* Fruit trees
Tree paint, 227
Trees: alkaline tolerance, 386;

arborvitae, 141; pruning, 106; beech, 141; birch, 87, 141; books on, 484–85; bracing, 151, *ill.* 149; broadleaved evergreens for California, 429–30; cherry, 141; Chinese elms, 87; for very cold climates, 411, 412–14; coniferous, for California, 430–31; crabs, flowering, 141; cultivated, for seashore, 433–34; deciduous, 140; list, 141; dogwood, flowering, 141 *ill.* 144; elm, 141; evergreens, 141; -deciduous difference, 140; list, 141; fertilizer, 98; fir, 141; fruit (*See* Fruit trees); growth rate, 138; guy wires, 151, 366; hardy, list, 399–410; hawthorns, 141; hemlock, 141; -pruning, 106; horse-chestnut, 141; juniper, 141; laburnum, 141; larches, 140, 141; linden, 141; locust, 141; magnolia, 87, 141; maple, 87, 141, 211; measuring shade from, 24, 25; mountain-ash, 141; native, for seashore, 433; oak, 141; ornamental: list, 141; for reclaimed desert areas, 431–32; oxydendron, 141; patio garden, 210–11; paulownia, 141; pine, 141; pin oaks, 87; planning before planting, 137, 139–40; planting, 137, 148–51; pruning, 104, 148, 150; purchasing, 140; Rocky Mountains, 412; sassafras, 141; selecting, 139–41; shade, 24–25, 87, 141, 211; for reclaimed desert areas, 431–32; silver bell, 141; size, 139; soil preparation, depth of, 95; for the South, 420–21, 423; species for locality, 139, 140; spruce, 141; sweet gum, 141; transplanting time, 138; tulip, 105, 138, 141; umbrella-pine, 141; "wells," 155; willow, 141; witch-hazel, 141; yews, 141

Tree-wound paint, 111

Treewrap, 128, 151

Trellises, 129, 147, *ill.* 130; climber roses, 219; grapes 262; rambler roses; 224; for tomatoes, *ill.* 244

Trench, roses in, 224

Trumpet creeper, 146

Trumpet-vine, 147

Tuberose roots, for the South, 426–28

Tuberous-rooted plants, propagation, 75, 76

Tubers: life cycle, *ill.* 55; for the South, 426–28; starting, 305

Tuffa, 197

Tulips, 186, 188–89, 215; bulb increase, *ill.* "forcing," 120; life cycle, 57

Tulip trees, 141; growth rate; 138; pruning, 105

Turf: edger, *ill.* 133; effect on grounds, 152–53. *See* Lawn

Turfing-daisy (*Matricaria tchihatchewi*), 169

Twiners, 146

U. C. Soil Mix B, 69

Umbrella-pine trees, 141

University of California, soil mixes, 68

University of Massachusetts, College of Agriculture, 43

Upkeep, 97–99

Utah: agricultural college and experiment station, 478; area, 292; gardens and parks, 460, 472; problems, 387–88

Utility area, planning, 22, 23–24

Vegetable garden, 232 ff; alkali tolerance, 385; annual, 251; asparagus, 235, 248–49; beans, 245–46; beets, 97; books on,

INDEX

483; broccoli, 241; celery, 97; chart, 250; corn, 97, 233, 241, 246–48; cucumber, 97; culture, 240–42; drainage, 234; fertilizer, 93, 98, 239; flavor, 233; in flower border, 235; freezing, 242; harvesting, 241, 300, 359; in herb garden, 235; leaders, 242–52; lettuce, 233, 242–43; melons, 249–50; mulching, 241; peas, 233, 241; perennial, 251; pests, 249; placement, 172; plan, 235–36, *ill.* 237; planning, 22–23, 27–28; planting, 238–39; preparation for, 236, 238; potatoes, 97; preliminaries, 234–36; reasons for growing, 232–33; rhubarb, 235; root, storing, 241; salinity tolerance, 385; setting out, 239; side-dressing, 240–41; site, 234; size, 234; storage, winter, 241–42; thinning, 240; tomatoes, 233, 243–45; watering, 91; weeds, 240; control of, 99, 450–51

Veltheimia, propagation, 75
Velvet bent, 163
Veneer grafting, 81
Ventilation: greenhouse, 276
Vermiculite, 78, 274, 280
Vermont: agricultural college and experiment station, 478; area, 292; problems, 390–91
Vetch, 36, 41, 93
Vinca minor, 170
Vines and other climbers, 145 ff; annual, 175–76, 437–38; bank garden, 200; books on, 484; for very cold climates, 416–17; cultivating, 147–48; fragrant, 443; grape, pruning, *ill.* 263; greenhouse, 272; patio garden, 211; planting, 137, 148–51; pruning, 145, 147, 148, 150; soil, 147; for South, 424–25; supports for, 145, 146–47, 177; window boxes, 216

Virginia: agricultural college and experiment stations, 478; area, 292; gardens and parks, 461, 473; problems, 390–91
Virginia creeper (*Parthenocissus quinquefolia*), 145, 146
Virus diseases, 450
Visqueen, 206

Walks, edging roses, 220
Wall gardens, 201–03; advantages, 192; books on, 483; natural settings for, 203; planning, 27; plants for, 201, 442; trailer roses, 219
Walls: climber roses, 219; free-standing, double faced, 201–03; temperature and, 86
Washington State: agricultural college and experiment station, 478; area, 292; gardens and parks, 461, 473; problems, 378–80
Water, 61; -ballast roller, *ill.* 133; greenhouse, 276–78; making most of, 87 ff; microclimates, 86–87; seed sowing devices, 70
Waterfall, 204; in patio, 213
Water features: in patio garden, 213–15. *See also* Pools, Streams *and* Water Gardens
Water gardens, 204, 208–09; annuals, 207; books on, 483; design, 205; perennials, 207; planning, 27; plants, 207, 208, 442; -pool difference, 208; water supply, 207–08
Watering: amount required, 90, *ill.* 90; in coldframe, 118; equipment, 91; grass seeding, 157–58; greenhouse seedlings, 280; measure for, *ill.* 90; method, 89–90; mistlike spray, 91; rock garden, 200; spray, 71, 280; vegetable gar-

den before planting, 236. *See* Hoses *and* Nozzles

Watering-can, 69

Watering system, 61; rose garden, 221–22

Water-lilies, tropical, 337

Wedge and cleft grafting, 80, *ill.* 82

Weeds: chickweed, 127; control of, 99, 450–51; cultivating, 126; mulching, 88; purslane, 127; seeds, elimination of, 282; surplus plants, 184; tools, 240; vegetable garden, 240

Weeks, Martin E., 43

West Coast, gardening problems, 378–80

West Virginia: agricultural college and experiment station, 478; area, 293; gardens and parks, 461, 473; problems, 390–91

Whetstone, 128

Whip and tongue grafting, 80, *ill.* 82

White Dutch clover, 165

White pine, 138

Willow, 141; propagation, 79

Wildflowers, 354

Wilt-Pruf, 128, 151

Wind barriers, 91

Windbreaks, 50, 366, 413–14

Wind burn, 299

Wind erosion, 50–51

Wind scald, 128, 315

Window boxes, 215–17; self-watering, *ill.* 216; watering, 298

Winter (care of): fish in pools, 209; lawn, 152; pools, 208; rock garden, 199–200; roses, 230–31

Winter-aconite, 186

Winter rye, 156

Winter shrubs, list, 143

Wisconsin: agricultural college and experiment station, 478; area, 293; gardens and parks, 461, 473; problems, 390

Wisteria, 146, 147

Witch-hazel trees, 141

Woman's National Farm and Garden Association, 481

Wood ashes: for acidity, 47, 297; for roses, 225

Woodland pool, 205

Wyoming: agricultural college and experiment station, 478; area, 293; gardens and parks, 461, 473; problems, 387

Yew trees, 141; pruning, 107–08

Zinnias, 175; seed sowing, 67

Zones, planting, 86

Zoysia grasses, 160, 162

Zoysias, 167